Asian-Pacific Security

The Asian-Pacific Region

Adapted from "The Nations of the Pacific," Current History 81, no. 474: 193. Used with permission of the publisher.

Asian-Pacific Security

Emerging Challenges and Responses

edited by
Young Whan Kihl
and
Lawrence E. Grinter

Lynne Rienner Publishers, Inc. · Boulder, Colorado

All of the chapters in this book are original and were written especially for inclusion in the present volume. Two chapters, however, have also appeared elsewhere as journal articles under slightly different titles. These are:

Chapter 4, by Sheldon Simon, under the title "The Great Powers and Southeast Asia: Cautious Minuet or Dangerous Tango?" _Asian Survey_ 25, no. 9 (September 1985):918–942.

Chapter 7, by Young Whan Kihl, under the title "Evolving Inter-Korean Relations: Security, Diplomacy, and Peace," _Korea & World Affairs_ 9, no. 3 (Fall 1985):441–468.

UA
830
.A84
1986

Published in the United States of America in 1986 by
Lynne Rienner Publishers, Inc.
948 North Street, Boulder, Colorado 80302

© 1986 by Lynne Rienner Publishers, Inc. All rights reserved

Library of Congress Cataloging-in-Publication Data

Main entry under title:

Asian-Pacific security

   Bibliography: p.
   Includes index.
   1. Pacific Area--Strategic aspects--Addresses,
essays, lectures. I. Kihl, Young W., 1932-
II. Grinter, Lawrence E.
UA830.A84 1986   355'03305   85-25631
ISBN 0-931477-51-4

Distributed outside of North and South America and Japan by
Frances Pinter (Publishers) Ltd, 25 Floral Street,
London WC2E 9DS England. UK ISBN 0-86187-85-25631

Printed and bound in the United States of America

To a safer world for this and future generations.

Contents

Illustrations

Acronyms

ABRI	Angkatan Bersenjata Republik Indonesia (Indonesian Armed Forces)
AFP	Armed Forces of the Philippines
ALP	Australian Labour party
ALRI	Angkatan Laut Republik Indonesia (Navy)
ANZUS	Australia-New Zealand-United States
ASDF	Air Self-Defense Force
ASEAN	Association of Southeast Asian Nations
ASW	antisubmarine warfare
AURI	Angkatan Udora Republik Indonesia (Indonesian Air Force)
BAM	Baikal-Amur Mainline
CAR	closer ANZAC relations
CENTCOM	U.S. Central Command
CINCPAC	Commander-in-Chief, Pacific
CITUU	Committee for International Trade Union Unity
CMEA	Council for Mutual Economic Assistance
COIN	counterinsurgency
COMECON	Council for Mutual Economic Assistance
CPP	Communist party of the Philippines
DCRK	Democratic Confederal Republic of Koryo
DEFCON	defense readiness condition
DPRK	Democratic People's Republic of Korea
DSP	Democratic Socialist party
EEZ	exclusive economic zone
FIP	Force Improvement Plan
GATT	general agreement on trade and tariff
GDP	gross domestic product
GNP	gross national product
GSDF	Ground Self-Defense Force
HF=DF	high frequency direction finding
IADS	Integrated Air Defense System
ICP	Indochina Communist party
JDA	Japan Defense Agency
JSP	Japanese Socialist party

KODAL	Komando Daerah Angkatan Laut (Navy Area Command)
KODAM	Komando Daerah Militer (Military Area Command)
KOSTRAD	Komando Strategic Angkatan Darat (Indonesian Army Strategic Command)
KOWILHAN	Komando Wilayah Pertahanan (Defense Regional Command)
KWP	Korean Workers party
LDP	Liberal Democratic party
MAF	Malaysian Armed Forces
MDB	Mutual Defense Board
MSDF	Maritime Self-Defense Force
NATO	North Atlantic Treaty Organization
NIC	newly industrialized country
NOIC	Naval Operational Intelligence Center
NOSIC	Naval Ocean Surveillance Center
NPA	New People's Army
OECD	Organization of Economic Cooperation and Development
PKP	Philippine Communist party
PLA	People's Liberation Army
PTUF	Pacific Trade Union Forum
RAAF	Royal Australian Air Force
RBAF	Royal Brunei Air Force
RIMPAC	Rim of the Pacific
RNZAF	Royal New Zealand Air Force
RNZN	Royal New Zealand Navy
ROK	Republic of Korea
RTA	Royal Thai Army
SAF	Singapore Armed Forces
SDF	Self-Defense Forces
SDI	Strategic Defense Initiative
SEATO	Southeast Asia Treaty Organization
SIGINT	signals intelligence
SLOC	sea-lanes of communication
SPNFZ	South Pacific Nuclear-Free Zone
STOL	short-takeoff-and-landing
USFJ	U.S. Forces, Japan
VCP	Vietnam Communist party
WFTU	World Federation of Trade Unions
WPC	World Peace Council
WTO	Warsaw Treaty Organization
ZOPFAN	Zone of Peace, Freedom, and Neutrality

Preface

The Pacific Ocean is no longer as much a physical barrier as it was once; today, travel and communication among the nations and people who share and border the ocean are easier to accomplish. The Pacific Ocean has become, in fact, the common lake for the Pacific-rim countries in this age of intercontinental air travel and instantaneous satellite communications.

The Asian-Pacific region, the focus of this book, is an arena in which the foreign and security policies of the Great Powers and their allies compete constantly. It is a region that is not only conflict ridden politically and heavily armed militarily, but also dynamic economically. Moreover, it is in East Asia in the mid-twentieth century that a major ideological confrontation between two different socioeconomic systems, socialism and capitalism, has occurred, and its outcome is far from clear.

Because security is one of the utmost concerns of the region's nations and people, it is natural and fitting that we have initiated this book on Asian-Pacific security affairs. The book assembles some of the leading analysts and specialists of East Asian affairs to identify the emerging security trends and challenges in the region. They have been asked to identify current and future trends and to give their views regarding the implications of these trends and the policy measures necessary to cope with these emerging challenges.

The origin of the volume stems from the two-tiered panel on Asian Security held during the 26th Annual Convention of the International Studies Association in Washington, D.C., March 5-9, 1985. The panelists, including Davis Bobrow, Lawrence Grinter, Richard Higgot, Sheldon Simon, William Tow, William Turley, and Donald Weatherbee, agreed to assemble their respective papers into a book format. Lynne Rienner was approached to publish the book. The group elected Lawrence Grinter as one coeditor of the book. Young Whan Kihl was subsequently recruited as the other coeditor. In addition to the panel participants mentioned above, several additional contributors were solicited: Leif Rosenberger and Marian Leighton, Robert Sutter, and Michael McKinley.

The two coeditors have given equal time and effort to the book. The select bibliography is the work of Young Whan Kihl and is based on his own research as well as references cited in individual chapters.

The editors wish to thank Lynne Rienner for her professional guidance and members of her editorial staff, especially Dianne Ewing and Janice Murray, for their dedication and skill. Young Whan Kihl also wishes to acknowledge the receipt of a faculty improvement leave grant from Iowa State University during the fall 1985 semester that enabled him to spend time at the University of California, Berkeley, Institute of East Asian Studies, to initiate new research on Pacific Basin issues including the completion of this book. Lawrence Grinter wishes to thank many of his faculty colleagues and students at Maxwell Air Forces Base, whose valuable comments over the years have sharpened his own appreciation of Asian-Pacific security problems. Finally, both editors wish to thank the associates and colleagues who contributed to this volume for their cooperation, support, and analytical skills, as well as their superb insights.

The coeditors and contributors hope that this volume will make a substantial contribution to understanding on both sides of the Pacific of East Asia's emerging security challenges and their implications for policy.

1 New Security Realities in the Asian Pacific: Perspectives, Purpose, and Approach

Young Whan Kihl
Lawrence E. Grinter

The Asian-Pacific area is one of the most dynamic regions in the world. It is a conflict-ridden region both politically and militarily where the interests of four major world powers--the United States, the Soviet Union, China, and Japan--intersect. It is also the site of the United States' last three military conflicts (World War II, the Korean War, and the Vietnam War). Yet the Asian Pacific is growing rapidly economically and in world trade, and it has grown in the 1970s and 1980s at rates not experienced elsewhere in the world. The Asian-Pacific region could become the world's most viable economic center in the not-too-distant future.[1]

The Pacific Basin region, defined broadly, includes the countries bordering on the Pacific: Australia, New Zealand, the United States, Canada, the ministates of the South Pacific, the Latin American states, and the East Asian and Southeast Asian nations. A subarea of the Pacific Basin is the Asian Pacific, which for the purpose of the present study consists of three main areas--Northeast Asia, Southeast Asia, and Oceania--including Australia, New Zealand, Japan, the People's Republic of China (PRC), South and North Korea, Taiwan, Hong Kong, the three Indochinese states of Vietnam, Laos, and Cambodia, and the six Association of South East Asian Nations (ASEAN) of Indonesia, Malaysia, the Philippines, Singapore, Thailand, and Brunei (the latter joining the organization in 1984).[2] The United States and the Soviet Union, which possess considerable regional ties and interests, are also included in the scope of the present study.

SECURITY ENVIRONMENT AND THE SHIFTING POWER BALANCE

The Asian-Pacific area is one of the most heavily armed regions in the world, and regional peace and security are still marred by continuing political and military conflicts. Since 1945, East Asia (or the Far

1

East) has been a center of the world struggle between the dominant adversarial systems of capitalism and socialism, and the Asian-Pacific region today continues to be a prime locus of contention for the main actors in the global balance of power.[3] East Asia has witnessed not only communist revolutions after World War II in China, North Korea, and Indochina, following prolonged civil and international wars, but conversely also some of the most impressive capitalist achievements in the postwar era in Japan, South Korea, Taiwan, Hong Kong, and Singapore. The economic "miracles" of the latter category have been credited to the dynamic forces of market-oriented capitalist economies.

The Asian Pacific is a region in search of peace and stability. The Korean Peninsula is an armed camp where a combined total of 1.5 million troops are stationed face to face across the 155-mile long Demilitarized Zone that separates the land into the communist North and the noncommunist South. In the three Indochinese countries of Vietnam, Cambodia, and Laos, some 1.3 million men are now under arms, and Vietnamese forces are face to face with Chinese forces across the Sino-Vietnamese border at the same time as Vietnamese forces also occupy Cambodia and deploy along the border of Thailand. About one-third of the 4 million men in uniform in China confront Soviet troops across the Sino-Soviet frontier, and approximately one-third of the Soviet ground forces--some 52 divisions--are garrisoned in the Soviet Far East.[4]

The steady increase in Soviet theater forces in the Far East since the U.S. withdrawal from Indochina and Thailand in 1974 and 1975 has been the major source of threat perception shared by most of the region's actors. The Soviet Pacific Fleet is now at its largest and Soviet airpower, both tactical and strategic, continues to grow. About one-third of the Soviet SS-20 intermediate-range ballistic missile battalions now threaten much of the Asian-Pacific region.[5] This concentration of military force is a source of considerable concern given the demonstrated willingness of the Soviet Union and its allies--in Afghanistan, Cambodia, and on the Korean Peninsula--to use their military power for political ends.

Fortunately, the Soviet Union has not yet been able to translate this growing military power into equivalent political influence. Its ideological appeal in the Asian Pacific remains negligible, and its economic leverage limited. Territorial disputes with Japan and China also limit prospects for accommodation with these most important Asian neighbors, and Soviet support for Vietnam fuels the suspicion with which all ASEAN states regard Moscow. As the Soviet facilities in Vietnam continue to expand, so the "reach" of Soviet naval forces extends beyond the West Pacific to the Indian Ocean.

REGIONAL DIVERSITY AND COMMONALITY

The Asian Pacific is a region characterized by great diversity of population size, economic wealth, and cultural tradition. Populations range from the world's largest, China, with over 1 billion people and almost 4 million square miles, to the world's smallest independent state, Nauru, in the South Pacific, with a population of 8,000 in 8 square miles. Economic size and influence also range from oil-rich Brunei, which gained independence in 1984, with a per capita GNP of nearly $18,000, to some of the island nations, with per capita GNPs of less than $180. Cultural, religious, and philosophical traditions cover the spectrum of the world's great heritages, ranging from Confucianism, Buddhism, and Islam to Christianity.

The Asian-Pacific region is also noted for several shared aspirations and attributes. Most of the countries in the region desire peace and stability, especially for economic growth and development. Human resources in the region are abundant and, given proper education and training, can be a productive force. The countries in the region with market-oriented systems have exhibited dynamic economic growth, aided by the U.S. economic recovery in 1983-84. The Asian-Pacific economies have displayed the greatest resilience and the world's highest rates of growth. U.S. trade with the region is growing, with U.S. exports to the Asian-Pacific countries valued at $54.6 billion in 1984 and U.S. imports from these countries at $114 billion. U.S. investments in the Asian-Pacific countries are conservatively valued at over $30 billion.[6]

NEW REALITIES: THREE DIMENSIONS

Three dimensions of the changing reality and emerging pattern in the Asian-Pacific region are particularly noteworthy. These are (1) Soviet and Soviet client power projection, (2) relative U.S. military disadvantage, and (3) noncommunist Asia's economic growth. The Soviet Union, for example, is projecting military forces and infrastructure into the area at a rapid pace. China, an adversary of the Soviet Union, is introducing a market economy into its countryside as well as into its cities and also is shopping for U.S. military equipment. Japan, totally defeated in World War II, has risen to possess the world's second largest GNP and has become East Asia's economic powerhouse. Other U.S. friends, such as South Korea, Taiwan, and Singapore, have vibrant economies and are running trade surpluses with the United States. Overall U.S. two-way trade with East Asia and the Pacific surpasses U.S. trade with Western Europe. But the United States stations fewer combat troops in the Asian-Pacific area today--only about 160,000 on shore and afloat--than in the last

forty years with the exception of the low point (about
140,000 under the Carter administration). The Soviets
have deployed another 100,000 troops in the region since
the United States exited Indochina in 1974 and 1975.
These developments create a rapidly changing security
environment, one increasingly independent of any single
country's control.

Dimension One: Soviet and
Soviet Client Power Projection

The Soviet Union since 1965 has steadily and con-
spicuously increased its military capabilities and
logistical infrastructure in the Asian-Pacific region.
Moscow's Far Eastern forces in 1985 are second in size
and quality only to the forces Moscow positions opposite
NATO. In 1985, the USSR positioned about 480,000 troops
on China's northern frontier and 110,000 troops on
China's western flank in Afghanistan. The Soviets'
largest fleet operates out of Vladivostock and Petropavlovsk to China's northeast. To the south, a squadron of
20 to 26 Russian warships and auxiliaries operates out
of Vietnam's Cam Rahn Bay. The Soviet Union also deploys in its eastern territories about two-fifths of its
ICBMs and ballistic missile firing submarines, one-third
of its SS-20 missiles, one-quarter of its tactical
fighter aircraft, more than one-third of its strategic
bombers, and one-third of its general purpose forces.
This enormous catalogue of modern military forces makes
the Soviet Union Asia's predominant military power in
sheer numbers alone, although equipment quality and
geostrategic disadvantages may reduce the force's
effectiveness.[7]

In geopolitical terms, it is perhaps not surprising
that the Soviets have chosen to heavily arm their Asian
territories. History and warfare have left a deep im-
print on the Russian view of East Asia. The Soviet
Union is an Asian as well as a European state: three-
quarters of Soviet territory lies east of the Ural
Mountains, and 80 percent of Soviet energy is produced
east of the Urals. Siberia holds up to one-fifth of the
world's coal, a virtually untapped storehouse of lumber,
and a huge stockpile of strategic minerals. However,
Siberia, as distinct from Central Asia, is a population
vacuum: only about 20 million Soviet citizens live in
Western Siberia, Eastern Siberia, and the Far Eastern
territories. In short, the USSR due east of the Urals
has a security problem: it pushes up against 1 billion
Chinese. For a variety of reasons, therefore, Moscow
approaches Asia and the Pacific from a position of
psychological insecurity compensated by territorial
expansion. More than ever, Asia occupies a central
position in Moscow's geopolitical priorities.[8]

The growth of Soviet military power on the Sino-
Soviet border has been steady. Since 1965, the number

of Far East forces has more then tripled, from 15 to 50 divisions. The Chinese oppose them with approximately 100 divisions that are much less well equipped. Over 2,400 Soviet combat aircraft are in the Far East, including 1,700 strike aircraft and 400 bombers, most of them highly modern. Of approximately 370 Soviet SS-20 mobile intermediate-range ballistic missiles, more than one-third are now deployed east of the Ural Mountains. By late 1981, seeking to head off more tension, the Chinese and the Russians sought ways of improving their strained relationship. In 1982, a limited rapprochement began, which resulted in an increase in bilateral trade to about $2.5 billion (in U.S. dollars) in 1984. A slowly improving, more stable, and less polemical relationship between Moscow and Beijing may be in the offing, but pervasive distrust and negativism between the two are not likely to dissipate.[9]

In contrast to the border buildup opposite China and its related negotiations, the Soviets are involved in a hot war on China's western flank in Afghanistan. One hundred ten thousand Soviet troops plus about 30,000 Kabul soldiers are fighting 80,000 to 100,000 Mujahideen --to date to a stalemate. The Russians test a variety of weapons in Afghanistan, some quite gruesome, against rebel personnel, encampments, and livestock.[10] More than 3 million Afghans (one-fifth of the population) have left their country, most of them crammed into dismal refugee camps in western Pakistan. As the Russians denude the Afghan countryside and garrison the towns, they do not seem likely to quit Afghanistan in the near future. It is a vicious war, but one whose costs to date are tolerable to both Moscow and the Mujahideen.

In Northeast Asia, the Soviet Pacific Fleet is the largest of the USSR's four fleets, exhibiting about 90 major surface combatants and 120 submarines. Overall Soviet naval tonnage in the Pacific is twice the U.S. tonnage. One of the principal objects of this enormous naval buildup has been Japan, Washington's main ally in the Asian-Pacific region and an historic Russian enemy. Prevented by U.S. policy from occupying Hokkaido at the end of World War II, the Russians settled for taking all of Sakhalin Island, occupying the northern half of Korea, and taking the southern Kuriles immediately adjacent to Hokkaido--what Japan calls the Northern Territories and has steadfastly claimed as its own. In order to deflect attention from the 100,000 Soviet troops on these islands, Moscow has kept up an endless barrage of propaganda about the alleged "remilitarization" of Japan.[11] On the Korean Peninsula, North Korea, allied with the Soviet Union and equipped largely by the latter, shows no change in its fundamental objective of reunifying the divided land, by force if necessary.

In Southeast Asia, the Soviets operate a southern naval squadron out of Vietnam's Cam Rahn Bay, part of a large naval-air-intelligence complex 800 miles across

the South China Sea from U.S. assets in the Philippine
bases at Subic Bay and Clark Air Base. At last count
twenty to twenty-six Soviet surface ships and four to
six submarines use Cam Ranh Bay. Bear and Badger aircraft also deploy out of Vietnam.[12] Vietnam's dependency on the Soviet Union is now striking--Hanoi's reliance
on the 1978 treaty with Moscow and membership in the
Soviet-bloc Council for Mutual Economic Assistance
(COMECON) continues. All gasoline, oil, major weapons,
logistics, and high technology in Indochina are of
Soviet or East European origin. Inside Indochina, the
Soviets may be spending $4 billion a year to prop up the
local economies and to fuel Vietnam's militarism. However, the relationship between Hanoi and Moscow shows
evidence of strain.[13] Vietnamese/Soviet militarism in
turn has produced a reaction among the ASEAN countries,
which together with the United Nations, the United
States, and China are attempting to press Vietnam to
leave Kampuchea.

Although it appears true that Soviet military power
projection has not translated into equivalent political
influence in the Asian-Pacific region and indeed tends
to engender backlashes, Russian behavior has not modified notably as a result. Indeed, the Soviets show no
desire to reduce their growing military presence in the
region. As the invasion of Afghanistan and the shooting
down of KAL flight 007 vividly demonstrate, the Soviets
will employ their forces where and when they please.
The effect has been to fundamentally challenge the peace
and stability of the Asian-Pacific region and the assumptions behind U.S. policy.

Dimension Two: Relative U.S. Military Decline

The second critical dimension of change involves
U.S. military force levels in the Asian-Pacific region:
they continue at one of their lower points since 1945.
With about 160,000 U.S. combat forces on shore and
afloat in the region, only Brunei, Singapore, Laos,
Kampuchea, Malaysia, New Zealand, and Australia have
fewer forces in East Asia.[14] However, under the Reagan
administration there has been an effort to modernize
U.S. Pacific forces. These initiatives include introducing F-16s into Japan and replacing F-4s assigned to
Okinawa and South Korea with F-15s and F-16s. The 7th
Fleet has also received more F-14s, and the aircraft
carrier <u>Carl Vinson</u> and the battleship <u>Missouri</u> are now
with the fleet. B-52s on Guam are being upgraded with
air-launched cruise missiles.[15] Nevertheless, the
United States is a military lightweight in terms of
manpower, and it is difficult to speak of the United
States maintaining a "balance of power" in East Asia and
the Pacific--unless U.S. ability to counter manpower
with firepower, or rapidly deploy more troops into the
area, or see its allies undertake substantially in-

creased efforts can make a difference. As we shall see, all of these contingencies are problematic.

The baseline for U.S. forward-deployed manpower in the Asian-Pacific area has tended to be about 180,000 personnel. That figure is 20,000 more than the 1985 levels. At the time of the Japanese attack on Pearl Harbor, the United States had approximately 160,000 troops in East Asia. By the end of World War II, the figure was more than 3 million (not counting the China-Burma-India theatre). After demobilization, force levels quickly fell only to rise by the end of the Korean War to 650,000. At the start of the Kennedy administration's Vietnam involvement, total U.S. forces in ,sia were back at about 185,000. Then with escalation in Vietnam, U.S. force levels rose to more than 855,000, peaking just after the 1968 Tet Offensive. By mid-1975, the total U.S. force figure had dropped to 175,000. Additional withdrawals from Thailand, Korea, and Taiwan, and some cutbacks in 7th Fleet personnel, reduced these forces by early 1979 to less than 140,000.[16] As indicated, the Reagan administration is attempting to overcome these disadvantages.

The fluctuating U.S. force presence in the Asian-Pacific area contrasts sharply with Soviet force deployments since the mid-1960s. They have been moving in only one direction: up. The numbers, an important measure of strength, are impressive. As of 1983 (see Table 1.1), the Soviets had more than 2,000 aircraft, including approximately 1,600 tactical aircraft and more than 400 bombers in the area, but the United States had less than one-fourth this amount--about 500. The Soviet surface navy outnumbered the U.S. surface navy in East Asia by a figure of 84 to 39. Soviet submarines were 122 compared to 13 for the United States. Since 1983, these Soviet advantages have increased. Finally, in addition to the massive Soviet force advantages in the region, there are the huge armed forces that North Korea and Vietnam bring to bear--785,000 and 1,227,000 active duty troops, respectively. Accordingly, to try and rebalance the scales, the United States must rely on the contributions of Asian allies and friends, in particular Japan's forces of 245,000, South Korea's 620,000 troops, and in Southeast Asia, Thailand's armed forces of 235,000.[17]

To maintain its forward presence in the Asian-Pacific region even at these reduced force levels, the United States continues to depend on critical bases in Northeast Asia, Southeast Asia, and in special areas such as Australia. Back-up and support bases and facilities are located in Guam, Hawaii, Alaska, and the western states of the United States. In mainland Japan these facilities include the U.S. 7th Fleet headquarters at the Yokosuka-Yokohama naval complex. U.S. 5th air force headquarters are at Yokota Air Base. On Okinawa the United States relies principally on air bases and facilities at Kadena and Futenma. In the Republic of

TABLE 1.1 U.S.-Soviet Military Balance in East Asia and
the Pacific, January 1, 1983

| | United States | | | |
	Western Pacific	Eastern Pacific	Total	Soviet Union
Divisions	1-2/3	2-1/3	4	35
Tanks	189	136	325	9,000
Bombers	14	0	14	435
Tactical aircraft	449	301	750	1,565
Naval aircraft	36	72	108	50
Naval ships				
Aircraft carriers				
Attack	3	3	6	0
Helicopter	1	5	6	1
Cruisers	5	9	14	13
Destroyers	13	18	31	20
Frigates	17	24	41	50
Total surface ships	39	59	98	84
Submarines				
Strategic	0	1	1	31
Attack	13	33	46	91
Total submarines	13	34	47	122
Amphibious	7	24	31	12

Source: Congressional Research Service, Report N. 83-153S, U.S./
Soviet Military Balance, August 1, 1983, pp. 127-128. Reprinted in
Stephen J. Solarz, "The Soviet Challenge in Asia," Asia Pacific
Community 24 (Summer 1984), p. 15.

Korea (ROK) the U.S. 2nd infantry division is headquartered at Camp Casey, and the U.S.-ROK Joint Command is
headquartered in Seoul. In the Philippines the United
States relies principally on Subic Bay Naval Base and
Clark Air Base, the 13th air force headquarters.[18] The
bases in the Philippines have become the subject of
drawn out and sharp negotiations in recent years, although a successful renegotiation in 1983 allows the two
governments a reprieve until 1987-88.
    In addition to these basing arrangements, the
United States also maintains defense treaties with the
countries in which it utilizes military facilities. The
United States originally signed bilateral defense pacts
with the Philippines, Japan, the Republic of Korea, and
the Republic of China on Taiwan (ROC). The Australia-
New Zealand-United States (ANZUS) Pact was signed in
September 1951. The Manila Pact, by which Thailand
comes under U.S. protection, was signed in September
1954 and the Southeast Asia Treaty Organization (SEATO)
was established shortly thereafter. SEATO has since
been disbanded, and the U.S.-ROC treaty was unilaterally
abrogated in January 1979 by the Carter administration.

Each of the remaining bilateral and multilateral treaties stipulates that an armed attack on any of the
parties would endanger U.S. peace and safety and that
each party is obligated to "act to meet the common
danger in accordance with its constitutional
processes."[19]

In spite of all the changes in the military equation in East Asia and the Pacific that occurred before
Saigon fell in April 1975--the huge Soviet buildup, the
low levels of U.S. forces, and the press of U.S. commitments in distant areas such as the Persian Gulf--U.S.
policymakers still argue that U.S. commitments remain
essentially unchanged.[20] Nevertheless, when Secretary
of State George Shultz recently addressed the changing
force balance in the Asia-Pacific, his tone was rather
somber:

> The Asian and Pacific region is one of enormous concen-
> trations of military power in the hands of regimes that
> have shown little hesitation to use force, either di-
> rectly or as a means of intimidation when provided with
> an opening. Vietnam has one million men under arms, a
> staggering number for a country of that size. North
> Korea is one of the most heavily militarized nations in
> the world, and it has shown no scruples about putting
> force to use. Beyond the strategic missiles on land
> and sea that threaten the United States itself, the
> Soviet Union has dramatically increased its forces in
> the Pacific region to include over 50 divisions, 3,000
> modern combat aircraft, its largest fleet, and 135
> intermediate-range nuclear missiles, poised against the
> nations of the Pacific area, including ourselves.[21]

Dimension Three: Noncommunist
Asia's Economic Growth

In contrast to the extraordinary buildup of Soviet,
Vietnamese, and North Korean military power in East Asia
and the decline of the U.S. force presence in the region
is the stunning economic growth of Asia's noncommunist
societies. For example, the Pacific Basin, led by the
"Gang of Five" countries (Japan, South Korea, Taiwan,
Hong Kong, and Singapore) is now the fastest growing and
most resilient trade region in the world. It is also
the fastest growing investment area. Add in the impact
of the United States, and the Asian-Pacific region also
becomes the high technology center of the world, bounded
by Silicon Valley on the U.S. West Coast, by Japan,
Taiwan, and Hong Kong in Northeast Asia, and by Singapore in Southeast Asia. Total U.S. two-way trade with
East Asia and the Pacific in 1984 was estimated to be in
the vicinity of $165 billion--greater than U.S. trade
with the European Common Market and almost one-third of
total U.S. trade.[22] U.S. investment in the area is
conservatively valued at more than $30 billion.[23] But

the United States is also running a serious trade deficit with the area--more than $60 billion.

U.S.-Japanese two-way trade alone was more than $75 billion in 1984. Japan now has the world's second largest GNP at $1.5 trillion in 1984. Together the United States and Japan account for almost one-third of all global economic productivity. Their combined share of world trade is about 22 percent. In Southeast Asia, the ASEAN countries also are generally showing remarkable progress. Their combined exports were more than $75 billion in 1984, and their per capita income growth has been very impressive. For example, compared to Vietnam's meager $180 annual per capita income, Thailand's is $800, Singapore's is over $5,000, and oil-rich Brunei's is nearly $18,000. ASEAN's combined population is almost five times Vietnam's. The association's combined Gross National Product (GNP) is over $210 billion, more than fifteen times Vietnam's.[24] Finally, as a group, the ASEAN countries now form the United States' fifth largest trade partner, and new reciprocal trade arrangements are under consideration. U.S. markets have opened liberally to ASEAN products in the past two years, and U.S. business investment in these countries was valued at $8 billion in 1984.[25]

These developments add up to something quite profound for the Asian-Pacific region's future: economically and politically the noncommunist countries (whether democratic or authoritarian) are dramatically outstripping the communist countries. By contrast, the economies of Beijing, Pyongyang, Hanoi, Phnom Penh, and Vientiane pale in comparison to the rest of East Asia. The region's two harshest regimes, Pyongyang and Hanoi, cannot hope to effectively develop as long as they rely on the Soviet Union, make war on their neighbors, spread terrorism, and divert 20 percent or more of their GNP to arms. Fortunately, Beijing no longer belongs to that mold and is rapidly modernizing its economy through programs of dramatic economic reform, free market incentives, and external trade and technology acquisitions. U.S. trade with the PRC went from $1.1 billion in 1978 to $4.4 billion in 1983 and may have reached $5.5 billion in 1984.[26] Having engaged with the West, China now has the chance to complete a new Long March--this time to economic maturity--if it can control its previous tendency toward political instability. In short, noncommunist Asia, plus the PRC, is making extraordinary economic progress.

THE SOVIET MILITARY CHALLENGE IN PERSPECTIVE

The rapid Soviet military buildup in the post-Vietnam War era is yet to be translated into a strategic environment in the region that is decidedly favorable to the Soviet Union. Several factors are responsible for the failure of the Soviet Union thus far to take advantage of the situation by consolidating its position of political influence in the Asian-Pacific region. These include, according to a noted scholar, the following seven regional developments in the early 1980s: (1) the new cold war between the communist states; (2) China's dramatic turn to the West; (3) the gradual reassertion of Japan; (4) the end of the period of U.S. drift; (5) the development of ASEAN; (6) the Korean standoff; and (7) the dynamic economic growth in the region that could eventually lead to a new Asian-Pacific trading community.[27] The possibilities for a Soviet comeback in the Asian-Pacific area in the immediate future, however, cannot and must not be ruled out. The five possible scenarios for the Soviet comeback in the region, according to the same scholar, are: (1) instability in the region; (2) further shifts in the military balance in Moscow's favor; (3) the unraveling of U.S. relations with China, Japan, or ASEAN; (4) a Soviet breakthrough with Japan; and (5) a successful Soviet reconciliation with China.[28]

Ultimately, it is the interplay of the forces within each country and between the major regional actors that will provide the stimulus for change and stability in the region. Domestic political trends and foreign policy directions of each regional actor will thus need to be surveyed with a view to determining the shape of the emerging pattern of regional developments in the Asian Pacific. The policymakers' perceptions of the external environment are particularly important in determining the pattern of policy response by individual countries in the region.

It is likely that the Soviet Union will not readily disengage or disassociate itself from its regional ties in the immediate future because of its heavy infrastructure, investment, and military buildup there. In fact, it is more likely that the Soviets are here to stay in the Asian-Pacific region for the foreseeable future. After all, the Soviet Union has longer coastlines along the Pacific Ocean than any ASEAN state. The implications of the Soviet presence and entrenchment in the region, in terms of impact on individual countries and the region as a whole, receives further analysis and interpretation in individual chapters of this volume. The meaning and significance of U.S. military decline vis-à-vis the Soviet Union in the Asian-Pacific region, although the trend has been reversed under the Reagan administration, also is analyzed. Also necessary is the discussion of the importance and future prospects of noncommunist Asia's economic growth in terms of regional stability and the power balance.

POLICY RESPONSES AND NEW U.S. ASIAN-PACIFIC POLICY

The Asian-Pacific area is a region of challenge and diversity that requires broadly gauged policy pronouncements and elicits creative policy responses by the

regional actors with regard to regional security and
welfare. The United States, for instance, was responsible for the shift in policy emphasis and attention in
the 1970s, which after Vietnam was reinforced by the
Carter administration's initial decision to withdraw
U.S. ground combat forces from South Korea, thus gener-
ating confusion and concern among U.S. Asian allies and
friends, including Japan.[29] President Reagan's unswerv-
ing support and shared optimism for the future of Asian-
Pacific cooperation, however, is manifested in a series
of unambiguous policy statements and acts regarding
future U.S. intentions toward the region. These include
President Reagan's addresses in November 1983 before the
Japanese Diet in Tokyo and the South Korean National
Assembly in Seoul, respectively, and his talks with
Chinese leaders during his visit to Beijing in April
1984. The policy agenda for promoting "a Pacific era,"
notwithstanding the concern of European allies, was also
put into effect in September 1984 when President Reagan,
during White House ceremonies, demonstrated his commitment to the future of Pacific cooperation by inaugurat-
ing the United States National Committee for Pacific
Economic Cooperation.

One U.S. government official, at the outset of
President Reagan's second term in office, perceived that
changes in the Asian-Pacific security environment and
regional development would offer the United States both
opportunities and risks in the future. He defined U.S.
opportunities in the region as follows: (1) expanding
commercial and investment opportunities; (2) associating
Japan even more closely with the West; (3) propelling
China toward closer cooperation with the United States;
(4) working constructively with regional groupings in
the area, particularly ASEAN; and (5) fostering a North-
South dialogue on the Korean Peninsula. Included in the
list of potential risks are: (1) burgeoning trade defi-
cits that will stimulate increased protectionist sentiment and protectionist trade measures in the U.S. Congress; (2) succession crises in several Asian-Pacific
countries that could lead to political instability adversely affecting U.S. financial flows, economic development, and strategic interests; (3) antinuclear sentiment that could check U.S. naval access to New Zealand
and vitiate a key alliance; (4) failure to address the
imbalance within the Cambodian resistance that would
undermine future possibilities for a political solution;
and (5) a Soviet policy that will continue to build its
military strength in Asia and play for any diplomatic
and political breaks that may come along.[30]

ORGANIZATION OF THE VOLUME

The present volume reflects varying views of Asian
security expressed in terms of each country's or subregion's perception of and response to the emerging secu-

rity environment in the remainder of the 1980s. Policy implications for the region, and especially for the United States, are then discussed in terms of past commitments, alliances, and treaties as contrasted with the current security realities and relationships. Each of the contributors has organized his (or their) chapter according to three concerns: (1) the country's (or sub-region's) perceived security threats or challenges; (2) the country's (or subregion's) emerging security re-sponse for the remainder of the 1980s; and (3) implica-tions of (1) and (2) for the region and especially for the U.S. national interests.

Although not all countries in the region (e.g., Taiwan) are included, most of the important regional actors are represented. The introductory chapter (Kihl and Grinter) presents an overview of regional security realities and emerging patterns as well as a framework for the subsequent individual analyses. Under the rub-ric of "the Great Powers as regional actors" in part 1, three separate chapters are included. The two super-powers, the United States and the Soviet Union, are examined separately in chapters 2 (Grinter) and 3 (Leighton and Rosenberger). The Great Powers' security role and their diplomatic and military interrelation-ships in the Southeast Asia subregion are examined in chapter 4 (Simon).

In part 2, the Northeast Asia subregion, whose major regional actors are China, Japan, and the two Koreas, is examined in terms of each country's security role and defense policies. China's perception of the strategic environment and its diplomatic policy are discussed in chapter 5 (Sutter). Japan's security role and continuing policy debates are examined in chapter 6 (Tow). North and South Korea's threat perceptions, diplomatic maneuvering, and prospects for inter-Korean negotiations are examined in chapter 7 (Kihl).

In part 3, the Southeast Asia and Oceania subre-gions, whose main regional actors are Vietnam, ASEAN and ANZUS, are examined. Vietnam's challenge to Southeast Asia's regional order, in terms of Hanoi's perception and ideological stands, is examined in chapter 8 (Tur-ley). The military and security policies of each ASEAN member state are examined in chapter 9 (Weatherbee). The prospects for ANZUS are examined in chapter 10 (McKinley).

In part 4, the concluding chapter (Grinter and Kihl) discusses the future prospects of Asian-Pacific security. The emerging regional trends are highlighted, and the policy implications are discussed for the region and for the United States. Both short-term and long-range prospects are introduced as probable future trends, and policy options are examined. The chapter closes with recommendations for U.S. policy.

14

NOTES

1. Recent studies on the economic prospect of the Asian-Pacific region include: Roger Benjamin and Robert T. Kudrle, eds., *The Industrial Future of the Pacific Basin* (Boulder, Colo.: Westview, 1984); Roy Hofheinz, Jr. and Kent Calder, *Eastasia Edge* (New York: Basic Books, 1982); Lawrence B. Krause and Sueo Sekiguchi, eds., *Economic Interaction in the Pacific Basin* (Washington, D.C.: Brookings Institution, 1980).

2. Excluded from the scope of the present study are Mongolia, Burma, Papua-New Guinea, and some island countries in the Pacific, such as Western Samoa, Tonga, and Fuji, and a large number of dependencies of the United States, France, and New Zealand in Oceania.

3. Jon Halliday, "Capitalism and Socialism in East Asia," *New Left Review* 124 (November-December 1980): 3-24.

4. In April 1985, China announced its intention of reducing troop size by as much as 1 million.

5. Department of Defense, *Soviet Miitary Power 1984* (Washington, D.C.: GPO, 1984).

6. Michael H. Armacost, *The Asia-Pacific Region: A Forward Look*, U.S. Department of State, Current Policy, no. 653, 29 January 1985.

7. Details are in Paul F. Langer, "Soviet Military Power in Asia," in Donald S. Zagoria, ed., *Soviet Policy in East Asia* (New Haven: Yale University Press, 1982), pp. 269-271; Patrick J. Garrity, "Soviet Policy in the Far East," *Asia-Pacific Defense Forum* (Summer, 1983):14-20; and Peter Polomka, "The Security of the Western Pacific: The Price of Burden Sharing," *Survival* (January-February 1984):4.

8. An insightful presentation is in John J. Stephen, "Asia in the Soviet Conception," in Zagoria, *Soviet Policy*, pp. 29-56.

9. See Chi Su, "China and the Soviet Union: 'Principled, Salutary, and Tempered' Management of Conflict," in Samuel S. Kim, ed., *China and the World: Chinese Foreign Policy in the Post-Mao Era* (Boulder, Colo.: Westview, 1984), pp. 155-156.

10. Details are in Claude Malhuret, "Report from Afghanistan," *Foreign Affiars* (Winter 1983-84):426-443.

11. Examples are shown in Langer, "Soviet Military Power in Asia," in Zagoria, *Soviet Policy*, pp. 261-262.

12. Donald S. Zagoria, "The USSR and Asia in 1984," *Asian Survey* (January 1985):27.

13. Donald S. Zagoria and Sheldon W. Simon, "Soviet Policy in Southeast Asia," in Zagoria, *Soviet Policy*, pp. 164-166.

14. "The Military Balance 1984-1985," as reprinted in *Pacific Defense Reporter*, 1985 Annual Reference Edition (December 1984-January 1985):137-147. The 160,000 U.S. combat, or combat support, troops in the Asian-Pacific are composed mainly of army divisions in Korea and Hawaii, a marine division and brigade in Okinawa and Hawaii, 7th Fleet assets, and U.S. Air Force strategic and tactical fighter squadrons. See Caspar W. Weinberger, *Annual Report to the Congress, Fiscal Year 1986* (Washington, D.C.: GPO, 4 February 1985), pp. 237-240.

15. Jonathan D. Pollack, "East Asia: A Positive Example for U.S. Interest," in Barry M. Blechman and Edward N. Luttwak, *Inter-*

national Security Yearbook 1984/85 (Boulder, Colo.: Westview, 1985), pp. 172-173.

16. Details are in Lawrence E. Grinter, The Philippine Bases: Continuing Utility in a Changing Strategic Context, National Security Affairs Monograph 80-2 (Washington, D.C.: National Defense University, 1980), p. 4.

17. Armed forces numbers are from "The Military Balance 1984-1985," pp. 139-147.

18. Details of all U.S. basing arrangements in East Asia and both the Western and Eastern Pacific are in William R. Feeney, "The Pacific Basing System and U.S. Security," in William T. Tow and William R. Feeney, eds., U.S. Foreign Policy and Asian-Pacific Security: A Transregional Approach (Boulder, Colo.: Westview, 1982), pp. 174-187.

19. A protocol of the Manila Pact defines "aggression by means of armed attack" as limited "only to Communist aggression." Article II of the 1954 ROC-U.S. Mutual Defense Treaty stipulated that the two "will maintain and develop their individual and collective capacity to resist armed attack and Communist subversive activities directed from without against their territorial integrity and political stability." The U.S.-Japanese Security Treaty of 1951 stipulated the United States would help defend Japan from both external attack and "large-scale internal riots and disturbances." The subsequent U.S.-Japanese Mutual Cooperation and Security Treaty of 1960 refers only to an "armed attack" against territory. Neither of the Japanese treaties nor the Korean or Philippine treaties specified communist aggression. Nor does the ANZUS treaty. See U.S. Department of State, United States Treaties and Other International Agreements, vol. 6, part 1, 1955, pp. 81-89, 322-343; vol. 3, part 3, 1952, pp. 3329-3340; vol. 2, part 2, pp. 1632-1635; vol. 5, part 3, 1954, pp. 2368-2376; vol. 3, part 3, 1952, pp. 3947-3951 and 3421-3425, published respectively in 1956, 1953, 1960, 1955, and 1953 by the GPO, Washington, D.C.

20. Ronald Reagan, in Shultz, Asia-Pacific and the Future, U.S. Department of State, Current Policy, no. 598, 18 July 1984.

21. Ibid.

22. George P. Shultz, Economic Cooperation in the Pacific Basin, U.S. Department of State, Current Policy, no. 658, 21 February 1985.

23. Armacost, Asia-Pacific, and Paul H. Kreisberg, "The United States and Asia in 1984," Asian Survey (January 1985):2.

24. Population and GNP figures are taken from "The Military Balance 1984-1985."

25. George P. Shultz, Challenge Facing the U.S. and ASEAN, U.S. Department of State, Current Policy, no. 597, 13 July 1984; and Shultz, Asia-Pacific and the Future.

26. Paul D. Wolfowitz, The U.S.-China Trade Relationship, U.S. Department of State, Current Policy, no. 594, 31 May 1984.

27. Zagoria, Soviet Policy, p. 5.

28. Ibid., p. 13.

29. See, for instance, Franklin B. Weinstein and Fujin Kamiya, eds., The Security of Korea: U.S. and Japanese Perspectives on the 1980s (Boulder, Colo.: Westview, 1980).

30. Armacost, Asia-Pacific.

Part 1

Great Powers as Regional Actors

2 The United States: Coping with the Soviet Buildup and Alliance Dilemmas

Lawrence E. Grinter

The Reagan administration perceives two fundamental trends in the Asian-Pacific region: (1) the vibrant economic growth of the noncommunist countries whose leader, Japan, nevertheless is seriously complicating the U.S. trade balance with the area; and (2) the growing Soviet and Soviet client military buildup in the region. In February 1985, Secretary of State George Shultz affirmed both perceptions when he commented:

> In economic development, in the growth of free institutions, and in growing global influence, the Pacific region has rapidly emerged as a leading force on the world stage. Its economic dynamism has become a model for the developing world and offers a unique and attractive vision of the future.

Shultz continued:

> While the prospects for the nations and people of the Pacific Basin are bright, politically and economically, we must bear in mind that this is one of the most heavily armed regions in the world, and Asian peace is still marred by continuing and tragic conflicts. In Vietnam, Cambodia, and Laos, some 1.1 million men are now under arms, while on the Korean Peninsula there is a combined total of 1.5 million troops. In addition to 4.4 million men in uniform in China, approximately one-third to one-half of the USSR's ground forces--some 52 divisions--are garrisoned in the Soviet Far East. Soviet air power, both tactical and strategic, continues to grow; the Soviet Pacific Fleet is now their largest;

Opinions, conclusions, and recommendations expressed or implied within are solely those of the author and do not necessarily represent the views of the Department of the Air Force, the Department of Defense, or any other U.S. government agency.

19

and about one-third of the Soviet SS-20 intermediate
range ballistic missile battalions overshadow much of
the population of the region. This concentration of
military forces is of considerable concern given the
demonstrated willingness of the Soviet Union and its
proxies--in Afghanistan, Cambodia, and Korea--to use
their military power for their political ends.[1]

These perceptions and concerns have been evident in
Reagan administration views of Asia and the Pacific
since Mr. Reagan took office in 1981. However, since
1984, as the Japanese trade surplus with the United
States has escalated, economic competition between the
United States and its allies as well as other alliance
difficulties have attracted more official comment than
the Soviet threat.

The Reagan administration's first major policy
statement on East Asia and the Pacific came in April
1981. In that statement, Under Secretary of State for
Political Affairs Walter Stoessel concentrated on U.S.
allies--assuring South Korea the new U.S. administration
would not reinitiate the Carter withdrawal plan; expressing confidence that U.S.-Japanese trade problems
could be handled; backing the attempts of the Association of South East Asian Nations (ASEAN) to get Vietnam
out of Kampuchea. The Soviet Union's military buildup
was mentioned in passing.[2] In June 1982, Stoessel gave
Soviet activities in East Asia more attention. He argued that the Soviet Union and its friends in Asia were
seeking "positions of maximum geopolitical strength from
which to project power and influence. . . . [They] put a
premium on military force as an instrument of geopolitical strength . . . and their force buildup far exceeds
any legitimate defense requirements.[3]

To counter these Soviet actions, Mr. Stoessel argued that U.S. policy should urge Japan to do more in
defense (especially in "air defense, antisubmarine warfare, logistics, and communications"); continue to rely
on Australia's and New Zealand's role in standing "guard
over a secure, if lengthy, line of communication between
the Pacific and Indian Oceans"; continue U.S. assistance
to South Korea, whose defense efforts "figure prominent-
ly in our broader objectives vis-à-vis the Soviet Union
in East Asia"; and be encouraged by China's "common
perception [with the United States] of threatening Soviet ambitions worldwide. . . . China's opposition to
Soviet and Soviet proxy aggression is an important factor in maintaining regional and global peace and
stability."[4]

Stoessel concluded by acknowledging the heavy Asian
defense burden that the United States carries in Asia,
and he indicated the apparent burden-sharing rearrange-
ments under way:

In summary, while our defense burdens are heavy and we
continue by necessity to make the largest single con-

tribution of any country, our allies and friends are continuing to assume an ever-increasing share of the burden. Given the increasing Soviet threat to our common interests, it is essential that we, our allies, and our friends transmit an unremitting signal of resolve to protect these interests for so long as they continue to be threatened. [5]

Thus, eighteen months into the Reagan administration's first term in office, four priorities in Asian policy had emerged: pushing Japan toward an increased security role, relying on Australia's and New Zealand's security contributions, depending on South Korea's critical military role, and relying on the People's Republic of China (PRC) as a "friendly, nonaligned country" with parallel strategic interests.

By 1984, these four priorities had enlarged to take into account ASEAN's anticommunist stance in Southeast Asia and U.S. problems with the Philippines and New Zealand. For example, in July 1984, Secretary of State Shultz told the ASEAN foreign ministers:

> ASEAN's record of progress over the past decade has been phenomenal. . . . U.S. investment in ASEAN, currently almost $8 billion . . . continues to increase, as American business sees new opportunities in ASEAN's expanding free-market economies. . . . ASEAN is now the fifth largest trading partner of the United States-- with total trade exceeding $23 billion.[6]

However, in April 1985, Assistant Secretary of State for East Asian Affairs Paul Wolfowitz addressed the problems in the Philippines and commented that the United States favored "free and fair local elections in 1986 and Presidential elections in 1987," backed "efforts to restore a free-market orientation in the economy," and would provide "enhanced military assistance in the expectation that reforms already begun will continue and expand."[7]

In February 1985, President Ronald Reagan spoke of the strains within the Australia-New Zealand-United States (ANZUS) alliance:

> We deeply regret the decision by the New Zealand Government to deny port access to our ships. . . . It's our deepest hope that New Zealand will restore the traditional cooperation that has existed between our two countries.[8]

Thus, as 1985 began, the United States had substantial problems with key allies. In early 1985, Secretary of Defense Casper Weinberger signed an article entitled "The Five Pillars of our Defense Policy in East Asia and the Pacific" in which he seemed to summarize the various challenges in the Asian Pacific. In it Weinberger cited five "foundation stones" underlying U.S. policy in Asia:

1. The key importance of the U.S. security relationship with Japan
2. The U.S. commitment to stability on the Korean
   peninsula
3. U.S. efforts to build an enduring relationship
   with China
4. U.S. support for ASEAN
5. The long-standing U.S. partnership with Australia and New Zealand[9]

By making these five relationships the foundations of
U.S. policy toward the Asian-Pacific region, the Reagan
administration has acknowledged Washington's dependence
on countries in the area to help produce the combined
economic-military-diplomatic strength necessary to contain and deter the Soviets and their clients. Little
commentary can be found on U.S. military forces alone
making the difference, any longer, in maintaining a
balance of power in the region. U.S. military assets in
the region are being modernized, although, as indicated
earlier in this book, they are at low levels. Thus,
more than ever before, the United States has become
dependent on its Asian-Pacific partners, rather than the
other way around, to maintain security in East Asia.
The remainder of this chapter examines these five relationships, the challenge they present, and the Reagan
administration's response, as it conducts its Asian-
Pacific policies.

U.S.-JAPANESE RELATIONS

By 1984, U.S.-Japanese relations, troubled by the
growing trade imbalance between the two partners (the
U.S. deficit was $37 billion in 1984 and approached $50
billion in 1985), became the single most commented on
aspect of U.S. relations with East Asia. Things did not
start out this way. In October 1981, nine months after
the Reagan administration came to office, the newly
appointed Assistant Secretary of State for East Asian
and Pacific Affairs, John Holdridge, concluded that
despite the burgeoning trade imbalance (about $15 bil-
lion in 1981)

> a continuing relationship of mutual confidence and
> credibility between Japan and the United States is
> essential to the maintenance of peace in East Asia. A
> solid foundation exists to sustain such a relationship.
> To ensure that the relationship will continue to serve
> the national interests of each, we must be aware of our
> mutual dependence; we must be considerate and patient;
> we must be willing to hear each other out. I think our
> record to date in sustaining and expanding this vital
> relationship holds solid promise for the future.[10]

Compare these assurances with the comments of the next
East Asian Assistant Secretary of State, Paul Wolfowitz,
three and one-half years later in April 1985:

> The striking increase in our bilateral trade deficit
> with Japan last year has provoked strong concern in the
> Congress, our business community, and the popular
> press. Pressures for protectionist action, which could
> have a major detrimental impact on this relationship as
> well as on the global trading system, have mounted on a
> dangerous level. Our relations with Japan are too
> vital strategically, politically, and economically for
> us not to resolve current and underlying difficulties
> on an urgent basis.[11]

What happened to Japanese-U.S. relations--"the core
element of our Asia policy"--in those four years?   The
answer is that U.S. consumers and industry bought about
$120 billion more of Japanese goods than U.S. businesses
and producers sold to Japan, and a political backlash
broke loose in the United States.   Three factors were at
work: (1) the relative disadvantage of U.S. manufacturing to Japanese manufacturing; (2) the historic protectionist sentiment in Japan; and (3) the free trade
philosophy of the Reagan administration versus a protectionist Congress. By 1984, it was almost as though the
executive branch of the U.S. government was acting as a
referee between Tokyo and the U.S. Congress.
    The problem initially began to mount in 1982: "The
movement of Japanese industry into industrial areas,
long considered the [United States'] preserve has . . .
caused a substantial increase in economic friction."[12]
By the fall of 1983, Reagan administration pressure on
Japan to reduce trade barriers was made public:

> Recently, the Japanese Government has taken several im-
> portant steps to reduce trade barriers in order to in-
> crease access and give more equal treatment for foreign
> goods in Japan. We welcome these steps. We encourage
> Japan not only to put them into effect expeditiously
> but also to pursue other measures for opening markets,
> for this will reduce serious stresses in our relation-
> ship.[13]

In early 1984, the serious U.S. backlash finally was
acknowledged by the executive branch:

> In the view of many Americans, the U.S.-Japan relation-
> ship is not characterized by global partnership and po-
> tential but by divisive problems, especially in trade
> and security. . . . A Gallup poll in September 1983
> found that fully 73% of the American public believed
> that Japanese imports pose a "serious threat now to the
> jobs of American workers."[14]

In June 1984, the administration sought to convey a conciliatory and optimistic attitude. Assistant Secretary Wolfowitz argued:

> When many people look at U.S.-Japan relations, the focus is on the problems in our relationship and not on its successes. But I believe that if we step back and take a look at our overall relationship, we would determine that it is the best that it has ever been and that the problems that we have are the exceptions and not the rule.
>
> First of all . . . our defense relationship with Japan has never been better.
>
> Second, we have with Japan one of the broadest and most diverse scientific relationships that we have with any country in the world--both in the private sector and between our governments.
>
> Our educational and cultural relationship with Japan is another aspect of our relationship that we hear little about--again, because everything is going so smoothly.
>
> Although the common perception is of a closed market, Japan actually is our largest overseas market. [15]

However, by April 1985, the administration conceded that pressures within the U.S. Congress and public for protectionist action had mounted to "a dangerous level."[16] To cope with it, the Reagan and the Nakasone governments singled out four trade sectors for special attention: telecommunications, electronics, forest products, and medical/pharmaceutical products. The Japanese prime minister pledged to take "dramatic steps" to open Japan's markets, but still the Japanese surplus mounted and as 1985 closed was estimated to be $50 billion for 1985.[17]

On the defense issue, an equally critical if less publicized problem in U.S.-Japanese relations was Japan's very low level of defense spending and capabilities compared to its enormous GNP. Japan, adjacent to the Soviet Union's largest fleet, would have consigned the Sea of Japan to Soviet domination if it were not for U.S. naval and air protection. Successive U.S. administrations have tried to prod Japan into substantial increases in its defense spending, its capabilities, or both. Under Presidents Ford and Carter, defense spending was pushed. Under President Reagan, the emphasis has been on "roles and missions." U.S. urging seems to have had little effect on Japan primarily because the Liberal Democratic party (LDP), which rules by way of internal party factions and periodic coalitions with other parties, simply has not given defense real priority. There are also constitutional prohibitions.

Japanese Prime Minister Yasuhiro Nakasone has rhetorically pushed for a strong defense, although like all
prime ministers, he is hemmed in by party politics. At
his first news conference after his November 1982 election, Nakasone said: "I believe that our country's defense efforts have not been adequate. And I understand
the argument put forward by the U.S. and its European
allies that Japan should increase its military spending
now that it has become a great economic power."[18] During his January 1983 visit to the United States, Nakasone talked about control of "the four straits that go
through the Japanese islands so that there should be no
passage of Soviet submarines," and he itemized Japan's
role in defending the sea-lanes out to 1000 miles.[19]

U.S. officials, in turn, have been candid about
Japan's minimal defense effort. In November 1982,
Commander-in-Chief, Pacific Admiral Robert Long stated:
"The Japanese are individually well-trained, well-
disciplined and technically very competent. The major
problem is that they lack adequate supplies of fuel,
ammunition and missiles. In my judgment, they lack the
ability to handle even a minor contingency."[20] In March
of 1982, Francis West, an assistant secretary of defense
in the first Reagan administration, testified to
Congress:

> By its own public analyses, [Japan's] Self-Defense
> Forces (SDF) cannot sustain its army divisions, de-
> stroyers, and tactical aircraft combat due to very
> limited supplies of ammunition, torpedoes, and mis-
> siles. The size and modernization of Japan's air and
> naval forces are not adequate to defend its air space
> and sea lanes to 1000 miles against the Soviet force
> levels of the 1980's, which even the Government now
> identifies as potentially threatening.[21]

All this controversy and the push to adequately arm
Japan stem in part from the stunning enlargement of
Soviet military capabilities in Asia. The Japan Defense
Agency's (JDA) analysis of the Soviet Union's capabilities is sobering. East of Lake Baikal, the USSR deploys
about 370,000 troops in 40 divisions compared to Japan's
160,000 troops in 13 divisions. Of the 2,400 Soviet
combat aircraft in Asia, the JDA indicates that more
than one-half are second or third generation, including
MIG-23/27 Floggers and SU-24 Fencers. On water, the
Soviet Pacific Fleet's 825 ships, with total displace-
ment of 1.7 million tons, outclass Japan's 132 ships at
400,000 tons. All three major Japanese straits, Tsushima, Tsugaru, and Soya, experience a large volume of
Soviet military aircraft movements and vessel passage.[22]
Japan's current Mid-Term Defense Program (1983-1987) has
not been able to accomplish its goals.[23] Various initiatives continue to be discussed in U.S.-Japan defense
circles. These include:[24]

Doubling Japan's Defense Budget

Doubling Tokyo's defense expenditures from 1 percent to
2 percent of GNP would raise the amount spent in 1985
to about $26 billion in 1985 dollars. This would allow
Japan to begin a competent defense of the Sea of Japan's eastern reaches including coordinated mining and
blockade activity with the United States.

Replacing Obsolete Equipment

Despite current modernization efforts, much of the SDF
equipment is still obsolete. In the ground forces, it
has been estimated that 60 percent are out of date. In
the maritime and air forces, the estimates run even
higher.

Improving Training

Training exercise areas and training funding for Japan's armed services are extremely limited. Because of
terrain, population density, environmental restrictions, and public moods, the ground forces have no
facilities for large unit maneuvers or for practice
firings of long range artillery and missiles. Naval
and air forces are also limited.

Increasing SDF Manpower

With an authorized manpower strength of some 272,000
men, the SDF is a relatively modest force, and its
forces are actually manned below this level. Ground
forces are presently manned at only 86 percent of the
authorized 180,000-man level. The air and naval forces
are at about 95 percent manning.

Increasing Ammunition Supplies and Logistic Support

U.S. estimates are that the Self-Defense Forces have
about three to five days of ammunition and logistics
stocks in the event of combat.

Developing an Integrated Strategy and Concept for Operations

Evidence indicates that Japan's armed forces have serious problems with a unified command system and a concept for integrated operations.

Expanding Transportation Capabilities

Japan's transport capabilities for troops and supply
movements are extremely limited. Even limited engagements would be difficult to handle under these circumstances.

Dealing with the economic and security aspects of
the relationship between Japan and the United States has
not been easy for either Washington or Tokyo. The
relationship constitutes the single most critical bilateral alliance for both countries. The conspicuous
imbalance in Japan's strengths--Japan is a global economic competitor but, in the face of the growing Soviet
threat, it is a military weakling--produces continual
frustration in the United States. This will continue
until and unless the imbalances are resolved. However
the imbalances are rectified--through reduction of
Japan's trade surplus with the United States, or increases in Japan's defense capabilities, or both--it
will probably prove to be the most delicate challenge
ahead for U.S. policy in the Asian-Pacific region.

U.S.-CHINA RELATIONS

Alexander Haig, when he was the Reagan administration's first Secretary of State, considered China crucial to U.S. strategic interests.[25] The perception was
not shared by President Reagan, at least not initially,
and it took almost a year for a consistent and strategic
China policy to emerge from the Reagan administration.
Ronald Reagan came to office intending that the United
States would not "abandon" Taiwan.[26] However, in June
1982, in a speech on Sino-U.S. relations, Under Secretary of State Walter Stoessel indicated new priorities
in U.S.-PRC relations:

> A strong U.S.-China relationship is one of the highest
> goals of President Reagan's foreign policy.
>
> Strong U.S.-China relations are not only critical for
> our long-term security but also contribute to Asian
> stability and global harmony.
>
> We view China as a friendly country with which we are
> not allied but with which we share many common inter-
> ests. Strategically, we have no fundamental conflicts
> of interest, and we face a common challenge from the
> Soviet Union.[27]

These priorities suggest that in the period between the
1980 campaign and 1982, the president came around to the
view that China should be considered the equivalent of a
strategic partner of the United States. Secretary Haig
did not last long enough to see the full fruition of his
(and others') efforts in this regard as he resigned in
July 1982, but he did remark in his memoirs that

> more than any other thing that happened in the eighteen
> months that I was Secretary of State, the China
> question convinced me that Reagan's world view was

indeed different from my own, and that I could not serve him and my convictions at the same time. [28]

It was the question of Taiwan that most complicated U.S.-China policy. After much debate within the administration and frustrating discussions with the Chinese ("an especially difficult and sensitive time for both sides" [29]), Washington and Beijing issued the Joint Communiqué of August 17, 1982. The document reflected the continuing and unresolved differences between the two countries--the ongoing U.S. "special relationship" (including arms sales) with the government on Taiwan, and the PRC's denial of legitimacy to that government. Those differences were further elaborated in a state department appraisal:

> Aware of our consistent and firm opposition to the use of force against Taiwan, the Chinese during these discussions agreed to state in very strong terms their policy of pursuing a peaceful resolution of the Taiwan issue and described this policy as "fundamental." The Chinese insisted, however, that we agree to the ultimate termination of arms sales [to Taiwan]. We refused. [30]

As finally hammered out, the communiqué reflected this U.S. position:

- The United States "has no intention of infringing on Chinese sovereignty."

- The United States "understands and appreciates the Chinese policy of striving for a peaceful resolution of the Taiwan question."

- The United States "does not seek to carry out a long-term policy of arms sales to Taiwan. . . . Its arms sales to Taiwan will not exceed, either in qualitative or in quantitative terms, the level of those supplied in recent years since the establishment of diplomatic relations between the United States and China, and that it intends to reduce gradually its sales of arms to Taiwan, leading over a period of time to a final resolution." [31]

This position on Taiwan continues to be Reagan administration policy, but U.S. policy is now further complicated by the question of arms sales to Beijing. In short, the United States has decided to sell arms to both Chinas and still encourage a peaceful resolution of their difficulties.

For over a decade, U.S. security thinking has considered the possibility of enlisting the People's Republic of China as an anti-Soviet surrogate. Statesmen and analysts have seen advantages to a Sino-U.S. "de facto strategic partnership in their parallel competition against the Soviet Union."[32]   Zbigniew Brezezinski, President Carter's national security advisor, expressed the idea during a May 1978 trip to the PRC: "We see our relations with China as a central facet of U.S. global policy. The United States and China share certain common interests and we have parallel, long-term strategic concerns. The most important of these is our common opposition to global or regional hegemony by any single power."[33] The then Vice President Walter Mondale, in Beijing in August 1979, expressed similar ideas.

However, during the 1980 election campaign, Ronald Reagan implied that he favored return to a Two Chinas policy (giving Taiwan an "official" status), and he included several pro-Taiwan specialists among his advisors. The Chinese, always touchy about Taiwan, found the initial Reagan position disappointing, and U.S. officials revealed that the United States faced "the threat of collapse of the entire structure of Sino-U.S. relations."[34]   PRC relations with the United States cooled. The Soviet military threat on China's border proved an added complication for Chinese foreign policy, and in late 1981 Beijing signaled a more flexible attitude toward the Soviet Union. Reconciliation talks between Moscow and Beijing began in early 1982 with the objective of recomposing their relations, defusing the border problem, and rebuilding trade and cultural exchanges.[35] China evidently had concluded there was "greater advantage for herself in maneuvering between the two superpowers."[36] Although Beijing characterized the cool relations with Washington as a function of U.S. ties to Taiwan ("interference in China's internal affairs"), it is likely that the need to defuse the Soviet threat was equally acute in PRC thinking. The Chinese remain touchy on all these subjects.[37]

At all events, Sino-U.S. relations hit a low in 1982 and early 1983. Trips in 1983 by Secretary of State Shultz and Secretary of Defense Weinberger helped to relax both sides' rhetoric on Taiwan. The notion of strategic cooperation had never really died, as concurrent events revealed:

- The late 1979 Carter administration agreement to establish a joint U.S.-PRC landsat missile monitoring station in Xinjiang (run by Chinese technicians)

- Secretary of Defense Harold Brown's January 1980 trip to the PRC and the subsequent U.S. agreement to sell China "nonlethal" military equipment

- Secretary of State Haig's June 1981 visit to the PRC and indications that the United States would increase technology sales to China and consider defensive weapons sales on a "case-by-case" basis

- The December 1981 U.S. lifting of barriers on munitions sales to the PRC

- The February 1982 visit to China by Secretary Shultz in which he sought to put Sino-U.S. relations "back on stable, realistic footing"[38]

- Secretary of Commerce Malcolm Baldridge's May 1983 visit to Beijing granting the Chinese liberalized dual-use technology access

With Secretary Weinberger's September 1983 visit, the notion of security cooperation between the two countries was back on track. Weinberger's visit opened up new areas of technology transfer as well as military equipment sales to China. In November 1983, new guidelines on technology transfer allowed the Chinese access to computers, scientific instruments, and microelectronic manufacturing equipment. In January 1984, Chinese Premier Zhao Ziyang signed a series of science, technology, and trade agreements in the United States. In April 1984 came President Reagan's lavishly publicized trip to the PRC that also resulted in the signing of a nuclear cooperation accord. In his April 27 address to Chinese leaders, the President acknowledged the two countries' mutual interests: "America and China both condemn military expansions, the brutal occupation of Afghanistan, the crushing of Kampuchea; and we share a stake in preserving peace on the Korean peninsula."[39]
Chinese Defense Minister Zhang Aiping came to the United States in June 1984; his trip coincided with press indications that the Chinese had received computers and radars for military use and that export licenses for antitank and antiaircraft weapons had been granted to U.S. firms dealing with China. Two months later, in August 1984, Secretary of the Navy John Lehman toured China amid indications that U.S. ships might make port calls in the future, and in January 1985, Chairman of the Joint Chiefs of Staff John Vessey made a widely publicized military tour of China. Seven months later, Chinese President Li Xiannian toured the United States. In short, the United States and the People's Republic of China have become de facto security allies in the political-military containment of the Soviet Union in the Asian-Pacific region. An anti-Soviet network of security relationships among Beijing, Washington, and Tokyo, backed by the military-technological-economic might of the United States, is in place.[40]
The issue now is arms sales: how much and what types? Beijing, Washington, and other capitals are moving to selectively modernize the PRC's huge and outdated ground, air, and naval forces with a variety of precision-guided weapons, missiles, radar systems, and training aids.[41] The Chinese require a quantum boost in lethality and mobility if they are to try and counter the Soviet's clearly better equipped forces on the Sino-Soviet border. Soviet forces on the border display nearly three times as many tanks and ten times the armored

fighting vehicles that China has, and they also have assured air superiority given that their airpower is nearly twenty-five years ahead of China's.[42]

In the last few years, the Chinese have conducted combined arms military exercises in northern China involving army, airborne, and air force units. There is also some evidence that Beijing may be developing tactical nuclear weapons in support of their conventional forces.[43] But defense still remains one of the lowest priorities in China's national programs. Thus, for the foreseeable future, it seems unlikely that the present military imbalance on the Sino-Soviet border can be dramatically altered.

It is from that perspective, and continuing United States ties to Taiwan, that U.S. arms sales policy toward China is being implemented. Selective U.S. arming of China should take place within the realization that it is not going to make a great deal of difference until the Chinese themselves upgrade their own defense commitment. Moreover, should the hostility between Moscow and Beijing diminish, U.S. weapons transfers to China would occur within an altered strategic climate. That possibility, though remote at this time, provides a second constraint on U.S. arms sales to China. There is also a third constraint: the concerns of other Asian governments.[44] Because air and naval forces would be the most likely Chinese instruments for use against Taiwan, it is prudent to place restrictions on equipment that could enhance a Chinese amphibious or airborne invasion of Taiwan. Thus ground force modernization is the most logical emphasis. Hawk ground-to-air missiles, TOW antitank weapons, air defense systems, anti-cruise missile defenses, attack helicopters, and armor piercing ammunition, already mentioned in press reports,[45] constitute the most logical kinds of defensive weaponry the United States could sell to China.

China is now a de facto U.S. partner in the political-military containment of the Soviet Union. But communist dictatorships can change policy overnight. Such realities must produce caution in U.S. arms sales policy toward both China and Taiwan. An arms race between the two Chinas, fueled by the United States, would not be in U.S. national interests nor would it contribute to Asian-Pacific stability.

STABILITY IN KOREA

The contrast between Carter and Reagan administration perceptions of the importance of South Korea, and how to ensure stability on the peninsula, is striking. Four months into his administration, Jimmy Carter announced he would withdraw all U.S. ground combat forces from South Korea. He did this against the private and public advice of every senior U.S. commander involved in Asian-Pacific security.[46] The announcement hit East

Asia and the U.S. national security community like a
bombshell. A year later, following much debate in which
leading congressional members of Mr. Carter's own Democratic party worked to stop the president's plan, the
president changed his mind. Eighteen months after his
May 1977 announcement, the withdrawal plan was shelved.
    The Reagan administration, on the other hand, from
its first weeks in office, sought to reassure South
Korea that it would never reinitiate the Carter withdrawal plan. For example, in April 1981, Under Secretary of State Walter Stoessel said:

> This Administration's approach to our relations with
> South Korea offers a solid demonstration of our
> intention to be a reliable friend and ally there, as
> elsewhere in Asia. In this regard we have moved
> quickly to affirm our security commitment to the
> Republic of Korea and to lay to rest any notion that
> this Administration will contemplate withdrawing U.S.
> forces from South Korea in the foreseeable future.[47]

High-level visits to South Korea, including the President's and Mrs. Reagan's own well-publicized trip in
November 1983, underscored the continuing importance to
U.S. interests of South Korea's security and stability.
Thus, with the exception of the 1977-1978 period, U.S.
policy toward South Korea since the end of the Korean
War has emphasized the need for U.S. combat forces
stationed between Seoul and the probable North Korean
invasion routes.
    The Korean Demilitarized Zone (DMZ) remains one of
the most heavily armed places in the world. Behind it,
on both sides, stand a total of 1.5 million armed men
who, unlike those in 1950, are now equipped with the
most modern conventional military weapons. In 1985,
North Korea is still led by Kim Il-Sung, and the Democratic People's Republic of Korea (DPRK) devotes more
than 20 percent of its meager GNP to the military. Its
784,000-man standing army contains 13 percent of all
North Korean males of military age (17 to 49).[48] This
force includes 100,000 commandos, the largest commando
force in the world. The DPRK fields over 2,600 tanks
and 4,000 to 5,000 artillery guns and howitzers, perhaps
three-fourths as many as the U.S. Army has worldwide.[49]
Russian-made Frog 5 and Frog 7 missiles close to the DMZ
could hit Seoul, just 35 kilometers away, in a matter of
seconds.
    Unmistakable evidence of North Korea's hostility to
peace on the peninsula continues: In October 1983, North
Korean officers attempted to kill South Korea's president and cabinet and in the process destroyed Rangoon,
Burma's most sacred historical monument. President Chun
Doo Hwan escaped, but 17 Republic of Korea (ROK) officials, including 4 cabinet members, died. A few weeks
later, North Korean agents resumed infiltration attempts
against South Korea.[50] North Korea in 1985 is governed

by what is perhaps the harshest Stalinist regime in the world; most power in North Korea remains concentrated in the hands of one man, Kim Il-Sung, who is lavishly praised in North Korean media and official communications as the "Great Leader," "Supreme Leader," "The Sun of the Nation," etc.[51]

In the mid-1980s, President Kim's son, Kim Jong-Il, has emerged as his father's successor with his own personality cult. North Korea's economy has made remarkable progress since the Korean War's destruction. Although most of the peninsula's heavy industry and mineral resources are concentrated in the North, North Korea suffers from a severe labor deficiency due to underpopulation and refugee flows to the South. The DPRK's economy has had to rely on massive foreign assistance despite the regime's policy of self-reliance (or juche).[52] In the 1970s, the DPRK sought to modernize its economy with a sharp turn outward to Western markets, but a serious hard currency debt resulted. A new technocratic elite is gradually emerging in North Korea and is now attempting to encourage limited foreign investment in the DPRK.[53]

South Korea, in turn, has experienced major political and economic changes. The assassination of ROK President Park Chung Hee in November 1979 temporarily halted stability and growth, but in 1981 and 1982 Park's successor, General Chun Doo Hwan, solidified his power through a substantial political and military housecleaning. South Korea's extraordinary economic performance was renewed. Three venerable political competitors in South Korea--Kim Chong Pil, Kim Young Sam, and Kim Dae Jung (who returned from exile in February 1985)--have been active in the last few years, but none has been able to seriously challenge Chun's power so far. President Chun has indicated he will not run for reelection in 1987 if security conditions are conducive to what he describes as a "stable" election environment. South Korea's GNP, now at almost $80 billion, reflects the country's enormous productivity, hard work, concentration of industrial capital, and technical ingenuity, in spite of a foreign debt of more than $40 billion in 1985--perhaps the fourth largest in the world.[54]

The question of Korean unification is a powerful issue in both South and North Korea, and it impacts on the rest of Northeast Asia. North Korea subscribes to three principles for Korean unification: (1) independent Korean efforts "without being subject to external imposition or interference"; (2) peaceful means, that is, "not through the use of force against each other"; and (3) a greater national unity "transcending differences in ideas, ideologies, and systems."[55] Debunking gradualist approaches to reunification as ways of perpetuating the peninsula's division, DPRK spokesmen propose rapid reunification aided by the elimination of "external forces" (i.e., the U.S. 2nd infantry division, the U.S. 5th Air Force elements, and the United Nations

Command), the easing of tensions and the "democratization" (i.e., radicalization) of South Korean society. A favored proposal of Pyongyang's is a "peace treaty" between the DPRK and the United States--thus dealing over Seoul's head.[56] By contrast, South Korea favors an incremental, step-by-step unification strategy designed to allow psychological adjustment by people on both sides prior to explicit reunification actions. This basic ROK position of "unification preceded by peace" understandably reflects caution over the tragic war of 1950-1953 that was started by North Korea as "the fatherland unification war."[57] As of late 1985, Red Cross, economic, and interparliamentary talks had occurred between the two Koreas.

Thus, in the late 1980s, U.S. policy toward the Korean Peninsula encounters major changes on both sides of the DMZ. There was some progress in 1985 on the diplomatic front between Seoul and Pyongyang. However, the arms race on the peninsula continues. Increased DPRK forward positioning near the DMZ, ROK purchases of U.S. F-16s, and DPRK receipt of MIG 23s are three of the most critical military developments. Can the Korean situation be guided toward more stability? Should an international conference on Korea be convened? Previous external proposals, such as Secretary of State Henry Kissinger's 1975 four-power conference proposal, or Marshal Tito's 1978 three-power conference proposal, met with lukewarm responses. Broadening the attendees to the six prime parties could prove unwieldy. U.S. policy continues to emphasize direct North-South discussions, although the Reagan administration has indicated it would consider a Chinese role useful.[58]

Conventional arms reductions in the two Koreas seem like a more logical and concrete problem to work on. There is little sense in the two Koreas continuing to pile up arms in what is already the most heavily armed 155-mile strip of land in the world. In the late 1970s, in anticipation of U.S. ground combat force withdrawals, South Korea's government made strong efforts to strengthen its defenses in order to catch up with North Korea. These efforts in turn may have triggered new defense spending by Pyongyang. Thus, the Carter withdrawal plan may have actually contributed to the arms race in the peninsula. There could come a point where the Korean arms race simply reaches the saturation point; it may already have. Both the ROK and the DPRK are receiving the most advanced U.S. and Soviet export fighters. As chief weapons suppliers to the two Koreas, should Washington and Moscow work to restrain, and then reduce, arms deliveries to their Korean clients?

There is also the issue of nuclear weapons on the Korean Peninsula. With the three most powerful nuclear states operating at close proximity in and around the Korean Peninsula--which already contains the most intense concentration of conventional armaments anywhere-- there are clear risks to peace. The Soviet Union, the

People's Republic of China, and North Korea have all
asserted that the United States stations tactical nuclear weapons in South Korea. Former Secretary of Defense James Schlesinger, when in office, once confirmed
this in public. In the past, Washington evidently has
had to press the South Korean government away from what
appeared to be pursuit of nuclear capabilities. Does
the United States pay a price for nonproliferation by
Seoul, given Pyongyang's military advantages on the
peninsula? The answer to that question might clarify
the degree to which the United States, the Soviet Union,
and China could possibly collaborate on a nuclear-free
zone in and around Korea. But the conventional arms
situation and the ongoing political hostility between
Pyongyang and Seoul will continue to bear closely on the
nuclear-free zone question.

Finally, there is the question of United Nations
admission of the two Koreas. Pyongyang continues to
reject any proposals that would legally acknowledge what
in fact is completely obvious: there are two independent, sovereign Korean states run by separate, recognized
governments. Pyongyang's traditional "Koryo" confederal
republic proposals have not met with much sympathy from
any corner; this includes the Russians who speak of
"both Korean states" and invite South Korean athletic
teams to Moscow, as do the Chinese to Beijing. At the
United Nations, both states remain in a diplomatic lim-
bo. But they are recognized by a total of about ninety
states, and close to seventy of these have recognized
both South Korea and North Korea.

Ultimately the key to peace in Korea rests with the
two Koreas, not the outside powers. The recent rounds
of dialogue between Seoul and Pyongyang are encouraging.
But, as always, the real motives of North Korea's ruling
elite are unknown. Whether Pyongyang is seriously interested in reaching an accommodation with Seoul or is
simply working to overcome the stigma of the Rangoon
terrorist attack is not known. As a result, Seoul and
Washington have no choice but to remain vigilant.

U.S.-ASEAN RELATIONS

U.S. policy in Southeast Asia encounters three
critical developments: (1) ASEAN's emergence as an economically dynamic, anticommunist regional association;
(2) Vietnam's military occupation of Kampuchea and Laos,
and concurrent Soviet power projection from Vietnamese
bases; and (3) the difficult political transition in the
Philippines. The Association of Southeast Asian Nations
has been one of the most encouraging regional developments among Asian-Pacific countries since the mid-1960s.
Currently with six members--Thailand, Malaysia, Singapore, Indonesia, Brunei, and the Philippines--ASEAN's
growth and strengthening have taken time, and association countries have had their problems. However, the

disputes within ASEAN, such as Indonesian-Malaysian-Philippine territorial squabbles or ethnic and religious differences between Malaysia and Singapore, have moderated. The unstable leaders of the past, like Soekarno, are gone. Each ASEAN country has strong or experienced leadership, and Vietnam's December 1978 invasion of Kampuchea accelerated ASEAN's strengthening. The association has much to protect: with the exception of the Philippines, all ASEAN economies have experienced real GNP growth of between 6 and 9 percent since 1970.[59] Their combined GNPs are fifteen times Vietnam's.

Secretary of State George Shultz assessed ASEAN's remarkable progress in July 1984:

> The accomplishments of all the ASEAN countries, individually and as a group, have captured worldwide attention and admiration. . . . Through disciplined and creative economic management your real growth rate has averaged over 7% a year for the last decade. Through realism and courage you have forced the world to address the threat to regional and world peace by Vietnamese aggression in Kampuchea.[60]

In July 1985, Shultz further noted that U.S. investment in ASEAN countries was almost $10 billion and that the association had become the fifth largest trading partner of the United States, the bilateral trade level having reached $26 billion.[61]

ASEAN's dramatic economic growth has occurred, however, at a time when threats to the region's stability have also increased. These threats include:

- The establishment and expansion of a large, confident, Soviet military presence on the South China Sea--based out of Cam Ranh Bay and Da Nang--and diplomatically anchored in a twenty-five-year treaty with the Socialist Republic of Vietnam. Will Soviet ships and aircraft move out into maritime and air power projection roles in insular Southeast Asia, perhaps pressuring ASEAN or threatening other countries' commerce?

- The possibility of expanded Vietnamese military aggression beyond the 230,000 combat troops already operating outside Vietnam's borders. Will the Vietnamese pursue Cambodian rebel remnants deep inside Thailand or grab pieces of Thai territory as bargaining chips against Bangkok's support of the Khmer resistance?

- The growing maritime security problems in the region. Offshore territorial claims and mineral deposits in the South China Sea, particularly among the Spratly Islands, where Vietnam, Malaysia, China, Taiwan, and the Philippines have all staked claims, have already produced military skirmishes.

• The continuing, though still low level, patterns of insurgency and/or communal threats against existing ASEAN governments. These include the Moro/New People's Army violence in the Philippines, the communist/separatist insurgencies in Thailand, the periodic appearance of communist cell activities in Indonesia, and communal/religious agitation in Malaysia and Indonesia.

The combined effects of these threats provide incentives for the ASEAN governments to take increased security measures.

ASEAN's responses to these multiple, emerging threats generally have been encouraging, although gradual and somewhat unfocused. As Donald Weatherbee documents in his chapter in this book, beginning in the late 1970s ASEAN armed forces have been changing from an internal, counterinsurgency emphasis to conventional capabilities focused on external threats. Substantial increases in defense expenditures have resulted. In 1980, ASEAN defense spending totaled about $5.5 billion, a 45 percent increase over 1979 and twice that of 1975. In 1983, spending reached $8 billion, and in 1984 it was estimated to have surpassed $8.25 billion.[62] Standardization of equipment also has occurred, and bilateral and trilateral military cooperation occur among ASEAN countries on a regular basis.[63] There is clearly room to broaden the exercises to include all six members.

Regarding Kampuchea, ASEAN governments note that Vietnam's army is one of the most formidable military machines in the Asian-Pacific region and is now right on Thailand's doorstep. In July 1981, at the UN-sponsored International Conference on Kampuchea, these proposals for a settlement in Kampuchea were made: (1) a ceasefire by all parties and withdrawal of all foreign forces under the UN's peacekeeping force/observer supervision and verification; (2) the holding of free elections under UN supervision; (3) prevention of intimidation by any Kampuchean faction during the election process; and (4) measures to maintain law and order before the establishment of a new government resulting from those elections.[64] Agreeing with the UN conference proposal, ASEAN sought to develop a framework for a political settlement that would preserve the legitimate security concerns of Kampuchea's neighbors, including Vietnam. However, Vietnam has rejected both the proposals of the International Conference on Kampuchea and ASEAN's proposals for phased territorial withdrawals, insertion of international peacekeeping forces and reconstruction aid, and commitments to elections.

The U.S. Department of State position is that "support for ASEAN and its approach to the Kampuchean problem is the cornerstone of U.S. policy in Southeast Asia." The U.S. Department of State continued:

The ASEAN members--the countries in the region most

threatened by Vietnamese aggression in Kampuchea--seek
a political settlement to the problem of Kampuchea
based on the complete withdrawal of Vietnamese troops
and the establishment of a neutral, independent
Kampuchea through internationally supervised elections.
. . . ASEAN's strategy includes applying political,
diplomatic, and economic pressures on Vietnam to
persuade Hanoi that a political settlement is in its
own interests. [65]

In July 1984, Secretary of State Shultz told the ASEAN
foreign ministers in Jakarta:

You have offered Vietnam a realistic proposal for a
negotiated political solution, one based on the
restoration of Kampuchea's sovereignty and the rights
of its people to choose their own government. Such a
solution safeguards the interests of the Khmer people
and all Kampuchea's neighbors. [66]

However, to date, no Vietnamese response has clearly addressed the underlying issue of withdrawal of Vietnamese forces from Kampuchea or creation of a free,
elected government in Phnom Penh. As William Turley's
chapter shows, the men who rule the Socialist Republic
of Vietnam evaluate their country's security interests
very differently than does ASEAN. The case for using
the carrot rather than the stick, that is, normalizing
U.S. or ASEAN relations with Vietnam before it withdraws
from Kampuchea, in hopes of "having positive impact on
Hanoi's policy toward the withdrawal of its military
forces from Kampuchea, its willingness to negotiate a
solution to the conflict there, and its general intentions with respect to Thailand and the rest of Southeast
Asia" [67] is not convincing. We simply have no evidence
that this will make any difference to Hanoi.
    The ability of the United States to maintain mili-
tary forces in the subregion and to project power from
Southeast Asia into the Indian Ocean is related to
ASEAN's security and Southeast Asia's development as a
whole. Of particular significance is the special situation in the Philippines and continued U.S. use of Subic
Bay Naval Base and Clark Air Base. It is from these
prime pieces of Asian military real estate that U.S.
power protects the interests of the United States and
the Philippines and underwrites the strategic balance in
Southeast Asia.
    Eight hundred miles west of Subic Bay, the Soviet
naval, air, and intelligence complex continues to expand. Critics at home of U.S. policy in the Philippines
have been curiously silent about the Soviets and Cam
Ranh Bay. But ASEAN, as we have seen, has been beefing
up its defenses. Although President Marcos's martial
law rule in the Philippines has had unfortunate results,
does it therefore make sense to "remove the bases from
the Philippines" as some critics advocate? [68] Subic Bay

and Clark Field cannot simply be packed up and reas-
sembled in less objectionable parts of Asia and the
Pacific. Strategic realities dictate otherwise.

Subic Bay is the finest deep water port in the entire Asian/Pacific/Indian Ocean region. With more than
60,000 acres of land and water, Subic is the major naval
base, ship repair, and storage facility west of Hawaii.
Guam, Palau, and Singapore are sometimes mentioned as
alternatives, but neither the small Apra harbor at Guam,
nor the primitive Malakal or Babelthuap harbors in the
Palau Republic, nor Singapore's commercial harbor are
viable as military substitutes for Subic Bay. Clark Air
Base is the largest airfield in the Asian-Pacific region. With 130,000 acres of land, all-weather runways,
and satellited electronic warfare and gunnery training
ranges, 13th air force headquarters is the major military communications center, air training, and transit
hub west of Hawaii. Are there alternatives? Tinian
Island, in the northern Mariannas, has some training
areas and several primitive runways. But the price tag
to modernize Tinian begins at $1 billion. Andersen Air
Force Base on Guam is more promising. Andersen could
absorb some traffic coming off Clark. The rest would
have to relocate to other parts of the region. In a
word, Subic and Clark remain extremely valuable.[69]

Hopefully, it is from this strategic perspective
that U.S. policy toward the Philippines, and the Marcos
administration, is being implemented. The Philippines
is changing from one-man authoritarian rule to a more
open, less centralized system. But there is no formula
for this process. The seriousness of the situation in
the Philippines ebbs and flows. The chief of staff of
the Philippine armed forces, General Fabian Ver, and
other senior officers have been on trial for a conspiracy to kill Benigno Aquino. Meanwhile President Marcos,
who has governed in the Philippines for twenty years,
has been able to tough it out as anti-administration
activism weakened during the long trial proceedings.
The political opposition is badly splintered and unable
to exploit the continuing popular resentment toward
Marcos. In the countryside, the New Peoples Army communist insurgents had grown, by 1984 U.S. estimates, to
about 10,000 active guerrillas, active to varying degrees in nearly all areas of the country.[70] July 1985
estimates placed the figure at 12,000 to 15,000.[71] The
Philippine economy continues its lackluster performance.
U.S. business investment--on terms favorable to both
sides--continues to prop up the Philippine economy.[72]

Encouraging constructive change in the Philippines,
Assistant Secretary of State Wolfowitz, in an April 1985
statement carefully coordinated with the White House,
indicated that future U.S. efforts would focus on backing free and fair local elections in the 1986 and 1987
elections; encouraging efforts to restore a free-market
orientation to the economy; and providing enhanced military assistance "in the expectation that reforms already

begun will continue and expand."[73] Wolfowitz indicated
that Philippine defense expenditures, at only 1.1 percent of Gross National Product (GNP), despite the communist insurgency, were the lowest in Southeast Asia. He
also mentioned shortages in logistics, transport, maintenance, communications, and training. His conclusion
was a thoughtful appraisal of the insurgency problem in
the Philippines:

> At the same time, we have made it clear that the
> Philippine military will not be able to stop the
> insurgency without basic changes. This aid proposal is
> premised on the full expectation that the incipient
> reforms we have seen will continue and expand. First
> and foremost, this requires an end to military abuse
> against civilians, perhaps the most fundamental
> explanation for the alarming growth of the insurgency.
>
> Nor can the insurgency be combatted effectively without
> addressing the political and economic problems that the
> communists exploit. The best antidote to communism is
> democracy.
>
> Should communists succeed in taking over the
> Philippines, however, there would be no alternative for
> 50 million Filipinos. The problems we see there today,
> serious though they are, pale in comparison to those
> that every communist regime in history has inflicted on
> its people. [74]

By late fall 1985, the Reagan administration was
also pressing the Marcos government for reform on a wide
range of political and economic issues--broadening the
political power structure and reintroducing market
forces into the collapsing economy.[75] Thus, U.S. policy
in the Philippines must take into account both the
changing strategic environment of Southeast Asia and the
responses of the Filipino government to its internal
problems. Much of Southeast Asia's continued progress
depends on the outcome in the Philippines.

THE ANZUS ALLIANCE

Australia's and New Zealand's importance to U.S.
Asian-Pacific policies derives from shared democratic
traditions, common ancestral roots, and the critical
geographic positions of New Zealand and Australia in the
South Pacific. These two middle- to small-sized
countries (in terms of population) are located on the
periphery of the Asian-Pacific region. Protected by the
U.S. nuclear guarantee, Australia and New Zealand, in
turn, have permitted the United States access to important facilities, air fields, and ports. This access
has enabled U.S. military projection and secure

communications across the southern zones of the Pacific and Indian Oceans.

The ANZUS alliance (security treaty between Australia, New Zealand, and the United States) was founded in 1951. Originally sought by Australia and New Zealand to prevent a repeat of circumstances that led to World War II, ANZUS has substantially evolved into an integral part of the Western security system. The alliance provides benefits to each member. There are, however, given the vast differences in size and power among the three countries, inevitable problems of "proportionality" in the triangular relationship. Neither the obligations nor the interdependencies have ever been equally distributed. Sensitivity to these points of difference, and policy shifts, has periodically disturbed the generally high quality of the alliance's partnership. The most recent example is the New Zealand Labor government's policy of banning U.S. (and UK) nuclear-armed or -powered vessels from New Zealand's ports despite the fact that allowing U.S. ships to dock in New Zealand is one of the very few obligations Wellington has as a part of ANZUS.

Although the governments of all three countries have had leadership changes since 1970 that have produced policies at times out of synchronization with each other (the Carter, Whitlam, and Lange administrations are the most obvious examples), nevertheless over the years shared perceptions of global and regional developments and the policies necessary to meet them have been the norm. "This includes," writes Henry Albinski:

> views about the interregional significance of rivalry between great powers, the ascription of mischievous motives to the USSR, and the need to appreciate the varieties and sensibilities of individual and regionally associated states that are not in direct line of First and Second World conflicts, as within the ASEAN community and in the South Pacific. Both Australia and New Zealand place a high premium on an effective and credible American presence in the region. Both feel that the United States should be encouraged and supported.[76]

These views, of course, tend to represent the positions of the more conservative governments among the three. Such views are less firmly held among the two Labor parties and the Democratic party in the United States. Indeed, the Labor party in New Zealand has advocated barring visits by U.S. nuclear-powered vessels for many years. There are differences as well between New Zealand's and Australia's Labor parties--the New Zealanders regard themselves "as less centrally placed, less vulnerable, and less threatened by great or intermediate powers than Australians do. New Zealanders also feel that they can do less about what happens overseas

with the special exception of the neighboring South
Pacific Community."[77]
    New Zealand's minor role in the alliance, compared
to the United States and Australia, is frequently mentioned, particularly by Australian commentators.[78]   Of
course, as Michael McKinley aptly demonstrates in chapter 10 of this volume, it is true that bilateral arrangements between Australia and the United States for
jointly managed defense facilities in Australia--partic-
ularly Pine Gap, Nurrungar, and North West Cape--make
very valuable contributions to allied communications,
navigation, satellite tracking, and intelligence acquisition. Prime Minister David Lange's position on nuclear ship visits is generally popular in the pastoral
southern Pacific country of New Zealand, but Lange, who
has been under criticism from both Washington and Canberra, also admits that he comes from a generation that
did not fight side by side with the United States and
Australia in World War II. With little leeway to move
on the issue, Lange appears to have had the policy
dictated to him by hardliners within New Zealand's left.
Not surprisingly, Lange misses no opportunity to emphasize that he believes the ban on ship visits does not
conflict with membership in ANZUS, calling it "antinuclear not anti-American or anti-ANZUS."[79]   U.S. and
Australian authorities do not agree with New Zealand's
prime minister.
    Alliances, to be successful, require sensitivity to
member interests, perceptions, and differences. So it
is with ANZUS, and the current U.S. Department of State
phrase for smoothing operation of the security treaty is
"managing ANZUS." In a speech in June 1984 (just before
the July election of the Lange government in New Zealand), Assistant Secretary of State Wolfowitz argued
that

>   for alliance managers, the essential task, whether in
>   Washington, Canberra, or Wellington, is to maximise
>   cooperation to mutual advantage when we are on common
>   ground and to contain differences--legitimate though
>   they may be--through the kinds of compromises necessary
>   in an effective working partnership. By so doing, we
>   can assure that competition in commerce and differences
>   in other areas do not threaten cooperation linked to
>   our most fundamental shared interest--mutual national
>   survival.[80]

    By the spring of 1985, with the effects of the
Lange government's nuclear ban in full view, Washington
and Canberra were taking a stronger stand. The Reagan
administration indicated to Wellington that the United
States has only one navy--not one conventional navy and
one nuclear navy; not one navy to accommodate one country's policy and another navy for the rest of the
world.[81]   Furthermore the United States indicated it
would not weaken its deterrent posture by advertising to

potential adversaries which U.S. ships are, and are not,
carrying nuclear weapons. As Assistant Secretary of
State Wolfowitz testified to Congress in March 1985:

> In sum, we believe that New Zealand's policy, whatever
> its intentions, is not good for the alliance or for the
> cause of peace. While we do not exaggerate the effect
> of that policy, we cannot ignore it.
>
> With words New Zealand assures us that it remains
> committed to ANZUS; but by its deeds New Zealand has
> effectively curtailed its operational role in ANZUS. A
> military alliance has little meaning without military
> cooperation--without some equity in sharing both the
> burdens and the rewards. New Zealand can't have it
> both ways.
>
> In light of New Zealand's dimunition of cooperation
> with us, we have reduced our own military and security
> cooperation with New Zealand. We have made these re-
> ductions with regret given New Zealand's history as an
> ally--one that has fought with us in four wars in this
> century. But unless our alliance partners bear a com-
> mensurate share of military cooperation essential to
> the alliance, our partnership cannot be sustained prac-
> tically or politically.[82]

It is unlikely that New Zealand's current nuclear
allergy will spread to Australia or affect other U.S.
allies in Asia and the Pacific that have more threatening security environments. But it is also likely that
the United States and Australia will insist on reduced
security cooperation with the government of New Zealand
until, and unless, Wellington seeks to return to its
previous degree of defense cooperation within ANZUS,
which, as Michael McKinley argues later in this volume,
is unlikely to occur.

CONCLUSION

What is striking about the U.S. position in the
Asian-Pacific region in the late 1980s is the extent to
which the United States has become dependent on countries in the area to assist in maintaining the region's
security and prosperity. The United States is no longer
able to assert itself as the most influential entity in
the region as it did in the 1950s, 1960s, and 1970s. As
is true at the global level, power and influence in Asia
and the Pacific have diffused and redistributed. Alliance capabilities have changed. Responsibilities are
shifting.

The Soviet Union is now the single strongest military power in East Asia. As in Europe, the USSR is
piling up armaments in Asia in redundant quantities. It
has surrounded China with military forces--some of them

in combat. However, Moscow has not been able to translate this determined military growth into equivalent political influence, and indeed, the Russians behave in ways that guarantee other countries' opposition. Japan, the most important U.S. ally in Asia and the Pacific, has grown to dominate the region's trade and investment and runs a steadily mounting and troublesome trade deficit with the United States. China, in turn, is opening rapidly to Western economic and technical development, but, unlike Japan, China's continued political stability cannot be predicted.

Recent changes and complications in the allied security system in Asia and the Pacific, first set up in the 1950s, have contributed to reduced U.S. dominance without, so far, having altered the main goal of the system--containing and deterring the Soviet Union and its allies. But, then, with 855,000 U.S. troops in East Asia in the late 1960s and a $200 billion plus combat expenditure over ten years, the United States was not able to ultimately change the outcome in one part of Southeast Asia. So perhaps, inevitably, the United States will find that having to use its ingenuity, rather than its power, is fortunate.

Among U.S. allies in the region, the Japanese economic challenge and the Philippine political transition are likely to carry the most serious consequences for U.S. interests. A poor handling of either problem will do substantial damage to U.S. interests and to the entire region's security system. On the Korean Peninsula, critical political transitions are under way in both the South and the North. In South Korea, whether a civilian or a military government is in power, the threat from North Korea is so well felt that it is unlikely a weak government will come to office in Seoul. Regarding U.S. policy toward the two Chinas, U.S. security arrangements with and assistance to both China and Taiwan will require delicate maneuvering in the years ahead. In Southeast Asia, assisting ASEAN as the principal stabilizer in this subregion will continue to be both a necessary and an intelligent U.S. policy. Finally, in the South Pacific, Australia and the United States will have to adjust to New Zealand's withdrawal from operational participation in ANZUS.

As the Soviet Union and its Asian associates expand their power and threaten their neighbors, the allied security system must adjust. Even as it redistributes its responsibilities and roles, the system has no choice but to maintain deterrence. No longer the dominant arbiter of the Asian-Pacific trends, the United States nevertheless--when the new partnership with China is factored in--has more friendly countries and more usable capabiltiies to work with than ever before. These facts, and the wisdom gained from the difficult U.S. experience in Indochina, should bode well for future U.S. policies in Asia and the Pacific.

45

NOTES

1. George P. Shultz, _Economic Cooperation in the Pacific Basin_, U.S. Department of State, Current Policy, no. 658, 21 February 1985.

2. Walter T. Stoessel, Jr., _Foreign Policy Priorities in Asia_, U.S. Department of State, Current Policy, no. 274, 24 April 1981.

3. Walter T. Stoessel, Jr., _Allied Responses to the Soviet Challenge in East Asia and the Pacific_, U.S. Department of State, Current Policy, no. 403, 10 June 1982.

4. Ibid.

5. Ibid.

6. George P. Shultz, _Challenges Facing the U.S. and ASEAN_, U.S. Department of State, Current Policy, no. 597, 13 July 1984. Also see Shultz, "Pacific Tides Are Rising," address to the World Affairs Council of Northern California in San Francisco on 5 March 1983.

7. From a speech by Assistant Secretary of State for East Asia and the Pacific, Paul D. Wolfowitz, as reprinted in _Wall Street Journal_, 15 April 1985, p. 29.

8. President Reagan is cited by Paul D. Wolfowitz, _The ANZUS Alliance_, U.S. Department of State, Current Policy, no. 674, 18 March 1985.

9. Caspar W. Weinberger, "The Five Pillars of Our Defense Policy in East Asia and the Pacific," in _Asia-Pacific Defense Forum_ (Winter 1984-1985):2-8.

10. John H. Holdridge, _Japan and the United States: A Durable Relationship_, U.S. Department of State, Current Policy, no. 337, 28 October 1981.

11. Paul D. Wolfowitz, _Protectionism and the U.S.-Japan Trade_, U.S. Department of State, Current Policy, no. 689, 17 April 1985.

12. John H. Holdridge, _Japan and the United States: A Cooperative Relationship_, U.S. Department of State, Current Policy, no. 374, 1 March 1982.

13. George P. Shultz, _Japan and America: International Partnership for the 1980s_, U.S. Department of State, Current Policy, no. 506, 2 September 1983.

14. Kenneth W. Dam, _U.S.-Japan Relations in Perspective_, U.S. Department of State, Current Policy, no. 547, 6 February 1984.

15. Paul D. Wolfowitz, _Taking Stock of U.S.-Japan Relations_, U.S. Department of State, Current Policy, no. 593, 12 June 1984.

16. Paul D. Wolfowitz, _Protectionism and U.S.-Japan Trade_, U.S. Department of State, Current Policy, no. 689, 17 April 1985.

17. Allen Wallis, _The Relation of Japan's Economic Inefficiencies to Its Balance of Trade_, U.S. Department of State, Current Policy, no. 763, 18 October 1985.

18. Nakasone cited in Steve Lohr, "Japanese Premier Urges an Increase in Armed Strength," _New York Times_, 28 November 1982, p. 1.

19. Nakasone's interview with the _Washington Post_ is summarized in the _Far Eastern Economic Review_, 15 December 1983, p. 30-31. Recall that it was Prime Minister Suzuki who first proposed the sea-lanes mission in May 1981.

46

20. Long interviewed in Niel Ulman and Urban C. Lehner, "Tokyo's Buildup," Wall Street Journal, 22 November 1982, p. 1.

21. U.S., Congress, House, Committee on Foreign Affairs, Francis J. West, Jr., U.S.-Japan Defense Cooperation and U.S. Policy, March 1982, pp. 7-8.

22. Japanese Defense Agency, Defense of Japan, 1984 (Tokyo: Japan Times, 1984), pp. 31-37; and The Military Balance 1984-1985 (London: IISS, 1984), p. 142.

23. Frank Langdon, "Japan and North America," Robert S. Ozaki and Walter Arnold, eds., Japan's Foreign Relations (Boulder, Colo.: Westview, 1985), p. 29.

24. The author is grateful to Major John Ebinger, USAF, for ideas concerning the issues that appear below. Major Ebinger completed a year in residence at the Air Command and Staff College in June 1985 and is the author of "Sharing the Defense Burden in East Asia: Japanese Defense Capabilities in the 1990s," ACSC Student Report 85-0735, April 1985. Also see Anthony H. Cordesman, "The Military Balance in Northeast Asia--The Challenge to Japan and Korea," Armed Forces Journal International (November-December 1983):27-37, 80-109; and Admiral Robert L. J. Long, USN (Ret.) in testimony before the Subcommittee on Asian and Pacific Affairs of the Committee on Foreign Affairs, House of Representatives, 98th cong., 2nd sess., 2 May 1984, p. 89.

25. Alexander M. Haig, Jr., Caveat: Realism, Reagan, and Foreign Policy (New York: Macmillan, 1984), pp. 194-217.

26. Haig: "Taiwan was a difficult question for Ronald Reagan. He is an anti-Communist. Reagan's emotions were deeply engaged in this question, and so was his sense of honor" (ibid, p. 198). Haig continued: "As late as March 1982, the President took the stance that we were going to sell spare parts to Taiwan whether the Chinese liked it or not; if they wanted to talk, then we would accommodate them, and if they did not, then there was nothing to talk about" (ibid., p. 213).

27. Walter J. Stoessel, Jr., Developing Lasting U.S.-China Relations, U.S. Department of State, Current Policy, no. 398, 1 June 1982.

28. Haig, Caveat, p. 195. However, when I discussed Haig's position, and other aspects of Reagan administration China policy, with senior U.S. officials in Beijing in June 1984, I found a genuine belief that it was Haig, more than anyone else, who had ultimately turned the President around on this issue.

29. John H. Holdridge, Assessment of U.S. Relations with China, U.S. Department of State, Current Policy, no. 444, 13 December 1982.

30. John H. Holdridge, U.S.-China Joint Communique, U.S. Department of State, Current Policy, no. 413, 18 August 1982.

31. Ibid.

32. Steven I. Levine, "China and the United States: The Limits of Interaction," in Samuel S. Kim, ed., China and the World: Chinese Foreign Policy in the Post-Mao Era (Boulder, Colo.: Westview, 1984), p. 113. Also see Henry B. Gass, Sino-American Security Relations: Expectations and Realities (Washington, D.C.: National Defense University Essay 84-2, 1984), pp. 1-11.

33. Brezezinski cited by Levine in Kim, China and the World, p. 113.

34. Holdridge, "Assessment of U.S. Relations with China."

35. The details are tracked in Chi Su, "China and the Soviet Union: 'Principled, Salutory, and Tempered' Management of Conflict," in Kim, China and the World, pp. 136-141.

36. Peter Polomka, "The Security of the Western Pacific: The Price of Burden Sharing," Survival (January-February 1984): 5.

37. See, for example, the argument in Zhang Jia-Lin, "The New Romanticism in the Reagan Administration's Asian Policy: Illusion and Reality," Asian Survey (October 1984):1007-1009.

38. Paul Wolfowitz, Developing an Enduring Relationship with China, U.S. Department of State, Current Policy, no. 460, 28 February 1983.

39. Ronald Reagan, "A Historic Opportunity for the U.S. and China," U.S. Department of State, Current Policy, no. 574, 27 April 1984.

40. See appraisals by Paul F. Langer, "Soviet Military Power in Asia," in Donald S. Zagoria, ed., Soviet Policy in East Asia, p. 258; and by John J. Stephan, "Asia in the Soviet Conception," also in Zagoria, ibid., pp. 46-47.

41. Evidently, Israeli advisors and weapons systems have entered the PRC through Hong Kong. Israel also supplies Taipei a variety of military items. Washington Times, 24 January 1985, p. 1.

42. A. James Gregor, "The Military Potential of the People's Republic of China and Western Security Interests," Asian Affairs (Spring 1984):1-24. Estimates of the cost to modernize China's 300 divisions range from U.S.$200 to 300 billion. Purchases abroad could require another $60 billion before a confident defense against the Soviets existed. Gass, Sino-American Security Relations, p. 31.

43. Robert S. Wang, "China's Evolving Strategic Doctrine," Asian Survey (October 1984):1044-1045.

44. As an Asian diplomat told Secretary Haig: "Rifles are okay, but not F-15s. Asians are counting on U.S. caution in military relations with China." As cited in Gass, Sino-American Security Relations, p. 23.

45. See, for example, Far Eastern Economic Review, 8 March 1984, pp. 12, 13, and 28 June, pp. 12-13; and Christian Science Monitor, 14 January 1985, pp. 9-10.

46. For example, on 8 January 1977, General John W. Vessey, Jr., commander-in-chief of UN, U.S., and ROK forces in South Korea, stated that removal of the remaining U.S. combat forces from South Korea would "increase considerably" the risk of war. Citing the 2nd infantry division's value, Vessey stated: "It's the one clear signal to Kim Il Sung that if he starts a war, he fights both the U.S. and the ROK armies." Washington Post, 9 January 1977, p. A-20. In May, General Vessey told reporters, on record, "I have told my superiors that no one here who is concerned with the military situation in Korea is in favor of U.S. troop withdrawal." Far Eastern Economic Review, 20 May 1977, p. 28. On 18 May 1977, Major General John Singlaub said that a U.S. force withdrawal "would lead to war"--a statement that led President Carter to relieve him of command. Washington Post, 19 May 1977, pp. A-1. Many more examples could be cited.

47. Walter T. Stoessel, Jr., Foreign Policy Priorities in Asia, U.S. Department of State, Current Policy, no. 274, 24 April 1981.

48

48. Tai Sung An, North Korea in Transition: From Dictatorship to Dynasty (London: Greenwood, 1983), p. 81.

49. C. I. Eugene Kim, "Civil-Military Relations in the Two Koreas," Armed Forces and Society (Fall 1984):12; and Paul D. Wolfowitz, The U.S. and Korea: Auspicious Prospects, U.S. Department of State, Current Policy, no. 543, 31 January 1984.

50. See Young Whan Kihl, "North Korea in 1983: Transforming the 'Hermit Kingdom'?" Asian Survey (January 1984):100-111.

51. See B. C. Koh, "The Cult of Personality and the Succession Idea," in C. I. Eugene Kim and B. C. Koh, eds., Journey to North Korea: Personal Perceptions (Berkeley: University of California Press, 1984), pp. 25-41; and Tai Sung An, North Korea in Transition, pp. 129-148.

52. For data on mineral, industrial, and hydroelectric resources, see U.S. Department of the Army, Area Handbook for North Korea (Washington, D.C., GPO, 1969), pp. 11-28, 286-289, 295, 368. During the 1970s and 1980s, North Korea still relied on the USSR and the PRC as its number one and two trade partners.

53. Young Whan Kihl, "North Korea in 1984: 'The Hermit Kingdom' Turns Outward," Asian Survey (January 1985):67-70.

54. Chae-Jin Lee, "South Korea in 1984: Seeking Peace and Stability," Asian Survey (January 1985):83.

55. Young Whan Kihl, "The Issue of Korean Unification: North Korea's Policy and Perception," in Kim, Journey to North Korea, p. 99.

56. Kihl, "Korean Unification," pp. 103-104; and Kihl, Politics and Policies in Dividend Korea: Regimes in Contest (Boulder, Colo.: Westview, 1984), pp. 209-212.

57. Kihl, Politics and Policies, p. 207.

58. Wolfowitz, "The U.S. and Korea: Auspicious Prospects"; also see Paul D. Wolfowitz, Recent Security Development in Korea, U.S. Department of State, Current Policy, no. 731, 12 August 1985.

59. ASEAN, Department of State Background Note, Washington, D.C., November 1983, relying on International Monetary Fund data.

60. George P. Shultz, Challenges Facing the U.S. and ASEAN, U.S. Department of State, Current Policy, no. 597, 13 July 1984.

61. George P. Shultz, The U.S. and ASEAN: Partners for Peace and Development, U.S. Department of State, Current Policy, no. 722, 12 July 1985.

62. Sheldon W. Simon, "U.S. Security Interests in Southeast Asia," in William T. Tow and William R. Feeney, eds., U.S. Foreign Policy and Asian-Pacific Security: A Transregional Approach (Boulder, Colo.: Westview, 1982), p. 125; Asia 1984 Yearbook (Hong Kong: Far Eastern Economic Review, 30 November 1984), p. 20; and The Military Balance, 1984-1985.

63. Robert L. Rau, "Southeast Asia Security in the 1980s: An Intraregional Perspective," in Tow, U.S. Foreign Policy and Asian-Pacific Security, pp. 97-98.

64. Paul D. Wolfowitz, Cambodia: The Search for Peace, U.S. Department of State, Current Policy, no. 613, 11 September 1984.

65. John C. Monjo, Kampuchea After Five Years of Vietnamese Occupation, U.S. Department of State, Current Policy, no. 514, 15 September 1984.

66. Shultz, Challenges Facing the U.S. and ASEAN.

67. Allen E. Goodman, "The Case for Establishing Relations with Vietnam," in William A. Buckingham, Jr., ed., Defense Planning

for the 1990s and the Changing International Environment (Washington, D.C.: National Defense University Press, 1984), p. 61. Dr. Goodman then reexamines his argument with this observation: "There is, of course, no actual evidence that [this] perspective is right. And there is a good deal of evidence that the current and projected leadership in Hanoi have a worldview shaped largely by the exigencies of maintaining their hold on power and not on the behavior and policies of superpowers, friend or foe" (pp. 61-62).

68. See, for example, George McT. Kahin, "Remove the Bases from the Philippines," New York Times, 12 October 1983.

69. A detailed case for retaining these critical bases is Lawrence E. Grinter, The Philippine Bases: Continuing Utility in a Changing Strategic Context, National Security Affairs Monograph 80-2 (Washington, D.C.: National Defense University, 1980). Also relevant is Francisco S. Tadad, "Keeping Philippine Bases," Washington Quarterly (Winter 1984); William H. Sullivan, "Relocating Bases in the Philippines," Washington Quarterly (Spring 1984); and Lawrence E. Grinter, "Pacific Military Installations Vital to U.S. Defense," Human Events (4 August 1984).

70. 1983 congressional testimony by James A. Kelly of U.S. Department of Defense as cited in David A. Rosenberg, "Communism in the Philippines," Problems of Communism (September-October 1984): 39-40.

71. Steve Lohr, "Filipino Insurgency: Out of Rice Paddies and Into the Cities," New York Times, 2 July 1985, pp. 1, 7.

72. A. James Gregor, "Some Policy Considerations" in Gregor, ed., The U.S. and the Philippines: A Challenge to a Special Relationship (Washington, D.C.: Heritage Foundation, 1983), pp. 67, 70-73.

73. Paul D. Wolfowitz, "U.S. Encourages Constructive Change in the Philippines," as adapted from a speech appearing in Wall Street Journal, 15 April 1985, p. 29.

74. Ibid.

75. Paul D. Wolfowitz, Developments in the Philippines, U.S. Department of State, Current Policy, no. 760, 30 October 1985.

76. Henry S. Albinski, "The U.S. Position in Asia and the Pacific: The Relevance of Australia and New Zealand," in Ramon H. Myers, ed., A U.S. Foreign Policy for Asia: The 1980s and Beyond (Stanford, Calif.: Hoover Institution Press, 1982), p. 290.

77. Ibid.

78. See, for example, F. A. Mediansky, "ANZUS: An Alliance Beyond the Treaty," Australian Outlook (December 1984):178-183; and Desmond Ball, The ANZUS Connection: The Security Relationship between Australia, New Zealand and the United States, SDSC Reference Paper, no. 105 (Canberra: Australian National University, 1983), p. 2.

79. David Lange, "New Zealand's Security Policy," Foreign Affairs (Summer 1985):1009-1019.

80. Paul D. Wolfowitz, The ANZUS Relationship: Alliance Management, U.S. Department of State, Current Policy, no. 592, 24 June 1984.

81. Australia's Labor Prime Minister Robert Hawke also told Prime Minister Lange, "We could not accept . . . that the ANZUS alliance had a different meaning and entailed different obligations for different members." Wall Street Journal, 6 February 1985, p. 26.

82. Paul D. Wolfowitz, The ANZUS Alliance, U.S. Department of State, Current Policy, no. 674, 18 March 1985.

3 The Soviet Union: Meshing Strategic and Revolutionary Objectives in Asia

Marian Leighton
Leif R. Rosenberger

With two-thirds of its landmass and the bulk of its mineral and energy resources in Asia, the USSR is focusing increasingly on the security environment beyond its eastern borders. It regards many of the trends there as adverse. Its pessimism is conditioned partly by deep-rooted ideological and psychological factors: a fear of capitalist encirclement, a conviction that capitalist hostility and "imperialist"-incited war are inevitable, and a paranoid attitude about the "yellow peril." The fact that the Soviet Union lacks a glacis of friendly and allied states along its Asian periphery contributes heavily to its sense of insecurity and vulnerability.

> Asia's spatial interpenetration with the Soviet Union is symbolized by the vast Eurasian plain, which stretches from the Urals to Mongolia. In the absence of major barriers, waves of migrations have moved across the plain for centuries, displacing or absorbing earlier inhabitants. . . . An awareness of the plain's permeability and ethnic evanescence leaves many Russians with a half-formed sense of territorial insecurity that manifests itself not only in the predilection for strong central authority but in what amounts to a national fixation on frontier defense.[1]

The Kremlin's paranoia about security is especially pronounced in Asia because of the peculiar geopolitical and demographic vulnerabilities that shape Soviet threat perceptions there. In sharp contrast with the United States, which looks out on vast expanses of ocean on its eastern and western flanks and friendly countries to the north and south of its borders, the Soviet empire is

----

This article reflects the views of the authors and not necessarily those of the U.S. government.

51

surrounded in most directions by hostile neighbors. In
Asia, China lies to the south of the USSR, Japan lies to
the east, and U.S. theater air and naval power cover the
Pacific region.

Logistical problems plague the Soviet military
position in the East Asia-Pacific arena. Enormous dis-
tances separate the resource-rich but sparsely populated
Soviet Far East from the major industrial and population
centers of European Russia. The Trans-Siberian Railway
constituted virtually the only link between the two
areas until the recent completion of sections of the
Baikal-Amur Mainline (BAM). The BAM runs parallel to
and a few hundred miles south of the Trans-Sib and would
be almost equally vulnerable to Chinese sabotage during
a Sino-Soviet war.

Soviet logistic vulnerabilities pertain on sea as
well as land. Siberian ports are limited in number and
are very congested. A new port at Nakhodka is designed
to handle civilian cargo so that Vladivostok can be
reserved strictly for military use. Although icebreakers (some of them nuclear-powered) have helped to keep
open the Arctic sea-lanes to the Soviet Far East, use of
that route to supply coastal villages (not to mention
such vital military installations as Vladivostok) remains time-consuming, extremely expensive, and ultimately unreliable. Vladivostok and Petropavlovsk, the two
principal bases for the Soviet Pacific Fleet, both suf-
fer from highly unfavorable weather conditions. Even
more importantly, Vladivostok has no direct access to
the open ocean. Naval vessels based there must transit
one of the three narrow chokepoints--the straits of
Tsushima, Tsugaru, or Soya--that provide ingress into
and egress from the Sea of Japan. Petropavlovsk, situated at the southern tip of the Kamchatka Peninsula,
faces the open sea but is too far north to be supplied
by land from Soviet territory.

In summing up the USSR's logistical difficulties as
they relate to potential military operations in Asia,
one scholar has pointed out that

> these logistical problems do not [pose] major con-
> straints on Soviet military power in East Asia, so long
> as any future conflict is geographically limited and of
> short duration. . . . Thus, a quick offensive action
> against a regional East Asian country in pursuit of a
> limited military objective along the Soviet periphery
> is possible. But Soviet logistical constraints mean
> that Moscow would experience extreme difficulty in any
> large-scale military involvement over a longer period
> of time outside the immediate Soviet periphery.[2]

This problem is compounded for the Soviet Union by the
fact that its Pacific Fleet is deficient in afloat
replenishment and supply capabilities and in sea-based
tactical airpower. The fleet would have to rely on

shore-based aircover in order to sustain a conventional
conflict with U.S. naval forces in the Pacific. Soviet
acquisitions of a naval base in Vietnam and the construction of aircraft and helicopter carriers are helping to remedy these deficiencies, as is a recent Soviet
focus on amphibious landing capability in the Pacific
area--reflected in the joint Soviet-Vietnamese naval
infantry landing exercise off the Vietnamese coast in
1984.[3]

Although Vietnam has emerged as a close Soviet ally
in Asia, Moscow appears to regard overall political-
military trends in the region as adverse. The Sino-
Japanese peace treaty of 1978, including an "anti-
hegemony" clause directed at the Soviet Union, was of
particular concern to the Kremlin. Soviet concern
mounted still further with China's decision not to renew
the Sino-Soviet treaty of thirty-years standing when it
lapsed in 1980. Moscow regularly denounces alleged
"collusion" among the United States, China, and Japan
and, increasingly, among the members of the Association
of Southeast Asian Nations (ASEAN). "Washington is
today seen as pushing China toward [confrontation with]
the USSR in the same way that Britain and France tried
to push Hitler toward the Soviet Union in the 1930's."
Moreover, regarding China's and Japan's alleged role in
the anti-Soviet conspiracy:

> Images of the Mongol conquest (the most traumatic his-
> torical experience of the Russian people) are triggered
> by shrewdly worded propaganda about the territorial
> appetites of "Great Han chauvinism." Japanese claims
> [to] the Kurile Islands are portrayed as following a
> tradition of predatory designs on the Russian Far East
> from the Siberian Intervention (1918-22) to the mini-
> wars around the Manchurian perimeter in 1937-39. Omi-
> nous motives are ascribed to the 19th-century American
> commercial interests in the Amur region, to American
> involvement in the Siberian Intervention, and to Wash-
> ington's wartime plans to occupy the Kurile Islands.[4]

In responding to what it apparently perceives as
threats to its security in Asia and the Pacific, the
Soviet Union itself has emerged as the greatest military
threat to this vast region. In view of the general
unattractiveness of communist ideology and of the Soviet
economic model to most Asian countries, the overwhelming
thrust of the Kremlin's policy in Asia has been
military.

SOVIET STRATEGY

The Soviet fear of a two-front war has led the USSR
to undertake military preparations that reflect a two-
front strategy. Having engaged since the mid-1960s in a

massive military buildup aimed largely at Europe, the Soviets have embarked on an unprecedented buildup of their forces in Northeast Asia. Unlike the 500,000 Soviet troops stationed along the Sino-Soviet frontier-- troops equipped to wage a land war with China--the new deployments in the Soviet Far East suggest acquisition of a capability to take on U.S. forces in the Pacific, neutralizing Japan in the process. Elements of Moscow's Asian-Pacific buildup include the emplacement of the latest generation of ground and air equipment (notably the nuclear-capable Backfire bomber), creation of a new theater high command, siting of some 140 SS-20 missiles, and the expansion and modernization of the Pacific Fleet. A Soviet strategic bastion is developing north of Japan on the Sea of Okhotsk and the Kamchatka Penin- sula. The Sea of Okhotsk, which is virtually encircled by Soviet territory, makes a natural strategic sanctuary and protective barrier for the USSR's Asian landmass. Blanketed with an air defense network consisting of radars, missiles, guns, and interceptor aircraft, the area has become so strategically sensitive that in 1983 the Soviets shot down a South Korean civilian jetliner with 269 passengers when it strayed off course there en route from Alaska to Japan.

The Soviet ring around the Sea of Okhotsk has been closed with the fortification of the southern Kurile Islands, which control passage from the Pacific to the Sea of Okhotsk. These islands, which Japan claims as its Northern Territories, were seized by the USSR at the end of World War II and have been a major bone of con- tention in Soviet-Japanese relations ever since. In 1983, Moscow deployed a squadron of supersonic MIG-23 fighter-bombers on Etorofu, one of the islands--a de- ployment that represented a significant upgrading of Soviet military power in the area and a strong signal that the Soviets intend to occupy the Northern Territo- ries permanently.

In addition to the military buildup around the Soviet Union's Far Eastern periphery, the Kremlin has moved to transform the U.S.-built naval base at Cam Ranh Bay, Vietnam, into the largest Soviet military installa- tion outside the USSR. Cam Ranh Bay is steeped in historical significance. It was the staging area for the Japanese Fleet during the Russo-Japanese War. The Japanese Fleet decimated the Russian Baltic Fleet in the Tsushima Strait in 1905 in the major naval battle of that war. This fact has led to speculation that Soviet naval strategists may be contemplating a Tsushima-in- reverse during a future conflict. Cam Ranh Bay has yet another historical connotation. It was the Japanese move into Cam Ranh Bay that led the United States to impose oil sanctions against Japan--a catalyst for World War II in the Pacific.

In 1985, Moscow's use of the base at Cam Ranh Bay enables it to project power far south of Japan and to

pose a threat to the vital sea-lanes and chokepoints
linking the Pacific and Indian oceans. The Soviets also
make use of the Vietnamese airbase at Da Nang and the
Cambodian port of Kompong Som, which lies on the Gulf of
Thailand. Bear-D long-range reconnaissance aircraft and
Bear-F antisubmarine warfare planes operate out of Vietnamese bases; they serve to enhance Soviet operational
and intelligence-gathering activities and to intimidate
the noncommunist states of Southeast Asia. In the
spring of 1984, Soviet and Vietnamese naval infantry
forces staged an unprecedented joint amphibious exercise
off the coast of northern Vietnam in the Gulf of Tonkin.[5] This episode presumably had a sobering effect on
China, which had threatened to teach Vietnam a "second
lesson" as punishment for its invasion of Cambodia.
(The "first lesson" consisted of a limited Chinese
cross-border attack into Vietnam in February 1979 and a
six-week-long occupation of some northern Vietnamese
areas.)

Moscow has used its military presence in Southeast
Asia for intimidation on other occasions as well. In
1980, for example, the aircraft carrier Minsk led a
four-ship flotilla on a precedent-shattering cruise
through the Gulf of Thailand. In February 1983, the
Minsk, carrying vertical takeoff YAK-36 fighter planes,
sailed virtually within view of Singapore's waterfront
business district. During his tenure as U.S. ambassador
to the Philippines, Michael Armacost told reporters that
Soviet aircraft carried out "hundreds of violations of
Philippine airspace."[6] Moscow's deployment of a permanent naval contingent in the South China Sea at a time
when the U.S. ability to retain use of bases in the
Philippines is in jeopardy constitutes still another
ominous portent for the region. The Soviets stand
poised to assert regional hegemony in this strategically
vital area. Meanwhile, the USSR stationed two aircraft
carriers in the western Pacific--formerly a U.S.
"lake"--during a period when the United States was
forced to denude its naval power there in order to
transfer carriers to the Indian Ocean and Persian Gulf
in response to the crises in Afghanistan and Iran.

As noted above, the Soviet Union's strategic nightmare envisages the formation of an alliance among the
United States, China, and Japan. However, the thrust of
the Kremlin's policy toward its foes has the effect of a
self-fulfilling prophecy. Its intransigence toward
Japan on the Northern Territories issue and vis-à-vis
China on concessions to bring about a Sino-Soviet reconciliation leaves those countries virtually no alternative but to recoil from the USSR and seek closer links
with each other, with the United States, and with ASEAN.
In short, the Soviet Union has created a situation in
which its provocative behavior is the catalyst for the
moves toward "collusion" among its foes that it pro-
fesses to recognize and deplore.

NORTHEAST ASIA: SOVIET RELATIONS
WITH CHINA, JAPAN, AND KOREA

U.S.-Soviet relations lie beyond the scope of this
chapter. Suffice it to say that the USSR regards the
United States as its main enemy (glavniy protivnik) in
Asia--and worldwide. The United States is viewed as an
actual, even imminent, threat as compared with the potential threat from China and Japan. Moscow's chief
concern, therefore, is that closer military links between Japan, China, and the United States will hasten
the day when those potential threats are transformed
into actual ones. As one scholar aptly pointed out:

> What the Soviets fear is a China industrialized and
> given military technology and assistance by Tokyo and
> Washington. . . . The Soviets are conscious of the high
> level of Japanese technology and of the danger that it
> might be applied to military ends. . . . Even if Japan-
> ese technological cooperation should remain outside the
> military sector, it could produce a quantum jump in
> Chinese industrial-military capabilities.[7]

As noted above, China, like Japan, seems to be
regarded by the USSR as a potential security threat. As
the Japanese might move during an international crisis
to mine the three straits through which the Soviet
Pacific Fleet would have to exit the Sea of Japan into
the open ocean, the Chinese might align themselves actively on the side of the United States and Japan in a
superpower conflict. Moreover, as one scholar has
pointed out, "Although China is no match for the Soviets
in a frontal, one-on-one conflict, its relatively obsolete weapons could turn into a formidable factor if the
Soviet Union were to exhaust itself in a major conflict
with the United States in East Asia."[8]

Moscow's concerns should be viewed against the
backdrop of the Sino-Soviet dispute, which, in turn,
evolved out of a long historical legacy:

> The Soviet security perspective in Asia and worldwide
> . . . bears the imprint of years of confrontation with
> the world's most populous, and Asia's largest, nation.
> The two countries share a border that stretches for
> more than 4,000 miles across Asia. Bitter ideological-
> political and territorial conflicts rooted in history
> going back to Czarist times have envenomed the . . .
> relationship. . . . Chinese military inferiority and
> technological backwardness are to some extent compen-
> sated for by China's enormous manpower resources, its
> proved tenacity in resisting foreign invaders, and the
> vastness of the country, where invading armies tend to
> bog down, as did those of the Japanese in the 1930's
> and early 1940's.[9]

Moscow's public attitude toward the Sino-U.S. rela-

tionship appears to be somewhat schizophrenic. Soviet
propaganda lambasts Beijing and Washington for alleged
collusion against Moscow, but at the same time Soviet
spokesmen profess to be unconcerned about a Sino-U.S.
rapprochement because the ideological gap between the
two nations seems unbridgeable.

Despite China's assertions that it is pursuing an
"evenhanded" policy equally critical of both superpowers, a Soviet Defense Ministry publication of late
December 1983--the eve of Chinese Premier Zhao Ziyang's
visit to the United States--accused Beijing of a pro-
U.S. bias. The publication argued that China was guilty
of complicity with U.S. "imperialism." It also chided
the Chinese for "forgetting" that "the entire Asian
continent is surrounded by U.S. military bases."[10] One
could spot traces of Soviet concern about Sino-U.S.
security ties in the wake of Zhao's U.S. visit in January 1984. Nevertheless, Soviet statements, although
exhibiting some unease about the development of Sino-
U.S. links, expressed relative optimism about the general course of Chinese foreign policy and the prospects
for Sino-Soviet relations. According to Moscow's assessment, underlying differences between the United
States and China would preclude "a comprehensive Sino-
U.S. strategic agreement."[11]

A short time later, Moscow's optimism gave way to a
more pessimistic outlook as a result of President Ronald
Reagan's official visit to China in April 1984. The
Soviet news agency Tass, for example, denounced Chinese
leader Deng Xiaoping for reportedly stating that "China
is not opposed" to a U.S. arms buildup.[12] Soviet policymakers and academics alike have periodically accused
Beijing of "tilting" toward Washington--Chinese claims
of "evenhandedness" notwithstanding.

The year 1984 was notable for the number of high-
level Sino-U.S. exchanges.[13] In January, as already
noted, Premier Zhao visited the United States, and in
March a group of Chinese defense industry specialists--
reportedly including Defense Minister Zhang Aiping's
son--paid a visit. The following month, President
Reagan journeyed to Beijing--a journey that the Soviet
Union viewed as a significant effort to upgrade Sino-
U.S. relations in preparation for Reagan's reelection
campaign.[14] The Soviets undoubtedly were relieved by
Beijing's rejection during Reagan's visit of Sino-U.S.
strategic cooperation, but they remained concerned about
the possibility that secret accords were signed at the
time of the visit.

Although Reagan received a warm welcome, the Chinese media deleted some of his strongest anti-Soviet
statements.[15] The censorship presumably reflected China's desire to avoid offending the Kremlin on the eve of
a planned visit by First Deputy Prime Minister Ivan
Arkhipov, who served as Moscow's chief economic adviser
in China during the Sino-Soviet honeymoon of the 1950s.
However, the Soviets postponed Arkhipov's visit in the

58

wake of escalating border clashes between Chinese and
Vietnamese armed forces. Moscow warned Beijing against
attempting to "teach Vietnam a second lesson" for its
invasion of Cambodia, while Beijing reiterated its three
preconditions for a normalization of Sino-Soviet relations: a Soviet drawdown of troops on the Sino-Soviet
border and in Mongolia; Soviet withdrawal from Afghanistan; and cessation of Soviet support for Vietnam's war
in Cambodia. China tried to reassure the Kremlin that
"China is not entering and will never enter into any
alliance with the United States against the USSR.
Never." [16]

The Soviet and Chinese foreign ministers conferred
at length during the UN General Assembly session in New
York in the autumn of 1984, and semiannual talks between
Soviet and Chinese officials on normalization of relations proceeded on schedule--albeit perfunctorily.
Arkhipov finally visited Beijing in December 1984. The
highest ranking Soviet official to come to China in
fifteen years, he negotiated a five-year trade accord
and an agreement providing for Soviet assistance in the
modernization of Soviet-financed industrial projects
dating from the 1950s.

Arkhipov's visit notwithstanding, Sino-Soviet
state-to-state relations have remained relatively chil-
ly, and party-to-party relations are nonexistent. Chinese party officials demand Soviet concessions on major
issues (troop levels, Cambodia, Afghanistan) before
"fraternal" ties can be restored. The Kremlin is unlikely to offer any concessions to Beijing so long as
Sino-U.S. ties become closer, particularly in the military field. As a U.S. scholar has emphasized: "Moscow
has feared that American advanced weapons technology and
weapons systems might make their appearance in China,
[thus] transforming a potential Chinese threat to Soviet
security into an actuality." [17] The United States reportedly already has agreed to sell the Chinese TOW
antitank and Hawk antiaircraft missiles. [18]

The Kremlin can be expected to play upon the concerns of those in Chinese officialdom who oppose the
U.S. connection and who, for ideological or other reasons, harbor nostalgia for the Sino-Soviet amity of
earlier times. Moscow's attempt to cultivate kindred
spirits in Beijing, however, will be accompanied by
continuing military pressure in the form of a tighter
encirclement of China from Mongolia, Vietnam, Cambodia,
Afghanistan, and perhaps, eventually, North Korea. Although the reinstatement of China into the Soviet-
controlled international communist movement would constitute a tremendous victory for the USSR, the Soviets
are unlikely to pay a price in the form of concessions
on what they view as important strategic interests elsewhere in Asia.

Moscow regards Japan, like China, as a potentially
serious threat to its security. As Soviet commentary
stated recently, "It is well known that it is primarily

a country's industrial base and . . . skilled manpower which constitute the foundation of military industry. Both these factors are present in Japan."[19] As Japan, under Prime Minister Yasuhiro Nakasone, has continued to increase its military expenditures, the Kremlin has displayed concern that Tokyo will harness its economic and technological prowess militarily to undermine Soviet security interests in Asia.

The uneasy relationship between the USSR and Japan, like that between Russia and China, has deep historical roots:

> The two powers have faced each other on the Korean Peninsula, on Chinese territory, and in areas tradi-tionally included in the Chinese zone of influence. They have clashed repeatedly in enormously costly and bloody land and sea battles: in the Russo-Japanese War, in confrontations triggered by the spread of the Bol-shevik Revolution into the Far East and leading to the Japanese armies' attempted occupation of Siberia, in the large-scale Soviet-Japanese tank battles of the 1930's, and in the sudden thrust of the Soviet armed forces into Japanese-occupied Manchuria during the closing days of World War II, a military operation that led to the capture and abduction of hundreds of thou-sands of Japanese into Siberian labor camps. . . . History has left in both nations a residue of psycho-logical attitudes that can be described only as dark suspicions of the neighbor's intentions. [20]

Although Japan represents an attractive trade and economic partner for the USSR, the Soviets seem to focus primarily on the military threat that they perceive in the U.S. security treaty and the U.S. nuclear umbrella over Japan.[21] In recent years, Moscow has expressed particular alarm over the increasingly close defense cooperation between Tokyo and Washington and over Ja-pan's willingness to assume greater burdens for its own defense.

In May 1981, Japanese Prime Minister Suzuki paid an official visit to Washington. He announced there that Japan would defend the seas and skies around the home islands and also contribute to the defense of the sea-lanes up to a distance of 1,000 miles. U.S.-Japanese military collaboration subsequently intensified and included, during 1982, a joint naval exercise in the Sea of Japan and a joint command post exercise on Hokkaido. In another recent development, U.S. and Japanese mili-tary staffs have been joint planning to provide for contingencies in the event of a Soviet attack on Japan. Tokyo also has agreed to export advanced military tech-nology to the United States and to increase its finan-cial support for the maintenance of the 45,000 U.S. troops stationed in Japan.

Prime Minister Nakasone's journey to the United States in 1983 reaffirmed Suzuki's pledge of helping in defending the sea-lanes up to 1,000 miles from Japan. He also told a Washington Post interviewer on 18 January that Japan should become "an unsinkable aircraft carrier" against Soviet Backfire bombers and should control the straits around the Sea of Japan to prevent Soviet warships from crossing between Vladivostok and the open Pacific. The following day, Tass declared:

> Is it not clear that in the present nuclear age there can be no "unsinkable aircraft carrier" and that by deploying "onboard the carrier" arsenals of armaments, including American [arms], the authors of such plans make Japan a likely target for a response strike? And for such a densely populated, insular country as Japan, this could spell a national disaster more serious than the one that befell it 37 years ago. [22]

Moscow's propaganda offensive against Japanese military policies intensified markedly after the arrival, on 22 March 1983, of the U.S. nuclear-powered aircraft carrier Enterprise at the port of Sasebo. On 25 March, a Radio Moscow commentator warned that "Japan will be the first victim in all disputes that arise in the Far East." On 5 April, Tass thundered that Japan's increasing military cooperation with the United States "threatens to transform Japan into an arena of nuclear combat and, in the final analysis, to bring about the country's destruction." [23] Soviet Foreign Minister Andrei Gromyko even charged that Japan was already "bristling with nuclear missiles." [24]

On 3 August 1983, Pravda summed up the prevailing Kremlin view of Tokyo's growing defense cooperation with Washington by contending that "after being an accomplice in the U.S. anti-Soviet strategy, Japan is increasingly becoming a co-participant." [25] Even more disturbing from Moscow's viewpoint, however, is the belief that Japan will become a de facto member of the North Atlantic Treaty Organization (NATO). According to an article on 11 March 1983 in Le Monde:

> Through various channels, with the active support of their American allies, the Japanese sounded out the members of the Atlantic Alliance early this year with a view to obtaining the status of "external associate," which would have enabled them to participate . . . in the operations and discussions of the regional organization which relate to East-West economic relations. . . . The French government . . . cut short the initiative, vetoing in principle any expansion or globalization of NATO. [26]

The La Monde article may have been referring to a tour in January of West European capitals by Foreign Minister Shintaro Abe, who reportedly also suggested the creation of a mechanism for informal consultations between Japan and NATO on political and security issues. [27]

In June 1983, Japan signed the declaration issued at the summit conference of the world's leading industrial powers held at Williamsburg, Virginia. The declaration dealt with both economic and political-military issues. It was the first time that Japan associated itself formally with NATO members on a document expressing support for a strong common defense. Moscow reacted, predictably, by proclaiming that "Tokyo is beginning to play increasingly clearly the role of NATO's Far Eastern flank." [28]

In seeking to further complicate Japan's relations with the West, Soviet propaganda continues to exploit Japan's "nuclear allergy" to the hilt. Tokyo adheres to a self-restraining policy in the form of the "three nonnuclear principles"--no manufacture, possession, or "introduction" of atomic weapons into the country. In 1984, when Prime Minister David Lange of New Zealand prohibited the entry of U.S. nuclear-armed ships into his country's waters, the reverberations were felt throughout Asia. The United States has a standing policy of neither affirming nor denying the presence of nuclear arms aboard its naval vessels, and the Japanese government to date has not challenged the comings and goings of U.S. warships in Japan's waters. Moscow presumably would welcome a U.S.-Japanese crisis over this delicate issue and has spared no effort in praising Wellington's antinuclear stance.

The Soviets have not confined themselves to propaganda in attempting to ward off what they view as a potential military challenge from Japan. Russian military forces in Northeast Asia have adopted an increasingly offensive and aggressive posture, and espionage and subversive activities, as revealed in great detail by KGB defector Stanislav Levchenko and others, have proceeded apace.

Soviet surface combatants and submarines sail along the very edges of Japanese territorial waters. Soviet minisubmarines of the type that have penetrated deep into Swedish waters now have appeared off Japan's coasts. These subs are capable of crawling along the seabed, where they leave track-like markings, and returning to their motherships after dropping off spies or other agents or engaging in sabotage operations. Soviet intelligence-gathering vessels (AGIs) ply constantly along Japanese shores. Soviet reconnaissance planes frequently appear simultaneously on both sides of the archipelago and approach so close to Japan's airspace that the self-defense forces and flights by reconnaissance and antisubmarine aircraft around Japan have become almost routine. The regular flights of Bear reconnaissance planes near Japan en route from the USSR to Vietnam have come to be dubbed the "Tokyo Express." [29]

In 1980, a Soviet TU-16 Badger long-range bomber, which is capable of delivering nuclear-tipped air-to-surface King Fish missiles, buzzed a Japanese naval vessel that was exercising in the Sea of Japan. Since that time, the Soviets have adopted an increasingly aggressive posture vis-à-vis U.S. as well as Japanese vessels in the area. The Soviet intention evidently is to demonstrate to Japan the vulnerability of the U.S. forces on which it depends for protection.

During an interview on 21 April 1981 with the Japanese daily Mainichi Shimbun, Aleksandr Bovin, a political commentator for the Soviet newspaper Izvestia, was asked about the continuing problem of the Northern Territories. "Is it for military reasons that the Soviet Union cannot return the 'northern territories'?" the questioner asked. Bovin's reply was as follows:

> This involves an important issue. It is a principled position of the Soviet Union that it will reject any proposal aimed at readjusting territorial delineations reached as a result of the Second World War. It took us 30 years to make Europe understand this position, which was at last recognized at the Helsinki Conference. . . . Our position of preserving political and geographical borders delineated after the Second World War is also applicable to Asia. [30]

Perhaps the chief underlying factor in Moscow's adamant refusal even to discuss the return of the Northern Territories, however, is its fear of creating a precedent for concessions on other significant territorial issues, particularly those involving the huge tracts of land that China claims were seized illegally by czarist Russia under the "unequal treaties" of the nineteenth century. At the height of the Sino-Soviet dispute, this question led to charges of "cartographic aggression."

As Moscow turns its attention to the Korean Peninsula, the Kremlin seems to have made considerable progress in wooing North Korea away from the Chinese orbit. Having long maintained a position of equidistance between Moscow and Beijing, Pyongyang appears to have strengthened its contacts with the USSR. In May 1984, Kim Il-Sung paid his first official visit to the Soviet Union in twenty-three years. He was accompanied by a high-ranking party and state delegation. From Moscow, he traveled to a number of East European bloc countries. Soviet statements and actions during Kim's visit suggested an effort to draw the Asian communist countries (notably North Korea and Vietnam) closer to the USSR and the East European bloc as part of a campaign to reinvigorate the international communist movement and to gain support for Soviet security objectives in Asia. Pyongyang reportedly is reluctant to strain its friendship with Beijing, however. North Korea has treaties of friendship, cooperation, and mutual assistance with both the USSR and China dating from 1961.

Kim's more forthcoming attitude toward Moscow was foreshadowed during an interview he gave to a visiting delegation from Tass in March 1984. In a rarely used formulation, he referred to the USSR and North Korea as "comrades-in-arms" and called the relationship an "alliance" (a startling term in view of North Korea's regularly self-proclaimed nonalignment). He also lauded Moscow's support for Third World "liberation struggles," in contrast with previous North Korean allegations that both the Soviet Union and the United States attempt to dominate the Third World.

Kim's sojourn in Moscow was marked by expressions of desire for closer bilateral relations and cooperation in the global arena. During a Kremlin banquet in his honor, Kim evinced a wish to learn from the success and advanced experience of the Soviet people and to extend cooperation between the two countries. In addition, he invoked "proletarian internationalism" (the code word for joint action by communist nations in support of "fraternal" states and revolutionary movements worldwide). In the latter context, North Korea, although not a Soviet proxy, "objectively" serves Moscow's interests by rendering military and propaganda assistance to the Sandinistas in Nicaragua, the Tamil rebels in Sri Lanka, and various anti-Western groups in the Middle East and Africa. North Korea also maintains friendly relations with Afghanistan, despite its initial criticism of the Soviet invasion.

Chernenko's banquet speech emphasized that Soviet-North Korean cooperation can be expanded beyond the economic field. He urged exchanges among party and state workers and interaction in the sphere of international activities. Kim toasted the international communist movement toward which North Korea has been aloof in recent years.

Kim held three rounds of talks with Chernenko, and North Korea's defense and foreign ministers met with their Soviet counterparts. Soviet officials in charge of foreign economic assistance also met the North Koreans. According to reports following Kim's visit, special emphasis was placed on questions of strengthening security in the Far East and Pacific. This formulation suggests that modernization of the North Korean armed forces may have been on the agenda. Persistent rumors raise the possibility that the USSR will provide MIG-23 warplanes to North Korea, thus reversing a decade-old policy of withholding offensive aircraft from Kim's militant regime.

In November 1984, Soviet Deputy Foreign Minister Mikhail Kapitsa visited Pyongyang. As was the case after Kim's Moscow visit, no formal military or economic agreements were announced, but the existence of secret accords cannot be precluded. Still another sign of the gathering momentum in Soviet-North Korean relations emerged with the announcement that Soviet Foreign Minister Gromyko would journey to Pyongyang in August 1985, presumably in order to reciprocate for a recent Moscow visit by North Korean Foreign Minister Kim Young Nam. Before the visit could take place, however, Gromyko was replaced by Eduard Shevardnadze. In the meantime, a

Soviet shipment of MIG-23 war planes arrived in North Korea for the first time, raising the question whether the Soviets had gained access to North Korean naval and airbases in return. Such bases would enable the USSR to thwart U.S.-Japanese control of the Sea of Japan in a crisis situation.[31]

Moscow seems to have abandoned its strong resistance to the transfer of power from Kim Il-Sung to his son, Kim Jong-Il--a dynastic succession at odds with Marxist-Leninist precepts. Befriending the younger Kim will smooth Soviet political relations with North Korea but is unlikely to temper the new leader's aggressive and independent nature. Kim Jong-Il, who is said to have masterminded the Rangoon bombing incident that killed several South Korean government officials and narrowly missed the president, reportedly is committed to the reunification of Korea--through military action if necessary. A new Korean war would plunge Asia into a crisis and almost certainly would lead to a direct U.S.-Soviet military confrontation. Thus, although Moscow would like to incorporate North Korea into a glacis of friendly communist states on the USSR's Asian borders, it would be loathe to endorse a new militant foreign policy of the Pyongyang regime. A MIGs-for-bases agreement could be the initial step in destabilizing Northeast Asia, which has enjoyed relative tranquility--despite severe underlying tensions--in recent years.

Soviet policies in Northeast Asia have been designed primarily to bolster the security of the USSR against the real and potential challenges that the Kremlin hierarchy perceives from the United States, Japan, and China. In Southeast Asia, on the other hand, the Soviets view the security environment more in terms of opportunities than of challenges.

SOVIET OPPORTUNITIES IN SOUTHEAST ASIA

The U.S. withdrawal from Vietnam left the Soviet Union with an irresistible opportunity to acquire the former U.S. base at Cam Ranh Bay. Although both Moscow and Hanoi denied vehemently that the Soviets enjoyed unrestricted use of the base, this fiction became increasingly difficult to sustain in the wake of the signing of the Soviet-Vietnamese friendship treaty of November 1978, followed by the Soviet-backed Vietnamese invasion of Cambodia. The quantity and quality of Soviet arms and equipment at Cam Ranh Bay have risen steadily. A squadron of TU-16 Badger bombers and a contingent of MIG-23 fighter bombers are among the weapons systems recently deployed there--evidently on a permanent basis.

Cam Ranh Bay serves the USSR admirably both as a means of projecting Soviet power into Southeast Asia for purposes of influencing and intimidating regional states and as a component of a worldwide network of staging areas for wartime use. Southeast Asia may be regarded as a missing link in the chain of military strong points with which the Soviet Union aspires to gird the globe. Soviet control of access to the Strait of Malacca, below the Malayan Peninsula, in particular would round off an arc of military facilities stretching from Murmansk to Vladivostok (across the northern sea route, which is kept open by icebreakers) to Indochina and southward through the Pacific into the Indian Ocean toward Soviet facilities in South Yemen and Ethiopia.

Pointing to Southeast Asia as a vital arena in Moscow's quest for global hegemony, an article in the Chinese Communist party's theoretical journal Red Flag contended that the Soviets seek to create a "bow-shaped navigation line" connecting the Mediterranean, the Red Sea, the Indian Ocean, the southwest Pacific, the Sea of Japan, and the continents of Europe, Asia, and Africa. According to the Chinese, such a navigation line would enable the Soviet Pacific and Black Sea fleets to conduct mutual support operations, would permit the Soviets to impede the U.S. 7th Fleet's entry into the Indian Ocean, would threaten China from the seas, and would leave the Soviet Navy poised to cut off maritime ties between the Far East and Australia and between the Far East and Europe, thus choking off Japan's commercial lifeline (and wartime resupply route).[32]

Aside from positioning itself for a number of wartime scenarios, the USSR is exploiting its growing military prowess in Asia for peacetime advantage. The Wall Street Journal aptly summed up this phenomenon in an editorial entitled "Ivan Knocking." Commenting on a recent Soviet offer to the ASEAN countries to act as a "guarantor" of peace in Southeast Asia, the Journal wrote: "The strategy is to build up armed strength, deploy those arms in threatening numbers, and then make an offer your 'partners' are afraid to refuse. In the gangster world, this is called a protection racket."[33]

Insofar as Vietnam remains a pivotal player in the Soviet Union's response to potential threats and opportunities in Southeast Asia, the nature of the Soviet-Vietnamese alliance must be examined and its future prospects assessed. The raison d'être of the alliance, which dates officially from the signing of the Treaty of Friendship and Cooperation on 3 November 1978, is mutual hostility toward China. Within weeks of the treaty's signing, Vietnam, bankrolled and supported materially and logistically by the Kremlin, invaded Cambodia and installed a puppet regime under Heng Samrin. In February 1979, Chinese forces launched an attack across the Sino-Vietnamese border--an attack for which Moscow claimed Beijing got the green light during Deng Xiaoping's visit to Washington at the end of 1978. In the aftermath of the invasion, which China claimed was designed to "teach Vietnam a lesson" on policy toward Cambodia, the Soviet Union sent military equipment that enabled Hanoi to bolster substantially the quantity and quality of its troops along the Sino-Vietnamese frontier. Moscow also warned Beijing against any attempt to administer a second lesson to Vietnam.

The Vietnamese have sought to straddle the fence in the Sino-Soviet dispute in order to enjoy the greatest potential for foreign policy maneuvering. Thus, Hanoi presumably applauded when the Sino-Soviet treaty expired in 1980 at China's initiative, but by the same token the initiation of normalization talks between the USSR and China in October 1982 was cause for Vietnamese concern. During the first round of talks, held in Beijing, the Chinese declared that the Soviet Union would have to meet three preconditions before a substantial improvement in bilateral relations could occur: a reduction of Soviet troops along the Sino-Soviet border and in Mongolia; a withdrawal of Soviet forces from Afghanistan; and a cessation of Soviet support to the Vietnamese war effort in Cambodia. China asserted that the last of these preconditions was the most urgent. Although the Soviets to date have indicated little receptivity to a settlement of the Cambodian issue on terms acceptable to China and have reiterated that improvement in Sino-Soviet relations would not come at the expense of third countries, Hanoi recalls past occasions on which Moscow sacrificed its interests on the altar of superpower politics. Vietnam thus fears that Soviet support for its policies would be a major casualty of a Sino-Soviet detente.

As an insurance policy, Vietnam has tried on a number of occasions to mend its relations with China. In turn, Moscow's concern that Hanoi might seek a deal with the Chinese behind its back evidently has induced the Soviet Union to remain inflexible on the Cambodian issue and not deviate from the Vietnamese position. To reassure Vietnam of continuing Soviet support, a delegation led by Politburo member Geidar Aliyev arrived in Hanoi in October 1983 to sign a new agreement updating the Soviet-Vietnamese friendship treaty. The new declaration (signed on 4 November 1983 and published in Pravda the following day) restated Soviet support for the Vietnamese communist regime. It stressed "the unchanged principled line of the USSR to provide support and assistance to fraternal Vietnam." In addition, it asserted that the Communist party of Vietnam "completely supports the principled line of the Soviet Union to normalize relations with the People's Republic of China." However, this assertion was accompanied by the contention that the existing government in Kampuchea (Cambodia) is the only legal one and that "the basic cause of the still existing tensions in the region is the hostile policy of the forces of hegemonism and imperialism which threaten the sovereignty and the territorial integrity of Vietnam, Laos, and Kampuchea." Hegemonism is a Soviet code word for Chinese policy, so that when the declaration states the necessity "first of all to stop foreign intervention into the internal affairs of the states of the region," it is clear at whom the remark is aimed. Although the gradual withdrawal of the Vietnamese occupation forces from Kampuchea was envisaged ("over a period of years"), the declaration backed Hanoi's call for "the unity of the Vietnamese, Laotian, and Kampuchean nations."[34]

Although the declaration seemed to reflect Soviet-Vietnamese harmony, the speeches delivered by Aliyev and Vietnamese Prime Minister Pham Van Dong on the occasion of its signing indicated that friction between the two allies persisted. Aliyev downplayed the Chinese threat and presented the United States as the greatest threat to world peace. He called on Vietnam to coordinate its policies with Moscow in facing the U.S. challenge. Dong, on the other hand, emphasized the Chinese peril.[35] Soviet-Vietnamese tensions on the economic front were alleviated with the signing, during Aliyev's visit, of a long-term agreement on economic development and scientific cooperation, which provided for mechanizing agricultural production, increasing energy and fuel production, expanding transportation and communication facilities, stepping up production of chemical fertilizer, and increasing overall Vietnamese exports to the Soviet Union.

Yuri Andropov's death in February 1984 and Konstantin Chernenko's accession to the top Soviet leadership post led to changes in the Kremlin's posture toward Vietnam and China. Unlike Andropov, Chernenko seemed strongly in favor of strengthening Moscow's relationship with Hanoi and using that relationship as a strategic asset against what the Soviets regarded as Sino-U.S. military collusion. Chernenko was particularly vehement in accusing China of aggressive activities in Afghanistan and elsewhere in Asia.

In the spring of 1984, worsening Sino-Vietnamese border tensions, increasing Soviet-Vietnamese military and naval cooperation, and Chinese naval maneuvers constituted both a cause and a symbol of deteriorating relations between Moscow and Beijing. (In an unequivocal gesture of militant solidarity, the Soviets and Vietnamese staged an amphibious exercise highlighted by the landing of some 400 Soviet naval infantrymen [marines] at Haiphong.[36]) In May, the Chinese countered with their own naval exercises in the South China Sea. Beijing's apparent purpose was to strain the Soviet-Vietnamese alliance by depicting the USSR as a paper tiger that would not protect Vietnam's security on the high seas.

Moscow cancelled Arkhipov's May visit to China, and the following month Vietnamese Defense Minister Van Tien Deng traveled to the USSR to meet with his counterpart, Dmitri Ustinov. Deng sought more Soviet military assistance to cope with mounting Chinese pressure on the Sino-Vietnamese border and to counter Chinese support for the Khmer Rouge in Kampuchea. The fact that Deng went to Moscow again six weeks later with the same agenda indicates that the results of the June meeting were unsatisfactory to the Vietnamese. Thus, Hanoi presumably realized that although Moscow was cooling its attitude toward Beijing, it intended to avoid military encounters with the Chinese on Vietnam's behalf. The Soviet Union, indeed, seemed to be acting like a paper tiger.

By the autumn of 1984, Chernenko's health was failing. Thus, he may have been able no longer to mobilize the anti-Chinese forces in the Kremlin against other officials who favored a more anti-Vietnamese, pro-Chinese policy. At any rate, anti-Chinese polemics in the Soviet media subsided markedly, and the Arkhipov visit was rescheduled for late December. Before the visit took place, however, the Soviets sent Vladimir Dolgikh, a candidate member of the Politburo, to Hanoi to reassure the Vietnamese that Moscow was not about to betray their interests.

The year 1985 witnessed a noticeable improvement in Sino-Soviet relations. Vietnamese President Truong Chinh, reputed during the Vietnam War to have been the leader of the pro-Chinese faction in Hanoi, journeyed to Moscow in March for talks with new Soviet party chief Mikhail Gorbachev. A Radio Moscow broadcast of 14 March lauded the "unshakeable cohesion" between the Soviet Union and Vietnam. The two countries were said to share a "complete identity of views," a formulation generally reserved only to describe relations between the USSR and its Warsaw Pact allies.

Nevertheless, strains persist in the Soviet-Vietnamese relationship, and China appears poised to exploit them. In May 1985, Deng Xiaoping averred that Beijing would tolerate a continuation of the Soviet military presence at Cam Ranh Bay if Moscow would halt its support for the Vietnamese war effort in Cambodia. Deng seemed to be offering the Kremlin an opportunity to accede to one of China's principal conditions for a normalization of Sino-Soviet relations (an end to Soviet support for the conflict in Cambodia) and maintain the strategic presence in Vietnam that enhances the USSR's capabilities in its global military competition with the United States. At the same time, Deng's statement provided the Soviets with an opportunity to curry favor with the ASEAN states, which strongly demand a Vietnamese withdrawal from Cambodia.

The USSR's impressive naval and air presence in Southeast Asia, its power-projection capabilities, and its alliance with Vietnam have created the preconditions for substantial logistical and other forms of "fraternal" assistance to communist insurrections in the area. Although Moscow's objectives in Southeast Asia do not necessarily entail the installation of communist regimes, the destabilization of pro-Western governments would add immeasureably to Soviet security goals in the region. During a 1983 visit to Singapore, Deputy Foreign Minister Mikhail Kapitsa warned that Vietnam would arm insurgents against Southeast Asian governments that continue to support the Cambodian resistance.[37] The implication was that Moscow would back Hanoi in such a policy. Evidence already is accumulating that the Soviets and Vietnamese are supporting a breakaway faction of the Thai Communist party and training Thai guerrillas in Laos.

Soviet support for the communist insurgency in the Philippines--a subject that has been virtually ignored by scholars and journalists alike--enables the Kremlin to promote two of its principal security objectives in Asia.[38] One is to fuel the campaign for the removal of U.S. military facilities from the Philippines, thus allowing the Soviets, through their Vietnamese bases, to acquire hegemony in the South China Sea and adjacent strategic areas. The other is to recapture the allegiance of Southeast Asian communist parties and movements that fell under China's sway during the Sino-Soviet schism. If the Philippine Communists win a military victory or a dominant place in a coalition government, both the U.S.-Philippine alliance and ASEAN will be damaged irreparably, and the "correlation of forces" in Asia will take a radical swing in favor of the Soviet Union. Soviet strategy in the Philippines, and elsewhere in Southeast Asia, combines minimal risks with the possibility of dramatic gains. Such gains, in turn, would have immediate and grave repercussions throughout Asia and would undo whatever progress the United States has made in the restoration of its prestige and influence since the debacle of the Vietnam War.

All too frequently, the Kremlin faces a dilemma in foreign policy decisionmaking. It must choose between furthering the national security interests of the USSR and enhancing Moscow's leadership role in the international communist movement. In the Philippines, the Soviets confront no such conflicting goals. Soviet security objectives would be advanced strongly by the end of U.S. military superiority in the Pacific. Supporting the communist insurgents, whose chief foreign policy goal is the expulsion of the U.S. military presence in the country, is an excellent means of promoting Soviet security objectives as well as bolstering Soviet ideological influence.

The Communist party of the Philippines (CPP) and its military arm, the New People's Army (NPA), have forged increasingly close links with the Soviet Union. Moscow formerly provided support exclusively to the Philippine Communist party (PKP), from which the CPP broke away in 1969 to espouse Maoist principles. A major issue in the Sino-Soviet dispute involved Soviet willingness to foster communist revolution in the Third World. Moscow argued that revolutions could not succeed unless the objective conditions were favorable. The Philippines was not judged ripe for revolution in Moscow's eyes. Thus, the Soviet Union and the PKP pursued a strategy of avoiding armed struggle and concentrating on political struggle and organizational activities.

The CPP and the NPA looked to Beijing, which argues that armed struggle itself could create the necessary conditions for communist victory in the Philippines. The Chinese accused the Soviets of selling out communist parties in Asia and elsewhere under a pretext of shunning "left-wing deviationism" and "adventurism."

During the latter half of the 1970s, Chinese support for the CPP/NPA evaporated steadily. China, determined to counter Soviet-backed Vietnamese expansion into Cambodia, cultivated close ties with Thailand and the rest of ASEAN. China also was obliged to improve relations with the United States in order to counter the Soviet buildup in Vietnam. Beijing, for example, supported the presence of U.S. military bases in the Philippines--a position that infuriated the CPP. By the early 1980s, the CPP appeared receptive to Soviet suggestions that it follow a united front strategy with the PKP and various front groups against the regime of President Ferdinand Marcos. With the active support and encouragement of the Soviet-controlled World Federation of Trade Unions, labor organizations of the CPP and PKP stepped up their cooperation bilaterally and with various ostensibly independent trade union groups. In 1982, Stanislav Levchenko, a former official of the Tokyo rezidentura of the KGB, testified before the House Select Committee on Intelligence that Soviet intelligence officers were funding the CPP on a fairly regular basis.[39]

The political turmoil that shook the Philippines in the aftermath of the assassination of popular opposition leader Benigno Aquino in August 1983 led Moscow to conclude that revolutionary conditions in the country were becoming increasingly favorable. The Soviets stepped up political and material support to the CPP and the NPA, which intensified their insurgency and spread their operations into the cities as well as rural areas. In the spring of 1984, the Kremlin assigned KGB disinformation expert Boris Smirnov to the Soviet Embassy in Manila. His task was to fan anti-U.S. sentiment in the Philippines.[40] A few weeks after Smirnov's arrival at his post, a bogus questionnaire "from the U.S. Information Service" was distributed among leading Filipinos that sought sensitive information on subjects such as their political leanings and military experience. Many of the recipients reportedly were outraged by the "American impertinence."[41]

Moscow conceals many of its sensitive covert activities in the Philippines under cultural, sports, or economic cover. There has been a marked increase in the number of visitors from the USSR and the East European bloc countries, according to a Philippine government official.[42] Meanwhile, the National Democratic Front, an umbrella group of anti-Marcos opposition elements, has dramatically stepped up its political and propaganda activities. The PKP and CPP work within this organization, as well as independently, and have devoted great efforts to winning over figures in the moderate opposition to communist positions on major political issues.

Soviet involvement in arms transfers to the NPA are more difficult to detect. The fact that the Philippines is an archipelago consisting of some 7,000 islands renders it virtually impossible for the government to monitor effectively any arms deliveries to the Communists. However, the Soviets evidently were involved in at least one recent shipment of arms from Eastern Europe that was made via South Yemen, a Soviet surrogate, to the NPA.[43]

From 30 November to 4 December 1984, the Soviet-controlled World Peace Council (WPC) and its Philippine affiliate, the Philippine Peace and Solidarity Council, co-sponsored the first International Conference on Peace and Security in East Asia and the Pacific. The conference took place at the University of the Philippines, a focal point of National Democratic Front activity. The parley coincided with a wave of protests and demonstrations throughout the Philippines that featured a common opposition to "American imperialism" and U.S. facilities in the country. _Pravda_ quoted an alleged participant at one of the rallies as saying:

> There were more than 5,000 people. We gathered in
> front of the American base at Clark Field, the largest
> in this region of the world. From here, the bombers
> flew to Vietnam. The Americans call the entrance to
> the base the "Gate of Friendship" but we call them the
> "Gates of Hell," since nuclear death lurks behind them.
> We demanded the removal from our land of all 23 U.S.
> bases, including Clark Field and Subic Bay.[44]

THE SOUTH PACIFIC: FISHING IN TROUBLED WATERS

Moscow has carried its political offensive against the U.S. presence in Asia and the Pacific southward to Australia and New Zealand and to the newly independent South Pacific islands. A U.S. observer of the USSR has written that "the Pacific is now an arena for Soviet military-political intrusion and subversion [with] the whole bundle of island ministates . . . up for grabs."[45]

Australia and New Zealand have traditionally harbored vocal pro-Soviet minorities in communist and other leftist (notably labor) organizations. However, the announcement by New Zealand Prime Minister David Lange, head of one of the country's leading political parties, that U.S. nuclear-armed and nuclear-powered ships would be banned from New Zealand's ports offered the Soviet Union a boon that it wasted no time in exploiting. A Soviet media blitz lauded New Zealand's newfound nuclear allergy and urged other Pacific nations to follow suit by banning U.S. nuclear arms in their waters or airspace, dismantling existing U.S. military installations on their territory, and preventing the establishment of new ones. Moscow, however, has not been averse to expanding its own naval presence in the South Pacific through such innocent-sounding proposals as treaties on fishing rights. Nor has the Kremlin offered to abandon its air and naval bases in Vietnam.

The Soviets evidently regard New Zealand's anti-nuclear policy as the opening wedge in the undermining of the Australia-New Zealand-United States (ANZUS) treaty, which links the United States, Australia, and New Zealand in the defense of the South Pacific. Soviet spokesmen are pressing for a nuclear-free zone in the Pacific--a topic on which they can draw support from a melange of nations that otherwise have little affinity for the USSR. The Soviet campaign is being waged not only in the media but also through various Soviet-dominated front groups. Perhaps the oldest of these groups is the Pacific Conference of Churches, founded in the 1960s and subsidized by the World Council of Churches. It propagandizes against U.S. military installations and exercises in the Asian-Pacific region and sponsors programs of "peace education." Another important front group is the Committee for International Trade Union Unity (CITUU), spawned in Sydney, Australia, by delegates to the 9th Congress of the World Federation of Trade Unions (WFTU) that took place in Czechoslovakia in 1978. According to a report in the Washington Times:

> CITUU has been organizing conferences and study programs in the Indian Ocean, Southeast Asia, and the Pacific regions. Pacific islanders have been sent to the Soviet Union, while Soviet and Vietnamese Communist officials have been the leading speakers at various area conferences.[46]

In 1980, three members of the Communist party of Australia attended the Third Nuclear-Free Pacific Conference in Hawaii, which brought together trade unionists from a number of Pacific nations and created an organization called the Pacific Trade Union Forum (PTUF). In 1981, the CITUU and PTUF held a joint conference in Vanuatu (formerly the New Hebrides) to which the Soviet Union sent observers. The following year the PTUF sponsored a Pacific-wide conference in Noumea at which peace and disarmament were the main issues. The Soviets and their new friends in the Pacific area have announced support for the NPA-led "liberation movement" in the Philippines and the anti-French Kanak Socialist National Liberation Front in New Caledonia and, for good measure, have recommended that Hawaii be returned to its "indigenous" peoples.[47]

Moscow's "peace offensive" in the Pacific can claim at least partial credit for New Zealand's action against U.S. naval vessels, for a similar ban by Vanuatu and the Solomon Islands on U.S. nuclear-armed and nuclear-powered ships, for Papua-New Guinea's rejection of a U.S. request to permit Philippine-based B-52s to overfly the country, and for a movement by politicians in Palau

to deny the United States a military base.[48]   The "peace
offensive" is occurring against a backdrop of growing
Soviet military power in the Pacific, large portions of
which used to be a U.S. lake.

CONCLUSION

Soviet concerns about a threat from the United
States and a potential challenge from China and Japan
notwithstanding, in our opinion the emerging security
environment in the Asian-Pacific region contains a host
of opportunities for the USSR. Furthermore, the accession of Mikhail Gorbachev, a relatively fresh, young
leader with an aura of dynamism, puts Moscow in its best
position in many years to exploit those opportunities.
The replacement of veteran Soviet Foreign Minister
Andrei Gromyko with Eduard Shevardnadze, who has little
experience in international affairs, not only suggests
Gorbachev's desire to take the lead in this realm but
also symbolizes a penchant for fresh initiatives abroad.
Gromyko, rightly or wrongly, was perceived widely as
obsessed with Soviet-U.S. relations and perhaps as advocating a superpower duopoly in world affairs. Gorbachev
may plan to deemphasize the relationship between the Big
Two and to seek improved ties with other major actors in
the global arena. China seems to be one of the primary
targets of his attention. In July 1985, Chinese Deputy
Premier Yao Yilin visited Moscow for talks with, among
others, First Deputy Prime Minister Arkhipov. The two
men initiated a five-year pact on barter trade that was
estimated at $14 billion.[49]   The accord also stipulated
that the Soviet Union would build seven new industrial
plants in China and would help to modernize a number of
enterprises that it financed during the heyday of Sino-
Soviet friendship in the 1950s. Arkhipov played a major
role as an economic adviser to China at that time. The
trade agreement was particularly significant because it
represented the first time in many years that bilateral
trade was placed on a long-term rather than an annual
basis.
According to the joint communiqué issued after
Yao's visit, the two sides discussed not only trade and
economic questions but also "some other problems of
mutual interest."[50]   In view of Deng Xiaoping's remark
that China would tolerate a Soviet military presence at
Cam Rahn Bay if the Soviets would halt their support for
Vietnam's war effort in Cambodia, Indochina may have
appeared on Yao's agenda in Moscow. The Kremlin undoubtedly has been feeling the pressure from the United
States (which was moving toward the provision of military assistance to the noncommunist elements of the
Cambodian resistance) and ASEAN on the Cambodian issue.
It undoubtedly felt still greater pressure following
U.S. Secretary of State George Shultz's summer 1985 tour
of Southeast Asia and meeting with ASEAN's foreign min-

isters. Vietnam, for its part, evidently hoped to head off a Sino-Soviet rapprochement at its expense by proposing high-level discussions with the United States on the unresolved issue of U.S. soldiers missing in action during the Vietnam War.

Hanoi's cautious overtures for the establishment of diplomatic relations with Washington have been spurned with the admonition that such a move was impossible before the withdrawal of Vietnamese troops from Cambodia. However, the greater the possibility of a Sino-Soviet reconciliation appears to the Vietnamese leaders, the more likely they are to persist in their campaign to bring all of Indochina under their control--even if Moscow withdraws military assistance for the Cambodian war. To allow Cambodia to drift into the Soviet or Chinese orbit would be an unacceptable threat to Vietnam's security interests.

Regardless of the outcome of the Cambodian conflict, Moscow's position at Cam Ranh Bay appears secure for at least the short-term future. Thus, Moscow may well be able to have its cake and eat it too by diminishing the threat from China through political and economic gestures and retaining Soviet military investment in Southeast Asia by means of its Vietnamese bases.

Gorbachev seems no more predisposed than his predecessors to making concessions aimed at improving Soviet relations with Japan. Sticks appear likely to prevail over carrots in Moscow's policy toward Tokyo. Japanese spokesmen, however, have reiterated that their country will not enter into any type of formal alliance or other strategic relationship with Washington and Beijing. Thus, the USSR's strategic nightmare of a Sino-U.S.-Japanese triangle is unlikely to materialize. Moreover, Moscow probably can take comfort in the thought that Prime Minister Nakasone's commitment to a substantial bolstering of Japanese military prowess may well be eroded by his successors.

Elsewhere in Asia the Soviets may worry about regional arms races, but they display no reluctance to participate. It was Soviet deployment of TU-16 Badger aircraft and MIG-23 fighter-bombers in Vietnam that brought about a U.S. decision to sell an upgraded version of the F-16 warplane to Thailand and Singapore.[51] Other ASEAN members may seek similar purchases. On the Korean Peninsula, tension almost certainly will mount as Moscow yields to Pyongyang's repeated requests for MIG-23s. The Soviets will justify such deliveries by citing South Korea's acquisition of F-16s. In surveying the overall military balance in the Asian-Pacific region, it is highly significant that the USSR and its allies possess an overwhelming superiority in manpower. The Soviets themselves deploy more than 500,000 troops on the Sino-Soviet border alone and have the capability to transfer forces relatively quickly from other theaters in any emergency situation short of an East-West war in

Europe. Vietnam's armed forces, totaling some 1.2 million, are larger than those of the six ASEAN countries combined. North Korea, like Vietnam, has one of the world's largest military establishments. One need not postulate combined action by Soviet, Vietnamese, and North Korean armies to appreciate the potential threat these forces pose to pro-Western nations in the Asian-Pacific region. If Sino-Soviet relations take a dramatic turn for the better, China's massive armed forces would be effectively neutralized from threatening Soviet security in Asia.

Much as the Kremlin would like to acquire reliable allies in Asia, it will continue to rely upon its own strength for expanding Soviet influence there. In view of the unattractiveness of communist ideology and of the Soviet economic model, the overwhelming thrust of the Kremlin's policy in Asia has been and will continue to be military. A long-time observer of Soviet affairs has aptly summed up this phenomenon by noting that

> a successful cultural diplomacy, an important means of policy, is virtually nonexistent in the Soviet case. Moreover, Soviet economic policy toward Asia is highly unsuccessful. . . . Most Asian states find Soviet goods unattractive, Soviet terms of assistance objectionable, and Soviet technology second-rate. . . . In terms of diplomatic style, Moscow's motives have been patently transparent, its manner heavy-handed and manipulative, and its appeal generally unsuccessful. . . . Soviet perfidy has come to be well known in Asia. . . . Effective Soviet policy instruments have been reduced to the military/conspiratorial tool, the only one in which it excels and to which it continues to devote most of its energies.[52]

NOTES

1. John J. Stephan, "Asia in the Soviet Conception," in Donald S. Zagoria, ed., Soviet Policy in East Asia (New Haven: Yale University Press, 1982), p. 31.
2. Paul F. Langer, "Soviet Military Power in Asia," ibid., p. 272.
3. Far Eastern Economic Review, 8 November 1984.
4. Stephan, "Asia," p. 32.
5. Far Eastern Economic Review, 8 November 1984.
6. See Marian Leighton, "Soviets Still Play Dominoes in Asia," Wall Street Journal, Op Ed page, 14 October 1983.
7. Langer, "Soviet Military Power," p. 266.
8. Tetsuya Kataoka, "Japan's Northern Threat," Problems of Communism (March-April 1984):6.
9. Langer, "Soviet Military Power," p. 259.
10. Krasnaya Zvezda, 31 December 1983.
11. See, for example, the article by I. Alekseyev and F. Nikolayev in International Affairs (Moscow, April 1984).

12. Tass, 3 May 1985.

13. These exchanges actually were kicked off by the visit of U.S. Secretary of Defense Caspar Weinberger in the autumn of 1983.

14. See Thomas P. Bernstein, "China in 1984," Asian Survey (January 1985):46.

15. Ibid., p. 45.

16. According to an interview that Chinese Communist party chief Hu Yaobang gave to the Italian Communist newspaper L'Unita, this assurance was passed by a high Chinese official to Rumanian President Nicolae Ceaucescu, who was asked to pass it on to Moscow. See Bernstein, ibid., p. 47.

17. Langer, "Soviet Military Power," p. 265.

18. Bernstein, "China in 1984," p. 46.

19. Quoted in Langer, "Soviet Military Power," p. 264.

20. Ibid., p. 261.

21. Interestingly, the treaty requires the United States to intervene militarily if Japan comes under Soviet attack but does not impose a parallel requirement on Japan. Thus, the USSR would be vitally concerned to prevent Japan from entering a NATO-Warsaw Pact war.

22. Tass, 19 January 1983.

23. Tass, 5 April 1983.

24. Asiaweek, 29 April 1983, p. 17.

25. Pravda, 3 August 1983.

26. Le Monde, 11 March 1983.

27. The Washington Times, 21 April 1983.

28. Izvestia, 10 June 1983.

29. Marian Leighton, "De-Coupling the Allies: Soviet Strategy Toward Northern Europe and Japan," Survey (Autumn-Winter 1983):134.

30. Mainichi Shimbun, 21 April 1984.

31. See Far Eastern Economic Review, 6 June 1985, p. 13; and Washington Post, 18 July 1985.

32. Ibid.

33. Wall Street Journal, 25 April 1985.

34. As cited in Leif Rosenberger, "The Soviet-Vietnamese Alliance and Kampuchea," Survey (Autumn-Winter, 1983):230.

35. Far Eastern Economic Review, 1984 Asia Yearbook, p. 285.

36. Far Eastern Economic Review, 8 November 1984.

37. Leighton, "Soviets Still Play Dominoes."

38. For a detailed study of this topic, see Leif Rosenberger, "Philippine Communism and the Soviet Union," Survey (Spring 1985).

39. U.S., Congress, House, Select Committee on Intelligence, Soviet Active Measures, 97th cong., 2nd sess., 13-14 July 1982, pp. 166-167.

40. Business Times (Kuala Lumpur), 5 December 1984.

41. Ibid.

42. Ibid.

43. Ross H. Munro, "Dateline Manila: Moscow's Next Win?" Foreign Policy (Fall 1984):186.

44. Pravda, 4 December 1984.

45. Arnold Beichman, "Trouble in Paradise," Washington Times, 19 June 1985.

46. Ibid.

47. Ibid.

48. Ibid.

49. Washington Post, 11 July 1985.

50. Ibid.

51. Reuter, 8 July 1985, Previous U.S. policy had been to sell only the export versions of the F-16.

52. Thomas W. Robinson, "On Soviet Asian Policy: A Commentary," in Robert H. Donaldson, ed., Soviet Union in the Third World: Success and Failures (Boulder, Colo.: Westview, 1980), pp. 298-299.

4   The Great Powers' Security Role in Southeast Asia: Diplomacy and Force

Sheldon W. Simon

Although Great Power relations are frequently described in geometric terms, suggesting structural balances in triangles and quadrangles, another perspective--at least in Southeast Asia--may be drawn from dance. Rather than viewing states confronting one another in a linear manner in tests of "power," it may be useful to think of them as engaged in a series of movements, some of which may be harmonious and graceful just as others could lead to serious collisions. A primary strategic goal of Great Powers (the United States, the Soviet Union, and China) is to avoid direct military confrontations with either of the others. However, secondary interests, for example, the protection of sea-lanes (the United States) or the establishment of new military positions (the USSR), require ties with regional members who may already be arraigned as antagonists. By assisting regional allies in attaining their security requirements, then, the Great Powers enter into relationships that may move them toward confrontation. Strategy depends on managing these relationships with sufficient skill that war is avoided and the interests of allies are advanced. This chapter assesses Great Power policies in Southeast Asia, focusing on their security ties with the region's major adversarial groups: the Association of Southeast Asian Nations (ASEAN) and Indochina. As in all alliances, each member hopes to acquire a measure of

----

This chapter was originally prepared for the National Strategy Information Center Conference on "Stability, Development, and Security in Southeast Asia," Port Dickson, Malaysia, November 12-14, 1984. Research for this paper was partially supported through travel grants from the U.S. Information Agency and the Earhart Foundation (Ann Arbor, Michigan). A slightly different version of this article was first published in Asian Survey, vol. 25, no. 9, September 1985, pp. 918-942, copyright 1985 by The Regents of the University of California.

policy support it could not afford to obtain by itself and minimize direct costs. In most instances of Great Power relations with smaller regional partners, the former finances the latter's military growth in exchange for strategic location (bases) and an understanding that the latter will provide neither facilities nor political support to the former's adversaries. Thus, alliances tend to polarize political relations, providing stability without resolving conflicts.

THE UNITED STATES: RELIABLE PARTNER
OR DECLINING POWER?

There are numerous claims that U.S. foreign policy has been erratic and reactive since the Second Indochina War (1965-1975), torn by conflicts between Congress and the executive branch, and flawed by a process that divides responsibility and lacks coherence.[1] Although it is true that U.S. foreign policy has been erratic on details and rhetoric, more remarkable has been that policy's overall consistency. As Kenneth Waltz recently observed:

> Who would have thought when the war ended in 1945 that 40 years later we would still be carrying West Germany and much of Western Europe on our backs at a cost recently estimated by Senator Sam Nunn at $90 billion a year? Who would have thought we would be proportionately outspending Japan for defense by about five to one, in considerable part to protect its vital interests? Seldom have a country's cost commitments abroad been sustained with the constancy or vigor that America has shown.[2]

This "constancy" is both a strength and a weakness--a strength in that it underscores U.S. reliability, a weakness because it may reflect a kind of strategic immobility or inability to adapt to changes in the international environment, to share burdens and power within the international system as the relative capacities of the United States diminish. Put another way, the maintenance of U.S. military hegemony may be accelerating its economic decline.

U.S. policy toward Southeast Asia is derivative of larger interests in the Asian region as a whole. Although the United States historically looked toward the Atlantic and Europe for its cultural heritage and social institutions, a political and economic reorientation to the Pacific began as early as World War II. Since 1945, Asia has been the locus of the United States' two major military confrontations (Korea and Indochina). More significantly, it has become the world region with which the United States has carried on the plurality of its international trade since 1978. In 1982, U.S. trade with the Pacific exceeded its Atlantic counterpart by some $15 billion. In 1983, Pacific trade accounted for approximately 30 percent of total U.S. trade. At the same time, U.S. investment in Asia has also grown at a faster rate than investment in any other world region. Pacific Basin countries currently produce 60 percent of the world's Gross National Product (GNP). For 1984, U.S. exports to the Asian-Pacific region were valued at $54.6 billion and imports at $114 billion. U.S. investments in the Pacific are currently valued at over $30 billion, and Asia now accounts for more than 50 percent of the U.S. global deficit. Asia is of prime importance, then, to U.S. prosperity, and U.S. Asian policy may in large part be explained by the desire to nurture these important economic considerations.

The primary components of Washington's East Asia policy appear to be an emphasis on close relations with market-oriented economies in Asia congenial to U.S. trade and investment and the development of military capabilities to protect the sea-lanes of international commerce. The military capabilities required to achieve these ends are primarily air and naval, which in turn necessitate regional base facilities through formal alliances.

Although most U.S. alliance commitments made in the 1950s (Japan, South Korea, the Philippines, Australia-New Zealand, and, to a smaller extent, Thailand) remain in force, the nature of these commitments has been somewhat degraded since the end of the Second Indochina War in 1975. That is, it is highly improbable that the United States will commit ground forces in future Asian conflicts (with the exception of the Korean Peninsula, which is characterized by an uneasy armed truce of more than thirty years' duration). As early as 1969, then-president Nixon enunciated a policy that holds to this day: that U.S. ground forces will not intervene in Asian domestic hostilities to protect incumbent governments from internal turmoil, even if that turmoil is externally backed. The single exception to this principle--Korea--is a special case. The 41,000 mostly forward-deployed U.S. forces there are not a significant military factor but serve rather as a political deterrent or tripwire comparable, say, to U.S. forces in Berlin. They constitute a guarantee that the United States would be involved in the early stages of a war on the peninsula if North Korea (Democratic People's Republic of Korea, or DPRK) launched an attack.

One other hypothetical case in which U.S. ground forces might be deployed should be mentioned: to protect U.S. facilities in the Philippines. Given the instability of Philippine politics, the country's economic crisis, and the growing unpopularity of the Marcos regime, U.S. military facilities in that country may potentially be at risk in the event of an internal uprising. It is noteworthy in this regard that the Philippine-U.S. mutual security agreement specifically prohibits the use of U.S. forces for action in the Philippines itself and that protection of the bases is the responsibility of the Philippine government because the bases are, under law, Philippine bases. In all probability, if the Philippine bases become a prime target for a popular uprising against Marcos or alternatively if Marcos himself turned against the bases and asked the United States to vacate as a nationalist ploy, U.S. forces would be withdrawn. It is inconceivable that the United States would fight Filipinos to maintain control of the bases. In fact, the United States is already examining possible alternatives to the Philippine bases for the twenty-first century (see discussion below).

Two major U.S. foreign policy concerns in Southeast Asia center on the ASEAN states and Indochina. ASEAN's importance is multifaceted, comprising economic, strategic, and political dimensions. The ASEAN states constitute precisely the kind of market-oriented, modernizing politicoeconomic systems that the United States hopes will come to characterize most of the Third World. An economically successful ASEAN is seen by Washington as both an examplar of the advantages in following international trade and investment-oriented development policies and an antidote to the failures of more radical autarkical systems such as Vietnam and North Korea. ASEAN as a group is America's fifth largest trading partner. In 1981, U.S. direct investment in ASEAN totaled $4.5 billion, a 48 percent increase over the level of U.S. investment in 1977.[3]

On the strategic level, the ASEAN states are situated astride Japan's most important trade route to the Persian Gulf. In the wake of the Soviet occupation of Afghanistan and the strongly anti-U.S. Shiite revolution in Iran, the United States has developed a new approach to security in the Indian Ocean area. By actively seeking to enhance its access to area-wide naval, air, and communications facilities, improving the naval and air operational capabilities of Diego Garcia, increasing the level of Indian Ocean deployments from the U.S. 7th Fleet to between one and two carrier task groups, and creating the Rapid Deployment Force (now known as the Central Command), the United States has substantially improved its capacity to project its forces into this region.

The ASEAN states are an integral component of this new strategy. The Indonesian archipelago, stretching for some 3,000 miles, and Malaysia sit astride a series of relatively narrow straits, the control of which could be used to both monitor and interdict ships moving between the Western Pacific and Indian oceans. Only a few of the channels through the Indonesia archipelago are wide and deep enough to permit the safe passage of submerged submarines (see Figure 4.1). These are the Sunda Strait with a governing depth of 120 feet and a minimum width of 12 nautical miles, Lombok Strait with a depth of 600 feet and width of 11 nautical miles, the Ombai Strait with a depth of 600 feet and width of 12

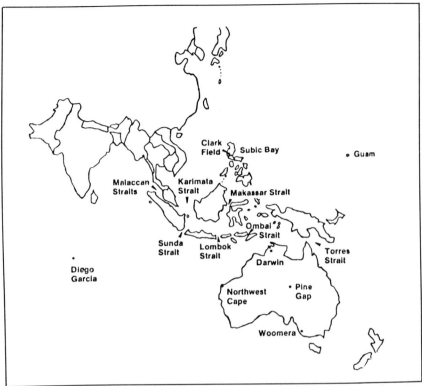

Figure 4.1. Strategic Straits and U.S. Military Bases in the Southeast Asian Region.

nautical miles, and the Straits of Malacca with a depth of 75 feet and minimum width of 8 nautical miles.[4]
It is assumed that U.S. SSBNs (NATO code for submarines carrying nuclear-ballistic missiles) from Guam sometimes transit these straits on their way to the Indian Ocean. Because the Soviet Union lags behind the United States in antisubmarine warfare (ASW) capability, these straits could be important chokepoints where the Soviets would have some chance to locate U.S. submarines through acoustic devices. Noteworthy in this regard was the 1982 arrest and expulsion of a Soviet espionage agent in Indonesia who was attempting to obtain exactly the kind of hydrographic data on the Makassar Strait necessary to position hunter-killer submarines in an interdiction mode.
In addition to ASEAN's strategic geography, the United States is also interested in its military growth. U.S. foreign military sales and credits to ASEAN in the early 1980s are around $4 billion for the acquisition of U.S. hardware, and U.S. military assistance is around $300 million (see Figure 4.2). The United States also plays a leading role in staging joint exercises as it is the dominant third country in the military maneuvers of ASEAN states.

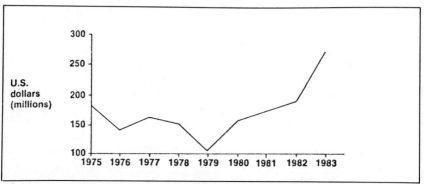

Figure 4.2   U.S. Military Assistance to the ASEAN Countries.

        U.S. military assistance has been instrumental in
providing Thailand with the firepower to resist Vietnamese encroachments along the Thai frontier.   Whereas
prior to 1983, Thai artillery lacked the range to suppress Vietnamese fire from across the border, the U.S.
supply of 155-mm howitzers in April 1983 enabled Thai
forces to repel Vietnamese incursions that spring.[5]
        There is a growing controversy, however, over
whether the ASEAN acquisition of some advanced U.S.
systems could fuel a regional arms race and/or skew
government budgets inordinately toward the military and
away from development expenditures.   Both Indonesia and
Thailand have asked to purchase a top-line U.S. fighter-
bomber, General Dynamic's F-16A.   As a general policy,
the United States has discouraged Third World countries
from buying the top-line F-16, urging instead that they
consider two new intermediate fighters developed specifically for Third World air forces: Northrop's F-20 and
General Dynamic's F-16/79.   Neither of these fighters
has yet to find a buyer, however.
        Proponents of F-16A sales to Thailand claim that
the fighter is necessary to balance the large number of
Vietnamese combat aircraft--485 including 180 MIG-21s,
versus 179 for the Thais, the top fighter being the F-5,
of which the Thais have 50.   Because the USSR has recently deployed MIG-23s in Vietnam, the argument goes,
then Thailand will need F-16s to be able to challenge
the Vietnamese in the air and possibly even to preempt
them on the ground.[6]   It should be noted, however, that
so far there is no evidence that the Soviets have given
MIG-23s to the Vietnamese Air Force.   The aircraft at
Cam Ranh Bay remain in Soviet hands.   Moreover, should
Thailand acquire the F-16A, in all probability Indonesia
would not be far behind.   The purchase of the F-16A
would enhance ASEAN's ability to develop a regional air
defense.   AWACs systems in Singapore could perform a
regional C^3 in this context and move ASEAN toward an
integrated air defense system.[7]   Singapore has recently
purchased several E-2Cs.

Opponents of the F-16A purchase believe that Thailand's F-5Es are more than sufficient to outmaneuver Hanoi's MIG-21s and that a squadron of F-16s, in any event, would have only a marginal effect on Vietnam's overall air superiority with their 207 MIG-17 and 21 fighters and SU-17 bombers. The enormous cost of an F-16A squadron--with spares and training--would be more than $500 million, money some say better spent on economic development. Furthermore, Thailand could acquire the F-20 at one-third of the F-16's cost.[8] Nevertheless, in July 1985, Thailand announced plans to purchase 12 F-16As at an initial cost of more than $300 million over a five-year period. To do this, the air force agreed to cut the rest of its operations--curtailing training, retiring older aircraft, and deferring developing of badly needed airlift capacity. Deliveries are scheduled to begin in 1988. As ASEAN defense budgets grow, the problem of trade-offs in other areas of public policy become increasingly salient. Is national security better served by acquiring big-ticket systems with a regional potential or by alleviating domestic, social, and economic conditions upon which insurgency thrives? Or alternatively, is security enhanced by adding less expansive military systems that would improve air-ground coordination as in the Thai case?

The primary confrontation between the powers in Southeast Asia for the past five years has been centered in Indochina. U.S. policymakers see several linkages between Indochina and ASEAN security. These include:

1. the threat posed by Soviet use of naval facilities at Cam Ranh Bay;
2. the threat to Thailand posed by the Vietnamese occupation of Kampuchea;
3. the danger of possible Vietnamese and/or Soviet support for communist insurgencies in ASEAN states; and
4. the destabilizing impact of large number of refugees, particularly in Thailand's eastern provinces.

Thailand and the other ASEAN states are particularly concerned that acceptance of Vietnam's domination of Kampuchea would remove the traditional buffer between the region's historic rivals, in effect turning Thailand itself into a buffer between a possibly expansionist Hanoi and Malaysia.[9] Although there is no evidence that Vietnam is currently attempting to subvert the Thai government, if Hanoi decided to do so, its domination of Kampuchea and past relations with the Thai Communist party could provide it with that capability.

ASEAN is particularly supportive of the maintenance of U.S. military forces in East Asia. Reversing its initial decision in 1978 to draw down U.S. forces in the aftermath of the Second Indochina War, the Carter administration, and then President Reagan, expanded U.S. naval and air capabilities. In effect, the U.S.

presence has prevented the polarization of Southeast
Asia into pro-Soviet and pro-Chinese blocs. Instead,
the United States is expanding the 7th Fleet, encouraging Japanese rearmament, and increasing arms sales to
ASEAN.

Although the U.S. presence provides ASEAN with
greater diplomatic maneuverability, ASEAN members are
uncomfortable with the de facto joint Sino-U.S. security
guarantee to Thailand. From ASEAN's perspective, Thailand's reliance on a combination of Chinese military
pressure on Vietnam's northern border and U.S. arms aid
to Bangkok has led Washington to adopt the intransigent
posture of the People's Republic of China (PRC) toward
any negotiated settlement to the Cambodian issue short
of a complete Vietnamese military withdrawal. The prospect of greater U.S. aid to the noncommunist segments of
the Cambodian resistance, however, is particularly welcomed by ASEAN (the Solarz proposal) because it increases the viability of a non-Khmer Rouge alternative
to Vietnam's occupation. The United States appears to
be less concerned about the future welfare of the Khmer
people than it is with consolidating Sino-U.S. cooperation against the Soviet Union. (One could speculate
about whether U.S. support for China's hard line on
Cambodia might change if Washington's security interests
began to diverge from Beijing's as China adopts a less
belligerent posture toward the Soviet Union.) At least
one U.S. observer during a recent visit to Hanoi found
some Vietnamese receptivity to the idea of negotiations
with the noncommunist elements of the Cambodian resistance if the Khmer Rouge were removed from the coalition.
According to former U.S. diplomat Anthony Lake, although
a Khmer Rouge exodus might lead to a marginal reduction
in military effectiveness,

> [t]he diplomatic advantages would be large, both in
> removing a stated Vietnamese objection to compromise,
> and a major Vietnamese propaganda issue, and in
> strengthening the ASEAN and American position before
> public opinion and at the United Nations, where current
> successes may not last forever.[10]

U.S. Force Deployments in Southeast Asia

The United States retains a considerable strategic
advantage in its relations with Southeast Asian states
(Table 4.1). With the exception of Indochina, all
states in the region are either tied into Western alliances, friendly to the West because of market-oriented
economies, or at least suspicious of Soviet intentions.
For the foreseeable future, the United States will be
able to deploy more forces throughout the region and
keep them on station for longer periods from bases in
the Philippines, Guam, Okinawa, and contingently from
Australia than can the USSR.

TABLE 4.1   U.S. Military Deployments in Asia

Army		Navy	
1 Infantry Division (Korea)		75 Air Squadrons	
1 Infantry Division (Hawaii)		21 attack	
		10 tactical early-warning	
Marines		7 early-warning	
1 Division (Okinawa)		14 fighter	
31 Air Squadrons (Pacific)		13 patrol	
2 attack helicopter		2 fleet air reconnaissance	
13 lift helicopter		2 fleet logistic support	
8 attack		6 antisubmarine warfare	
7 fighter attack			
1 photo reconnaissance		Air Force	
		1 strategic bomber wing	
Navy Seventh Fleet		1 air reinforcement wing	
7 aircraft carriers		15 Air Squadrons	
86 surface combatants		10 tactical fighter	
32 amphibious ships		2 tactical air support	
38 attack submarines		1 tactical reconnaissance	
2 ballistic missile submarines		2 tactical airlift	
marine amphibious units			

Source: New York Times, 26 October 1983.

The centerpiece for U.S. force deployments in
Southeast Asia is, of course, the air and naval bases at
Clark and Subic Bay--the largest and most complete U.S.
military facilities outside the United States. These
bases constitute a source of considerable political
controversy given the instability of the Marcos government and demands from some Philippines opposition quarters that the bases agreement not be renewed in 1991.[11]
   Briefly, the bases are positioned to provide maximum flexibility in responding to crises anywhere from
the Indian Ocean to the Sea of Japan. Clark, for example, is home base for a tactical airlift squadron of
C-130s that can move men and supplies through the Indian
and Pacific oceans. It is also an important C^{3I} center
for the Pacific. Subic's major wharves can service all
ship types in the U.S. Navy, including its largest
carriers--the basic component of U.S. maritime deployments in Asia. The ASEAN states openly (and China
privately) have urged the United States to retain the
Philippine bases.[12] On the other hand, Philippine opponents of the bases claim they are there solely to but-
tress U.S. global competition with the Soviets, they
contribute nothing to Philippine security. Because the
Philippines face no external threat and in the event of
a global war Philippine bases would become a Soviet
nuclear target, the bases place the Philippines at risk
and should be terminated.[13] This argument ignores, of
course, U.S. overseas military facilities as a deterrent
to a Soviet-U.S. confrontation, but it does reflect the

conflict between a Great Power with global concerns and the more parochial responsibilities of smaller states. The same principle was manifested in New Zealand's objections to U.S. Navy nuclear ship port calls.

At bottom, criticism of U.S. facilities in the Philippines may be explained more accurately in terms of domestic Philippine politics than external security concerns. Marcos' opponents argue that $900 million in aid provided under the 1983 bases agreement allows the regime to substitute repressive capabilities for responsive capabilities. U.S. aid has supplied the wherewithal for the Philippine armed forces to increase threefold in size and tenfold in budget since the declaration of martial law in 1972.[14] Although the bases may be important for the maintenance of U.S. forces in the Western Pacific, they are harmful to bilateral relations with the Philippines, for they are seen as the means whereby a repressive regime is maintained in power. Herein lies the dilemma for U.S. policy. Should Washington risk the possibility of being precipitously forced out of the bases by a post-Marcos regime, or should it plan now for other alternatives--the latter requiring new political negotiations with Australia, Japan, Thailand, Singapore, and/or the costly expansion of facilities on Guam and the Marianas?[15]

In 1985, with the Philippine bases, the United States dominates the waters of the South China Sea and eastern Indian Ocean. An average of seven to eight 7th Fleet vessels transited the Strait of Malacca each month of 1981-82 compared with three Soviet ships. Some eleven fixed-wing aircraft carriers cruised the region for the United States compared to none for the Russians. Finally, the Russians deployed four destroyers and two frigates compared with ten U.S. destroyers and thirteen frigates over the two-year period.[16]

If U.S. naval supremacy is to be maintained in South and Southeast Asian waters, prudence requires that alternatives to the Philippine bases be investigated. The Pentagon estimates that the construction of alternative facilities on Palau, Guam, and/or Tinian to the east of the Philippines would realistically require ten years lead time and cost anywhere from $3-4 billion. Moreover, relocation of Philippine base facilities to the western Pacific would place U.S. forces farther from the crucial Persian Gulf region or require the construction of additional ships to maintain the same level of deployment.[17]

On the other hand, those such as Admiral Gene La Rocque, (Ret.) USN, and Air Force Colonel William Berry, who advise the phasing-out of U.S. facilities in the Philippines by 1991, believe that U.S. facilities in Okinawa and the mid-Pacific are sufficient to sustain a U.S. naval presence throughout the region. Any loss in bases support could be compensated by greater reliance on at-sea logistics (the primary resupply mode of the

Soviet Pacific Fleet in the Indian Ocean). Major re-
pairs could be undertaken at Yukosuka, Japan, though
labor costs would be considerably higher than in the
Philippines. Ship repair facilities at Sembawang Ship-
yard in Singapore, already available to the U.S. Navy,
could also be enlarged. Tengah Air Field, from which
U.S. P3C-Orions fly to monitor Soviet submarine activity
in the Indian Ocean, could accommodate other aircraft in
the U.S. inventory as well. Moreover, Singapore is
1,300 miles closer to the Indian Ocean. Air and naval
bases in northern and western Australia, including Darwin, Learmoth, Tindal, Townsville, and Perth, could also
be used for deployment into the Indian Ocean.[18]
     With more modern aircraft, such as F-15s, the com-
mander of the 13th air force was reported as stating
that the air force could operate as effectively in the
Indian Ocean/Persian Gulf from Guam--with one inflight
refuelling--as it currently does with older planes from
Clark Field.[19] Moreover, both the drydock and airstrip
facilities in Guam can handle the largest U.S. ships and
planes. As long-range Tomahawk cruise missiles are
added to the 7th Fleet, U.S. ships can steam farther to
the east without losing the capability of striking East
Asian targets.
     In sum, although most specialists agree that the
loss of U.S. facilities in the Philippines could not be
fully replaced at a reasonable price through base diversification in the Indian Ocean, Southwest Pacific, and
Southeast Asia, opinions differ about whether such diversification would degrade the U.S. presence and render
it less credible to both friend and foe. Those who
support the status quo insist that the combination of a
superb infrastructure, low-cost labor, and geopolitical
location astride the major Asian sea-lanes cannot be
replicated. Critics of this position believe, however,
that the U.S. presence in the region can be maintained
from other locations and that the political risk of
being asked to leave the Philippines precipitously by a
post-Marcos nationalist regime requires the United
States to embark upon a systematic phasing out of the
bases during the next several years.
     Other avenues that might be explored as an alterna-
tive to a complete withdrawal from the bases include a
change in the legal relationship whereby the United
States leases some of the base facilities in concert
with the diversification plan discussed above. Another
possibility would be the multilateralization of the
bases whereby ASEAN forces would be invited to use some
of the facilities. Such a policy would reduce political
allegations that the bases serve only U.S. interests.
Moreover, a multilateral ASEAN presence in the Philippines could be an initial step toward a greater capacity
for local states to undertake more responsibility in
their own regional defense.

THE SOVIET UNION: SUPERPOWER ENTANGLED

Like the United States, the USSR, too, views Southeast Asia's importance as part of broader Asian concerns. Overall, the Soviet political position is decidedly inferior because of (a) the USSR's intractable conflict with China; (b) Moscow's poor relations with Asia's most powerful economy, Japan; (c) a relative stability throughout East Asia, except for Indochina, that provides few opportunities for Soviet influence; and (d) the lack of appeal in the Soviet model for either development strategies or revolutionaries.

Nevertheless, Soviet competitive involvement against the United States, encirclement of China, and the establishment of an important client with base facilities for its growing naval force seem worth the disadvantages that have accrued to Soviet policy. Although perceived as the patron of a state (Vietnam) that has violated the independence of its neighbor, the Soviets seem prepared, nevertheless, to write off relations with the rest of the region for the time being. The gains Moscow sees in Southeast Asia are the increase of Soviet influence in Indochina and the facilitation of Soviet naval passage. Moscow views these gains as stepping stones toward the enhancement of its total Asian presence.

Although the Soviets are prepared to accept negative relations with ASEAN and China, they are concerned that sustained high levels of tension could bring about a grand coalition among China, Japan, ASEAN, and the United States that opposes Soviet buildup in the region. Beginning in 1981 under Brezhnev and continuing with Andropov and to a smaller extent Chernenko, Moscow has essayed a peace offensive, the primary goal of which is to relax Soviet relations with its adversaries sufficiently to weaken incentives toward security collaboration. Nevertheless, it is difficult to pursue a peace policy convincingly and simultaneously continue a military buildup, occupy one nation with armed force, and support the military suppression of another. The Asian states are not convinced.

Furthermore, there is minimal likelihood that Soviet-U.S. relations will moderate in Asia during a second Reagan term. Sensing in the incumbent U.S. administration a coherent policy to undermine Soviet political legitimacy at home and abroad and to restore U.S. military superiority in violation of the Russian view of détente, the Soviets have little incentive to negotiate superpower differences in Asia, much less other global regions.

Instead, typically, the Soviets rely on a single element of influence--the deployment of force. The Southeast Asia/Indian Ocean nexus falls within the purview of the Soviet Pacific Fleet, currently the largest in the Soviet Navy, with over 720 ships, including 200 combatants, 65 of which are nuclear-powered submarines.

Many of these are attack vessels tasked with hunting the U.S. 7th Fleet and possibly interdicting Southeast Asian straits in the event of a crisis. The Pacific Fleet possesses a modest amphibious assault capability in the Ivan Rogov, the largest such craft in the Soviet Navy, capable of carrying 500 troops, 30 APCs, and 10 tanks. According to Commander-in-Chief, Pacific (CINCPAC), if provided with sufficient aircover and antisubmarine warfare (ASW) protection (the former particularly deficient in the Pacific Fleet) the Ivan Rogov would be a significant means of projecting Soviet or client state forces into local conflicts.[20]

In April 1984, Soviet amphibious forces staged landings on the Vietnam coast involving both the Ivan Rogov and the Minsk. This was the first time Soviet Marines operated outside Soviet coastal waters. Pentagon officials stressed the timing, noting that a message was being sent to both ASEAN and China--to Beijing at a time when its People's Liberation Army (PLA) forces were probing the Vietnamese border.

Soviet naval forces are supplemented by some 2,000 land-based combat aircraft, including 70 Tupolev Backfires with an operational radius of 3,400 miles. In both 1981 and 1982 in Southeast Asia and northern Pacific waters, Backfires staged simulated attacks on U.S. carriers, the first demonstration of a Soviet anticarrier warfare capability in Asia.[21] In addition, Moscow's theater nuclear capability has been enhanced by the deployment of over 130 SS-20 mobile, MIRVed (3 warhead) IRBMs in Soviet Asia. Their range could encompass Thailand and the Philippines.

Although Soviet basing facilities at Cam Ranh Bay and Da Nang provide logistics sufficient for Pacific Fleet vessels to remain on station in the Indian Ocean double the time they could prior to 1980, these bases cannot repair major battle damage; nor do they provide aircover for Southeast Asian operations. Indeed, the fleet's greatest deficiency is the absence of fixed-wing aircraft carriers. The Minsk, which has operated out of Cam Ranh Bay, and a newly commissioned short-takeoff-and-landing (STOL) carrier, the Novorossisk, being deployed in the Pacific, are primarily ASW vessels. Nevertheless, by 1984, the Soviet level of naval operations out of Cam Ranh Bay had reached twenty to twenty-five ships daily.[22]

Perhaps as important as Soviet facilities for naval craft is the construction at Cam Ranh Bay of one of the largest communications and electronic surveillance stations outside Soviet territory. It is used to monitor Chinese and U.S. military activities and to communicate with fleet headquarters at Vladivostok.[23] Soviet reconnaissance aircraft and electronic eavesdropping ships from Vietnam penetrated the Gulf of Thailand to observe the summer 1984 Thai-U.S. Cobra Gold exercise.[24]

A navy has three roles in a wartime environment: first, to deny the enemy free access to and use of a

particular sea area; second, to control a sea area so
that its own ships have safe passage; and third, to use
naval assets either to invade or devastate a particular
onshore area. The U.S. 7th Fleet deploys systems for
all three roles, but so far the Soviets are able to
undertake only the first on a regular basis. This
capability should not be underestimated, however. For
the first time, the Soviets could interdict at sea U.S.
and other countries' efforts, say, to supply friendly
states under attack. Moreover, the Soviets could impede
7th Fleet access to the Indian Ocean via the Strait of
Malacca, threaten China from the south, and cut off
maritime arteries to Japan from both Australia and
Europe. In February 1983, the Minsk, carrying Yak-36
VSTOL fighters, sailed virtually within view of the
waterfront business district of Singapore.[25]

Despite their growth in numbers, Soviet naval
forces in South and Southeast Asia experience serious
deficiencies. Reinforcements from Europe could be
blocked at such chokepoints as Bab al-man-deb and Suez
in the Middle East and from Vladivostok at the Japanese
straits of Soya, Tsushima, and Tsugaru. Moreover, the
Badger and Bear aircraft deployed at Cam Ranh are old
and slow, useful for peacetime reconnaissance but clearly ineffective in combat situations. Similarly, Soviet
Pacific Fleet ships generally deployed in the Indian
Ocean are among the least sophisticated in the navy.
They possess primarily "day-sailing" capability with
minimal electronics. The best ships are kept instead
near Soviet home waters where they can be protected by
land-based aircraft and are able, in turn, to protect
the homeland and their own SSBNs.[26]

Because neither the size nor firepower of the
forward-deployed elements of the Pacific Fleet are sufficient to interfere with the major Asian shipping
lanes, there must be other roles for the Soviet fleet.
A persuasive case can be made that the fleet's utility
for Soviet policy lies more in the politicoeconomic
realm, including the protection of its own extensive
commercial fleet that supplies Soviet Asia via a Black
Sea-Mediterranean-Indian Ocean route. The presence of
the fleet also provides the USSR with a presumptive
claim to participate in any negotiations leading to
regional peace or control zones. Indeed, the Soviets
have more interest in upholding freedom of navigation
through all straits than in any act of interdiction.
(Both the USSR and the United States argued successfully
for a free passage provision in the 1982 Law of the Sea
draft treaty.)

In sum, there is no need to be alarmist about the
Soviet naval presence in Southeast Asia. Its effectiveness depends on the maintenance of maritime peace. In
the event of war, U.S. 7th Fleet surveillance and firepower would be sufficient to destroy Soviet surface
ships and ultimately interdict most of their submarines
at Japanese chokepoints. In the event of war, according

to U.S. military analysts, the Soviets would probably not even attempt to reinforce their presence in Vietnam. Rather they would concentrate their fleet in the Sea of Okhotsk, the North Pacific, and the northern part of the Sea of Japan.[27]

In Vietnam, the USSR has acquired its first major Southeast Asian client. Although Hanoi and Moscow will probably share parallel strategic interests against China for some time, there are longer term prospects for divergence based on a number of past, current, and incipient conflicts and differences. Just as Hanoi argued that Beijing's record of support for Viet Minh victory in the First and Second Indochina wars is tarnished, a comparable allegation could be made against the Soviets. The Soviets, for example, proposed the admission of both Vietnams to the United Nations in 1955, a proposal, which had it been implemented, would have destroyed any prospect for reunifying the country under the terms of the 1954 Geneva Agreements.[28] Nixon's warm welcome by Brezhnev during the May 1972 mining of Haiphong Harbor also demonstrated to Hanoi's leadership where Moscow's priorities lay. Even after the Soviet-Vietnam Friendship Treaty was signed in 1978, the Soviets initiated sharp cutbacks in economic aid to Vietnam and raised the price of petroleum in 1980 from $4 to $16 per barrel. The subsequent decrease in Soviet oil shipments contributed to the serious Vietnamese food situation as vehicles were without fuel to transport rice from the surplus South to the deficit North. Vietnamese tractors also were idle for lack of fuel.[29]

The Soviets have pressed the Vietnamese for domestic economic/administrative reforms that make more efficient use of aid and allow the presence of large numbers of Soviet advisers (some 7,000 were estimated to be in country by 1983). The Soviets have used their aid, then, as a form of political leverage to exploit Vietnamese vulnerabilities and isolation. They have used the debt issue to acquire a long-term mortgage on the Vietnamese economy, thereby bargaining their financial aid in return for receipt of coal and even scarce grain, which could have been used to meet internal reconstruction needs. In 1982, the USSR still supplied 200,000 tons of grain, all of Vietnam's oil, and 90 percent of Vietnam's other imports. Hanoi's options were few.[30]

Moreover, the USSR has refused to go through Vietnam in dealing with Laos and Kampuchea. Opposed to the creation of blocs not under its control, the Soviet Union has sent advisers to the other components of Indochina as well. The Soviets have signed a long-term economic aid agreement with Laos (1981-1985), providing Vientiane with some $600 million in goods and services. There are 1,000 Soviet advisers in Laos; and the Laotian Air Force has acquired 20 MIG-21 fighters, infantry weapons, and new radar and SAM sites near Vientiane and the Sino-Lao border. Soviet military instructors are also in Kampuchea.[31] Japanese sources claim that the

Soviets are converting Phsar Ream in Kampuchea into a
new naval base.[32]

Although the Soviets may have ambivalent feelings
about Vietnam's hegemonial position in Laos and Cambodia, they continue to add to Hanoi's military capacity
for domination. In 1984, according to U.S. Assistant
Secretary of Defense Richard Armitage, Moscow supplied
Hanoi with MI-24 combat helicopters (the same kind the
Soviets use in Afghanistan), SU-22 swing-wing fighters,
missile coastal attack boats, SAMs, and tanks.[33] Nevertheless, there is evidence the Russians are also pressing Vietnam to reach a settlement of the ASEAN-Indochina
confrontation over Kampuchea. Vietnam is constantly
aware of a possible Sino-Soviet deal at Hanoi's expense;
therefore, both Moscow and Hanoi are sensitive to the
possibility of each playing a "China card" in their
political maneuvers concerning the future of Cambodia.
(This issue is discussed below.)

The Soviets have hinted to ASEAN independently that
they could support a neutral Cambodia so long as Soviet
bases were undisturbed. Indonesia has argued that a
return to the 1954 Geneva Agreements status of neutrality and nonalignment for Cambodia should satisfy the
defensive security needs of both China and Vietnam.
Nevertheless, Foreign Minister Andrei Gromyko apparently
concluded discussions with Indonesian Foreign Minister
Mochtar in April 1984 by reluctantly demurring: "The
clock cannot be turned back in Cambodia. The society . . . is entirely different from the one in which
people of the like of Sihanouk used to function."[34]

It is noteworthy that the Soviets have not condemned ASEAN directly for resisting Vietnam's control of
Indochina but rather claim that the association is acting against its own interests under Chinese and U.S.
pressure. Instead, the Soviets insist that ASEAN's
future security lies in accepting Hanoi's fait accompli
and creating a peaceful relationship with a Soviet-
backed Indochina. From Moscow's perspective, this development would move its long-held "collective security"
plan a giant step forward.

There are strategic differences between Moscow and
Hanoi with respect to ASEAN. The Kremlin probably favors a more conciliatory attitude. Hanoi's use of force
serves only to cement the ASEAN-China-U.S. relationship.
Moscow seems prepared to see the war of attrition continue at a low level, however, because this seems to
maximize Soviet influence, though Moscow would prefer a
settlement that leaves Russia on good terms with both
Vietnam and ASEAN. Thus, the USSR has shown particular
favor to the partial troop withdrawal proposal first
broached by Hanoi in July 1982. The USSR also views the
creation of a safety zone on the Thai-Kampuchean border
as an initial step toward a solution of the Kampuchean
issue.

Despite these efforts, the Soviet role in Southeast
Asia is treated with considerable hostility by ASEAN.

Not only do Soviet actions obstruct the realization of the Zone of Peace, Freedom, and Neutrality (ZOPFAN), but they have probably accelerated the development of security cooperation between ASEAN states and outsiders. The Soviet Pacific Fleet presence, for example, led Malaysia to agree to the basing of Australian P3-C reconnaissance aircraft that follow the Soviet fleet through the South China Sea and Indian Ocean.

ASEAN leaders also fear that the larger the Soviet presence becomes the more active will be China's efforts to subvert it. Malaysian Foreign Minister Ghazali Shafie believes that Soviet moves to develop an independent Soviet position in Laos and Kampuchea will encourage China to accelerate aid to the resistance movements in both countries, thus ensuring constant turmoil and involving both the Chinese and Russians in territory adjacent to Thailand.[35] Ominous, given this line of reasoning, are reports from Thailand that for the first time, the Soviets are backing a breakaway movement (Phak Mai) of the factionalized Thai Communist party. This group has reportedly set up three operational zones in Thailand's north and northeast that border Laos with training centers located in Lao military garrisons across the border.[36]

CHINA: THE INTRACTABLE PARTNER/ADVERSARY

Although the USSR and the United States view Southeast Asia as a region into which they project military power and political influence from afar, the Chinese solution is quite different. For China, Southeast Asia is a vital neighboring area that must not be controlled by regimes hostile to Beijing. China would prefer that Southeast Asia be ruled by states that acknowledge China's historical and current eminence. Traditionally, China's dynasties essayed tributary relations with southern neighbors, exchanging Confucian cultural and political forms for acquiescence. At times, China intervened directly in regional affairs, particularly in what is today Indochina, and supported one contending kingdom against another. Reacting to this history of Chinese intervention and indirect control became a basis for Southeast Asian nationalism, which in the nineteenth and twentieth centuries centered around both anti-European and anti-Chinese sentiments. Even today, the region's fear of China extends to the overseas Chinese communities born out of nineteenth century migrations. These communities number approximately 17 million, their members play a central role in almost all of the region's economies and have engendered an abiding concern among Southeast Asian governments that Beijing might seek to influence its ethnic kinsmen's behavior to political ends.

Central to China's foreign policy calculations in Southeast Asia is the belief that Vietnam has become a

surrogate for the USSR through Hanoi's membership in the
Council for Mutual Economic Assistance (COMECOM) and
through the 1978 Treaty of Friendship and Cooperation
that confirmed Vietnam's client status. Vietnam's political and economic dependence on the Soviet Union combined with the former's depredations against Vietnam's
Chinese community precipitated China's limited military
intervention into Vietnam in February 1979 and subsequent pressure in the border region.

China employs coercive diplomacy against Vietnam
(with indifferent results so far). This strategy uses
military force in "an exemplary, demonstrative manner,
in discrete and controlled increments, to induce the
opponent to review his calculations and agree to a
mutually acceptable termination of the conflict."[37]
Beijing's earlier invasion and current probes are designed to restore China's credentials as a regional
military power after they had been diminished in light
of the defeat of China's Khmer Rouge client. China
believed it had to demonstrate that Soviet forces deployed along its northern border had not rendered the
People's Liberation Army (PLA) militarily impotent.[38]
Nevertheless, from the coercive dilomacy perspective,
China's efforts have not been successful. The Vietnamese have neither withdrawn from Cambodia nor severed
their ties to the USSR.

China derived some benefits from its use of military force, however. The myth of Vietnam's military
invincibility was exploded as PLA forces leveled parts
of the country's six northern provinces. Hanoi also
learned that a treaty with the USSR would not necessarily deter a limited but costly Chinese military attack.
To this end, China demonstrated it was prepared to
sacrifice lives and treasure in order to restore Chinese
credibility to both friend (Thailand and the United
States) and foe (Vietnam and the USSR). Nevertheless,
on balance, China's coercive diplomacy may be judged a
failure. Vietnam has been driven deeper into a Soviet
embrace, thus distorting Chinese political priorities--
the object of the exercise had been to counter Soviet
influence, not to promote it.[39] Moreover, in 1985,
China's military credibility was further eroded when
China refrained from reacting to the Vietnamese destruction of Kampuchean resistance base camps and temporary
occupation of Thai territory in several locations along
the Thai-Cambodian border.

To balance the Soviet-Vietnam alliance, China
turned to the United States and ASEAN. By 1982, sensitive to Soviet and Vietnamese allegations that Beijing
had become too dependent on Washington for its security
and that its commitment to the Third World had been
eroded, China began to balance its diplomacy. China
sought to reduce the level of tension with the USSR and
to distance itself somewhat from the United States politically, but still retain its actual dependence on U.S.
trade and investment for economic development and the

deployment of U.S. forces regionally for security. Although China's declaratory policy became more critical of the United States, there was no evidence that Beijing wished to reduce economic ties or ask the United States to draw down its naval and air forces in the region. It is important to note that Soviet hegemony directly threatens China's security; U.S. hegemony only offends its moral sensibilities.

As Jonathan Pollack notes, China's more evenhanded approach to the superpowers is best explained through long-term modernization considerations that include (1) diminishing direct Soviet pressure against China, thereby making defense needs less imperative; (2) devising a credible, consistent basis for heightened economic and technological exchanges with the West; and (3) creating a stable and peaceful international environment that would be congruent with orderly economic development.[40] Thus, China defines its security relations with the United States in terms of a coalition or a loosely fashioned united front, not an alliance. The two states may undertake parallel, mutually supportive actions without more formal kinds of security collaboration. In this way China avoids being linked directly to a superpower's global strategy and to the Soviet-U.S. confrontation.

At the same time, however, China understands that East Asia is no longer a peripheral military front for the USSR, a fact formalized by the establishment by the Soviet Union of an independent theater command for the region in late 1978. The Soviet political and military presence to the north (Mongolia and the Sino-Soviet border), the east (the Soviet Pacific Fleet), the south (in Vietnam), and to the west (in Afghanistan) reflect an underlying strategy of containing China. Beijing's problem is to devise a means of managing this long-term geopolitical threat.[41]

The United States is a useful partner in this endeavor because, according to Xinhua Deputy Editor-in-chief Mu Guangren,

> the U.S. will continue to need China to tie down the
> million Soviet soldiers on the north, and the several
> hundred thousand Vietnamese soldiers on the south. And
> it will need to coordinate with China on Afghanistan
> and Kampuchea in support of those people's resistance
> and of ASEAN's effort against the Soviet and Vietnamese
> threat. The U.S. will also need to coordinate with
> China on any and all steps that may bear on global
> strategic situations.[42]

In short, the United States now needs China's strategic position as much as China requires U.S. economic assistance and also benefits from U.S. regional military presence. Thus, China is once again able to declare a policy of nonalignment toward both the United States and the Soviet Union, thereby improving its diplomatic credentials with the Third World but knowing that, in fact, the United States will still maintain a close relationship with China because of its own Asian security concerns.[43]

The most artful issue in China's diplomacy is undoubtedly the Kampuchean conflict. ASEAN members, most particularly Indonesia and Malaysia, are skeptical of China's long-term objectives in the region and are not convinced that Vietnam is a greater threat than China. If this view persists, ASEAN solidarity could be sorely strained over time and might even unravel over the issue of reaching an accommodation with Vietnam. The ASEAN states are particularly concerned that the United States in its zeal to contain the Soviet-Vietnamese alliance not help lay the basis for Chinese predominance in Southeast Asia.

ASEAN and PRC objectives differ over Cambodia. Although the former seeks a Vietnamese withdrawal, it is opposed to a Khmer Rouge return to power--hence, the belief that truly free UN-supervised elections in Kampuchea after a Vietnamese exit would eliminate any role for the Khmer Rouge in a popularly elected government. Indefinite military forays from the Thai border areas, according to this line of reasoning, with no diplomatic progress will only increase Sino-Soviet rivalry and influence in Southeast Asia to the detriment of the region's independence. Vietnam, of course, attempts to reinforce these underlying ASEAN-China differences by insisting that it is willing to withdraw its forces from Kampuchea as soon as "the cessation of the Chinese threat and the use of Thai territory by guerrillas hostile to the Government in Phnom Penh [occurs]."[44]

Vietnam's primary fear is the possibility of a Soviet sellout in a negotiated Sino-Soviet détente. If the financial costs of underwriting Hanoi's Indochina hegemony seem to exceed the strategic benefits of access to Vietnamese bases, the Russians might consider a withdrawal of support from Vietnam just as Moscow has betrayed its interests in the past. The Vietnamese are undoubtedly apprehensive every time Chinese and Soviet delegations meet to discuss their full range of relations.

China's policy is best interpreted as a long-term undertaking. Its geopolitical position enables it to apply persistent pressure on Vietnam and Laos directly as well as on Cambodia via the Khmer Rouge through Thailand. China's objectives are to prevent the consolidation of the Heng Samrin government and the Vietnamization of Kampuchea via the installation of Vietnamese advisors and the emigration of Vietnamese farmers, fishermen, and tradespeople to Cambodia. Although the PRC has not achieved these goals to date, it has forced Vietnam to pay an exceedingly heavy price (by waging the border war in 1979) in lagging construction, staggering debt, and dependence upon the USSR, from which grows, in part, the genuine possibility of economic collapse.

In effect, China refuses to contemplate a political settlement that does not entail a Vietnamese withdrawal from Kampuchea and some kind of acknowledgment that China possesses legitimate interests in helping to determine regional order in states contiguous to its southern boundaries. Although the PRC's armed forces are qualitatively inferior to the Soviet-supplied Vietnamese military, its superiority in numbers and growing regional navy make it more than a sufficient match. A thorough evaluation of the Falkland Islands War in which several British naval vessels were sunk by Argentina's electronically guided missiles led China in 1982 to acquire advanced naval equipment including Sea Dart SAMs, sonars for ASW, and navigational and fire control radars for its Ludaclass destroyers. The South Sea Fleet has been reinforced by additional destroyers and landing craft. China maintains regular sea patrols around both the Paracels, which it occupies, and the Spratly Islands, which it claims in competition with Vietnam (and others).[45]

China's disputes with Vietnam over regional status on the mainland and territorial control in the South China Sea appear both intractable and dangerous. Intractable because they deal with historical questions of national independence on Vietnam's part and regional superiority on China's. Dangerous because China has not shrunk from military confrontation with a more powerful neighbor, the USSR, and can hardly be expected to retreat from a relatively small nation such as Vietnam, which China also sees as an ungrateful and arrogant tributary. For its part, Vietnam seems equally intransigent. If Hanoi was prepared to challenge China's claims in the South China Sea even before the end of the Vietnam War and risk Beijing's enmity in the war's aftermath by expelling tens of thousands of ethnic Chinese at a time when it was economically destitute and politically overburdened, there is little reason to believe Hanoi will make concessions now when the country is politically unified, enjoys the strong backing of the USSR, and is consolidating control over Indochina.[46]

For China, the dispute with Hanoi about the future governance of Kampuchea and control of the South China Sea islands and surrounding waters is a question of which state will be preeminent in the region. Although unable to regain control of the Paracels, sovereignty over the Spratlies has become Vietnam's minimum demand, backed up by the fortification of the six islands it occupies. If the Soviets are willing to back Vietnamese claims with support from its Pacific Fleet at the same time that China is increasing its own naval strength in the same region, the potential for armed conflict will loom larger toward the end of the decade. China is developing the Paracels as a naval base. The precipitating issue could well be petroleum exploration and development in areas of overlapping jurisdiction. Noteworthy in this regard is U.S. caution with respect to naval protection for U.S. oil company operations. Washington has made it clear to both the oil companies and China that it has no intention of intervening in disputed areas.[47] But it is important to realize that a future area of Great Power confrontation in Southeast Asia may be on the waters rather than the land.

NOTES

1. An excellent example of this argument is I. M. Destler, Leslie H. Gelb, and Anthony Lake, Our Own Worst Enemy: The Unmaking of American Foreign Policy (New York: Simon & Schuster, 1984).
2. Kenneth Waltz, "How Foreign Policy Went Off the Rails," New York Times Book Review, 9 September 1984, p. 7.
3. These figures and other measures of the profitability of U.S. investment in ASEAN are cited in John W. Garver, "The Reagan Administration's Southeast Asian Policy," in James Hsiung, ed., U.S.-Asian Relations: The National Security Paradox (New York: Praeger, 1983), pp. 86-88.
4. Ibid., p. 89.
5. U.S., Congress, House, Committee on Armed Services, Report of the Delegation to East Asia, 98th cong., 1st sess., 16 November 1983, p. 13.
6. Jeffrey Gayner and Gregory Hung, "New Opportunities for U.S.-Thai Relations," Asian Studies Center Backgrounder (Washington, D.C.: Heritage Foundation, 9 April 1984), p. 5.
7. This prospect is discussed in Merdeka (Jakarta), 1 March 1984; and in FBIS, Daily Report: Asia/Pacific, 12 March 1984, N1.
8. Nayan Chanda, "Countdown on F-16s," Far Eastern Economic Review, 5 April 1984, pp. 42-43.
9. This concern was expressed to the author by Malaysian specialists in a 1981 visit to Kuala Lumpur.
10. Anthony Lake, "Dealing with Hanoi: What Washington Can Do," Indochina Issues 49 (August 1984):6.
11. This position was articulated by exiled opposition leader Senator Jovita Salonga in an address in Phoenix, Arizona, February 24, 1984. It is also reportedly held by Senator Jose Diokno, the leader of the Anti-Bases Movement in the Philippines. On the other hand, in an interview by the author with then newly elected opposition member of the Batasan Kabangsan, Aquilino Pimentel, May 20, 1984, in Cagayon de Oro, the view was expressed that an opposition-led government would probably renegotiate the bases agreement because of its economic importance to the country.
12. Statement by Assistant Secretary of Defense Richard Armitage in U.S., Congress, House, Subcomittee on Asian and Pacific Affairs, Hearings: United States-Philippine Relations and the New Base and Aid Agreement, 98th cong., 1st sess., 17, 23, and 28 June 1983, pp. 33 (hereafter cited as Hearings). See also William Feeney, "The United States and the Philippines: The Bases Dilemma," Asian Affairs 10, no. 4 (Winter 1984):63-85.
13. Salonga takes this position (see fn 11). It may also be found in the testimony of the late Benigno Aquino, Jr., in Hearings, pp. 87, 89. See also Walden Bello, "U.S. Military Bases in the Philippines," Southeast Asia Chronicle 89 (April 1983):3-19.
14. Testimony of Professor Lela Noble in Hearings, p. 137.

101

15. The most detailed case for alternatives to Clark and Subic Bay is made by Rear Admiral Gene R. LaRocque, USN (Ret.) in Hearings, pp. 174-188. See also George McT. Kahin, "Remove the Bases from the Philippines," New York Times, 12 October 1983.

16. A Malaysian military surveillance report as carried in The New Straits Times (Kuala Lumpur), October 1983.

17. See Admiral Robert Long's testimony in Hearings, pp. 16, 18, 19, 39, 40.

18. Ibid., pp. 178, 183, 184, 205.

19. Ibid., p. 226.

20. A May 1983 CINCPAC report cited in F. A. Mediansky and Dianne Court. The Soviet Union in Southeast Asia, Canberra Papers on Strategy and Defense, no. 29 (Canberra: Australian National University, 1984), p. 25.

21. Ibid.

22. The Christian Science Monitor, 14 February 1984.

23. Mediansky, The Soviet Union, p. 28.

24. "Intelligence," Far Eastern Economic Review, 20 September 1984, p. 11.

25. Joseph G. Whelan, The Soviets in Asia: An Expanding Presence (Washington, D.C.: Congressional Research Service, 27 March 1984), p. 111.

26. For analyses that deprecate Soviet naval capabilities in the Indian Ocean, see Richard Remnak, "Soviet Strategic Interests in Africa" and Howard Hansel, "Soviet Interests in the Indian Ocean," both papers presented at the International Studies Association annual meeting, Atlanta, 28 March 1984.

27. Author's discussions with U.S. Defense Intelligence Agency analysts, Washington, D.C., 2 May 1984.

28. Carlyle Thayer, The Origins of the National Front for the Liberation of South Vietnam (Unpublished Ph.D. diss., Australian National University, 1977), p. 561.

29. Leif Rosenberger, "The Soviet-Vietnamese Alliance and Kampuchea," Survey 27, nos. 118/119 (Autumn-Winter 1983):214-215.

30. Ibid., p. 218; and Paul Keleman, "Soviet Strategy in Southeast Asia: The Vietnam Factor," 24, no. 3 (March 1984):342.

31. Rosenberger, "Soviet-Vietnamese Alliance," pp. 224, 225.

32. Research Institute for Peace and Security, Asian Security, 1982 (Tokyo: RIPS, 1983), p. 66.

33. Nayan Chanda, "The Uneasy Alliance," Far Eastern Economic Review, 6 September 1984, p. 40.

34. Robert Trumbull, "Indonesian Says Soviet Supports Cambodian Plan," New York Times, 23 April 1984; and Far Eastern Economic Review, 19 April 1984, p. 30.

35. Nayan Chanda, "United We Stand," Far Eastern Economic Review, 11 August 1983, pp. 24-25.

36. The Nation Review (Bangkok), 8 November 1983, p. 5.

37. Alexander George, David K. Hall, and William E. Simon, The Limits of Coercive Diplomacy (Boston: Little, Brown, 1971), p. 118.

38. For a discussion of China's use of coercive diplomacy, see Paul H. B. Godwin, "Soldiers and Statesmen in Conflict: Chinese Defense and Foreign Policies in the 1980s," in Samuel Kim, ed., Chinese Foreign Policy in the 1980s (Boulder, Colo.: Westview, 1984).

39. For an excellent analysis of the costs and gains of

China's Southeast Asian policy, see Michael Leifer, "Conflict and Regional Order in Southeast Asia," in Robert O'Neill, ed., Security in East Asia (New York: St. Martin's, 1984), pp. 139-142.

40. Jonathan D. Pollack, China and the Global Strategic Balance (Santa Monica, Calif.: Rand Corporation, P-6952, January 1984), p. 13.

41. Ibid., pp. 19, 21.

42. Mu Guangren, "The Current U.S. Policy Toward China," Ban Yue Tan (Tab Biweekly) 16 (1981):53.

43. For a typical statement on China's independent foreign policy, see Foreign Minister Wu Xueqian's address to the 39th UN General Assembly, Xinhua, 26 September 1984, as reported in FBIS, Daily Report/China, 29 September 1984, A2-A3. For a U.S. statement to Thai Prime Minister Prem that the United States believes China's continued opposition to Vietnam is an important component of Indochinese diplomacy, see Nayan Chanda, "Take-off for F-16s," Far Eastern Economic Review, 26 April 1984, pp. 17-18.

44. SRV Foreign Minister Nguyen Co Thach's statement to the Press Trust of India cited by Agence France Presse, 1 September 1984, in FBIS, Daily Report Asia/Pacific, 13 September 1984, K2.

45. Donald McMillen, "Chinese Perspectives on International Security," in Donald McMillen, ed., Asian Perspectives on International Security (London: Macmillan, 1984), pp. 186-188. See also June Dreyer, "China's Military in the 1980's," Current History (September 1984):276-278.

46. For an insightful discussion, see Chang Pao-min, "The Sino-Vietnamese Territorial Dispute," Asia Pacific Community 24 (Spring 1984), especially pp. 43-48.

47. Mark Valencia, "Oil Under the Troubled Waters," Far Eastern Economic Review, 15 March 1984, pp. 30-33.

Part 2

Northeast Asia

5 China: Coping with the Evolving Strategic Environment

There is no consensus among specialists as to which factors--internal or international--are more important at any given time in determining the course of Chinese foreign and security policy. Thus, there is no agreement as to whether or not Chinese policy tends to be more reactive to outside events or tends to evolve as a result of forces inside China. Some analysts have tried to bridge the gap between those specialists who stress foreign and those who stress domestic determinants in Chinese foreign and security policy. Some point to "policy packages" of mutually reinforcing and compatible foreign and domestic policies advocated by a particular group of leaders and note how these leaders fare in promoting their approaches in the face of opposition from other leaders with competing foreign-domestic policy arrangements. Others have tried to isolate those aspects of Chinese foreign and security policy (e.g., certain aspects of security policy) that are more likely to be reactive to international pressures from those foreign policy concerns (opening Chinese society to Western economic contact) that are more likely to be affected by Chinese domestic determinants.[1]

The record of Chinese foreign and security policy since the late 1960s has shown a fairly consistent Chinese effort to deal with often difficult changes in the strategic environment surrounding China. It depicts China emerging from a period of serious dislocation and ideological excess during the violent stage of the Cultural Revolution and its attendant Red Guard "diplomacy." Faced with dangerous international circumstances, Beijing felt compelled to begin a more conventional and rational balance-of-power approach to foreign affairs that would shore up its national security and foreign

----

The views expressed in this chapter are the author's and not necessarily those of the Congressional Research Service, Library of Congress.

policy interests and ensure a more favorable environment
for restoring disrupted political order inside China and
pursuing the development of national wealth and power.
Key aspects of this balance-of-power approach involved
the perceived power and policies of the Soviet Union and
the United States. [2]
     Moscow's persisting military buildup and search for
greater political influence around China's periphery
have represented the strategic center of gravity for
Chinese foreign and defense policy since the late 1960s.
Top level Chinese leaders of whatever background or
ideological inclination were forced by Soviet actions to
focus their foreign policy on the fundamental question
of how to deal effectively with Soviet military threat
and political intimidation without compromising Chinese
security and sovereignty or mortgaging Chinese aspirations for independence and development. Initially,
Chinese leaders came up with strikingly different approaches, leading in the late 1960s to the most serious
leadership dispute over foreign and security policy in
the history of the People's Republic of China (PRC). [3]
     The death of Defense Minister Lin Biao and purge of
a large segment of the Chinese military high command in
1971 markedly reduced the political importance of Chinese leadership differences over how to handle the Soviet Union. From that time on, China developed a fairly
consistent strategy, at first under the leadership of
Premier Zhou Enlai and Chairman Mao Zedong, and later
under Deng Xiaoping. It attempted to use East-West
differences pragmatically to China's advantage. The
Chinese leaders recognized that China--only at tremendous cost and great risk--could confront the Soviet
Union on its own. It relied heavily on international
counterweights to Soviet power, provided mainly by the
United States, its allies, and associates. As the U.S.
reevaluated its former containment policy directed
against China, and no longer posed a serious military
threat to Chinese security, Beijing maintained a col-
laborative relationship with the United States and the
West as a key link in Chinese security policy against
the USSR.
     Meanwhile, Chinese internal policy increasingly
focused on economic development and modernization. Chinese leaders, especially in the post-Mao period, saw
that these goals would be best achieved through closer
economic relations with the West. The United States,
Japan, and other noncommunist developed states had the
markets, technology, managerial expertise, and financial
resources that were seen as crucial in speeding and
streamlining China's heretofore troubled modernization
efforts so as to increase material benefit to the Chinese people and thereby sustain their political loyalty
and support.
     This simple outline of a framework for recent Chi-
nese foreign and defense policy clearly portrays China
as often reactive to the actions of foreign powers,

especially the Soviet Union and the United States. It shows that Chinese leaders were well aware of China's internal weaknesses and wished to remedy those flaws through a prolonged effort at economic modernization. In the meantime, these leaders recognized that China needs to secure its international environment in order to focus energies internally, and that although China influences the situation around it in the Asian-Pacific region to some degree, the USSR, the United States, and their friends and allies exert far greater influence there. As a result, China was forced repeatedly to adjust to perceived changes in the international situation around it.

Indeed, the record shows that many of the changes in Chinese policy during this period were caused chiefly by Chinese reactions to perceived shifts in the international balance of forces and influence affecting Chinese security and development. Salient examples include:[4]

• August 1968 The Soviet invasion of Czechoslovakia and Moscow's subsequent announcement of the so-called Brezhnev doctrine of limited sovereignty caused China to view the recently expanded Soviet military presence along the Sino-Soviet border in a more ominous light. It prompted at least some Chinese leaders to advocate a more activist, conventional Chinese approach to foreign affairs in order to enhance Chinese international leverage in the face of Soviet power.

• August 1969 Six months of Sino-Soviet military conflict along the frontier reached a climax as the largest Sino-Soviet border clash on record resulted in a serious Chinese military defeat and was followed by Soviet warnings about possible military "preventive strikes" against China. This pressure tipped the scales in the ongoing policy debate in Beijing against those, led by Lin Biao, who held out for uncompromising opposition to the Soviet Union. China eventually favored a tactically more flexible posture advocated by Premier Zhou. The fruits of Zhou's efforts were seen in the use of Sino-Soviet talks and Chinese diplomatic maneuvers, along with Chinese defense preparations, to deal with Soviet pressure. Zhou's strategy included the start of Sino-U.S. diplomatic contacts focused on the two sides' common opposition to Soviet attempts at dominance in Asia--contacts that led directly to President Nixon's landmark visit to China.

• 1975 The rapid collapse of U.S.-supported governments in Indochina prompted China to adopt a much more active approach throughout East Asia in order to shore up a united front against the perceived danger of Soviet expansion around China's periphery as the United States withdrew.

Concurrent signs of U.S. weakness in the face of

growing Soviet military power and breakthroughs by
both countries in negotiating East-West accords over
arms control and European security caused China to
raise vocal opposition to U.S.-Soviet detente to unprecedented heights. In the process China underlined
its keen suspicion that Western accommodation with
Moscow would allow the Soviets a free hand to deal
with China.

- 1978 Soviet gains in the Third World, especially the
areas of direct importance to China (i.e., Vietnam),
enhanced Chinese interest in fostering a common front
with the United States, Japan, and other Western
states against the USSR. Prospects for such cooperation increased as opinion in the U.S. government gradually shifted from the view advocated by Secretary of
State Cyrus Vance that gave priority to U.S.-Soviet
arms control to the view favored by National Security
Adviser Zbigniew Brzezinski that advocated confronting
Soviet expansion in sensitive Third World areas.

- April 1979 China's efforts to confront Soviet expansion focused on Vietnam and led to direct Chinese
military intervention; that intervention produced
mixed results for Chinese interests and left Beijing
dangerously exposed in the face of increasing Soviet
military pressure. Chinese leaders were compelled to
change tactics, moderate their anti-Soviet stance, and
open a political dialogue with Moscow in order to
manage the danger of Soviet military power.

- January 1980 The Soviet invasion of Afghanistan and
stiffened Western opposition to Soviet expansion
prompted China to change direction again: China re-
verted to a firmly anti-Soviet posture and suspended
talks with the USSR.

- 1981-1982 A Chinese perceived shift in the international balance of power against the Soviet Union, and
a revival of U.S. power and determination against the
USSR under the Reagan administration, gave China more
freedom to maneuver. These changes allowed China to
distance itself from the Reagan administration over
Taiwan, Third World and other issues, reopen talks
with the Soviet Union, and adopt an ostensibly more
independent posture in foreign affairs.

- 1983-1984 Beijing's growing concern over a projected
long-term downturn in Sino-U.S. relations at a time of
increasing Soviet pressure on China prompted China's
leaders to compromise for a time. They modified their
hard line on sensitive bilateral disputes with the
United States in order to solidify relations with the
Reagan administration in preparation for a period of
difficult relations with the USSR.

- **1984-1985** Following consolidation of relations with the United States, Beijing was in a good position to respond in a forthcoming way to the rise of power of the Gorbachev leadership in the USSR, thereby attempting to encourage Moscow to curb its military buildup in Asia and its pressure against China.

Despite such repeated examples of reactive Chinese foreign and security policy, especially with regard to perceived changes in the international balance of power affecting Chinese interests in Asia, there are instances that vividly demonstrate that wellsprings of particular Chinese policies also lie within China. For one thing, Chinese views of their surroundings and the international balance of power are filtered through lenses colored by Chinese history, culture, and ideology. The strength and unity of China's political leadership has had a profound effect on security whether or not China can take the initiative in international security affairs or merely respond passively to international circumstances. Domestic demands for economic development, military modernization, and political control often have had a vital impact on the course of such Chinese decisionmaking. Meanwhile, Chinese leaders have demonstrated a desire to manipulate international events and to maneuver more freely among competing outside pressures in order to enhance their particular interests within China, especially their leadership standing.

Key examples of such domestic determinants influencing the course of Chinese foreign policy since the late 1960s include: [5]

- **February-August 1969** Intense competition for political power in China led to debate over competing approaches to international developments, especially concerning relations with the United States and the Soviet Union. Lin Biao and others advocating a tough line toward both powers were able to reverse the opening to the United States initiated by Zhou Enlai and other leaders a few months earlier, which had called for revived political discussions with the United States. They succeeded in following their hard-line posture for seven months.

- **1973-1974** Leadership conflict over internal political and development questions rose during the intense political campaign against Confucius and Lin Biao. The campaign spilled over into foreign policy, resulting in an across-the-board toughening of China's approach to the Soviet Union, the United States, and their allies and associates and a cutback in China's interest in greater economic and cultural contacts with the West.

- **1976-1977** Beijing's preoccupation with post-Mao

leadership transition and major economic problems resulted in a much less active Chinese approach to most foreign issues, even those having a direct bearing on China's security, such as increasing Soviet-Vietnamese collaboration.

• 1979 Some Chinese leaders questioned China's previous emphasis on establishing close ties with the West in order to better confront the USSR. They stressed China's need for "breathing space" in competition with the USSR, emphasized that defense modernization would have to be prolonged for the sake of speeding higher priority economic modernization, and wished to reestablish China's flagging ties with the developing countries and the international communist movement. They were successful for a time in advocating an easing of Chinese confrontation with the USSR and a cutback in China's developing strategic alignment with the United States and the West.[6]

• 1981-1982 These same leadership decisions helped push China to reassert its policy independence of the United States, adopting in the process a more balanced stance between the superpowers and adhering more closely to Chinese nationalistic principles on sensitive issues like Taiwan.

DETERMINANTS OF RECENT CHINESE FOREIGN AND SECURITY POLICY

In assessing the relative importance of the strategic environment and domestic developments in the recent Chinese approach to international security affairs, the scales appear to tip decidedly in favor of strategic factors. In effect, the two sets of factors appear to interact in the following manner.

The objectives of Chinese foreign and security policy have been determined by a small group of top-level Chinese leaders who have reflected the broad interests of the Chinese state as well as their own parochial concerns. In the past, Mao Zedong, Zhou Enlai, and other senior leaders exerted overriding control over foreign policy. In recent years, there has been an increase in the number of officials involved in advising about Chinese foreign policy, but key decisions remain the preserve of a small group of leaders, especially Deng Xiaoping.[7]

The primary concerns of these leaders have been to guarantee Chinese national security, maintain internal order, and pursue economic development. Especially since the death of Mao in 1976, the top priority of Chinese leaders has been to promote successful economic modernization. This development represents the linchpin determining the success or failure of their leadership.

Thus, Chinese officials have geared China's foreign and security policy to help the modernization effort.[8]

But in order to accomplish economic modernization as well as to maintain national security and internal order, Chinese leaders recognize the fundamental prerequisite of establishing a relatively stable strategic environment, especially around China's periphery in Asia. The alternative would be a highly disruptive situation requiring much greater Chinese expenditures on national defense and posing greater danger to Chinese domestic order and tranquility. Unfortunately for China, it does not control this environment. Despite some Chinese influence, the environment remains controlled more by others, especially the superpowers and their allies and associates. As a result, China's leaders have been required repeatedly to assess their surroundings for changes that could affect Chinese security and development interests. They have been compelled repeatedly to adjust Chinese policy to take account of such changes.

At the same time, Chinese leaders also have nationalistic and ideological objectives regarding irredentist claims (e.g., Taiwan). They have a desire to stand independently as a leading force among "progressive" nations of the Third World. These goals have struck a responsive chord politically inside China. Occasional leadership discussion and debate over these and other questions regarding foreign and defense policy have sometimes had an effect on the course of Chinese policy. Since the early 1970s, the debates have become progressively less serious, and the policy differences raised in these debates have become more moderate and less of a challenge to the recent dominant objectives of national development and security.

Thus, China's top foreign and defense policy priority has remained the pragmatic quest for the stable environment needed for effective modernization and development. Chinese leaders in the fifteen years prior to 1985 have seen the main source of negative change in the surrounding environment as the Soviet Union. At first, China saw Soviet power as an immediate threat to its national security. Over time, it came to see the USSR progressively as more of a long-term threat, determined to use its growing military power and other sources of influence to encircle and pressure China into accepting a balance of power in Asia dominated by the USSR and contrary to PRC interests.[9]

China's strategy against the Soviet threat has been both bilateral and global. Bilaterally, China has used a mix of military preparations and tactical political moves to keep the Soviets from attacking China, but without compromising China's basic security interests. Globally, China's strategy has focused on developing--either implicitly or explicitly--an international united front designed to halt Soviet expansion and prevent the consolidation of Soviet dominance abroad.

As the most important international counterweight to Soviet power, the United States has loomed large in Chinese calculations. Once the United States, under terms of the Nixon Doctrine announced in 1969, seemed determined to withdraw from its past containment policy in Asia and thereby end its threat to China's national security, the PRC was prepared to start the process of Sino-U.S. normalization. The process has been complemented in recent years by China's enhanced interest in pragmatic economic modernization, which has emphasized the importance of Western markets.

Closer Chinese ties with the United States continue to be complicated by Chinese nationalistic and ideological concerns about such issues as Taiwan and Third World questions as well as by fundamental differences between the social-political and economic systems of the United States and the PRC. Most notably, U.S. support for Taiwan is seen as a continued affront to China's sense of national sovereignty. But Chinese leaders have differentiated between substantive threats to their security, posed by the USSR, and threats to their ideological sense of national sovereignty, posed by U.S. support for Taiwan. [10]

China sees the Soviet strategy as an expansionist one in which military power is used relentlessly but cautiously in order to achieve political influence and dominance throughout the periphery of the USSR. China has long held that the focus of Soviet attention is in Europe, but that the North Atlantic Treaty Organization's (NATO) strength requires Moscow to work in other areas, notably the Middle East, Southwest Asia, Africa, and East Asia, in order to outflank the Western defenses. China is seen as relatively low on Moscow's list of military priorities, although Chinese leaders clearly appreciate the dire consequences for the PRC should the USSR be able to consolidate its position elsewhere and then focus its strength to intimidate China. [11]

China's strategy of deterrence and defense, therefore, aims basically to exacerbate Soviet expansion in general and to raise the possibility of a multifront conflict in the event the Soviet Union attempted to attack or intimidate China in particular. Chinese leaders see China's cooperation with the United States as especially important in strengthening deterrence of the Soviet Union and in aggravating Soviet strategic vulnerabilities. Beijing also encourages anti-Soviet efforts by so-called Second World, developed countries--most of whom are formal allies of the United States--and by developing countries of the Third World. At the same time, Beijing uses a mix of political talks, bilateral exchanges, and other forms of dialogue to help manage the danger posed by the USSR.

Meanwhile, within this overall strategy to establish a stable environment in Asia, Chinese leaders have employed varying tactics to secure their interests,

depending on international variables, such as the perceived strength and intentions of the superpowers, and
Chinese domestic variables, such as the status of leadership cohesion. For example, when Chinese leaders have
judged that their strategic surroundings were at least
temporarily stable, they have seen less immediate need
for close ties with the United States and thus have felt
freer to adopt strident policies on Taiwan and other
nationalistic issues that appeal to domestic constituen-
cies but offend the United States. (This type of logic
was in part responsible for China's tougher approach
toward the United States about Taiwan and other issues
in 1981-1983.) But when the Chinese leaders have judged
that such tactics could seriously alienate the United
States and thereby endanger the stability of China's
environment, they have put them aside in the interests
of preserving peaceful surroundings. (This kind of
logic was in part responsible for China's moderate approach toward the United States in 1983-1984.)[12]

At bottom, therefore, Beijing leaders have placed
first priority in foreign and security affairs on securing a stable environment in Asia that will allow internal reform and modernization to proceed smoothly. The
recent record shows that other factors influencing Chinese policy (domestic politics, ideology, and nationalistic goals, for example) have not been allowed to upset
seriously China's continued efforts to deal pragmatically with the Asian balance, and especially the superpowers' influence in Asia, from what is clearly seen as a
position of relative weakness. The result is a Chinese
policy in Asia quite responsive to and dependent upon
Soviet and U.S. actions in the region.

CHINA'S RECENT CALCULUS IN THE
GREAT POWER TRIANGLE IN ASIA

China's changing response to the Great Power
relations has been amply illustrated by the adjustments
in China's "independent" stance in foreign affairs in
1983 and 1984.[13] At that time, Beijing moved to halt the
decline in Sino-U.S. relations and attempted to
consolidate relations with the Reagan administration on
an anti-Soviet basis.

The changes in Chinese policy were based largely on
perceptions of shifts in the international balance of
power affecting China. Chinese leaders became increasingly concerned about the stability of the nation's
surroundings in Asia at a time of unrelenting buildup of
Soviet military and political pressure along China's
periphery. They also were concerned about what they
considered a serious and perhaps prolonged decline in
China's relations with the United States. Chinese leaders decided that the foreign policy tactics of the
previous two years, designed to distance China from the
policies of the United States and to moderate and

improve relations with the Soviet Union, were less likely to safeguard the important Chinese security and development concerns affected by the stability of the
Asian environment. They recognized in particular that
Beijing would have to stop its pullback from the United
States for fear of jeopardizing the maintenance of
China's security and development interests in the face
of persistent Soviet pressure in Asia. Thus, in 1983,
Beijing began to retreat from some of the previous
tactical changes made under the rubric of an independent
approach to international and security affairs. The
result was a substantial reduction in Chinese pressure
on the United States concerning Taiwan and other issues;
increased Chinese interest and flexibility in dealing
with the Reagan administration and other Western countries across a broad range of economic, political, and
security issues; and heightened Sino-Soviet antipathy.

By employing such foreign policy tactics effectively, Beijing was able to secure its concerns without
substantially disrupting efforts to modernize internally. Thus, economic reforms continued to receive high
priority as military modernization received relatively
low priority. Plans to streamline and reduce the size
of the Chinese army could move ahead; these plans held
out the hope that overall defense spending could be held
down, and selective modernization of military equipment
and organization could be funded by savings generated by
a cutback in personnel and other related expenses.[14]

The key element in China's decision to move toward
the United States was an altered Chinese view of the
likely course of Sino-U.S.-Soviet relations over the
next several years. When China began its more independent approach to international events and its concurrent
harder line toward the United States in 1981 and 1982,
it had hoped to elicit a more forthcoming U.S. attitude
toward issues sensitive to Chinese interests, notably
Taiwan. Beijing almost certainly knew that there were
serious risks to be incurred by alienating the United
States, which had provided an implicit but vital counterweight against the USSR for more than a decade and
had assisted more recent Chinese economic development
concerns. But the Chinese seemed to have assessed that
their room to maneuver had increased because the United
States had reasserted a balance of East-West relations
likely to lead to a continued major check on possible
Soviet expansion. In addition, the Soviet ability to
pressure China had appeared to be at least temporarily
blocked by U.S. power as well as by Soviet domestic and
international problems, and at least some important U.S.
leaders continued to place a high strategic value on
preserving good U.S. relations with China as an important element in U.S. efforts to confront and contain
Soviet expansion.

By mid-1983, China saw these calculations upset.
In particular, the United States adopted a new posture
that publicly downgraded China's strategic importance to

the United States.[15] U.S. planners now appeared to
consider improved relations with China less important
than in the recent past because:

- China seemed unlikely to cooperate further with the
United States (through military sales, security consultations, etc.) against the Soviet Union at a time
when the PRC had publicly distanced itself from the
United States and had reopened talks on normalization
of relations with the USSR.

- At the same time, China's continued preoccupation with
pragmatic economic modernization and internal development made it appear unlikely that the PRC would revert
to a highly disruptive position in East Asia that
would adversely affect U.S. interests in the stability
of the region.

- China's demands regarding Taiwan and other bilateral
disputes, and Beijing's accompanying threats to down-
grade U.S.-China relations if its demands were not
met, appeared openended and excessive.

- U.S. ability to deal militarily and politically with
the USSR had improved, particularly as a result of the
large-scale Reagan administration military budget
increases and the serious internal and international
difficulties of the USSR.

- U.S. allies, for the first time in years, were working
more closely with Washington in dealing with the Soviet military threat. This was particularly true in
Asia where Prime Minister Yasuhiro Nakasone took positions and initiative underlining common Japanese-U.S.
concerns against the Soviet danger.

- Japan and U.S. allies and friends in Southeast Asia--
unlike China--appeared more immediately important to
the United States in protecting against what was seen
as the primary U.S. strategic concern in the region:
safeguarding air and sea access to East Asia, the
Indian Ocean, and the Persian Gulf from Soviet attack.
By contrast, China did not appear as important in
dealing with this perceived Soviet danger.

In effect, the U.S. shift meant that Chinese ability to exploit U.S. interest in strategic relations with
China, in order to compel the United States to meet
Chinese demands on Taiwan and other questions, had been
sharply reduced. Underlining this trend was the continued unwillingness of the United States throughout this
period to accommodate high-level PRC pressure over Taiwan, the asylum case of Hu Na, the Chinese representa-
tion issue in the Asian Development Bank, and other
questions.
    Moreover, Beijing perceived its political leverage

in the United States to be small. Chinese press reports
noted the strong revival in the U.S. economy in 1983 and
the positive political implications this had for President Reagan's reelection campaign.[16] China also had to
be aware through contacts with leading Democrats, notably Speaker O'Neill, that Beijing could expect little
change in U.S. policy toward Taiwan under a Democratic
administration.[17]

Meanwhile, although Sino-Soviet trade, cultural,
and technical contacts were increasing, Beijing saw
little sign of Soviet willingness to compromise basic
political and security issues during the vice foreign
ministerial talks begun in October 1982. The Soviet
military buildup in Asia--including the deployment of
highly accurate SS-20 intermediate-range missiles--
continued unabated.

In short, Beijing faced the prospect of a period of
prolonged decline in Sino-U.S. relations, which could
last until the end of Reagan's second presidential term,
if it continued to follow the hard line of the previous
two years in relations with the United States. This
decline ran the risk of cutting off the implicit but
vitally important Chinese strategic understanding with
the United States in the face of a prolonged danger
posed by the USSR.

China's incentive to accommodate the United States
was reinforced by Beijing's somber view of Sino-Soviet
relations. Disappointed with China's inability to elicit substantial Soviet concessions--or even a slackening
in the pace of Soviet military expansion in Asia--during
the Andropov administration, Beijing saw the Chernenko
government as even more rigid and uncompromising. In
response, China hardened its line and highlighted public
complaints against Soviet pressure and intimidation--an
approach that had the added benefit of broadening common
ground between China and the West, especially the Reagan
administration.

The Sino-Soviet vice foreign ministerial talks,[18]
revived in October 1982, met semi-annually, alternating
between Beijing and Moscow. Although some progress was
made on secondary issues, these talks were unable to
bridge a major gap between the positions of the two
sides on basic security and political issues. Thus,
Beijing stuck to its preconditions for improved Sino-
Soviet relations: withdrawal of Soviet forces from the
Sino-Soviet border and Mongolia (later China added specific reference to Soviet SS-20 missiles targeted
against China); end of Soviet support for Vietnam's
occupation of Kampuchea; and withdrawal of Soviet forces
from Afghanistan. Beijing sometimes said that Soviet
movement on only one of these questions would substantially open the way to improved Sino-Soviet relations.
But Moscow remained unwilling to compromise, stating
that the USSR would not discuss matters affecting third
countries.

In part to get around this roadblock, a second channel of vice foreign ministerial discussions was begun in September 1983. Progress in both sets of talks came only in secondary areas of trade, technical trans- fers, and educational and cultural exchanges. Both sides attempted to give added impetus to progress in these areas coincident with the exchange of high-level Sino-U.S. visits in early 1984. In particular, Moscow proposed and Beijing accepted a visit to China of Soviet First Deputy Prime Minister Arkhipov, reportedly to discuss longer term economic and technical assistance to China.[19]

Nevertheless, both sides proved willing to disrupt these contacts when more important strategic and politi- cal issues were at stake. Beijing in particular was disappointed with the new Chernenko regime. China had sent its ranking Vice Premier Wan Li as its representa- tive to the funeral of Andropov in February 1984-- marking a substantial upgrading from Beijing's dispatch of Foreign Minister Huang Hua to Brezhnev's funeral in 1982. But Wan received only a cool welcome in Moscow. Moreover, the Soviets then appeared to go out of their way to publicize strong support for Mongolia and Vietnam against China, and they underlined Soviet unwillingness to make compromises with China at the expense of third countries.

Beijing also saw Moscow resorting to stronger mili- tary means in both Europe and Asia in order to assert Soviet power and determination at a time of leadership transition in the Kremlin. Chinese media portrayed Moscow as on the defensive on a whole range of interna- tional issues, particularly its failure to halt the deployment of U.S. Pershing and cruise missiles in West- ern Europe, or to exploit the peace movement in Europe as a way to disrupt the Western alliance over the de- ployments and other issues. They now saw Moscow--faced with ever-growing Western military power and greater solidarity in the face of the Soviet threat--lashing out with new demonstrations of Soviet military power.[20] In Asia this perceived Soviet approach directly affected Chinese security and ultimately appeared designed to bring China to heel. Thus, in February and March, the Soviet Union deployed two of its three aircraft carriers to the Western Pacific; one transited near China in late February on its·way to Vladivostok.[21] In March, the USSR used an aircraft carrier task force to support its first joint amphibious exercise with Vietnam, which was conducted fairly close to China and near the Vietnamese port city of Haiphong. This followed the reported sta- tioning of several Soviet medium bombers at Cam Ranh Bay in Vietnam in late 1983--the first time such Soviet forces were reported stationed outside areas contiguous with the USSR.[22]

Meanwhile, the Chinese escalated their military pressure against the Vietnamese--taking their strongest action precisely at the time of President Reagan's visit to China in late April and early May 1984. The result was the most serious downturn in Sino-Soviet relations since the Soviet invasion of Afghanistan in late 1979. Both Moscow and Beijing revived polemical exchanges, trading particular charges about issues involving sensitive security matters in Asia, East-West arms control in Europe, and the international communist movement. Their bilateral diplomatic dialogue was disrupted for a time, as the USSR--presumably concerned and irritated by China's closer relations with the United States and tougher posture toward Vietnam--postponed for an indefinite time the visit of First Deputy Prime Minister Arkhipov to China. Sino-Vietnamese military confrontation along their common border continued into the summer of 1984, well beyond the usual period of fighting coincident with the annual Vietnamese dry season campaign against Chinese-supported resistance forces in Kampuchea. Sino-Soviet political competition heated up in Korea as both sides maneuvered to improve relations with Kim Il-Sung and his successors. In particular, Moscow welcomed Kim Il-Sung in May--the Korean leader's first visit to the USSR since 1961. At the same time, Beijing continued to move ahead in establishing closer economic and military ties with the United States despite the absence of ostensibly balancing progress in Sino-Soviet relations.

China was still anxious to manage the Soviet threat without recourse to force, however. It held out the option of resumed Sino-Soviet border talks: Hu Yaobang reportedly told visitors that a border settlement could be reached with relative ease. [23] China agreed to remark frontier lines with the Soviet satellite, Mongolia, and agreed to set up joint economic commissions to discuss economic exchanges with Moscow's close East European allies. Moscow of course had long proposed renewed border delineation agreements and the establishment of similar joint economic commissions with China. Beijing also said that it was willing to receive Arkhipov whenever the USSR would send him, and it was also willing to conduct foreign ministerial consultations with the Soviets during the UN General Assembly in September.

Moscow moved to respond to the Chinese gestures and to resume forward movement in less sensitive economic and technical areas. The Soviets sent Arkhipov to China in late December. He was warmly received and signed three economic agreements that would provide for a broad array of economic cooperation, including the exchange of production technology, the construction and revamping of industrial enterprises, and technical training and exchanges of experts and scientific data under the supervision of a new Sino-Soviet economic trade, scientific, and technological cooperation committee. It was announced that the two countries would sign a five-year trade agreement and that their trade level in 1985 would be 60 percent greater than their trade in 1984.

PROSPECTS AND IMPLICATIONS FOR ASIA AND THE PACIFIC

The advent of the Gorbachev administration has led to further Sino-Soviet efforts to improve exchanges, reduce acrimony, and otherwise manage bilateral tensions in a more moderate fashion. But Beijing still grounds its policy toward the USSR and its demands for Soviet compromise on the "obstacles" in the relationship--all of which involve Soviet military actions around China's periphery. This testifies to the likelihood that Beijing will remain fundamentally concerned with this perceived Soviet pressure in Asia and the Pacific.

Even though the Soviet Union, along with China, has made recent efforts to improve the atmosphere and increase exchanges in Sino-Soviet relations, it has thus far not reduced its military pressure around China's periphery. Indeed, the USSR has used a continued military buildup and support for such key allies as Vietnam, Afghanistan, and Mongolia as the critical means to help secure its interests in the region. This has been done in part because Moscow has been unable to build substantial economic or political influence in the area. As a result, it is highly likely that China will continue to perceive a growing danger of Soviet military dominance and a strong need to work with the United States, Japan, and other countries to provide a counterweight that would keep the Soviet power in check and preserve a balance of influence in Asia favorable to Beijing's security and development concerns.

In fact, prospects for widening Sino-Soviet differences to include Korea have increased as Moscow has feted Kim Il-Sung in 1984 and sent advanced fighter aircraft to North Korea in 1985.[24] Beijing has been trying hard--in conjunction with North Korea--to foster a North-South Korea dialogue and an easing of military tensions on the peninsula. Nevertheless, apparent differences between Beijing and Pyongyang have emerged as the North Koreans have repositioned themselves between Moscow and Beijing. The implications of this change for China's past favorable influence on North Korea remain unclear, but it may open the way for greater Soviet influence in Pyongyang.

On balance, however, China is likely to remain preoccupied internally with major leadership and economic changes for the remainder of the 1980s. These proposed changes have been set forth in recent Chinese pronouncements promising major shifts in the urban economy, in Chinese party ranks, and in the Chinese military. It seems logical that under these circumstances China would not be inclined to upset the prevailing acceptable balance in Asia or otherwise exacerbate tensions along its periphery in ways that would upset the modernization and reform process. China would probably prefer, if possible, to encourage Soviet moderation in Asia and a curb in Moscow's military buildup there.

China's incentive to continue this balanced, relatively moderate approach to security policy issues in Asia will likely be underlined by the anticipated continuation of military reforms, including the major cutback in the size of the Chinese armed forces projected for 1985 and 1986. The resulting savings presumably will be used to modernize Chinese military equipment and thereby make the Chinese armed forces more streamlined and effective in the longer run. But the short-term effect of such changes will likely be a reduction in Beijing's inclination to confront its adversaries militarily and a strengthening of China's reliance on effective diplomacy to meet national security problems.

Beijing, of course, retains the option of attempting to reach, on its own, a serious accommodation with Soviet power in Asia. This path could help China's modernization and reform by reducing the need for extensive defense expenditures to deter Soviet power, thus allowing greater Chinese resources to be applied to economic development. But the Chinese leadership is doubtless aware that any serious Chinese effort to accommodate the USSR in Asia would cause the United States, Japan, and their allies and friends in Asia to reassess their policies toward China and would run the risk of leaving China isolated as it dealt with the USSR. Under these circumstances, China almost certainly would risk mortgaging its longer term development and independence to the dictates of Soviet power and influence.

China therefore is unlikely to pursue such a risky course unless it perceives that Soviet leaders are no longer interested in using military power to exert dominating influence over China. The proof of such intent would be seen in Soviet efforts to curb military power in the region. Whether or not the Gorbachev administration will adopt such policies is doubtless a key determinant in the future course of Sino-Soviet relations and China's response to its perceived security threat in the Asian-Pacific region. Although some Chinese officials may hope for such a reduction in Soviet power, sober analysis would suggest such prospects are remote. A Soviet military pullback from Asia at this time would seriously jeopardize Moscow's ability to protect Soviet territory and the interests of Soviet allies and friends, not only against possible threat from China, but against the continuing military buildup of the United States, Japan, and their associates.

IMPLICATIONS AND OPTIONS FOR THE UNITED STATES

The overall result of China's efforts to deal with its strategic environment in the Asian-Pacific area and its concern with domestic political and economic reform is that Chinese foreign and defense policy is likely to

remain aligned with the interests of the United States,
at least during the next few years. In fact, it seems
fair to say that Chinese policy will continue in a
direction more favorable to U.S. interests than at any
time in the past.

China probably will continue to work cooperatively
and in parallel with the United States and its allies
and friends in the Asian-Pacific region to check the
expansion of Soviet power and influence in the region.
Beijing will play, as it has in the past, an important
role along the Sino-Soviet and Sino-Vietnamese borders,
and an indirect role in Indochina, and to a lesser
degree in Afghanistan. At the same time, China will
probably continue to use bilateral political, economic,
and other contacts with the USSR--in part to insure that
Sino-Soviet tensions do not get out of hand and endanger
China and the stability of the region. Although there
remains a danger that the recent Sino-Soviet contacts
may develop to a point where they could undermine China's utility as an anti-Soviet counterweight in Asia,
the likelihood of that happening appears remote as long
as the USSR continues to use increasing military power
to assert its influence in Asia.

China also appears likely to sustain a moderate
approach toward its noncommunist Asian neighbors and to
seek closer economic and political ties with them. Many
of these states are allies or close associates of the
United States that in the past required direct U.S.
military support against the "China threat"--notable
examples are Thailand and South Korea. In particular,
Beijing seems determined to complement its avowed peaceful approach toward Taiwan with recent unprecedented
efforts to work with the United States to ease tensions
between North and South Korea, something that until
recently China has been loathe to do for fear of alienating North Korea.

In general, China can be expected to follow a path
toward becoming a greater source of stability in Asia
and an important source of economic expansion there.
Thus, Chinese economic growth and rapidly expanding
foreign economic exchanges have promoted opportunities
for U.S. entrepreneurs and those of its friends in Asia
and elsewhere to invest and trade with the PRC.

U.S. policymakers may be inclined under these circumstances to follow policies more in accord with Chinese interests. They could

• Reduce arms sales and sensitive political contacts
  with Taiwan in order to help ease this long-standing
  source of irritation in Sino-U.S. relations;

• Be more forthcoming with economic and technical as-
  sistance and supplies and with military supplies.
  This could include increased willingness to train
  Chinese in the United States (there are over 12,000 at

present) and willingness to follow the example of path
breaking U.S. management schools in China (e.g., the
Dalien Institute) with more such institutions;

● Avoid policies toward the USSR that could be seen by
China as endangering the balance of power in Asia so
essential to China's ability to focus on internal
economic modernization;

● Encourage a more forthcoming attitude on the part of
other capitalist powers and international financial
organizations regarding economic interchange with
China. This would involve avoiding restrictions on
Chinese imports.

But each of these options has important, potentially negative trade-offs for U.S. interests. Thus, for
example, a sharp reduction in arms sales and contacts
with Taiwan could be seen as contrary to the Taiwan
Relations Act, upsetting to the stability of Taiwan, and
damaging to the U.S. reputation as a reliable supporter
of allies and friends. U.S. military exchanges with
China could unnerve Taiwan and other noncommunist
friends in Asia and might complicate U.S. efforts to
reach understandings with the USSR on arms control.
More extensive economic exchanges with China could come
at the expense of U.S. manufacturers or economic support
elsewhere in the developing world. U.S. encouragement
of greater Western and UN involvement with China might
require greater outlay of U.S. aid funds for such endeavors, a potentially unpopular trend at a time of U.S.
budget constraint.

As a result, unless the United States sees a greater need for accommodating Chinese interests than it has
recently, it is unlikely to make rapid policy changes
more favorable to Beijing. A more evolutionary approach, consistent with recent policy, appears more
likely as the Reagan administration and the U.S. Congress continue to value good relations with China but do
not place the heavy emphasis on the importance of those
ties, as was done in the late 1970s and early 1980s.

NOTES

1. This chapter relies heavily on the research conducted by
the author for his book, Chinese Foreign Policy Developments After
Mao (New York: Praeger, 1985). On the concept of "policy packages," see Carol Hamrin, "Emergence of an 'Independent' Chinese
Foreign Policy and Shifts in Sino-U.S. Relations," in James Hsiung,
ed., U.S.-Asia Relations (New York: Praeger, 1983). On differen-
tiating between aspects of Chinese foreign and security policy, see
Michael Yahuda, Towards the End of Isolationism: China's Foreign
Policy After Mao (New York: St. Martin's, 1983).
2. For a full discussion of events in the period, see Sutter, Chinese Foreign Policy. For a different perspective on Chi-

nese foreign policy at this time, see Harry Harding, ed., <u>Chinese</u> <u>Foreign</u> <u>Relations</u> <u>in</u> <u>the</u> <u>1980s</u> (New Haven: Yale University Press, 1984).

3. For background, see Thomas Gottlieb, <u>Chinese</u> <u>Foreign</u> <u>Policy</u> <u>Factionalism</u> and <u>the</u> <u>Origins</u> <u>of</u> <u>the</u> <u>Strategic</u> <u>Triangle</u> (Santa Monica, Calif.: Rand Corporation, 1977).

4. Assessments particularly useful in charting these in-stances in Chinese foreign and security policy are: A. Doak Bar-nett, <u>China</u> and <u>the</u> <u>Major</u> <u>Powers</u> <u>in</u> <u>East</u> <u>Asia</u> (Washington, D.C.: Brookings Institute, 1977); Joseph Cammilleri, <u>Chinese</u> <u>Foreign</u> <u>Policy:</u> <u>The</u> <u>Maoist</u> <u>Era</u> and <u>Its</u> <u>Aftermath</u> (Seattle, Wash.: Universi-ty of Washington Press, 1980); Harry Gelman, <u>The</u> <u>Soviet</u> <u>Far</u> <u>East</u> <u>Buildup</u> and <u>Soviet</u> <u>Risk-Taking</u> <u>Against</u> <u>China</u> (Santa Monica, Calif.: Rand Corporation, 1982); Richard Solomon, ed., <u>Asian</u> <u>Security</u> <u>in</u> <u>the</u> <u>1980s</u> (Santa Monica, Calif.: Rand Corporation, 1982). See also Robert Sutter, <u>Chinese</u> <u>Foreign</u> <u>Policy</u> <u>After</u> <u>the</u> <u>Cultural</u> <u>Revolution</u> (Boulder, Colo.: Westview, 1978); and Robert Sutter, "Realities of International Power and China's 'Independence' in Foreign Affairs, 1981-1984," <u>Journal</u> <u>of</u> <u>Northeast</u> <u>Asian</u> <u>Studies</u> (Winter 1984).

5. For background, see sources cited in notes 3 and 4, as well as Jonathan Pollack, <u>The</u> <u>Sino-Soviet</u> <u>Rivalry</u> and <u>Chinese</u> <u>Security</u> <u>Debate</u> (Santa Monica, Calif.: Rand Corporation, 1982).

6. See Hamrin, "Emergence." See also Kenneth Lieberthal's article in Harding, <u>Chinese</u> <u>Foreign</u> <u>Relations.</u>

7. See, in particular, A. Doak Barnett, <u>The</u> <u>Making</u> <u>of</u> <u>For-eign</u> <u>Policy</u> <u>in</u> <u>China</u> (Boulder, Colo.: Westview, 1985).

8. For background on this change in priorities, see U.S. Central Intelligence Agency, <u>China:</u> <u>The</u> <u>Continuing</u> <u>Search</u> <u>for</u> <u>a</u> <u>Modernization</u> <u>Strategy</u> (Washington, D.C.: CIA, Report No. ER-80-10248, April, 1980).

9. For a clear articulation of this view, see Banning Gar-rett and Bonnie Glaser, <u>War</u> and <u>Peace:</u> <u>The</u> <u>Views</u> <u>from</u> <u>Moscow</u> and <u>Beijing</u> (Berkeley: University of California Press, 1984).

10. For background, see Jonathan Pollack, <u>The</u> <u>Lessons</u> <u>of</u> <u>Coalition</u> <u>Politics:</u> <u>Sino-American</u> <u>Security</u> <u>Relations</u> (Santa Monica, Calif.: Rand Corporation, 1984).

11. These themes have occurred repeatedly in the author's conversations with Chinese officials over the past eight years.

12. See Sutter, <u>Chinese</u> <u>Foreign</u> <u>Policy.</u> See also Sutter, "Realities of International Power."

13. For background on this period, see Sutter, <u>Chinese</u> <u>For-eign</u> <u>Policy,</u> chapter 9. See also Jonathan Pollack, <u>The</u> <u>Lessons</u> <u>of</u> <u>Coalition</u> <u>Politics.</u>

14. This calculus was clearly evident in statements by Deng Xiaoping and other Chinese leaders leading up to the Chinese Commu-nist party conference of September 1985.

15. For background, see Robert Manning, "Reagan's Chance Hit," <u>Foreign</u> <u>Policy</u> (Winter 1984); and Richard Nations, "President Ronald Reagan Charts a New Course in Asia," <u>Far</u> <u>Eastern</u> <u>Economic</u> <u>Review,</u> 21 April 1983.

16. See Chinese coverage of U.S. developments replayed in the U.S. Foreign Broadcast Information Service, <u>Daily</u> <u>Report,</u> <u>China</u> (April-June 1983).

17. See Speaker O'Neill's official report in the U.S. Con-gress, House of Representatives, <u>The</u> <u>United</u> <u>States</u> and <u>China</u> (Wash-ington, D.C.: Government Printing Office, 1983).

18. For background, see article by Chi Su in Samuel Kim, ed., Chinese Foreign Policy in the 1980s (Boulder, Colo.: Westview, 1984).

19. See note 18 and also see Chi Su, "China and the Soviet Union," Current History (September 1984).

20. These themes were common in Chinese media coverage during March-May 1984.

21. These ship movements were disclosed in the Japanese press and replayed in U.S. Foreign Broadcast Information Service, Daily Report, Asia and the Pacific (March 1984).

22. Beijing published U.S. and Japanese references to these Soviet activities in March, April, and May 1984.

23. Washington Post, 22 June 1985.

24. On the latter subject, see Sankei Shimbun, 28 June 1985.

6 Japan: Security Role and Continuing Policy Debates

William T. Tow

Since the Sino-U.S. rapprochement in 1972 and the re-
traction of U.S. military forces from Vietnam beginning
in 1969, East Asia's strategic environment has become
increasingly multidimensional. Elements of the United
States' traditional postwar containment network as represented by its alliances with various Asian-Pacific
regional actors are still intact. But significant
forces of strategic change are also at work in the
region; the Sino-U.S. rapprochement and the Soviet
Union's development of a formidable military power projection capability in the Far East are two recent illus-
trations of how crucial international systemic changes
may originate from Asian sources.

How effectively the people of Asia and the Pacific
adjust to regional political and cultural changes engendered by rapid economic growth and national development
trends will be of particular strategic significance in
the coming years. From a U.S. perspective, East Asia--
even more than Europe--has functioned as the primary
catalyst since 1945 for changes in the U.S. strategic
doctrines and outlooks. The Korean War, for example,
precipitated the North Atlantic Treaty Organization's
(NATO) Lisbon Declaration; the 1954 Geneva conference on
the status of Indochina foreordained later rifts between
NATO members concerning allocation of land forces in
central Europe; and the failure of U.S. military efforts
in Vietnam even more than ostpolitik eventually compelled Washington to seek detente with Moscow on both
European and extra-European geopolitical questions.

As has been the case throughout most of the postwar
era, however, it is Japan that constitutes the central
focus of Washington's strategic outlook on the Pacific.
This is true despite Japan's constant tendency to downplay its own involvement in Western collective defense
and to project a security image of war avoidance under
the guise of "omnidirectional foreign policy" of "comprehensive security."[1] From the Japanese vantagepoint,
Asian security can be best attained through Tokyo's

projection of an economic rather than a strategic image toward the outside world. This approach is the product of a conscious decision reached early on by the country's postwar leadership to pursue national survival through concentrated economic reconstruction and through the building of trade relationships on a global scale. Japan's expectation was that by pursuing this policy, its wartime enemies would eventually feel comfortable in permitting Japan a legitimate reentry into the international system. Tokyo's low strategic profile was also embodied in Article 9 of its national constitution (ratified in 1947), which clearly states that no land, sea, or air forces as well as other war potential would be maintained--a seemingly explicit "no war" clause.

But the interpretation of Article 9 over the years by successive Japanese governments as well as by the general populace has been subject to increased ambivalence and debate. This trend has led many observers to ask why Japan has refused to amend Article 9 at the same time it has strengthened its Self-Defense Forces (SDF) to meet perceived outside security threats. Most Japanese, according to public opinion polls recently conducted by the news daily Asahi Shimbun, the Jiji Press, and other sources indicate the Japanese electorate tends to support SDF buildups only if Washington initially moves to define the threat against which Japan must prepare and only if subsequent SDF reinforcement is accomplished under the strict auspices of the Mutual Security Treaty with its various provisions for shared protection.[2]

The Japanese tactic of maintaining a benign security identity, couched within the overall rubric of the U.S. defense posture, remained effective as long as the world was strategically bipolar. As the global and East Asian military balance shifted in Moscow's favor, however, during the mid to late 1970s, the Japanese preference for relying on signals from Washington to determine its defense efforts became more conspicuous and less credible within the framework of overall Western alliance politics. Japan has thus come under increasing criticism from those in the West who contend that Tokyo cannot remain immune much longer from a changed international environment. Indeed, Washington now asserts that Japanese strategic reciprocity in Asia must evolve in the form of greater defense expenditures and more formidable military capabilities as the Soviet, Vietnamese, and other potential security threats confronting noncommunist Asian-Pacific states grow. The Nunn Resolution, which was considered by the U.S. Congress during 1984 and called upon NATO to upgrade its defenses in an era of rising trade imbalances, has reflected what is certain to be similar U.S. impatience over Tokyo's reluctance to play a security role more in keeping with its economic influence throughout the world.[3]

The importance of evaluating divergent Japanese and U.S. security approaches is related to the need for understanding how any upgrading of Japan's security posture will affect overall power balances in Asia and beyond. In essence, what Japan does in terms of developing a military outlook to regional security threats on its own as opposed to what the United States continues to do in terms of underwriting Japanese security must be weighed seriously. Those decrying U.S. pressures on Japan to accelerate its defense efforts assert that not only will the Japanese continue to resist a militaristic future but that neither the United States nor its other Asian-Pacific allies would really want a remilitarized Japanese state acting independently.[4]

Yet, ultimately, Japan must be viewed as an increasingly critical factor within the Asian-Pacific's politicostrategic framework. How successful the United States and Japan will really be in adjusting their security relations without seriously disrupting the underlying premises of their military cooperation is the major concern of this chapter. More specifically, the question of what Japan really perceives as security threats to itself is considered. Also of concern is what means of defense the Japanese are now pursuing in response to any such perceived threats. Finally, the implications of an upgraded Japanese security role in the overall Asian-Pacific security environment is discussed in relation to that region's overall power balance.

JAPANESE GOVERNMENT THREAT PERCEPTIONS AND THE STRATEGIC BALANCE IN THE ASIAN-PACIFIC REGION

U.S. threat assessments based on traditional balance of power calculations and Japanese tendencies to downplay threats posited by military capabilities in favor of diplomatic harmony remain inherently contradictory. Current Japanese public perceptions of a "Soviet threat" emanate primarily from sociocultural factors related to Japan's postwar determination to avoid war. Indeed, many in Japan feel that Soviet military expansion is a natural historical development stemming from the USSR's sense of cultural and geopolitical inferiority. Japanese conciliatory tactics toward Moscow throughout the postwar era often seemed to be the most expedient means of pursuing strategic survival against Soviet military power. The abhorrent legacy of Japan's own imperialism preceding World War II, moreover, has reinforced in the minds of many Japanese the futility of the Soviets (or anyone else) using military means to coerce others into long-term compliance with their own geopolitical objectives.[5]

Recent Japanese foreign policy doctrines have therefore emphasized diplomatic and economic means for interacting with all other states. This trend reflects a fundamental postwar Japanese interest in rejecting "politicophobia" and in keeping the nation's overall

approach to international affairs "value free."[6]   If
Japan actually does conduct its policies based on such
reasoning, U.S arguments that Japan should be more responsive militarily to closing the power gap between the
USSR and the West throughout the Asian-Pacific and elsewhere would be largely irrelevant.

The extent to which Japan's global and regional
strategic perceptions move closer to those of the United
States will depend in large part on the future course of
Soviet-Japanese relations. Notwithstanding Japan's publicly stated objective of conducting good relations with
the USSR as well as with all other states, Tokyo has
little real interest in placating Soviet needs for economic development or diplomatic inroads as long as the
United States remains Tokyo's major ally. The prospect
of long-term Siberian development projects or of a larger Russian market is attractive to Japan but is more
than counterbalanced by Tokyo's fears that Moscow's
political price for attaining these would be too high.
The question of sovereign control over the Northern
Territories, for example, remains unsolved because the
Soviets fear that any move to return the four contested
islands of the southern Kuriles to Japan would open up a
plethora of other Asian claims against territory now
held by the USSR, especially because Japan continues to
regard the islands as a symbol of Soviet hegemonic
designs against Japan and the entire East Asian area.[7]

Territorial disputes, however, are only one dimension of Soviet-Japanese tensions. Since the middle of
the nineteenth century, Japanese strategists have viewed
their large northern neighbor as potentially their most
troublesome threat. Such feelings are reciprocal in
Moscow: the Russians regard the Japanese as potential
militarists of the first order.[8] Past wars and occupa-
tions between the two nations have created a difficult
legacy of relations that exacerbate current differences
between Tokyo and Moscow. Soviet military expansion in
East Asia has been characterized in the 1984 Japanese
Defense White Paper as an "unrelenting buildup," and the
1984 Japanese foreign ministry Diplomatic Bluebook describes Soviet military power in Asia as the "cause of
the harsh climate around Japan."[9]

Aside from increasing their military deployments on
the Northern Territories to division level (16,000 men),
the Soviets are believed to have developed higher level
attack capabilities against Japan's air and sea-lane
approaches out to several hundred miles. Although Japan
maintains four military divisions of its own with air
support on Hokkaido, the level of Japanese resistance
possible without U.S. help in the event of a concerted
Soviet amphibious operation against Hokkaido remains
largely uncertain. Japan's former secretary-general of
the Defense Council asserts that Japan's air defense
could be eliminated by any combination of over 2,200
Soviet military aircraft situated in the Far East and
that Japanese forces would be defeated in two to three

days by elements of the Soviet Pacific Fleet (40 MIG-23
Floggers are stationed on the contested Northern Territories alone, and recent reports assert that even the
latest Soviet fighter model--the MIG-31 Foxhound--has
been emplaced there).[10]
    The Russian's military deployment patterns and
military assistance programs to North Korea and Vietnam
are also considered highly threatening by Tokyo. Kim
Il-Sung's North Korean regime still intermittently
threatens to invade South Korea; if carried out, a North
Korean takeover of the South could deprive Japan of its
only geographic buffer zone in Northeast Asia. The
heightened presence of Soviet naval and airpower in
Vietnam's Cam Ranh Bay and Da Nang airfield, moreover,
could (in times of war or high crisis) sever continued
Japanese access to Southeast Asian markets, Persian Gulf
oil supplies, or to the other critical sea-lanes of
communications (SLOCs) both in the Indian and Pacific
oceans. The Soviet presence at Cam Ranh has become
particularly worrisome to Japanese defense planners
because for the first time the USSR's Pacific Fleet sits
astride the South China Sea oil conduits. These conduits, with permanent port facilities, service, on the
average, a dozen Soviet warships and submarines and
seven auxiliary vessels with maintenance, munitions,
communications, and intelligence-gathering facilities on
Vietnam's shores.[11]
    Accelerated Soviet military power concentrations in
Northeast Asia and in the East and South China Sea
areas, moreover, are complemented by the deployment of
some 80 supersonic Backfire bombers (with a range of
4,000 kilometers), 120 SS-20 intermediate range ballistic missiles (with a maximum range of 5,000 kilometers),
and some 24 ballistic missile submarines with backup
cruise missile subs all east of Lake Baikal. These are
seen by both U.S. and Japanese defense planners as part
of an accelerated Soviet effort to split the United
States from Japan and from other pro-Western states in
East Asia through intimidation. The U.S. Assistant
Secretary of Defense for International Security Policy,
Richard Perle, underlined this point in an early 1985
interview, and the Japan Defense Agency (JDA) specifically applied the "Soviet divide and rule" hypothesis to
its own reading of how future Japanese defense policy
should be forced.[12] (Appendix B, which summarizes and
contrasts the general purpose force deployments in and
around Japan, seems to validate Japanese and U.S.
concerns.)
    At the nuclear level, Japan's survival certainly
would be dependent on the mutual restraint of the USSR,
the United States, and/or China in introducing nuclear
weapons on or near Japanese territory in the event of a
major war in the Asian-Pacific region. Such restraint,
however, would by no means be guaranteed; bases in Japan
constitute a primary means by which Washington would
project its own military power throughout East Asia.

130

TABLE 6.1 Japan's Regional Security:
Selected Nuclear Capability Indices

Soviet Union	China	United States
• A number of ICBMs capable of hitting Japanese/East Asian targets • 135 SS-20 IRBM launches in Far East • 80 nuclear-capable Backfire bombers • Assorted TU-16 Badgers and TU-22 Blinder mid-range bombers (latter directed toward naval aviation role) • Assorted nuclear-capable surface-to-ground missile launchers • Assorted cruise-missile submarines carrying SS-N-7, SS-N-9, and SS-N-12 number cruise missile warheads	• Limited number of East Wind DF-4 and DF-5 ICBMs (range: 10,000-13,000 km) • 60 DF-3 and 50 DF-2 ICBMs (range: 1,800-5,500 km) • 1 Daqingyu (Xia) SSBN with 12 CSS-NX-3s with 4 more Daqingyu SSBNs on order (range: 2,800 km) • 120 H-6 medium range bombers • 500 H-5 light bombers • Assorted atomic demolition munitions on Sino-Soviet border	• 2 Trident SSBNs • 2 attack carrier task forces with assorted nuclear-capable firing systems, fighter-bomber aircraft, etc. (backed by 4 other task forces in the central and eastern Pacific) • Battlefield nuclear weapons deployed with South Korean land-force division • 2-3 refurbished battleships with nuclear cruise missile delivery systems • B-52 squadron on Guam with nuclear-capable short-range attack missiles • Tomahawk nuclear-controlled cruise missiles coming on line for development on U.S. air and naval elements in late 1980s • 59 marine air fighter and attack aircraft, at least some deploying nuclear-capable attack systems (backed by 127 marine air fighters and attack aircraft in California, Hawaii, and Arizona)

Sources: International Institute of Strategic Studies, London, Military Balance, 1984-1985, and Research Institute for Peace and Security, Tokyo, Asian Security, 1984

The quid pro quo for such U.S. access is the extension of the U.S. nuclear deterrent to Japan. Yet this extended deterrent only confirms, in Moscow's estimate,

Japan's tacit acceptance of U.S. nuclear strategic operations in the region as precedental over a more strict
constructionist Japanese adherence to Article 9 of its
"peace constitution." (Table 6.1 details the nuclear
forces surrounding Japan.)

JAPANESE PUBLIC PERCEPTIONS AND
FORCE STRUCTURES IN TRANSITION

Japanese public opinion, however, still remains
lukewarm to any argument that the Mutual Security Treaty
needs to be reshaped so as to allow for more U.S.-
Japanese reciprocity in military burden-sharing. An
October 1984 poll conducted by the Yomiuri Shimbun noted
that only 2 percent of those polled responded that Japan
needs to shoulder a bigger share of expenses for the
stationing of U.S. forces in Japan, and only 5.4 percent
agreed that Tokyo should accept U.S. arguments about
strengthening Japan's defense power. Fully 38.9 percent
advocated sustaining only current levels of Japanese
cost supports for U.S. forces stationed in Japan (29.8
percent wanted decreases in such support), and a combined 51.9 percent said Japan should not accept U.S.
arguments concerning the necessity for Japan to accelerate its own defense buildup.[13] These poll results, in
keeping with a wide range of previous ones, indicate
that the Japanese public continues to resist extensive
remilitarization in the form of increasing national "war
potential" (and respected U.S. analysts still find it
impossible to entertain in-depth discussions with their
Japanese counterparts about any possible scenario for
actual war fighting by Japanese forces).[14]

Under such circumstances, even Prime Minister Yasuhiro Nakasone is required to temper his normally enthu-
siastic support of U.S. defense policies in Asia (when
he visits Washington) with an acute sensitivity to Japanese domestic political concerns. In general, Nakasone has upheld Japanese international trade policies
instituted by previous governments that tend to work for
Japanese businessmen, farmers, and exporters, even at
the expense of their U.S. counterparts. He has also
maintained fairly subtle, if not ambiguous, positions on
particularly divisive defense issues: e.g., whether to
oppose superpower arms control deals that might discount
Asian or Japanese interests in the process of stabilizing the nuclear balance in Europe, or whether to support
the Reagan administration's Strategic Defense Initiative
(SDI), which many Japanese worry could eventually under-
cut Washington's extended deterrence commitments to its
allies.[15]

The presence of a growing antinuclear movement in
East Asia also affects Japan's defense outlook. In
August 1984, for example, during the ceremonies held to
honor the memory of those who died as a result of the
atomic bombing of Hiroshima and Nagasaki, Prime Minister

Nakasone pledged that Japan would refuse to allow U.S.
warships carrying Tomahawk nuclear cruise missiles to
enter its ports.[16]   Six months after the Tomahawk statements, and perhaps sensitive to U.S. uncertainties,
Nakasone seemed to make a conceptual aboutface when he
announced that Tokyo would allow the United States to
use nuclear weapons in joint U.S.-Japanese defense operations if Japan's actual survival were at stake.   The
Mutual Security Treaty was again cited as the rationale
for applying what, in this case, was regarded as an
extremely flexible interpretation of Japan's non-nuclear
principles, i.e., not to allow production, introduction,
or storage of nuclear weapons on Japanese soil.[17]
    On the other hand, Japan received the crisis in the
Australia-New Zealand-U.S. (ANZUS) alliance, which involved New Zealand's refusal to admit into its ports
British or U.S. warships that could be carrying nuclear
weapons, with what one Australian newspaper has labeled
"deeply considered silence."[18]   The Japanese are especially concerned that if the United States continues to
exercise a hard line against New Zealand's antinuclear
stand, the cohesion and credibility of the West's strategic planning throughout the Asian-Pacific region will
decline in light of increased Soviet military activities
in Indochina and along the Indian Ocean littorals.   Conversely, any U.S. concessions to New Zealand or to other
Asian-Pacific nuclear-free-zone factions would be quickly seized upon by Japanese political opposition parties
to pressure the United States into a more literal interpretation of Japan's non-nuclear principles than is now
the case.
    At present, both the United States and Japan have
opted to treat the sensitive issue of U.S. naval port
calls with public silence because, as noted by Japan's
Research Institute for Peace and Security, "[if] the
United States were ever prepared to disclose the existence of nuclear weapons it would presumably not consult
[the Japanese] either, since Japan is [publicly] bound
to reject any request."[19]   Intense debate did materialize in the Japanese Diet during February and March 1984
about the pending docking of the nuclear-capable U.S.S.
New Jersey and the right of Japan to enjoy "prior consultation" regarding U.S. nuclear-armed cruise missiles
flying through Japanese airspace.   To date, however,
both the United States and Japan have found it mutually
advantageous to avoid directly forcing the issue.
    How long this "agreement to disagree" will continue
is open to serious question when the growing momentum of
the Asian-Pacific free-zone movement is considered.   In
August 1984, the fourteen nations of the South Pacific
Forum unanimously approved a resolution calling for a
nuclear-free-zone treaty that would prohibit the manufacture, use, storage, or acquisition of nuclear weapons
in their region as well as the dumping of nuclear waste
there.[20]   New Zealand and Australia were among the participants in this group, and the Association of South-

east Asian Nations (ASEAN) later went on record supporting the extension of this nuclear-free-zone criteria to
its own region.[21]
    Doubts over Japan's continued willingness to assist
U.S. forces will only increase if, as a result of such
antinuclear initiatives, the Japanese public becomes
more resistant to the SDF's "offensive potential" in its
relation to U.S. nuclear-capable military elements.
Even pro-defense factions of the Liberal Democratic
party (LDP) during past crises involving the interpretation of Mutual Security Treaty were prone to use time-
honored techniques for humoring Washington without demonstrating actual doctrinal compatability between U.S.
and Japanese defense policies. As a June 1980 U.S. Arms
Control and Disarmament Agency report to the Congress
concluded:

> The security policy that is envisioned by most of the
> Japanese populace is therefore an eclectic one which
> seeks to assure continued access to resources and ener-
> gy as well as internal political and economic stabili-
> ty, largely by avoiding any abrupt changes in Japan's
> foreign or military posture. . . . The public view
> seems to endorse the status quo, requiring that the
> future growth of the JSDF, potential increases in de-
> fense spending, and possible changes in Japan's overall
> military posture be incremental and unobtrusive.[22]

This same Japanese tendency to resist significant military doctrinal change, however, also tends to work in
favor of upgraded U.S.-Japanese defense ties. Indeed,
any explicit adoption of a "no first use" nuclear posture by Japan would deny it the full protection of U.S.
military power and deprive it of the benefits currently
available through the U.S. "nuclear umbrella." No responsible Japanese leadership would seriously consider
risking such deterrence guarantees.
    Moreover, Moscow's crude use of military power for
purposes of regional intimidation seems to have had a
largely counterbalancing effect. The Japanese public
seems increasingly willing to modify postwar war-avoid-
ance sentiments in favor of greater resistance to accommodation with the Soviet Union. Sixty percent of those
questioned in a 1984 JDA poll, for example, feel Japan
is in danger of being attacked by the USSR, and 80
percent of the Japanese public support the Self-Defense
Forces; only 12 percent resist SDF outright.[23] Although
attitudes have yet to be transformed into support for
greater Japanese defense burden-sharing, it does seem
that high levels of public support of SDF would allow
for its incremental strengthening against Soviet military intimidation.
    In fact, marked improvement in Japan's defenses has
been reflected in the National Defense Program Outline
and the Standard Defense Force Concept, both in effect
since October 1976. Under the outline's directives,

Japan has extended its parameters of defense from its
own shorelines to several hundred miles out to sea and
has initiated the upgrading of its warning, surveillance, and intelligence-gathering capabilities so as to
be able to ward off small-scale, limited conventional
attacks without the assistance of U.S. Forces, Japan
(USFJ). Qualitative improvements within the SDF, moreover, have been emphasized over quantitative expansion
in order to preclude the type of increases in successive
annual Japanese defense budgets that would inevitably
catapult their measurable annual level to considerably
more than 1 percent of Japan's Gross National Product
(GNP).

But the outline has also reflected Tokyo's belief
that other regional powers, including the Soviet Union,
are still sufficiently nonthreatening. If such were the
case, there would be little necessity for Japan to
increase its own military power based strictly on what
force levels other military powers active throughout
East Asia might deploy.[24]

Accordingly, defense procurement patterns have
reflected more abstract concepts of general maritime and
air corridor defense commensurate with Japan's unique
geographic identify: an island-archipelago dependent on
imports and raw materials from many sources for its own
survival. For example, the Maritime Self-Defense Force
(MSDF) is invested with securing and sustaining two
major SLOCs: (1) an eastern sea-lane extending 1,000
nautical miles southward from Tokyo/Osaka bays toward
(but not reaching to) Guam; and (2) a western sea-lane
stretching 1,000 nautical miles to the southwest as far
as the Bashi Channel between Taiwan and the Philippines.[25] In the event of specific Soviet aggression,
the MSDF would also assist elements of the U.S. 7th
Fleet in blockading the Soya, Tsushima, and Tsugaru
straits. The MSDF, however, would not be expected to
sustain long-term missions related to either sea-lanes
of communication (SLOC) control or straits closure.
Most Western defense analysts seriously doubt that Japanese naval capabilities, as they are now constituted,
would come close to actually defending a 1,000-mile SLOC
radius even though Japan's determination to do so would
remain an important factor in the West's overall defense
strategy as it applies to Asian-Pacific contingencies.

The JDA has determined that at least 4 escort
flotilla must be maintained as mobile operating ship
units, comprised of some 60 antisubmarine surface vessels (the MSDF now only has 34 destroyers and 18 frigates), 16 submarines (only 14 are currently on patrol),
a separate mine-sweeping naval component operating off
both the eastern and western shores of Japan, and 220
combat aircraft focusing on antisubmarine warfare (ASW)
operations.[26] Moreover, in order for MSDF to operate
effectively offshore up to 200 nautical miles, as Washington would like, present inventories of submarines,
destroyers, and large frigates would have to be in-

creased by 50 percent, and an array of fixed-wing ASW aircraft--estimates run as high as 125--needs to be added to the 13 P-3Cs and 90 obsolescent P-20 maritime patrol aircraft now in service.[27] Japan also remains somewhat overdependent on U.S. electronics and C^3I related systems for the manning of its own naval communications systems. However, Japan is beginning to produce indigenous shipborne electronics and sonar systems (the NOLQ-1 ESM/ECM threat analysis system, NOLR-6, OLR-9 ESM, and OLT-9 ESM) at a more credible pace.[28] Japanese naval aviation capabilities beyond purely ASW components are well regarded with some 81 combat aircraft and 63 combat helicopters divided into 6 air wings.[29]

A major emphasis in Japan's Air Self-Defense Force (ASDF) procurement is to build sufficient inventories of fighter aircraft (eventually 13 full-strength squadrons as opposed to the 10 now deployed) to block seaborne and airborne landing invasions and to support Japanese ground defenses with adequate cover critical to achieving such missions.[30] Also deemed critical is the upgrading of air refueling capabilities. Consideration is now being given to purchasing the Boeing KCE-3J refueling tankers to supply the MSDF's F-4EJ Phantom and ASDF F-15J Eagle all-purpose jet fighter squadrons.[31] A countervailing factor, however, is the Japanese wish to ensure that any air refueling or air transport modernization undertaken will not be perceived as a threat by Japan's Southeast Asian neighbors. Such consideration has restrained the Diet, to date, from approving the building of an MSDF-proposed "invincible" class-type aircraft carrier.

In March 1985, Prime Minister Nakasone announced that a new JDA program for improving the Ground Self-Defense Force (GSDF) would be incorporated into Japan's forthcoming 1986-1990 defense plan.[32] The GSDF would be given stronger defense systems designed for coping with amphibious operations or with similar attacks where it would be required to fight back an enemy "at the water's edge." The four GSDF divisions now stationed at Hokkaido (out of twelve deployed in the country) would be armed with heavier weapons--i.e., more main battle tanks with advanced 220-mm guns and greater survivability than the current Type 74s anad Type 61s already deployed, more AH-15 antitank helicopters, and greater ammunition stocks--and backed with greater air mobility. The objective of this buildup on Hokkaido and of the overall strengthening of GSDF components is "to maintain a quick and effective system capable of launching systematic defense operations from the start of aggression in any section of Japan."[33]

In summarizing the overall pace and scope of Japan's current force structure and programs, it is clear that the Japanese have acquiesced to U.S. pressures for doing more in the security realm. They have qualified their compliance, however, by delicately calibrating defense budget increases at relatively small levels and

subtly timing public declarations reaffirming the basic
rationales of the Mutual Security Treaty. Japanese
security policy, therefore, seems to be one of coping
with and parrying against U.S. pressures to change
Japan's postwar security identity and reconciling U.S.
pressures with the generally anti-defense outlook of
Japan's own population.

U.S. BURDEN-SHARING PRESSURES:
THE JAPANESE RESPONSE

Both the Carter and Reagan administrations have
contested the reticent Japanese interpretation of and
response to external security threats. In 1978, President Carter secured commitments from the NATO allies to
increase their defense budgets by 3 percent annually (in
real terms after inflation), and the United States simultaneously implored Tokyo to underwrite even greater
defense expenditures, considering the favorable state of
its economy in relation to most West European states.
The U.S. and Japanese military establishments subsequently moved to adopt the Guidelines for Defense Cooperation that authorized bilateral military planning
studies geared to larger Japanese defense outlays. By
late 1980, however, most prominent U.S. officials were
criticizing the Suzuki government's disclaimers that an
overall national budget deficit in Japan would not allow
that country to attain an originally (and admittedly
overoptimistic) 9.7 percent increase in defense spending
for fiscal year 1981.[34]
The Reagan administration has attempted to avoid
the trap of measuring the relative merit of U.S.-
Japanese defense ties on the basis of such narrow criteria as incremental fiscal commitments. Although they
have pushed the Japanese to spend "substantially greater
amounts" on its defense forces, Secretary of Defense
Caspar Weinberger and other U.S. officials have preferred to emphasize Japan's gradual assumptions of
greater defense missions within the parameters of the
1976 National Defense Program Outline. The United
States has continued to insist, however, that Japan move
gradually to incorporate a wider geographic area in its
overall military responsibilities. This would ideally
be accomplished so Japan could supplement or even replace the United States in fulfilling selected defense
missions throughout the Pacific.[35] Although such a
policy approach has helped to address past Japanese
criticisms that Washington has failed to specify what
more it actually wanted Japan to do in the defense
sector, policy critics in both the United States and
Japan argue that by pushing the Japanese to assume
greater responsibilities, the United States is destabilizing East Asia's overall security environment.
Presently, however, U.S. officials have toned down
their burden-sharing rhetoric by noting that all they
are really demanding from Japan is a greater effort to

defend itself and that the Japanese should ultimately
determine what military roles their country will ful-
fill. Yet, at the same time, these spokesmen have
insisted that the United States should benefit from
whatever increased defense efforts Japan does make because Tokyo would inevitably focus on sea-lane coverage
and "create room for the U.S. to be able to [better]
cope with Soviet military power in the Far East."³⁶

For its part, Japan has become more sensitive to
Western accusations that Tokyo still enjoys a "free
ride" from the United States by continuing to exercise a
low military profile. But Tokyo also faces the dilemma
that if it does invest more heavily in weapons, it risks
provoking fears throughout East Asia. Even within Japan
such concerns are still held by the nation's major
political opposition group--the Japanese Socialist party
(JSP). This remains true despite a recent effort by
Party Chairman Masashi Ishibashi (in 1983 and 1984) to
shift the JSP from its traditional position that SDF
forces are "unconstitutional and illegal" to a new line
of "unconstitutional but lawful."

Yet Ishibashi's tactics were attacked not only by
his own party's theoreticians but by Komeito (Clean
Government), Japan's other major opposition party, as
implicitly endorsing an "unchecked expansion" of the
SDF.³⁷ Komeito itself, however, actually supports the
Mutual Security Treaty on the basis that the international situation will eventually eliminate the need for
both the Mutual Security Treaty and the SDF. Within the
current domestic political scene, only the Democratic
Socialist party (DSP), along with the Liberal Democrats,
supports the need for Japanese national defense in unambiguous terms. The LDP still prefers to steer a middle
course between intermittent U.S. burden-sharing demands
and the Japanese public's overall pacifist sentiments.

In reality, both those U.S. officials who insist on
imposing set quantitative criteria for Japan's defense
efforts and those Japanese political opposition groups
that criticize what they see as submission to U.S.
demands are backing arguments of only tentative credibility. Most U.S. and Japanese decisionmakers recognize
the challenges of cultural and historical diversity
within the alliance and tend to find ways to deal with
those challenges.

For example, in early 1980, Japanese Foreign Minister Saburo Okita told the Diet that Japan would allow
the United States to use bases in Japan for the movement
of U.S. troops to trouble spots in the Middle East and
Indian Ocean based on their "transit status," which did
not technically violate Japan's peace constitution.³⁸
The Nakasone government has broadly interpreted Article
6 of the U.S.-Japan Mutual Security Treaty, which stipulates that the mission of United States Forces, Japan
(USFJ) is to contribute to the security of Japan and
maintain international peace and security in the Far
East. Threats to Japan's survival may emanate not only

from Soviet activities in Northeast Asia but also from
the future closure of oil routes in Southeast Asia, the
Indian Ocean, and/or the Persian Gulf by undesignated
combatants.[39]   In September 1984, therefore, a modest
detachment of U.S. Special Forces was allowed to be
deployed at Okinawa to augment the 3rd marine division.[40]   Japan also continued its indirect participation
as an "observer" in the Rim of the Pacific (RIMPAC)
exercises held in the central Pacific in May and June
1984, which involved 80 ships, 250 aircraft, and more
than 50,000 personnel from, in addition to Japan, the
United States, Australia, New Zealand, and Canada.[41]

   U.S. and NATO optimism concerning Japan's increased
readiness to become actively involved in Persian Gulf/
Middle East defense efforts must be tempered, however,
by the realization that Tokyo remains extremely sensitive to the use of USFJ components beyond Japan's immediate perimeter of defense.   One Western skeptic of
Japan's burden-sharing intentions viewed the 1980 Okita
statement cited above as the Japanese doing nothing more
that "decid[ing] not to decide."   By allowing USFJ to
use Japanese staging posts at Washington's discretion,
Tokyo, according to this viewpoint, was shifting the
decisionmaking for Middle Eastern oil supplies to U.S.
shoulders and not really committing Japan to the support
of such basing use.[42]   A Japanese analyst further notes
that a literal interpretation of constitutional restraints embodied in the language of Article 9 would
restrict his countrymen from even cooperating with U.S.
Rapid Deployment Force/Central Command (CENTCOM) units
in ferrying troops or material from Japan into the
Persian Gulf or Indian Ocean.[43]   It appears that overall
consensus on any Japanese defense burden-sharing role in
the defense of Persian Gulf oil supplies will have to
await a more definitive atmosphere.

   A second area of expanded U.S.-Japan defense relations emerging as a burden-sharing factor is advanced
weapons-related technology transfer from Japan's industrial concerns to the U.S. Department of Defense.   In
September 1980, the Japan-U.S. Systems and Technology
Forum was created to allow for regular discussions on
mutual technology transfer arrangements.   Within three
years (January 1983), in response to a number of U.S.
requests for access to Japanese high-tech elements, the
Japanese government determined that a two-way defense
technology flow under the auspices of the Mutual Security Treaty has priority over other kinds of restrictions
on technology transfers.[44]   On November 8, 1983, a Mutual Defense Assistance Agreement was signed between the
United States and Japan, to implement mutual technology
transfer and regular consultations between representatives constituting a Joint Military Technology Commission that was formed as part of the agreement.   The
long-term policy implications of U.S.-Japan military
technology transfers have been assessed by this writer
more extensively elsewhere.[45]   It should be noted, how-

ever, that by mid-1985, Japan had gradually acquiesced
to U.S. Department of Defense requests to transfer between thirty-six and thirty-eight military-related high
technology items to U.S. recipients over the next few
years.[46]

ASSURING JAPAN'S SECURITY
THROUGH NONMILITARY MEANS

Although in economic terms Japan now stands as a
global power, its geopolitical identity remains limited
to a regional context. If Japan can follow an effective
strategy along ideal lines, its leadership can exercise
creative policy innovations with developing countries,
in international political-economic questions, and in
regional cultural developments and eventually forge the
nation's identity in harmony with an increasingly interdependent world. Consensus is now building in Japan to
address the country's energy and geographic vulnerabilities and simultaneously use the country's economic
wealth and cultural homogeneity to fashion a more benign
international strategic environment.[47]

In East Asia, the Japanese have recently adopted a
new, more politically oriented vision of Pacific Cooperation, emphasizing Tokyo's willingness to realize a
"balanced" interaction between Asian-Pacific and extraregional actors. This somewhat fluid, all-inclusive
outlook supplanted the former Pacific Community concept
that tended to emphasize a specifically regional and
strictly economic leadership role for Japan.[48] Accordingly, Japanese leaders in government and business now
endorsing the Pacific Cooperation approach have opted to
avoid unqualified endorsement of various ASEAN proposals, noting that Southeast Asian capitals not be too
eager to appropriate Japan's postwar development experience in lieu of other Western development models that
may be more applicable to their own unique situations.[49]
But Japan also remains sensitive to the chronic problem
of imbalance in Japanese-ASEAN trade and investment.
During the 1980s, Japan's economic assistance profile
toward the Association of Southeast Asian Nations
(ASEAN)--dramatically labeled "heart to heart relations"
by former Japanese Prime Minister Takeo Fakuda--has been
maintained, although with a lower profile as the visits
of Prime Minister Suzuki (1981) and Nakasone (1983)
produced only small-scale Japanese commitments to ASEAN
economic assistance.[50]

Notwithstanding increased Japanese sensitivities to
ASEAN's economic development problems, Malaysian Prime
Minister Mahathir has forcefully argued that in its
efforts to emulate Japanese industrialization, Malaysia,
and other ASEAN states, often has become more, not less,
dependent on Japanese heavy industry and high technology
to broaden its own manufacturing and commercial infra-
structures. Future Japanese access to Southeast Asia's

natural resources may well depend on Tokyo's ability to
demonstrate more affinity toward ASEAN economic problems
than has been the case to date.[51]

To some extent, residual economic tension with
other East Asian nations has overshadowed Japanese efforts to play a more visible role in backing ASEAN's
security concerns. In July 1984, Japanese Foreign Minister Shintaro Abe told his ASEAN diplomatic counterparts that Japan was determined to seek a peaceful
solution to the Cambodian crisis, consistent with
Tokyo's and ASEAN's mutual aspirations for a lasting
peace in Indochina. In October, Japan hosted Vietnamese
Foreign Minister Nguyen Co Thach and urged a prompt
Vietnamese military withdrawal from Cambodia as well as
immediate Vietnamese negotiations with ASEAN states to
find a common basis for settlement.[52] The Japanese,
however, also had other motives in bringing Hanoi to the
negotiating table than merely to derive a Cambodian
settlement for ASEAN's benefit. These included enhanced
stability for Thailand, which is a guardian of key SLOCs
that stretch to the easternmost parts of the Indian
Ocean (via the Andaman Sea), less probability of a long-
term arms race between the Vietnamese and ASEAN states
spanning the Strait of Malacca as well as other key oil
routes, and the encouragement of greater Vietnamese
strategic independence from the USSR through the lessening of overall regional tensions. The amelioration of
Indochinese tensions could also reduce U.S. pressures on
Japan to sustain or increase its own maritime defenses.

Similar rationales lay behind Japan's efforts to
defuse tensions on the Korean Peninsula. A May 1984
visit to Moscow by North Korean President Kim Il-Sung to
seek additional military assistance from the USSR cul-
minated in Soviet leader Konstantin U. Chernenko's
statement that such assistance would be extended by the
USSR to stem "the rise of militaristic moves" by the
U.S. and Japan in Northeast Asia.[53] The Japanese public's continued animosity toward the Soviet Union has
remained more constant (see Table 6.2) than the attitudes of Japan's successive governments. The government
has tended intermittently--and unsuccessfully--to initiate negotiations concerning territorial and political
differences as a means to break into the Soviet market-
place. Continued tensions on the Korean Peninsula will,
however, only reinforce Japan's overall view that a high
level of strategic dependence on U.S. military power
stationed in or adjacent to Japan is necessary. Japan
will be less able to facilitate a more independent
strategic image as might be construed from the somewhat
obfuscated projections contained in the July 1980 Comprehensive National Security Task Force report's
recommendations.

Beyond the Asian-Pacific region, Japan is asserting
itself more in Middle East diplomacy. Economic and
strategic incentives have reinforced this policy. In
1983, Japan surpassed the United States as the leading

TABLE 6.2 Japanese Public Opinion of Security Threats

Inquiry: Is there any country which you especially think of as a threat to Japan's security recently? From among the following, list as many as you like.

Country	Percentage of Responses
United States	7.8
South Korea	2.9
North Korea	5.4
China	2.3
USSR	53.5
Others	0.1
Threat, but no specific threat	16.0
No threat	13.5
No answer	10.5

Source: Yomuri Shimbun, 8 October 1984, reprinted in DJSP, 19 October 1984, p. 13-14.

supplier of goods to Saudi Arabian markets (U.S.$7.7 billion to $7.6 billion), and the bulk of Japanese oil supplies continue to originate from the Persian Gulf area. In June 1984, Nakasone reportedly had drafted his country's first postwar diplomatic initiative independent of U.S. encouragement. This was a three-step peace plan for ending the Iran-Iraq war to be presented at the annual economic summit of seven industrialized countries in London.[54] Reports also surfaced that the Japanese might even consider using SDF units in a UN peacekeeping role as a preferred alternative to the scenario of Japanese naval convoys escorting U.S. naval units through Asian-Pacific waters en route to a Persian Gulf defense operation. The Iran-Iraq war's negligible effect on global oil supplies, however, has removed some sense of urgency for the Japanese in finding a diplomatic solution to that conflict singlehandedly. In the government's annual foreign policy address delivered at the Diet's opening session on January 25, 1985, Foreign Minister Abe concluded that "our country is in no position to mediate or arbitrate the conflict" but that Japan would work through the United Nations to realize a peaceful settlement to Middle Eastern disputes.[55]

THE JAPANESE DEFENSE TRANSITION: IMPLICATIONS FOR THE REGION AND THE UNITED STATES

U.S.-Japan military burden-sharing trends will be followed closely in the ASEAN region. Assuredly, the Soviet Union continues to provide the communist

Indochinese states with generous levels of military
assistance and has dispatched thousands of military
advisers to Vietnam, Cambodia, and Laos. Yet any significant increase of Japanese military power in East or
Southeast Asia would be regarded by most ASEAN nations
with trepidation.

Specifically, U.S. pressures for greater naval
patrolling by Japan to its southwest would complicate
ASEAN's efforts to implement a Zone of Peace, Freedom,
and Neutrality (ZOPFAN) by introducing yet another significant naval power into their region. Of additional
concern is the possibility that Japan could establish an
independent strategic foothold along Southeast Asian oil
routes in the event of further decline in U.S. offshore
power in the region. Finally, the prospect of Japanese
defense firms reaching out to cultivate new markets
raises fears that regional ethnic or territorial disputes and confrontations in Southeast Asia could become
more exacerbated. As Francis Lai Fung-wai observed in
assessing Nakasone's January 1983 trip through ASEAN
countries to allay fears about Japanese military
intentions:

> The diplomatic language of support [for Japan's defense
> buildup] . . . [has] seemed to be expressions of cer-
> tain reservations rather than of enthusiastic endorse-
> ment. Most of the ASEAN leaders made it clear that
> they were only endorsing Japan building up its self-
> defense force, but definitely not an active military
> role in the region. . . . The ASEAN leaders seemed to
> agree that . . . it is not desirable for Japan to
> involve its military forces directly, either in pro-
> tecting sea lanes or patrolling the region.[56]

If this interpretation is valid, the United States'
continued willingness to deploy a strong military presence on or proximate to the ASEAN neighborhood may
remain the best hope for noncommunist Southeast Asia to
eventually realize its long-term security goal of regional neutrality. Washington would have great difficulty in justifying to ASEAN the need for Japan to take
over sea-lane patrols in various parts of the region.[57]

Japan's security policy toward the Korean Peninsula
is thus also relevant to any upgraded defense role it
might undertake in partnership with Washington. In
September 1984, South Korea President Chun Doo Hwan
journeyed to Japan as his country's first head of state
to ever formally visit that country. Economic problems
and the issue of Japanese wartime atonement toward the
Korean people highlighted Chun's trip (although a Japanese loan of $4 billion to Seoul was extended earlier in
the year). In addition, a joint statement was issued by
Chun and Nakasone, urging direct talks between North and
South Korea. The chairman of the South Korean Joint
Chiefs of Staff also accompanied President Chun to Japan, and his SDF counterpart, General Keitaro Watanabe,

announced that he would return this "courtesy visit" by touring Seoul in the fall of 1985. Yet both sides were emphatic in their denials that any Japanese-South Korean military alliance was forming.[58]

Although Japan had signed a joint military plan with the United States in December 1984 that is thought to have some relevance to the defense of South Korea, Tokyo and Seoul seem content at present to work through their mutual U.S. security partner in achieving common defense objectives rather than through more direct security ties with one another.[59] Some basis for South Korean-Japanese defense coordination could materialize, however, if Soviet airpower continues to be deployed in great quantities in the Northeast Asian perimeter. Any Backfire bomber strikes directed against Japanese or U.S. naval elements in the area would have to fly past South Korean territory to reach the Sea of Japan, Okinawa, and the Philippines. South Korean air defenses could coordinate a forward air defense line of F-16 interceptors stationed at Cheju Do or other appropriate bases in conjunction with U.S. and Japanese forces operating from Misawa Air Base, Okinawa, and other sites. This multilayered air defense screen would be even more effective if and when Japan deploys a truly formidable early warning air defense system for its home islands. The South Koreans could also upgrade their minelaying aircraft and naval vessels with the intent of closing off the Korean Strait to Soviet surface ships, thereby freeing Japan and the United States to concentrate on the Tsugaru and Soya straits to the north.[60] As is the case in Southeast Asia, however, the U.S. military presence in Northeast Asia remains the paramount instrument of deterrence against aggression directed at the Korean Peninsula.

It seems clear that the Reagan administration, and, most probably, its successors will continue to pressure the Japanese into accepting greater defense responsibilities rather than merely demand increases in Japanese fiscal commitments that may or may not be related to a well-integrated regional defense effort by both allies. U.S. proposals will focus on achieving greater Japanese sea control capabilities in Southeast Asia and the Pacific island-states; achieving straits control by credibly mining and blockading the Tsushima, Tsugaru, and Soya straits through which the Soviet Pacific Fleet must pass during wartime to reach open waters; and structuring more sophisticated air defenses that could inflict significant losses on Soviet attack aircraft operating from the USSR's Far Eastern Command. Japan's recent willingness to accept greater defense burden-sharing during Prime Minister Nakasone's tenure of office has been encouraging, but Washington must have more permanent indications that future Japanese leaders will be as committed to accepting a broadened Japanese defense role.

CONCLUSION

Japan's approach to security problems may be perceived as part of a strategy to move through a difficult transition period in which an almost exclusive emphasis on economics under the protection of U.S. deterrence is widening to include independent Japanese diplomatic and security efforts. Extended politicostrategic activities, whether carried out on a global or regional level, however, must still be justified by Japanese leaders to their electorate in largely nonmilitary terms; these activities must be seen as facilitating positive economic, social, and cultural development. In the final analysis, both the United States and Japan still hold largely the same broad objectives for ensuring their national well-beings: to stabilize the Third World so as to guarantee their mutual access to critical national resources and markets; to preclude radical forces such as the Soviet Union or fundamental Islamic movements from undercutting such Western access; and to minimize the polarization of ASEAN or Middle Eastern societies into pro-Western and anti-Western factions. The key question is to what extent Washington and Tokyo will be able to pursue their collaboration in military planning, technological support, and other avenues of strategic cooperation given the shift of economic and even political influence in East Asia from Washington to Tokyo during the past decade.

Although Japan will most likely become neither neutralist nor nonaligned--at least in the short term-- it is clear that the Japanese will be less prone to support tight bipolar security coalitions or other blocs fashioned by the superpowers. Certainly, the Mutual Security Treaty will undergo at least some shifts and changes in the years ahead because collective security, as the Japanese now interpret it, "is not . . . confined to [concern about] the defense of frontiers . . . [and] . . . the purely military dimension [is] seen as of limited importance."[61] Continued relaxation of regional and global tensions through promotion of economic and diplomatic harmony will remain the essence of Japan's overall national security policy, and this reality must be considered in future U.S. strategic policy deliberations. In turn, the acceptability of U.S. strategic deterrence in Japan will remain credible only so long as Tokyo remains confident that Moscow cannot be diverted by any other means from pressuring Japan into submission. This acceptance is a most difficult compromise for Japan to make in both cultural and historical terms. It also, however, stands as a reluctant acknowledgment by the Japanese people that the West's traditional strategic geometry is still a better guarantee of Tokyo's security aspirations than is the more idealistic yet amorphous politics of interdependency.

NOTES

1. Joachim Glaubitz has characterized the omnidirectional approach adopted by Japan throughout the 1970s as a "policy of peace to all sides" (zenhoi - heiwa-gaiko) or, as critics would term it, a "be nice to everybody policy." The diplomatic strategem was to compensate for Japan's strategic vulnerability by cultivating the best possible relations with every country in the world. See Glaubitz, "Japanese Foreign and Security Policy," Aussenpolitik (English edition) 2 (1984):176. For in-depth assessments of the more recent comprehensive security approach found in the July 1980 special task force report presented to the Japanese government and entitled "Report on Comprehensive National Security," see Robert W. Barnett, Beyond War: Japan's Concept of Comprehensive National Security (New York: Pergamon-Brassey's, 1984), pp. 1-6.

2. See the data incorporated by Shinkichi Eto, "Japanese Perceptions of National Threats," in Charles E. Morrison, ed., Threats to Security in East Asia-Pacific (Lexington, Mass.: Heath, 1983), pp. 53-64.

3. See, for example, "Japan-U.S. Defense Relations Entering a New Stage," Yomuri Shimbun, 29 June 1984, p. 3 as translated and reprinted in Daily Summary of the Japanese Press (hereafter cited as DSJP), U.S. Embassy, Tokyo, Political Section--Office of Translation Services, 6 July 1984, pp. 3-4; "Security Consultations: No Basic Change in U.S. Requests," Sankei, 29 June 1984, p. 13, translated and reprinted in DSJP, 7-9 July 1984, p. 1; "Japan-U.S. Joint Defense and Self-defense Power," Mainichi Shimbun, 29 June 1984, p. 2, translated and reprinted in ibid., p. 2; "Japan-U.S. Defense Cooperation Reaches Limit," Tokyo Shimbun, 29 June 1984, p. 5, translated and reprinted in ibid., p. 3. Also see Mike Tharp, "Softly Does It," Far Eastern Economic Review, 31 May 1984, pp. 42, 43. The entire U.S.-Japan burden-sharing history in a 1980s context is well covered by Peter Polemka, "The Security of the Western Pacific: The Price of Burden-Sharing," Survival 26, no. 1 (January-February 1984), especially pp. 11-12; and by Robert F. Reed, The U.S.-Japan Alliance: Sharing the Burden of Defense (Washington, D.C.: National Defense University Press, 1983), especially pp. 58-59.

4. A representative criticism along such lines is that of R. B. Byers and Stanley C. M. Ing, "Sharing the Burden on the Far Side of the Alliance: Japanese Security in the 1980's," Journal of International Affairs 37, no. 1 (Summer 1983):163-175.

5. Taketsugu Tsurutani, Japanese Policy and East Asian Security (New York: Praeger, 1981), pp. 89-90.

6. Ibid., pp. 118-125; and Fuji Kamiya, "Japan's Security and the International Environment in the 1980's," in Donald Hugh McMillan, ed., Asian Perspectives on International Security (New York: St. Martin's, 1984), especially p. 29.

7. Reciprocal Soviet-Japanese tensions along such lines are well described by Edward A. Olsen, U.S.-Japan Reciprocity (Stanford, Calif.: Hoover Institution Press, 1985), pp. 46-47.

8. See analysis of Paul F. Langer, "Soviet Military Power in Asia," in Donald S. Zagoria, ed., Soviet Policy in East Asia (New Haven: Yale University Press, 1982), pp. 260-261.

9. Japan Defense Agency, Defense of Japan 1984 [Boei Hakusho--English edition] (Tokyo: JDA, 1984), p. 30; Japanese Ministry

of Foreign Affairs, Diplomatic Bluebook 1984 Edition [in English] (Tokyo: Foreign Press Center, 1984), p. 12; and Robert Y. Horiguchi, "Vigorous Soviet Buildup," Pacific Defense Reporter 11, nos. 6/7 (December 1984-January 1985):33-37.

   10. Horiguchi, "Vigorous Soviet Buildup," p. 34; Larry A. Miksch, "Japanese Defense Policy: Issues for the United States," Background Paper, Congressional Research Service, Library of Congress, 15 December 1984, pp. 3-4; Langer, "Soviet Military Power," pp. 268-269; and G. Jacobs, "North Asian Naval Forces," Asian Defense Journal (January 1985):65.

   11. "Camranh--A Threat to Japan," Mainichi Daly News, 1 March 1985, p. 1, discusses U.S. Pacific Command Intelligence estimates placed before the seapower subcommittee of the U.S. Senate Armed Services Committee. Also see The International Institute for Strategic Studies, Strategic Survey 1984-1985 (London: IISS, Spring 1985), p. 87.

   12. The Perle interview is reprinted as "Moscow Out to Divide the Western Alliance," Pacific Defense Reporter 11, no. 11 (May 1985):35-36; the JDA affirmation is in Defense of Japan 1984, p. 54.

   13. "Results of Yomiuri Shimbun's Public Opinion Survey on Japan-U.S. Defense Relations (extracted from 29 October 1984 edition)," DSJP, 7 November 1984, pp. 11-12.

   14. Barnett, Beyond War, p. 126.

   15. In late April 1985, Nakasone indicated that he would take a "cautious stand" over the SDI issue within the framework of Japan's no-war constitution and, as such, not necessarily comply with President Reagan's request for Japanese funding and technological support for that project. See "Nakasone Comments on Bonn Summit, SDI Project" as reported by Kyodo, 27 April 1985, and reprinted in Foreign Broadcast Information Service (hereafter cited as FBIS), 29 April 1985, p. C-1. In a March 25, 1984, press conference in Beijing between Prime Minister Nakasone and Chinese Communist Advisory Committee Chairman Deng Xiaoping, both leaders stated that Japan and China wanted to promote "nuclear disarmament on a global scale" and that the increasing Soviet deployment on SS-20s is a major problem facing both China and Japan. Asahi Shimbun, 26 March 1984, p. 2, as translated and reprinted in DSJP, March 31-April 2, 1984, p. 11. Japan and China also announced an agreement "to trade their own information" on SS-20 deployment.

   16. "Japan Ban Includes U.S. Warship," The Times (London), 10 August 1984, p. 5; and "Nakasone to Deny Nuclear-Armed Ships Protocols," FBIS, Asia & Pacific (Daily Report), 9 August 1984, p. C-1.

   17. Robert Whymant, "Tokyo Sets Out Conditions for Nuclear Defense," The Guardian, 20 February 1985, p. 4; and "Nakasone Approves U.S. Nuclear Defense of Japan," FBIS, Asia & Pacific (Daily Report), 19 February 1985, p. C-1.

   18. "Japan Keen for N.Z., U.S. to Stay on Even Keel," The Australian Financial Review, 12 February 1985, p. 14.

   19. Research Institute for Peace and Security, Asian Security 1984, (Tokyo: RIPS, 1984), p. 205. Also see comments by Masamichi Inoki, chairman of the Board of Directors, RIPS, in an interview conducted by the Japanese Magazine Jitsugyokai [date, place, and identity of interviewer not specified] (1 February 1983), pp. 24-27, as reprinted in Joint Publications Research Service (JPRS), JAR-84-006, Japan Report, 23 March 1984, especially pp. 26-28.

20. "14 Countries in Area Back Nuclear-Free Pacific Zone," International Herald Tribune, 28 August 1984, p. 5; and "Nuclear Free Zone To Be Set Up in Pacific," Daily Telegraph (London), 29 August 1984, p. 6.

21. "ASEAN Ministers Communiqué," FBIS, Asia & Pacific (Daily Report), 12 July 1984, p. A-7.

22. U.S., Congress, Senate, Subcommittee on East Asian and Pacific Affairs of the Committee on Foreign Relations, Japan's Contribution to Military Stability in Northeast Asia, 96th cong., 2nd sess., June 1980, pp. 43-44.

23. As cited by Denis Warner, "Japan's Global and Regional Strategic Perceptions," Pacific Defense Reporter 11, no. 11 (May 1985):31.

24. The National Defense Program Outline is summarized in comprehensive terms by Nishihara, "Expanding Japan's Credible Defense Role," International Security 8, no. 3 (Winter 1983-1984), especially pp. 180-185.

25. See Jacobs, "North Asian Naval Forces," p. 66, for a comprehensive map-graph of the proposed Sea-Lane Defense Concept. Also see Niksch, "Japanese Defense Policy: Suzuki's Shrinking Options," Journal of Northeast Asian Studies 1, no. 2 (June 1982):84; and Defense of Japan 1984, p. 56.

26. Defense of Japan 1984, p. 67.

27. Jacobs, "North Asian Naval Forces," p. 66.

28. Ibid.

29. International Institute for Strategic Studies, The Military Balance, 1984-1985 (London, IISS, 1984), p. 101.

30. As outlined by Defense of Japan 1984, p. 67.

31. Kensuke Ebata, "Japan Considers Contenders for Air-Refueling Tanker," Jane's Defense Weekly, 23 February 1985, pp. 313-318.

32. "Nakasone Calls for SDF Buildup," Japan Times Weekly 25, no. 14 (6 April 1985):3; and "Nakasone, Kato Discuss New Defense Program," FBIS, Asia & Pacific (Daily Report), 15 April 1985, p. C-4.

33. Defense of Japan 1984, p. 66.

34. The progressive attacks of the Carter administration against the quantitative deficiencies of Japan's 1980 and 1981 defense budgets are best surveyed by Chae-Jin Lee and Hideo Sato, U.S. Policy Toward Japan and Korea: A Changing Influence Relationship (New York: Praeger, 1982), pp. 134-135.

35. Perhaps the most definitive statement of the Reagan administration's approach was offered by then Assistant Secretary of Defense for International Security Affairs, Frances J. West, Jr., testifying in Hearings before the Committee on Foreign Affairs and its Subcommittees on International Economic Policy and Trade and on Asian Pacific Affairs, United States-Japan Relations, 97th cong., 2nd sess., 1 March 1982, p. 26:

The Reagan Administration [has] adopted a policy of not criticizing its allies in public and of discussing defense cooperation on the basis of roles and missions rather than on arbitrary statistical indices such as percentages of GNP, which by themselves are not necessarily meaningful.

36. "Interview with U.S. Deputy Assistant Secretary of Defense [James Blaker]; Expectations Placed on 'Easing of Tension on Korean Peninsula'; Soviet Nuclear Weapons Excessive; Japan Should Complement Strategy Toward USSR," Mainichi Shimbun, 22 November 1984 and translated in DSJP, 4 December 1984, p. 1.

37. Background on the domestic Japanese political debate is provided by Olsen, U.S.-Japan Reciprocity, pp. 98-101; and International Institute for Strategic Studies, Strategic Survey, 1984-1985 (London: IISS, 1985), p. 94. On overall Japanese political opposition party strengths, see Fukuoka Masayuki, "The Ailing Opposition," Japan Echo 12, no. 1 (Spring 1985):45-50. On the specific issue, consult remarks of JDA Director-General Yuko Kurihara in Tokyo Shimbun, 3 January 1984, as translated and reprinted in DSJP, 12 January 1984, pp. 3-4.

38. See "Trouble Spots: Japan's Yes to U.S. Troops," New Straits Times, 2 February 1980, p. 32.

39. Nishihara, "Credible Defense," p. 196.

40. Robert Whymant, "Green Berets Stretch Defense Pact with Japan," The Guardian, 3 August 1984, p. 5.

41. Defense of Japan 1984, p. 179.

42. Olsen, U.S.-Japan Reciprocity, pp. 16-17.

43. Yatsuhiro Nakagawa, "The WEPTO Option: Japan's New Role in East Asia/Pacific Collective Security," Asian Survey 24, no. 8 (August 1984):837.

44. Defense of Japan 1984, pp. 171-172; and William T. Tow, "U.S.-Japan Military Technology Transfers: Collaboration or Conflict?" Journal of Northeast Asian Studies 2, no. 4 (December 1983):10-14.

45. See Tow, ibid., pp. 3-23.

46. "U.S. Interested in Japan's Military Technology," The Japan Economic Journal (International Weekly of Nihon Keizai Shimbun), 23, no. 1162 (4 June 1985):1, 19; and William J. Holstein et al., "The Pentagon Heads for a Shopping Spree in Japan," Business Week (8 July 1985):40-41.

47. Barnett, Beyond War, pp. 1-14, provides useful analysis on this point.

48. Bruce Roscoe, "A New New Order," Far Eastern Economic Review, 31 January 1985, pp. 28-30, provides background on this revised Japanese regional approach.

49. As noted in Lim Hua Sing's "Japanese Perspectives on Malaysia's 'Look East' Policy," Southeast Asian Affairs, 1984, especially pp. 244-245.

50. For background on Japanese economic initatives to ASEAN during recent years, see Charles E. Morrison, Japan, the United States and a Changing Southeast Asia (London: University Press of America with The Asia Society, 1985), pp. 35-38. Also see Chris Sherwill, "ASEAN Crosses Swords with Japan," Financial Times, 3 September 1983, p. 3.

51. For assessments on Mahathir's overall outlook see Jurek Martin, "Japan and its Neighbors," Financial Times, 31 August 1984, p. 11; and Ahmad Rejal Arbee, "Pros and Cons of Ties with Japan," Japan Times, 30 October 1984, p. 18.

52. "Thach, Abe Agree Hanoi Should Meet with ASEAN," Japan Times, 4 October 1984, p. 1; and Whymant, "Japan and Hanoi Poles Apart," The Guardian, 4 October 1984, p. 7.

149

53. Sam Jameson, "Fears Grow in Seoul of New North Korea Buildup by Soviets," Los Angeles Times, 9 June 1984, p. 2.

54. Geoffrey Murray, "Japan Tries Out More Active Diplomatic Role in Persian Gulf War," The Christian Science Monitor, 13 June 1984, p. 13; Jurek Martin, "Japan May Play More Active Role in Bid to End Iran-Iraq War," Financial Times, 5 June 1984, p. 11; and Stuart Auerbach, "Japan Surpasses U.S. as Saudi's Chief Supplier," International Herald Tribune, 11 February 1984, p. 2. For background on emerging Japanese policies in the Gulf, consult M. Yoshitsu, Caught in the Middle East: Japan's Diplomacy in Transition (Lexington, Mass.: Lexington Books, 1984).

55. "Abe Outlines Foreign Policy at a Diet Session," FBIS, Asia & Pacific (Daily Report), 30 January 1985, p. C-13.

56. Frances Lai Fung-wai, "Japan's Defense Policy and Its Implications for the ASEAN Countries," in Institute of Southeast Asian Studies, Southeast Asian Affairs, 1984 (Singapore: ISAS, 1984), p. 60.

57. Southeast Asian fears of Japanese naval expansion are discussed by Takashi Oka, "Southeast Asia Wary of Changing Roles of Japan and U.S. in Pacific," The Christian Science Monitor, 10 July 1984, p. 10. A more optimistic assessment is a report asserting that "Japan Sea Lane Defense Doesn't Worry Mahathir," Japan Times, 26 January 1983, p. 1. During his January 1983 tour of the ASEAN Region, Nakasone discussed prospects of limited Japanese naval expansion with all his Southeast Asian counterparts without raising visibily sharp opposition in the context of Japan's limited patrolling objectives capabilities.

58. A Japanese account of the limited nature of tacit Japan-South Korea security relations is "Forward Looking Attitude Toward Settlement of Pending Matters: New Era Marked by President Chun's Visit to Japan," Sankei, 9 September 1984, as translated and reprinted in DSJP, 21 September 1984, p. 5. Also see Horuguchi, "Vigorous Soviet Buildup," p. 35; and Asian Security 1984, p. 180 for more general summaries.

59. See "U.S.-Japan in Joint Military Plan," Asian Defense Journal (February 1985):88.

60. Niksch, "South Korea in Broader Pacific Defense," Journal of Northeast Asian Studies 2, no. 1 (Spring 1983):94-95; and "Strengthening of Soviet Military Power and Deploymet of F-16s," Mainichi Shimbun, 5 April 1985, p. 5 as translated and reprinted in DSJP, 11 April 1985, pp. 2-3.

61. Wolf Mendl, Western Europe & Japan Between the Superpowers (New York: St. Martin's, 1984), p. 153.

7 The Two Koreas: Security, Diplomacy, and Peace

Young Whan Kihl

The precarious military balance on the Korean Peninsula is complicated by recent diplomatic activities concerning Korea. With the inter-Korean arms race intensified, any move toward reduction of tensions on the Korean Peninsula would be welcomed and regarded as encouraging. However, any attempt to break the stalemate in inter-Korean relations through diplomatic maneuvering will also introduce new elements of uncertainty and risk--as well as resistance to change by vested and entrenched interests--thereby increasing the danger of unstability and potential war between the two halves of divided Korea.[1]

The arms race in Korea has reached the point of no return--the Korean Peninsula in the 1980s has turned into an armed camp. As one of the most heavily militarized and fortified spots in the world, divided Korea has become a dangerous powder keg where slight provocation might ignite and involve the outside powers.[2] The relatively evenly matched military and power balance between the two Koreas in the 1980s may shift and favor one side over the other as a result of the dynamic interplay of several factors: increased Soviet military activities and presence in the region; Chinese diplomatic pressures on North Korea to improve its relations with South Korea and also with the United States; and the dynamics of inter-Korean dialogue and competition regarding the future of Korea.[3]

KOREA AND THE CHANGING SECURITY ENVIRONMENT

The shifting major power relations in the region have had a great impact on Korea and especially on the diplomatic alignment of the respective Korean regimes.

This article appears as "Evolving Inter-Korean Relations: Security, Diplomacy, and Peace," Korea & World Affairs, vol. 9, no. 3 (Fall 1985), pp. 441-468.

151

The two Koreas' security environment, like that of any
other country, is shaped by a host of factors, some of
which are fixed, such as geography, and others that are
constantly changing, such as politics, economics, and
military capabilities.[4] Changes in Korea's security
environment, moreover, are also affected by developments
within each Korean state and between the two Koreas.

Geopolitically, the Korean Peninsula is the strategic fulcrum of East Asia where the interests of four
major powers--the Soviet Union, China, Japan, and the
United States--converge and crisscross. It is not surprising, therefore, that in the one hundred years prior
to 1985 three major international wars have been waged
over the control of the Korean Peninsula: the Sino-
Japanese War of 1894-1895, the Russo-Japanese War of
1904-1905, and the Korean War of 1950-1953, the last one
involving the United States and China, among others, as
major belligerents.

As a peninsula, Korea is not only vulnerable to
attack by sea but also is deeply affected by the latest
developments in naval warfare as support from any ally
not on the Asian mainland must arrive by sea or air.
Because the Korean Peninsula is poor in natural resources, its economic well-being depends on world trade:
its import and export activities depend on the supply
line from the sea. The fact that South Korea controls
one side of the important Strait of Korea (Tsushima),
which is one of the four main chokepoints for entrance
into the Sea of Japan from the Pacific, also enhances
South Korea's strategic value.[5]

In the 1980s, the strategic environment in Northeast Asia surrounding the Korean Peninsula is fluid and
uncertain due to the heightened tension in U.S.-Soviet
relations, the continued Sino-Soviet conflict, and the
improvement in U.S.-Sino and Sino-Japanese relations.
More specifically, the security environment on the Korean Peninsula is rapidly changing because of increased
Soviet military activities in the region, a heightened
Soviet concern about developments in North Korea, and an
evolving de facto triple entente between the U.S., China, and Japan (to the extent that such major power
relationships produce a negative impact on Korea).

Soviet and U.S. Force Deployment

Both North and South Korea are considered strategic
assets by the major powers and by the countries that
border the two Koreas: in the case of a major war, both
Korean states could provide excellent naval support
facilities and air bases to outside powers in the
region.

The Soviet Union presently maintains no naval support facilities, ground forces, or air bases in North
Korea. However, the Soviet Pacific Fleet headquartered
in Vladivostok (across from the Soviet-North Korean

border) could easily use several of North Korea's excellent port facilities in the Sea of Japan. North Korea's
port cities, such as Chogjin, Unggi, and Najin, could
very well serve as subsidiary loading points for cargo
destined for the Soviet maritime province.

The recently negotiated North Korea-Soviet border
treaty, signed in 1984 and put into effect in 1985, may
give both countries better access to each other's territory, economically and militarily. Although the common
border shared by both countries runs only for fifteen
miles along the Tumen River in the northeastern corner
of the Korean Peninsula, several crossing points act as
vital connecting transportation links, both railway and
highway, between the two countries. With Soviet technical support, the port facilities of Najin have been
expanded and modernized. An oil refinery was built in
Unggi, halfway between Najin and the Soviet border.[6]

Recently, Japan's _Sankei Shimbun_ reported a Soviet
test-flight across the narrow neck of North Korea's
east-west corridor along the DMZ, a flight that may have
political as well as strategic significance.[7] This may
have been one of the results of Kim Il-Sung's 1984
Moscow visit and the subsequent border treaty negotiated
in 1984. Politically, North Korea has now agreed to
support Soviet access to North Korea, as it did with
China in 1983. In that instance, North Korea made the
port city of Chongjin available for cargo transshipment
for Japan-China trade in order to serve the interior of
China's northeast province.[8]

Strategically, Soviet access to North Korea's airspace also is important because it provides the Soviets
with an alternative route and channel for the transair
link between the Soviet Far East and Soviet stations in
the Cam Ranh air bases in Vietnam. Prior to this access, the Soviet air route had been over the narrow
Strait of Tsushima between the Sea of Japan and the
South China Sea. Now with the cooperation of North
Korea, the Soviet Air Force can proceed from the Sea of
Japan to the Yellow Sea via North Korea, thereby bypass-
ing and avoiding the dangerous corridor between Japan
and South Korea.

The Soviet interest in Korea is closely tied with
its overall global strategic designs.[9] Although the
Soviet force deployment in the region--both conventional
and nuclear--is aimed primarily at the countries surrounding the Soviet Union, such as China and Japan, it
has recently extended beyond the traditional line of
defense to include countries like Vietnam and possibly
North Korea. Intermediate-range nuclear delivery systems maintained by the Soviet Union in Asia include the
SS-20, a mobile missile with a range of about 5,000
kilometers, and the TU-22M Backfire, a high-performance
bomber capable of penetrating airspace at low altitudes
and high speeds. Of the 351 SS-20s (carrying three
MIRVed warheads) deployed since 1977, about 144 are
deployed in the Far East, and 80 of the more than 200

Backfire bombers are in Asia, according to the 1983
white paper on defense published by the Japan Defense
Agency.[10] The Soviet Union also has deployed considerable conventional forces in the region east of Lake
Baikal, with approximately 370,000 troops, 820 vessels
displacing over 1.6 million tons, and 2,100 aircraft.
The main components of the Soviet weaponry include MIG-
23s, long-range 130-mm cannons, and MI-24 Hind ground
attack gunship helicopters.[11]

By comparison, the United States maintains no naval
support facilities in South Korea, perhaps because the
United States has access to Japan's nearby naval facilities in Sasebo and Yokosuka. But the United States has
extensive use of air bases in South Korea in four locations: Kunsan, Osan, Suwon, and Taegu. Together with
other air bases in Japan and Okinawa, such as Iwakuni,
Atsugi, Yokota, Misawa, Futenma, and Kadena, U.S. planes
on Korean air bases provide tactical support not only to
U.S. ground forces in Yongsan and along the DMZ in Camp
Casey but also to Republic of Korea (ROK) defense
forces.

Total U.S. forces in Korea currently number about
40,462. Of these, about 29,232 are assigned to the U.S.
8th Army, which includes the 2nd infantry division, the
19th support command, supporting aviation and engineer
groups, and various smaller support units. The other
component of U.S. forces is the 314th air division, with
tactical fighter wings and squadrons located in four
separate air bases already mentioned.[12]

The U.S. deployment of forces in the region is
considerably less in number than that of the Soviets.[13]
The mainstay of the U.S. force in East Asia are U.S.
forces in Korea, with 40,000 troops and approximately
100 aircraft, and the U.S. 7th Fleet, with 230 aircraft
and 65 vessels amounting to some 670,000 tonnages. Also
about 33,000 U.S. Marines are on Okinawa assigned to the
7th Fleet. In addition, the United States can rely on
Japan Self-Defense Forces (SDF) consisting of 156,000
troops, 350 aircraft, and 166 vessels amounting to some
232,000 tons.[14] The United States can also rely on
Taiwan and possibly China for support against the Soviet
threat in the region. Whereas Taiwan maintains sizeable
military forces consisting of 330,000 troops, 547 aircraft, and 170 vessels amounting to a tonnage of 86,000,
China is Asia's largest military power with 4,000,000
regular troops, 6,100 combat aircraft, and 2,650 vessels
amounting to a tonnage of 665,000.[15]

No known deployment of nuclear warheads exists in
North Korea. However, the United States reportedly
maintains a nuclear weapons system in South Korea consisting of more than 1,000 warheads. Establishing a
nuclear-free zone for the Korean Peninsula, proposed so
far by various peace movement groups, may be a viable
option in the future, but now it is an ideal plan rather
than a practical alternative.

155

The Major Powers' Policies Toward Korea

The major powers surrounding the Korean Peninsula generally maintain an active interest in the overall situation and specific developments in each Korean state, and they actively pursue a publicly stated policy of promoting peace and stability on the peninsula. Security ties that both North and South Korea maintain with their respective allies are an indication of the strategic values and importance that the major powers attach to the Korean Peninsula. North Korea, for instance, is the only communist country that is allied with both the Soviet Union and China, by virtue of a Treaty of Friendship, Cooperation, and Mutual Assistance signed with each country in 1961. South Korea likewise is an important U.S. ally in East Asia, with the Mutual Security Treaty signed in 1954. The U.S.-ROK Joint Combined Forces (which replaced the United Nations Command) as well as annual U.S.-ROK security consultative meetings are institutional manifestations of the close security ties established between the two countries.[16] Neither North Korea nor South Korea, however, is party to multilateral defense agreements, such as the North Atlantic Treaty Organization (NATO) or the Warsaw Treaty Organization (WTO).

The United States
U.S. policy toward Korea focuses on maintaining a stable strategic and political environment through the prevention of armed conflict between the two hostile Korean states and the avoidance of hegemony on the peninsula by any outside power. Renewal of armed conflict in Korea would pose a potentially grave threat to the security of Japan, to regional stability, and to U.S. interests.[17] The presence of U.S. combat forces in South Korea is thus an important means of preserving stability on the Korean Peninsula.

In the wake of rapid change in the Asian strategic environment following Sino-U.S. rapprochement in the early 1970s, the United States has not always followed a consistent policy toward Korea, as the reversal of the ill-fated Carter administration policy on ground troops withdrawal from Korea illustrates.[18] Nevertheless, the basic U.S. policy goal of maintaining a security alliance with South Korea has remained consistent, and the Reagan administration stresses the continuing importance of close U.S.-ROK cooperation for regional stability and for bilateral trade.[19]

Japan
Japan shares a common interest with the United States in preserving regional stability and reducing tension on the Korean Peninsula as a means of promoting Japanese security and economic interests. Because of its constitutional restrictions, and the absence of defense

arrangements with either of the two Korean states, however, Japan depends heavily upon the United States to
preserve security and stability on the Korean Peninsula.
In fact, the Japanese leadership was quite reluctant to
see the withdrawal of U.S. forces under Carter, from
South Korea.[20]

The Soviet Union
Soviet policy toward the Korean Peninsula was governed
less by its bilateral relationship with North Korea than
by its concern about Sino-Soviet conflict and Soviet
rivalry with the United States and Japan.[21] The USSR's
strategic-military offensive in the Asian-Pacific since
the Vietnam War, however, seems to have led to the
reversal of its usual posture from one of limited logistic and military support to a more active and aggressive
military assistance to North Korea. As a result of this
changed Soviet policy toward North Korea under Gorbachev, in May and June 1985 the Soviet Union modified its
hitherto restraining posture by supplying North Korea
with its latest weaponry system, including MIG-23s.
Moscow, at some point, may also encourage and support a Pyongyang hardline policy toward the South, in
the hope that a major military confrontation in Korea
could split the Sino-U.S. détente and the implicit Sino-
U.S.-Japanese coalition. Furthermore, as some analysts
point out, if strategic circumstances seem favorable, as
was the case in Vietnam in the 1970s, the Soviets may
attempt to help create one large Korea dominated by pro-
Soviet Communists in order to reinforce dramatically the
Soviet position in the Western Pacific.[22]
Strategic considerations may therefore be more
important in the Soviet calculus of the Korea policy.
Conflict in Korea fostered by Soviet military and economic support, however, would accelerate pressures for
Japanese remilitarization, cause anti-Soviet collaboration among the United States, Japan, and China, and
thereby exacerbating Sino-Soviet relations. In fact,
Soviet perception of such an eventuality may underlie
the Soviet (and North Korean) criticism of an evolving
"Asian NATO" or "U.S.-Japan-ROK triangular military
alliance."

China
The People's Republic of China (PRC) appears momentari-
ly satisfied with the status quo and stability on the
Korean Peninsula. North Korea, as China sees it, serves
as an important buffer between the PRC and Western
powers, and the U.S. forces in South Korea may also help
to counter Soviet expansionism. Military confrontation
in Korea would place China in the strategic dilemma of
either supporting the Democratic People's Republic of
Korea (DPRK) and thereby jeopardizing U.S.-PRC relations
or abandoning North Korea totally to Soviet influence.
Beijing, therefore, has consistently discouraged Pyongyang's belligerence.[23]

In recent years, the Chinese have gradually increased their military and economic aid to North Korea,
including A-5 aircraft and oil supplies, and the relationship between the two countries has improved significantly, as shown by the mutual exchange of state visits
by the respective leaders. Between December 1981 and
May 1985, a total of seven mutual visits by high-level
leaders took place between the two countries and involved Kim Il-Sung and Kim Jong-Il (for North Korea) and
Deng Xiaoping, Hu Yaobang, and Zhao Ziyang (for China).
Although Chinese efforts are aimed at preventing near
total North Korean dependence on the Soviet Union, it is
uncertain whether such a policy will continue to be
successful. Due to limited Chinese industrial and military capabilities, Chinese support has not significantly
affected the security balance on the Korean Peninsula.
If China's Korea policy fails, it will no doubt undermine the Chinese efforts at countering Soviet encirclement of the PRC.

Korea's Shifting Balance of Power

North and South Korea, as allies of the Soviet
Union and the United States, respectively, are valuable
strategic assets because they would most likely provide
support to the war efforts in a future hypothetical war
between the two superpowers in the region. Therefore,
the shifting power balance between the two hostile Korean states will have broader security and strategic implications, not only for the Korean Peninsula but also
for the contingency planning of the superpowers.

The Military Balance
The military balance between communist North Korea and
noncommunist South Korea in the 1980s, according to many
analysts, favors North Korea over South Korea. However,
the successful completion of the ongoing Force Improvement Plan (FIP) II (1982-1987) in the ROK may eventually
lead to a situation whereby the South will come to
surpass the North. Nevertheless, the military balance
between the two Koreas will remain relatively constant
and evenly matched for the remainder of the 1980s.[24]
Both Korean regimes maintain a huge military establishment that is undoubtedly beyond their individual
means of support. In 1984, North Korea, for instance,
maintained a large military force consisting of a total
of 784,000 troops, 740 aircrafts, and 490 vessels
amounting to 66,000 tonnages, and South Korea had a
military force consisting of 622,000 troops, 440 aircrafts, and 110 vessels amounting to 89,000 tonnages
(see Table 7.1).[25]
At the time of this writing, North Korea is said to
possess a substantial advantage over the South in overall quantity of military equipment as a result of its
intensive defense buildup during the 1970s. North Korea,

TABLE 7.1   Comparison of North and South Korean
            Military Postures, 1984

	North Korea	South Korea
Population, 1984	19,600,000	41,600,000
Total Active Forces	784,500	622,000
Total Reserve Forces	300,000	1,540,000
Paramilitary Forces[a]	4,138,000	4,400,000
Military Expenditures as % of GNP		
1980 estimate	18.9	6.6
1982 estimate	21.6	6.9
Army	700,000	540,000
Armored Divisions[b]	2	0
Mechanized Divisions[b]	3	2
Infantry Divisions[b]	34	20
Navy	33,500	49,000
Submarines	21	0
Destroyers (Frigates)	0(4)	11(8)
Naval Bases	9	8
Air Force	51,000	33,000
Combat Aircraft	740	440
	incl. 290 MIG-15/17	incl. 260 F-5A
	100 MIG-19	70 F-86F
	160 MIG-21	72 F-4D/E

Sources: The International Institute for Strategic Studies, The
Military Balance, 1984-85 (London: IISS, 1984), pp. 102-104; U.S.
Arms Control & Disarmament Agency, World Military Expenditures &
Arms Transfers, 1972-1982 (Washington, D.C.: Arms Control and Dis-
armament Agency, April 1984), p. 33.

[a]paramilitary forces include security forces, border guards, militia, etc.
[b]North Korean divisions are modeled after USSR/PRC divisions and
number about 10,000 men, about 65 percent of the strength of a
South Korean division. The latter follows U.S. division organization. Most of the manpower differences lie, however, in combat
support and logistics troops, and the North Korean divisions are
roughly equivalent to the combat strength of South Korean
divisions.

for instance, has allocated some 20 to 25 percent of its
Gross National Product (GNP) to military spending. In
1984, North Korea's 784,000-man armed force (out of a
population of 19.6 million) was highly disciplined. The
stockpile of North Korean military equipment in major
categories--armor, artillery, ships, and aircraft--was
also estimated to be more than twice that of the South.
The North was judged by military analysts to hold a
clear military advantage, with offensive capabilities
fashioned precisely to the battlefield's tactical contours.   North Korea is also believed to maintain a
large commando force of approximately 100,000 men (the

8th special corps) whose primary mission is to create a second front in rear areas of the South.

South Korea has been expanding its military modernization program since the late 1970s under FIP I (1976-1982) and FIP II (1982-1987), in a delayed response to the North's military buildup. South Korea's military budget has been increased substantially and is almost 6 percent of the GNP. South Korea's 622,000-man armed force in 1984 (out of a population of 41.6 million) was well trained, and the South might retain a qualitative advantage in military equipment, including aircraft and ground weapons. These are not sufficient, however, according to military analysts, to offset the quantitative disadvantages of South Korea's military establishment.

The arms race and existing military imbalance between the two Korean states will continue, however, as each Korean regime outspends its opponent in defense and also acquires the latest advanced equipment from the respective allies. These include the promised sale of 36 F-16s and 1,000 M55-1 light tanks to the South and the acquisition of MIG-23s and T-72 tanks for the North.[27]

The Economic Race

South Korea generally enjoys far more advanced economic and industrial capabilities than the North.[28] In 1982, the South Korean GNP (U.S. $70.8 billion) was more than four to five times that of the North (U.S. $13.6 billion), and the total volume of the South's foreign trade was more than ten times that of the North.[29] South Korean technology is also far superior to that of the North in almost every category.

Both Korean economies suffered in the wake of worldwide economic recession in the early 1980s. High inflation, worldwide oil shocks, and uncertain supplies of other key raw materials all adversely affected South Korean economic growth and stability. Due to the rising pressures of protectionism in world trade, South Korea's export of manufactured products did not increase as rapidly as in the 1970s. North Korea's economic problems appear to be even more serious as a result of heavy defense expenditures, increasing foreign debts (approximately $3.5 billion), and lagging technology.[30]

Soviet and Chinese economic aid to North Korea is not sufficient to enable the North to catch up with South Korea's economic and industrial advances. Under such circumstances, the North seems to have no alternative but to turn outward economically, patterning itself after China's successful program of economic reform measures and the four modernizations. The new joint venture law enacted on September 8, 1984, together with "the trade development resolution" adopted on January 26, 1984, by the 3rd Session of the 7th Supreme People's Assembly is an expression of North Korea's altered economic development strategy.[31]

THREAT PERCEPTION AND DIPLOMATIC MANEUVERS

The changing security environment in East Asia is perceived by the respective Korean leaderships to be potentially destabilizing and threatening to the viability of their system. To overcome the perceived threat, the two Korean states took measures to strengthen their security and security ties with their allies and also initiated a series of diplomatic maneuvers vis-à-vis the major powers in the region. Legitimacy, security, and development are the strategic goals pursued by both Korean regimes ever since their establishment in 1948. The abnormal partition of the Land of the Morning Calm into two hostile and antagonistic political systems has accentuated the security concerns of the ruling elites of North and South Korea. Both Korean states and their citizens have been gripped by a "siege mentality"--deep-seated anxiety and fear prevail in both North and South Korea. Diplomatic moves and initiatives, including the recently revived inter-Korea dialogue and negotiation in 1984, are attempts, both psychological and political, by the leadership in each state to cope with the rapidly changing environment surrounding the Korean Peninsula.[33]

North Korea Vis-à-vis the Major Powers

Threat Perception and Security Policy
From Kim Il-Sung's perspective, "U.S. imperialism" is North Korea's number one enemy and the main stumbling block to Korea's reunification.[34] It is no wonder, then, that U.S. troop withdrawal from South Korea is North Korea's first foreign policy objective. North Korea's strategic objectives vis-à-vis South Korea, consistently upheld throughout the 1970s and 1980s, are: (1) withdrawal of U.S. troops from the South; (2) "democratization" of South Korea, i.e., via a communist-sponsored revolution, if necessary; and (3) building the "revolutionary" base of operation in the North through the "socialist revolution and construction" under the Korean Workers party (KWP) auspices.[35]

North Korea's chaju (independence) and juche (self-reliance) posture on the Sino-Soviet rivalry is greatly strained because of the diplomatic moves that grew from the Sino-U.S. rapprochement in 1971 and normalization of diplomatic relations between Washington and Beijing in 1979. Pyongyang's delicate relations with Beijing and Moscow, neither of which appears to be perceived by the North Koreans as a truly reliable ally, have been strained in the 1980s. In an attempt to assert North Korea's independence and to exercise diplomatic leverage, Kim Il-Sung initiated a series of diplomatic moves to enhance his personal prestige and status that included the exchange of mutual visits with China in 1983, 1984, and 1985 and the visit by Kim to Moscow and Eastern Europe in May-June 1984.

One of the tangible outcomes of Kim's Moscow visit, although no joint communiqué was issued at the time, was the Soviet assurance of assistance to North Korea in upgrading military hardware and equipment. As a result of the subsequent thirteen-day visit by Soviet Deputy Foreign Minister Mikhail Kapitsa to Pyongyang in November 1984, the Soviet Union reportedly agreed to supply North Korea with advanced MIG-23 jetfighters and T-72 tanks.[36]

North Korea's threat perception in the 1980s was accentuated by a series of military exercises involving both ROK and U.S. troops in South Korea. North Korea specifically criticized the annual U.S.-ROK joint military exercises called Team Spirit, objecting to what it calls the policy of reviving "Japanese militarism" as well as the forming of a U.S.-Japan-South Korea "triangular military alliance."[37]

North Korea's response to its perceived security threat was to beef up its own defense posture and to initiate diplomatic moves to counter the perceived security threat. Thus, in a major operation during the three-year period between 1983 and 1985, North Korea has reportedly redeployed large numbers of troops into approximately one hundred underground bunkers close to the Demilitarized Zone (DMZ).[38] Three underground bunkers, reportedly located twelve to eighteen miles from the DMZ, also can accommodate large numbers of men and supplies. These new troop movements will greatly reduce the length of time it would take the North Koreans to launch a large-scale invasion, if they so desire. The troop movements, however, do not seem to represent an increase in overall North Korean military strength, according to U.S. officials; instead, it represents a redeployment of rear-echelon troops to new positions near the DMZ.[39]

Diplomatic Initiatives and Maneuvers
Pyongyang's tripartite talks proposal, involving South Korea in what basically appears to be a two-way discussion between the United States and North Korea, was officially made public on January 10, 1984, and clearly represents its latest effort to negotiate a U.S. troop withdrawal from the South. North Korea's primary objective is also to replace the existing armistice agreement with a peace treaty. The tripartite talks proposal was interpreted by many Western observers as a tactical move, especially after the October 1983 Rangoon bombing, to achieve one of Pyongyang's triple strategic goals.

Pyongyang first moved diplomatically to improve its security and diplomatic ties with both Beijing and Moscow. Kim Il-Sung paid a nine-day state visit to China in September 1982, followed by an unofficial visit to China by his son, Kim Jong-Il, in June 1983.[40] The Chinese party leader Hu Yaobang paid an eight-day official visit to North Korea in May 1984 and was greeted by "the greatest welcome in Korean history," according to

the North Korean media.[41]   In addition, the leaders of
the two countries exchanged numerous "informal" mutual
visits for continuous policy consultation, such as Kim
Il-Sung's "unofficial" four-day visit to Beijing (October 23-27) in 1984 and Hu Yaobang's three-day unofficial
visit (May 4-6) to Shinuiju, North Korea's border town,
in 1985.
     The agenda and agreements of these and other simi-
lar meetings are not known to outsiders.   One South
Korean source speculated, however, regarding the May
1985 Hu-Kim meeting, that North Korea had strenuously
objected to China's relaxed posture toward South Korea
as evidenced by South Korea's negotiation with China in
March 1985 over the return of the latter's PT boat and
its crew.   North Korea also pressured China, according
to the same source, to reverse China's contemplated
approval of U.S. fleet vessels' visit to Shanghai on May
18, 1985, a decision that was subsequently rescinded by
China on the grounds of disagreement over the nuclear
disclosure issue.[42]   If this speculation about Pyongyang's role in pressuring China to reverse its decision
regarding the U.S. visit to Shanghai is correct, it
means that North Korea still exercises leverage in major
power relations.
     Five days after Hu Yaobang left North Korea in May
1984, Kim Il-Sung embarked upon an ambitious forty-five-
day trip abroad that took him to Moscow and to the East
European countries.   Although no joint communiqué was
issued following a three-day stay in Moscow and meetings
between Kim Il-Sung and the Soviet President Konstantin
Chernenko, Kim's 1984 Moscow visit was important as it
was his first visit to Moscow in twenty-three years.   It
signified his willingness to improve close ties with the
Soviets.   Soviet Deputy Foreign Minister Mikhail Kapitsa
was also in North Korea on November 11-27, 1984, to
negotiate a new border treaty, which was signed in
Moscow by North Korean Foreign Minister Kim Young Nam in
April 1985.
     Soviet First Deputy Premier Geidar Aliyev led a
twenty-three-member government delegation to Pyongyang
in August 1985 to attend the celebration of the fortieth
anniversary of Korea's liberation from Japan on August
15, 1945.   He was accompanied by First Deputy Minister
of Defense Marshall Vasily Petrov, who reportedly agreed
to offer "around 40" MIG-23s and future delivery of SAMs
to North Korea.[43]   To underscore the importance of the
new Soviet-North Korea military cooperation, three Soviet warships arrived on August 13 in Wonsan on the Sea of
Japan, the first Soviet naval visit to a North Korean
port.
     Noteworthy in this regard is the fact that China
did not receive an invitation from North Korea to attend
the ceremony commemorating Korea's liberation.   China's
absence during the celebration was clearly an expression
of North Korea's diplomatic disfavor of the PRC.   If and
when North Korea permits a similar visit of Soviet

warships to its port in the Yellow Sea, such a move will
clearly indicate a pro-Soviet stance by North Korea
because North Korea's nearest port lies less than 200
miles from the home port of the Chinese Northern Fleet
in Qingdao.[44]   All of these diplomatic maneuvers by
North Korea vis-à-vis its allies are an ominous sign of
North Korea's continued strategic role as the balancer
between Beijing and Moscow, and of North Korea's effort
to remain independent in the Sino-Soviet hegemonic
conflict.

South Korea Vis-à-vis the Major Powers

Threat Perception and Security Policy
To South Korea's Fifth Republic, the security goal also
overrides all others, including legitimacy and development. Once the question of legitimacy had been temporarily set aside, with the founding in 1981 of the Fifth
Republic, the question of South Korea's national security vis-à-vis North Korea reemerged as the foremost priority for South Korea's policy.   In his inaugural speech
on March 3, 1981, President Chun Doo Hwan affirmed the
importance of national security when he said that "no
matter how fine our goals, they are meaningless unless
our national security is unflinchingly preserved. We
must not relax our guard for even the most fleeting
moment; in light of our unique geopolitical position, we
must keep an unblinking watch on the volatile situations
surrounding the Korean Peninsula, as well as on the
unpredictable global scene in the 1980s."[45]
    The source of South Korea's threat perception is,
of course, the alleged "aggressive" intentions of North
Korea. "We live under constant threat of military invasion from the north" because, as Chun put it, "during
the past 10 years, North Korea has aggressively built up
arms, dug infiltration tunnels, and set guerrillas and
provocateurs into the south."[46]   The United States is
considered an ally that could help South Korea overcome
the perceived security threat from the North.   From
South Korea's perspective two matters are particularly
worrisome: increased Soviet military assistance to North
Korea and possible reduction in the level of U.S. security commitment to South Korea.
    South Korea has come to be less fearful of China
ever since the U.S.-China diplomatic normalization of
1979, but it is increasingly more fearful of the Soviet
Union.   A series of dramatic events led to Seoul's
differing perceptions of the USSR and the PRC. The
shooting down of KAL flight 007 on September 1, 1983,
over the Sea of Japan off Sakhalin Island, reinforced
South Korea's fear of the Soviet Union and reinforced
its image of the USSR as a "militant" and "dangerous"
country hostile to South Korea. The negotiation on the
release of China's civil airliner and its crews in 1983,
after it was hijacked and forcibly landed on South

Korea's soil, gave South Korea an invaluable diplomatic
opening for official contacts with Beijing. This was
followed in March 1985 by another successful negotiation
of the return to China of China's PT boat and its crew
after the boat had been taken into South Korea's port
city of Kunsan.

South Korea's image of the Soviet Union as a hostile power is of long standing. The U.S. military
presence in Korea is defended on the grounds that it
plays a "strategic role" in the U.S.-Soviet rivalry.
Korea, according to Chun Doo Hwan, "is after all a
bulwark of defense for the Free World, especially Japan
and the United States in the Pacific Basin. So, working
together, we and the U.S. forces serve to restrain,
serve the stay of hands of Soviet expansionism in Northeast Asia, and particularly to diminish the possibility
of Soviet Russia using North Korea as a proxy and creating major strife in that critically important region.
That is the role, that is the strategic role, that the
United States forces are playing."[47]

Diplomatic Initiatives and Maneuvers
Two important diplomatic trips were initiated by President Chun Doo Hwan in 1984 and 1985: a three-day state
visit to Japan in early September 1984 and a working-
level visit to the United States in late April 1985.
These trips were ostensibly to strengthen South Korea's
relationship with Japan and security ties with the
United States. Earlier in 1983, Japan's Prime Minister
Yasuhiro Nakasone paid a state visit to Seoul in January; U.S. President Ronald Reagan came to South Korea in
November 1983.

Chun's Japan visit, his first foreign travel since
the October 1983 Rangoon incident that killed seventeen
South Korean officials and narrowly missed him, was the
first state visit to Japan ever made by a Korean head of
state. Although Chun was able to extract the Emperor's
expression of "regrets" and Prime Minister Nakasone's
"apology" for Japan's thirty-five-year colonial rule of
Korea (1910-1945), he failed to obtain Japan's conces-
sion on the trade imbalance between the two countries,
an imbalance that amounted in 1983 to $2.8 billion in
Japan's favor. Nevertheless, Chun received the Japanese
prime minister's pledges not only to help promote
Seoul's overtures toward China and the Soviet Union but
also to support Chun's proposal for direct talks between
North and South Korea.[48]

President Chun's 1985 Washington visit, the second
such visit in four years, was low key and meant to
institutionalize political consultations between the two
countries. Included on the agenda of consultations was
Seoul's desire to receive extra military credits and to
extract trade concessions from the United States. President Reagan, in his welcoming remarks, reiterated U.S.
support for "Chun's commitment to a peaceful transfer of
power at the end of his term in 1988" and also reaf-

firmed the "strong and multifaceted ties" with Seoul
that "remain the linchpin of peace in Northeast Asia."[49]
At a subsequent news conference on board a special plane
returning to Korea, Chun claimed that President Reagan
agreed to his view that the coming three to four years
would be "most crucial to the security of the Korean
peninsula."[50]
    Chun's meeting with Reagan was followed by a regu-
lar, annual security conference in Washington, D.C., on
May 7-8, 1985, between the defense ministers of the two
countries. Included on the agenda were possible coun-
termeasures to be taken against North Korea's recent
acquisition of eighty-seven Hughes helicopters, trans-
mitted by a third country in violation of U.S. law.
Seoul reportedly mentioned AWACS and new electronic
identification gear as a way of preventing North Korean
helicopters from sneaking into the South, which also is
equipped with the Hughes helicopters. On the trade
front, South Korea's complaint about growing U.S. protectionism was not well received in Washington, which in
turn reminded South Korea of its trade surplus with the
United States, which rose 39 percent in 1984, and its
"closed market" to certain U.S. products.[51] In spite of
these trade disputes, Seoul was able to reaffirm its
strong security ties with the United States.

Inter-Korean Dialogue and Negotiation

    North-South Korean Red Cross talks to bring about
the possible reunion of 10 million dispersed families
were resumed after a twelve-year lapse as the two sides
agreed to hold the eighth regular meeting in Seoul on
May 28-29, and the ninth meeting in Pyongyang on August
26-27, 1985. Inter-Korean economic talks were also held
in Panmunjom on May 16, 1985, after a lapse of six
months since the first historic meeting.[52] This was
followed by the third economic talks in July and a
preliminary meeting of the interparliamentary talks in
Panmunjom in July 1985. These developments represent
efforts by both Korean regimes to move ahead on the
front of inter-Korean dialogue and negotiations.
    The North-South Korean dialogue, initiated in 1971,
remained deadlocked and stalemated throughout the pre-
1984 period because of conflicting interests and expectations. The South Korean policy, for instance, was
based on a posture of incrementalism, a "step-by-step"
approach toward gradual integration of North and South
Korea through cultural and economic exchanges during the
initial stage and political negotiations at later
stages. The North Korean policy, on the other hand, was
based on a posture of simultaneous problemsolving--
dramatic steps taken on several fronts that are aimed at
achieving immediate unification, such as the founding of
the Democratic Confederal Republic of Koryo (DCRK).[53]
    Underlying the divergent unification policy

positions is a difference in strategic calculation and estimation shared by "two regimes in contest." The position outlined by the South, for instance, emphasizes greater security and the guarantee of stability as preconditions in the unification process. The North, in turn, declares that the prerequisites for unification include the withdrawal of U.S. forces from South Korea, the scrapping of South and North Korean defense treaties with third countries, and the replacement of the armistice agreement of 1953 with a peace treaty.[54]

South Korea's "peace first, unification later" position is closely tied with and reflected in its military-strategic policy toward North Korea. South Korea's posture basically is defensive and reactive, stressing deterrence, i.e., prevention of any armed conflict on the Korean Peninsula. North Korea's "unification first, peace later" position, on the other hand, is based on its assessment that the U.S. military presence in Korea is the main obstacle to Korean unification and poses the primary threat to North Korean security. For this reason North Korea, in 1973, adopted a new strategy by boycotting the North-South negotiation process and seeking, instead, direct bilateral talks with Washington in 1974 and, since 1984, tripartite talks that involve South Korea in the process.

The divergent perceptions and expectations underlying the negotiation strategies are clearly present in the current round of inter-Korean dialogue in 1984. An important breakthrough suddenly occurred in September 1984 when the South Korean Red Cross Society announced that it would accept the North Korean Red Cross Society's offer to send relief goods to flood victims in the South. As a result, on September 29-30, 1984, North Korea delivered 50,000 suk (14,300 tons) of rice, 100,000 tons of cement, 500,000 square meters of textiles, and medical supplies by truck via the land route through Panmunjom and by cargo vessels docking at the port cities of Inchon on the west coast and Pukpyong on the east coast.[55]

Included in the list of North Korea's latest peace initiatives is the proposal of April 9, 1985, to hold talks between the two legislative bodies of North and South Korea to deliberate the possibility of issuing a North-South joint declaration of nonaggression. South Korea responded positively on June 4, proposing that preliminary contact between the two sides be established in July in Panmunjom to deliberate the possibility of drafting a united constitution for North and South Korea. The economic talks in Panmunjom and the Red Cross talks in Seoul and Pyongyang are welcome developments in the service of lessening tensions on the Korean Peninsula.

These initiatives are also positive news for the prospect of normalizing inter-Korean relations and for promoting peace and eventual reunification of divided Korea. However, these steps, like the earlier tripartite talks proposal of January 1984, may not bear the intended fruit unless they are positively reinforced by both sides and are seen as genuine measures for promoting peace and unification rather than smokescreens for disguising aggressive intentions.[56]

The strategic environment in Northeast Asia has improved considerably in 1985 for the prospect of a breakthrough in inter-Korean relations. The two Korean regimes have carried out intensive policy consultation with their respective allies in recent years, and they also appear to be ready to face each other in a series of serious intergovernmental negotiations and in bargaining on the issues of peace and unification. President Kim Il-Sung of the DPRK, as noted, paid numerous visits to China, both official and unannounced, in 1983 and 1985, as well as the long-awaited official visit to Moscow in May 1984. President Chun Doo Hwan of the ROK also paid an official visit to Japan in September 1984 and a working-level visit to the United States in April 1985. The recent series of moves to allow South Korean diplomats to visit China, and North Korean journalists and athletes to visit Japan, are further evidence of readiness on the part of the major powers to accommodate the interests of the respective Korean regimes for the sake of improving peace and stability on the Korean Peninsula.

PROSPECTS AND IMPLICATIONS

What are the future prospects for peace in divided Korea? What are the possible scenarios and contending issues? What policy implications follow from recent diplomatic activities that directly and indirectly concern the Korean Peninsula?

Prospects

Broadly speaking, either war or peace is the option facing the Korean Peninsula. Between these two theoretical possibilities are a number of probable intermediary situations including (1) confrontation; (2) coexistence; (3) cooperation, either limited or active; (4) integration, either sectoral or broad; and (5) unification. The situation that prevails in the mid-1980s is one of confrontation, which if the current inter-Korean negotiation is successful, may lead to coexistence or even to limited cooperation.

The policy issues confronting the respective Korean regimes in the future are also political, economic, social, and cultural in nature, and they also have time dimensions that are either short term or long term. From a short-term perspective, both Korean regimes are likely to face the challenge of assuring the political stability and continuity of their political systems.

Both North and South Korea must resolve the issue of how to allow a smooth transition of power by enabling an orderly and predictable political succession of the leadership. Kim Il-Sung has already designated his son, Kim Jong-Il, to succeed him in a manner resembling the hereditary, or dynastic, succession of the old regimes. Whether such an arrangement is acceptable to the people of North Korea, assuming that "the masses are masters of their own destiny" as Kim Il-Sung's preaching of mass-line politics would lead us to believe, will be known only after the death of Kim Il-Sung. Chun Doo Hwan also announced that he would not seek a second presidential term after completing his first seven-year term in 1988. The next president of each Korea, and the segments of the population he or she represents, is an important political issue for the future survival of both Koreas.

Other short-term issues that South Korea faces include reconciliation on the issue of the 1980 Kwangju Uprising, for which President Chun Doo Hwan's government was charged by the opposition as responsible; successful completion of the 1988 Summer Olympics in Seoul, which North Korea announced it would boycott and oppose, although it lately proposed to "cohost" the Olympics with South Korea; taming of the hard-line military faction that may not go along with many of the Chun Doo Hwan policies; finding a solution to the student activism, which has resulted in continuous anti-government campus demonstrations; and sustaining the momentum of economic growth by expanding the export sector of the economy and holding inflationary pressures down.

North Korea likewise faces a number of short-term policy issues: invigorating the stagnant economy by obtaining new technology and enticing investment capital from abroad; reconciling the old ideology of self-reliance as symbolized by the juche idea with a new policy of promoting joint ventures with foreign capital; and transition from the old to the new generation of leadership in the party, army, and bureaucracy. The latter concern was manifest in the Three Revolution Team movement, a campaign organized and led by Kim Jong-Il.[57]

In the long run, only time will tell whether any or most of these short-term issues will be resolved smoothly and successfully and thereby lead to the survival and viability of the respective political systems beyond the life span of their incumbent leaders. Assuming that no second Korean war will occur in the foreseeable future, and that inter-Korean coexistence and limited cooperation will continue, the respective Korean states will emerge as economically developing and industrializing countries. South Korea's emergence into a NIC (newly industrializing country) status will enable it to join the ranks of the mature and developed industrialized countries, so that South Korea now will be eligible for membership in the Organization of Economic Cooperation and Development (OECD). North Korea's turn outward economically, which emulates China's new economic policy, may also provide a new stimulus to the centrally planned and stagnant economy by injecting new technology and capital from the outside world under the joint venture laws recently enacted.

The long-term prospects for a unified Korea through economic integration or political union seem less sanguine and likely from the perspective of 1985. The existing arms race and heightened tension on the Korean Peninsula, unless disarmament and arms control measures are taken immediately, will continue to persist and make Korea one of the most sensitive and dangerous security flashpoints in the world. It is hard to believe that the Korean conflict has been prolonged for so long. It is more than forty years since the initial partitioning of the peninsula in 1945 and more than three decades since the Korean War ended in 1953. The Korean armistice agreement is one of the oldest truce regimes in effect and still observed, so the necessity for concluding a peace treaty to replace the armistice agreement, when and if circumstances are right, has not diminished.

In the absence of a breakthrough in the current inter-Korean dialogue and negotiation on unification, however, there is no compelling reason to assume the existing armistice regime will cease to function or the current tensions will end in the near future. Without first abandoning mutual suspicion and distrust and restoring political will and mutual confidence, no positive and meaningful inter-Korean interaction is likely to occur in the forseeable future. Because of the delicate balance between domestic political issues and foreign policy issues, especially in relation to diplomacy and national security in the South, the future problems of Korean politics will become more complex and difficult to resolve. Given the geopolitical role and significance that the Korean Peninsula occupies in global and regional politics, no major powers surrounding the Korean Peninsula seem to favor a drastic and abrupt change in the status quo prevailing on the Korean Peninsula. The more it changes, the more it seems that the Korean situation symbolized by the current "regimes in contest" will remain the same, insofar as the long-term prospect of Korea is concerned.[58]

Implications

What implications arise from the preceding analysis, especially in terms of the possible impact of a divided Korea on regional and U.S. policies? If the scenario of "continued confrontation" between the two Korean regimes proves to be valid, the situation in the Korean Peninsula for the rest of the century will remain similar to what has transpired since 1945, i.e., heightened tension and institutionalization of the war system.

On the other hand, if the scenario of "limited cooperation" and even active inter-Korean interaction

result from successful North-South Korean dialogue and
negotiation on unification, the prospect for peace in
Korea will improve measurably, although the situation
may also become increasingly complex and volatile. More
conflict issues will prove difficult to resolve because
of a greater tendency in both Koreas to link domestic
politics and security-diplomatic policy issues.

The two Korean societies will become more integrated into a system of mutual dependence psychologically and culturally, so that each will be increasingly
subject to pressures emanating from the opposite side.
Although both systems will grow more sensitive to each
other's strength and weakness, pluralistic South Korea
will be more vulnerable to outside pressures, at least
in the short run, than monolithic North Korea.

Future development on the Korean Peninsula will
also influence the major powers' policies and attitudes
toward the respective Korean states. Because the United
States is an architect and active participant in the
current system of divided Korea, the future direction of
U.S.-Korea relations will affect the situation on the
Korean Peninsula. From a broader historical perspective, U.S.-Korea relations have had many ups and downs
characterized by both initial aloof contact and subsequent intimacy, or what Bruce Cumings in 1980 called "a
century of contact and thirty-five years of intimacy." [59]
The current active phase of U.S.-Korea policy, one of
"involvement and intervention," is motivated largely by
U.S. perception of Korea's geopolitical role and importance as part of the post-World War II "internationalist policy" of the cold war era.[60]   During the post-
World War II era "no Asian nation has been in more
intense, sustained, and conflictual relations with the
United States than Korea," as one noted student reminds
us.[61]

From the macroscopic and structural perspective,
however, no nation's policies, including the U.S.-Korea
policy, may be considered "enduring," in the sense that
diplomatic policies are never permanent but are more
likely a reflection and interpretation of particular
sets of interests. From this realistic perspective,
then, U.S.-Korea policy is bound to change as it has in
the past. In fact, "Korea has never mattered much to
Americans for its intrinsic interest or characteristics,
but only as it relates to some broader concern," Cumings
observed. "Indeed, one can question whether it is proper to speak of mutuality in this relationship at all,
since the influence has been so strongly one-way." [62]
How long the United States will continue as the single
most influential global power, especially in the face of
U.S. response to Soviet expansion in the Pacific, remains to be seen. As long as the United States remains
the principal global power, however, the intrinsic value
of the Korean Peninsula will continue to be obvious and
so Korea will continue to be an important piece on the
chessboard of U.S. geopolitical strategy.

CONCLUSION

Both Korean states share similar, although diamet-
rically opposed, perceptions of security concerns and
threats from the outside. Soviet expansion in the Pacific is naturally a matter of serious concern and a
security threat to South Korea. But South Korea shares
such a concern with other major powers in the region,
such as the United States, Japan, and China. The continued U.S. military presence in South Korea is the
dominant security concern of North Korea, which genuinely feels threatened. It also feels increasingly isolated because China, its foremost ally, has turned toward the West and joined a de facto anti-Soviet entente
with the United States and Japan. North Korea has
sought Soviet support in its denunciation of the U.S.-
ROK military exercises (Team Spirit), the revival of
"Japanese militarism," and the emerging "triple military
alliance" of the United States, Japan, and the ROK.[63]
The primary source of external threats to each
Korea is, of course, the presence of an antagonistic and
rival regime on the opposite side of the DMZ that divides the peninsula into the two "regimes in contest."[64]
But both Korean regimes are basically cautious and suspicious of outside forces, lest the Great Power "scheme
and machination" would be done, once again, at the
expense of the future welfare and interest of the Korean
people.
This is why both Korean states have agreed to
pursue inter-Korean dialogue and negotiation on unification. Since territorial partitioning of Korea by the
Great Powers at the end of World War II in 1945 was
imposed upon the Korean people as a fait accompli,
without participation of the Korean people in the decisionmaking, the nationalist-minded Korean people desire
reunification of their divided land as a matter of right
and justice. The threefold principle of national unification, as contained in the July 4, 1972, Joint Communiqué of North-South Dialogue to which both Korean regimes
subscribe, represents the broad consensus of the Korean
people. These principles stipulate that Korean unification will be achieved by (1) independent efforts, without interference by and resort to external forces, (2)
peaceful means, without resort to war or the use of
force, and (3) through a greater national unity that
transcends ideas, ideology, and systems.
The reality of Korea's strategic value and importance will, nevertheless, continue to dominate the deci-
sionmaker's perspective and perception of Korea's place
in the region. Korea's geopolitics will continue to
ensnare both Korean regimes in a web of complex and
complicated alliance systems. As long as major power
relations surrounding the Korean Peninsula, i.e., U.S.-
Soviet, Sino-Soviet, and Japan-Soviet relations, do not
improve, but remain basically hostile and antagonistic,
the respective Korean states will be unable to decouple

172

themselves from the entangled alliance network. Korea, under the circumstances, will remain more of a dependent than an independent variable in the equation and on the altar of power politics.

NOTES

1. Recent studies on Korean security, in English, include: Sang-Woo Rhee, Security and Unification of Korea (Seoul: Sogang University Press, 1984); Young Choi, "The North Korean Military Buildup and Its Impacts on North Korean Military Strategy in the 1980s," Asian Survey 25, no. 3 (March 1985):341-355; Young-Ho Lee, "Military Balance and Peace in the Korean Peninsula," Asian Survey 21, no. 8 (August 1981):852-864; Edward N. Luttwak and Steven L. Canby, "The Defense of Korea," in Robert L. Downen, ed., Northeast Asia in the 1980s: Challenge and Opportunity (Washington, D.C.: CSIS, 1983); William Scully, "The Korean Peninsula Military Balance," Backgrounder No. 2 of Asian Studies Center (Washington, D.C.: Heritage Foundations, 1983); Franklin B. Weinstein and Fuji Kamiya, eds., The Security of Korea: U.S. and Japanese Perspectives on the 1980s (Boulder, Colo.: Westview, 1980); Joseph A. Yager, "The Security Environment of the Korean Peninsula in the 1980s," Asian Perspective (Seoul) 8, no. 1 (Spring-Summer 1984):85-105.
2. Young Whan Kihl, Politics and Policies in Divided Korea: Regimes in Contest (Boulder, Colo.: Westview, 1984), pp. xi-xii, 145-150.
3. Military analysts disagree as to whether the military balance between North and South Korea is evenly matched or is in favor of the North. The trend, however, seems to be toward an arms equilibrium between the two Koreas.
4. Yager, "Security Environment," p. 85.
5. Ibid.
6. Young Whan Kihl, "North Korea: A Reevaluation," Current History 81, no. 474 (April 1982):181.
7. Sankei Shimbun, 18 April 1985, as cited in Korea Herald, 18 April 1985.
8. Young Whan Kihl, "North Korea in 1983: Transforming 'The Hermit Kingdom'?" Asian Survey 24, no. 2 (January 1984):105.
9. Donald S. Zagoria, ed., Soviet Policy in East Asia (New Haven: Yale University Press, 1982); see, especially, Ralph N. Clough, "The Soviet Union and the Two Koreas," in Zagoria, Soviet Policy, pp. 175-200.
10. Japan Defense Agency, Defense of Japan, 1983, as cited in Japan Economic Institute Report, no. 8A (Washington, D.C., JEI, 1985), p. 8.
11. Ibid.
12. Scully, "Korean Military Balance," p. 14; also, see Appendix B.
13. For details, see chapters 2 and 3 of this book.
14. Defense of Japan, 1983.
15. Far Eastern Economic Review, Asia 1985 Yearbook, 20 November 1984, pp. 26-27, 30; also see Appendix B.
16. Chae-Jin Lee and Hideo Sato, U.S. Policy Toward Japan and Korea (New York: Praeger, 1982).

17. Nathan N. White, U.S. Policy Toward Korea: Analysis, Alternatives, and Recommendation (Boulder, Colo.: Westview, 1979).

18. Larry Niksch, "U.S. Troop Withdrawal from South Korea: Past Shortcomings and Future Prospects," Asian Survey 21, no. 3 (March 1981):325-341.

19. Paul D. Wolfowitz, Recent Security Developments in Korea, U.S. Department of State, Current Policy, no. 731, 12 August 1985.

20. Weinstein, Security of Korea.

21. Young Whan Kihl, "Sorenno Kanhanto Seisaku" [Soviet Policy Toward the Korean Peninsula], Koria Hyoron 270 (November-December 1984):3-15; Clough, "The Soviet Union," pp. 175-176.

22. White, U.S. Policy Toward Korea.

23. Young Whan Kihl, "North Korea in 1984: The 'Hermit Kingdom' Turns Outward!" Asian Survey 25, no. 1 (January 1985):65-79.

24. Scully, "Korean Military Balance."

25. Defense of Japan, 1983; The International Institute for Strategic Studies, The Military Balance 1984-85 (London: IISS, 1984).

26. Choi, "North Korean Military Buildup,"; U.S., Congress, Senate, Committee on Foreign Relations, U.S. Troop Withdrawal from the Republic of Korea, A Report to the Committee by Senators Hubert H. Humphrey and John Glenn, 95th cong., 2d sess., 9 January 1979.

27. Scully, "Korean Military Balance," p. 14.

28. U.S. Central Intelligence Agency, Korea: The Economic Race Between the North and the South: A Research Paper (Washington, D.C.: National Assessment Center and the Library of Congress, 1978).

29. National Unification Board, A Comparative Study of the South and North Korean Economies (Seoul: ROK National Unnification Board, 1984), p. 32.

30. Kihl, Politics and Policies, pp. 155-157.

31. Kihl, North Korea in 1984, pp. 69-70.

32. Byung Chul Koh, The Foriegn Policy Systems of North and South Korea (Berkeley: University of California Press, 1984), pp. 8-14.

33. On inter-Korean dialogue and negotiation in the 1970s, see Young Whan Kihl, "Korean Response to Major Power Rapprochement," in Young C. Kim, ed., Major Powers and Korea (Silver Spring, Md.: Research Institute on Korean Affairs, 1973), pp. 139-164; Young Whan Kihl, "Korea's Future: Seoul's Perspective," Asian Survey 17, no. 11 (November 1977):1064-1076.

34. Koh, Foreign Policy Systems, p. 88; also see Young C. Kim, "North Korean Foreign Policy," Problems of Communism (January-February 1985):1-17.

35. Young Whan Kihl, "The Issue of Korean Unification: North Korea's Policy and Perception," in C. I. Eugene Kim and B. C. Koh, eds., Journey to North Korea: Personal Perceptions (Berkeley: University of California Institute of East Asian Studies, 1983), pp. 99-117.

36. IISS Report on May 3, 1985, as cited in Korea Herald, 5 May 1985.

37. On Kim Il-Sung's criticism of Japan, see the text of his banquet speech in Moscow, Pyongyang Times, 26 May 1984; also see New York Times, 26 May 1984.

38. Washington Times, 2 May 1985, quoting a U.S. State Department official.

174

39. Ibid.
40. Kihl, North Korea in 1983, pp. 70-71.
41. Pyongyang Times, 9 May 1984; Beijing Review 27, no. 20 (14 May 1984).
42. Naewoe Press, 435 (17 May 1985).
43. Far Eastern Economic Review, 29 August 1985, pp. 22.
44. Ibid.
45. Chun Doo Hwan, 3 March 1981, as cited in Koh, Foreign Policy Systems, p. 104.
46. Chun Doo Hwan, speaking before the National Press Club in Washington, D.C., on February 2, 1981, as cited in ibid.
47. Ibid., p. 106.
48. Chae-Jin Lee, "South Korea in 1984: Seeking Peace and Prosperity," Asian Survey 25, no. 1 (January 1985):80-89.
49. Far Eastern Economic Review, 16 May 1985, p. 46.
50. Korea Herald, 30 April 1985.
51. Far Eastern Economic Review, 16 May 1985, pp. 46-49.
52. Kihl, North Korea in 1984, pp. 77-78.
53. For details, see Kihl, Politics and Policies, pp. 206-212.
54. Ibid., pp. 228-230.
55. Kihl, Noth Korea in 1984, pp. 76-77.
56. The tripartite talks proposal was not successful because the timing, among other factors, was not right following the October 1983 Rangoon bombing episode. See ibid., pp. 66-67.
57. Kihl, Politics and Policies, p. 243.
58. Ibid., pp. 242-245.
59. Bruce Cumings, "Korean-American Relations: A Century of Contact and Thirty-Five Years of Intimacy," in Warren L. Cohen, ed., New Frontiers in American-East Asian Relations (New York: Columbia University Press, 1983), pp. 237-282.
60. Bruce Cumings, The Origins of the Korean War: Liberation and the Emergence of Separate Regimes, 1945-1947 (Princeton: Princeton University Press, 1981).
61. Cumings, "Korean-American Relations," p. 136.
62. Ibid., p. 277.
63. "Team Spirit, Three-Way War Game," Pyongyang Times, 9 March 1985.
64. See Kihl, Politics and Policies, especially chapter 9.

Part 3

Southeast Asia and Oceania

8 Vietnam/Indochina: Hanoi's Challenge to Southeast Asian Regional Order

William S. Turley

In an era of power diffusion and waning Great Power hegemony, local actors have greater opportunity than previously to shape political and security arrangements for their regions. Such is the case in Southeast Asia, the other strategic fulcrum of Asia where the interests of the United States, the Soviet Union, China, and Japan now converge, if less directly than in the northeast. Local rivalries have reemerged after a century of colonial rule, and despite an overlay of Great Power competition, initiative belongs to states of the region. Vietnam in particular has responded to its own national reunification, the U.S. retreat from the mainland, and a reassertive China by seeking to consolidate a new pattern of relations with its neighbors and with extraregional powers. This striving already has affected security in Southeast Asia and the strategic positions of Great Powers in the Western Pacific. Significant long-term policy implications for a variety of affected countries hinge on the goals, perceptions, determination, and capabilities of the Vietnamese. In this chapter, "Viet-centric" views of strategic security and regional order are examined in order to determine what some of these implications might be.

Attention necessarily focuses on the conflict that centers on Cambodia. There, it will be remembered, Pol Pot's Khmer Rouge broke away from Vietnamese tutelage even before the Second Indochina War ended. As Hanoi tilted toward Moscow, China supported the Khmer Rouge

----
Research for this paper, including two trips to Hanoi, was conducted when I was visiting professor in American Studies, Chulalongkorn University, Bangkok, under the auspices of the Fulbright-Hayes Program and the John F. Kennedy Foundation of Thailand. I also wish to acknowledge the support given to me by the International Relations Institute, Hanoi, during my visit to Vietnam in 1984.

against the Vietnamese. Finally, in 1978, Hanoi obtained reassurance from Moscow and intervened in December of that year to suppress a Cambodian regime it
judged to be subservient to China.[1] That intervention
provoked attack by China and opposition from the noncommunist Association of Southeast Asian Nations (ASEAN)
supported by the United States and Japan. The ensuing
conflict facilitated Soviet efforts to consolidate a
closer relationship with Vietnam, as it deepened Vietnamese dependence on the Soviet Union. Obviously, the
conflict was entangled from the beginning in the Sino-
Soviet dispute and has potential to create a deep regional cleavage subordinate to the rivalry of Beijing
and Moscow.

However, the trilateral Great Power competition
permits regional actors a greater degree of flexibility
than they had during the period of U.S. hegemony. Great
Powers supply local contestants and thus sustain the
latters' conflicts, but they obtain little leverage over
them in return. Vietnam's dependency on the Soviet
Union, for example, is matched by the Soviet dependency
on Vietnam to extend the range of its largest fleet into
waters hitherto a preserve of the United States and to
gain a foothold on China's southern flank. The Soviet
Union has no other viable way besides cooperation with
Vietnam to be a major player in this part of the world.
However dependent Vietnam may be on the Soviet Union,
Soviet dependency on Vietnam assures Hanoi of stable
support for its own goals in Indochina. Those goals are
incompatible with the Thai perception that Thailand's
security is threatened by a Vietnamese military presence
in the Mekong Basin; protracted conflict disturbs other
ASEAN states because it provides opportunities for Great
Powers, principally China and the Soviet Union, to gain
influence in the region. For the policymaker or the
analyst to respond effectively, it is necessary to understand Hanoi's goals in some detail and to gauge its
commitment to attaining them.

THE SETTING

Without implying geopolitical determinism, certain
environmental features of Southeast Asia must be given
their due. Though Vietnamese communist leaders hold
conceptions that distinguish them from other elites that
have governed Vietnam, geography and history shape their
views and provide continuity. These continuities help
to explain the local and most enduring features of the
current conflicts.

The dominant geopolitical feature of Southeast Asia
is the region's political fragmentation combined with
its location on China's periphery. China historically
has sought to keep regional powers weak, divided, or
deferential and to exclude competitors in order to mini-

mize threat from this quarter. Except in the ultimately unsuccessful attempt to conquer Vietnam, China pursued this strategy before the colonial period by manipulating trade privileges, mediating disputes, inviting tribute, and engaging in limited military forays. China pursued this strategy through the late nineteenth century (even though directly challenged on its own territory) in an attempt to avert the unification of Indochina by France. Following the Chinese Revolution, for lack of alternatives as long as the Western presence was still strong, Chinese tactics emphasized support of insurgencies, but their strategy was the same. Ironically, the Vietnamese were the first to benefit as China sought to terminate the French presence on its southern flank and then to prevent the United States from obtaining a second foothold on the Asian mainland.

Over the years, China has supported insurgencies in virtually every Southeast Asian country. It has given this support sometimes to weaken regimes and sometimes to secure leverage over them, e.g., to enforce Burma's neutrality. In 1979, China suspended support of insurgencies in the ASEAN countries in exchange for improved state-to-state relations but since then has sponsored or supported insurgencies in Laos, Cambodia, and Vietnam in an effort to break up any pro-Soviet emergent bloc and to deter alliance between that bloc and the Soviet Union. China is the only Great Power supplying direct military support to insurgencies in Southeast Asia today. Only internal upheaval and external challenge have ever stayed China's striving for predominance within the region. Of all Southeast Asian countries, Vietnam has most often fallen within the scope of China's strategic concern--whether as beneficiary or victim.

A second important geopolitical feature is the process of state consolidation that has taken place in Southeast Asia over a period of 2,000 years. For the Vietnamese, this process occurred in the context of repeated attempts by China to subjugate them. China's attempted subjugations have implanted in the Vietnamese a deep antipathy to China and may have both propelled and steeled the Vietnamese for southward expansion at the expense of weaker neighbors. The Thai likewise expanded southward, and with the same result. By the seventeenth century, Vietnam and Thailand had emerged as the leading contenders for power on the Southeast Asian mainland and commenced a rivalry for influence in the buffers between them. The root of conflict was the shared perception that the Mekong Basin comprising lowland Laos and most of Cambodia was a line of unity, not division, that neither power could let fall to the other without threat to security.[2] Sporadically, during two centuries beginning in 1623, the two countries supported rival claimants to the Cambodian throne and attempted to enforce exclusive claims to suzerainty. These interventions involved armed action inside Cambodia, supply of

arms and troops to the Khmer contestants, one outright
military occupation (by Vietnam), the annexation of
Cambodian territory (by both), and general warfare.
Colonial rule suspended Asian international politics.
It also unified Indochina under a single administration
for the first time in history, to the Thais' advantage
of having escaped direct rule as Vietnam went through
two devastating wars. Rivalry resumed as the Thais
seized this opportunity to work for the fragmentation of
Indochina and weakening of Vietnam. Between 1959 and
1973, the Thais sent twenty-five battalions of "volun-
teers" into Laos and facilitated the U.S. bombardment of
Vietnam from Thai territory. Vietnam responded by aid-
ing an ongoing insurgent movement in Thailand.

Last is Vietnam's construction as a thin sliver of
land on the edge of the Asian landmass. Open deltas at
either end of this sliver support dense populations, but
these are flat, vulnerable, and separated by more than a
thousand kilometers of cross-running ridges. Between
these ridges lie small compartments of human settlement
and coastal enclaves. The terrain is hostile to internal communication and traditionally has made Vietnam
difficult to govern and defend. Whereas Thailand is
held together by its topography, Vietnam is divided by
it; Thailand has flourished under incohesive state
structures, but Vietnam has relied on bureaucracy to
hold the country together.[3] The sea can be a link, but
the concentration of people along the coastline also
places the bulk of resources within easy range of seaborne attack. The Vietnamese consequently have felt it
necessary to control the mountainous hinterland shared
with Laos and Cambodia in order to have a secure rear
and linkage between regions. This requirement has
seemed to the Vietnamese to grow in importance because
in modern times three Great Powers, two of them with
Thai connivance, have intervened in Laos and Cambodia to
obstruct a struggle for national independence and unity
in Vietnam.

These contexts encourage Vietnamese communist leaders, as they did their predecessors, to view Vietnam as
the principal repository of advanced universal values
(Chinese in the past, Marxist-Leninist in the present)
in Southeast Asia and the region's bulwark against China's political and military power. They also make it
easy for the Vietnamese, as long as there is no revolution in Thailand, to interpret Thai policy partly as a
traditional pursuit of power and expansion, now aided by
a hostile United States and China. Lastly, Vietnam's
geography makes the Vietnamese extremely sensitive to
threats against their internal lines of communication;
therefore, they insist on unimpeded access to the territory of Laos and Cambodia. Such perceptions, however,
are only a substratum as compared with others that
reflect the current Vietnamese leadership's experience
on the road to power, strategic aims, and ideology.

INDOCHINA IN VIETNAMESE COMMUNIST STRATEGY

The most common assumption about Vietnamese strategy is that it aims to establish Hanoi's dominion over
all of Indochina, perhaps in a federal structure. Evidence for this view is found in precolonial Vietnamese
relations with Laos and Cambodia, in the Communist party's claim to responsibility for revolution in all three
countries up to 1951, and in references to an Indochina
Federation in early party documents. It is reinforced
by the fact that the French colonial regime relied, in
part, on Vietnamese to administer Laos and Cambodia,
that liberation movements worldwide have sought to fill
out the boundaries of their colonial predecessors, that
the Vietnamese have tutored Lao and Khmer Communists
down to the present, and that Le Duc Tho boasted in
secret talks with Henry Kissinger, according to Kissinger, of "his people's destiny not merely to take over
South Vietnam but to dominate the whole of Indochina."[4]
The conventional view, however, rests on simplistic
historicist premises. It also assumes a uniformity of
experience among Vietnamese elites that did not exist.
The true inheritors of the French mandate, it should be
pointed out, were Vietnamese employees of the French
colonial administration, and these wound up in Saigon
not Hanoi in 1954. For these reasons the evolution of
communist strategy as regards Indochina, though familiar
in broad outline, deserves close attention.
That evolution began with a dispute over the party's name at the time of its founding. In February
1930, representatives of four Vietnamese communist
groups met at a "merger conference" at the behest of Ho
Chi Minh to found the Vietnam Communist party (VCP).
The name reflected a wish to concentrate on achieving
independence for Vietnam just as it reflected low esteem
for the revolutionary potential of Laos and Cambodia.
Delegates from northern Vietnam also asserted that "in
accordance with Leninist self-determinism they could not
make the Cambodian and Lao proletariats enter the party
with them."[5] The idea of assuming responsibility for
revolution in all of Indochina seems to have had little
support. That responsibility was assumed later to bring
VCP policy into line with the Comintern principle of
matching parties in the colonial world with colonial
(not ethnic) jurisdictions. Accordingly, the 1st Plenum
of the Central Committee, held in October 1930 principally to correct the "errors" of the merger conference,
gave considerable attention to the question of the party's name. The plenum resolution stated that "instructions from the Comintern" were to "drop the name 'Vietnam Communist Party' and take the name 'Indochina Communist Party (ICP).'"[6]
An intensive campaign had to be mounted within the
party to explain this change, as the reasons for it were
by no means obvious to the membership. The explanation

was that despite differences of custom, language, and
"race," the Vietnamese, Cambodian, and Lao "proletariats" had formed a close political and economic relationship due to their joint subjugation by French colonialism. Because the colonial administration was a "unified
concentrated force," it was necessary to "have a single
Communist Party to concentrate the force of the prole-
tariat in all of the countries of Indochina."[7] A letter
from the Central Committee to party branch committees
further explained that because the three countries had
grown interdependent under colonial rule, each required
the support of the other two to overthrow colonial rule
and "if separated each would lack sufficient conditions
for economic activity. Erroneous recognition of these
conditions," the letter sternly concluded, "has resulted
in many dangerous interpretations of the party's ideology. The 'name' problem may seem only a matter of form,
a small matter, but in reality it has importance because
it can influence the thought and actions of the Party."[8]

Though this affair took place when the party had
only 200 to 300 members, it had lasting importance
because these founders, who were to lead the party down
to the present, passed on views formed in this period to
the membership as a whole. The incident revealed important formative elements in Vietnamese communist orienta-
tions toward Indochina. First, the perception of Indochina as a unity did not come naturally to the apparent
majority of party members who tended to dismiss the
revolutionary potential of Laos and Cambodia. Whether
national liberation or proletarian revolution was the
primary objective, the need to involve Laos and Cambodia
was not evident. The requirements of ideological ortho-
doxy and subservience to Moscow, however, assured a
split within the party on this issue.[9] Second, in 1930,
Vietnamese Communists perceived little threat emanating
from Laos and Cambodia, apart from that which "internationalists" associated with French colonial rule.
Third, ideology reshaped if it did not completely sup-
plant traditional Vietnamese attitudes toward the Lao
and Khmer. Although low esteem for the revolutionary
potential of these peoples resonated with an older Vietnamese belief in Lao and Khmer cultural backwardness,
the evidence given to support this view was that they
lacked the requisite class structure to sustain a prole-
tariat party. Such reasoning implied poor prospects for
a Marxist mission civilisatrice and ruled against organizing proletarian revolutions in Laos and Cambodia con-
temporaneous with that of Vietnam. Fourth, the concept
of trinational unity embodied in the name Indochinese
Communist party grew out of general guidelines on organizing against colonial rule.

These guidelines were drawn up by Comintern officials (a few of whom were Vietnamese) and imposed on
those who attended the "merger conference" in 1930.
There is no evidence that the concept was camouflage for

an ancient ambition of the Vietnamese to dominate all of Indochina. Last, the assertion that the three countries had become economically interdependent implied that their ties should be preserved in some form past the end of colonial rule. With little foundation in fact, the significance of this assertion was unclear except as an echo of a Comintern theme, though the assertion was to be made again in the postrevolutionary era.

For the rest of the 1930s, the ICP did little to live up to its name. Very little effort was made to recruit members in Laos and Cambodia, and virtually all of those who joined were Vietnamese residents of those countries, not Lao and Khmer. Directives from the Comintern to extend organizing work among non-Vietnamese went largely ignored as members focused on people whose language and patriotic aspirations they shared. Federating Indochina after independence appeared among the goals laid down at the 1st Party Congress in 1935 and again in the resolution of the 8th Plenum in 1941, but this goal was otherwise disregarded. Party members were too concerned with their own survival to take interest in the practical implications of what some say was a vague expression of solidarity, not a concrete objective.

The first serious attempt to broaden the revolution cross-nationally flowed from support for Lao residing in Vietnam who were swept up in the anti-French fervor of 1945. The event that did most to awaken Vietnamese Communists to the unity of Indochina was the opening of attacks by France from bases in these countries against the Viet Minh's mountain redoubts in 1947. This experience forced the Vietnamese to see revolutions in Laos and Cambodia as means to tie down the French from the rear. The Comintern's instructions, in retrospect, must have seemed extraordinarily prescient. The views of "internationalists" in the party were vindicated. Indochina henceforward was to be considered a "single strategic unit," though principally for military reasons. As Vo Nguyen Giap put it in 1950:

> Indochina is a single strategic unit, a single battle-field, and here we have the mission of helping the movement to liberate all of Indochina. This is because militarily, Indochina is one bloc, one unit, in both the invasion and defense plans of the enemy. For this reason, and especially because of the strategic terrain, we cannot consider Vietnam to be independent so long as Cambodia and Laos are under imperialist domination, just as we cannot consider Cambodia and Laos to be independent so long as Vietnam is under imperialist rule.

> The colonialists used Cambodia to attack Vietnam. Laos and Cambodia temporarily have become the secure rear areas of the enemy and simultaneously their most

vulnerable area in the entire Indochina theatre. Therefore, we need to open the Laos-Cambodia battle-field resolutely and energetically.[10]

It was against this background that the ICP decided to push revolutions in Laos and Cambodia. In 1951, the party invited a number of Lao and Cambodian leaders to attend its 2nd congress, which proclaimed the formation of the Vietnam Worker's party to replace the ICP and unveiled a Viet-Lao-Khmer alliance. References to an Indochina Federation disappeared from party texts, and separate Lao and Cambodian Communist parties appeared shortly thereafter. The purpose was to capitalize on nationalist sentiment in all three countries and to mobilize joint struggle against French colonialism and U.S. interventionism.[11] By the end of the war, as the Viet Minh strove to link up their far-flung base areas, they also noted that the central highlands were of "extreme strategic importance." "Only by developing into the Central Highlands," observed the Political Bureau's military committee in November 1953, "is it possible to obtain the most important strategic position in the South. If the enemy controls that strategic zone, it will be very difficult to improve the situation in the South." [12]

The validity of perceiving Indochinese unity as a function of others' strategies seemed, to the Vietnamese, confirmed by subsequent events. Even before the Second Indochina War got under way, the United States with Thai connivance took advantage of instability in Laos to secure a foothold in the same lowland from which the French had attacked the Viet Minh. The United States and Thailand systematically undermined Laotian neutrality and equipped the Royal Lao Army and hill tribes to attack the Ho Chi Minh Trail. The United States also capitalized on Prince Noradom Sihanouk's overthrow in 1970 to attack Vietnamese sanctuaries in Cambodia. Although the Vietnamese were hardly innocent of provocation, the implications for Vietnam's security and unity seemed clear. By 1977, as relations between Beijing and Hanoi deteriorated, the Vietnamese could not but view Chinese support for the Khmer Rouge as the third attempt by a Great Power in modern times to en-circle and attack Vietnam from the west. The Vietnamese thus were satisfied in their own minds that their re-sponses were, first, defensive, and then, in December 1978, preemptive.

Hanoi's Indochina strategy grows principally out of the perception that the three countries are security interdependent. This perception is expressed both pri-vately and publicly by Hanoi officials as a "law": because adversaries must gain a foothold in at least one of the states in order to attack another, the three states must be joined in alliance to guarantee the peace and independence of each. In the words of the commander of Vietnamese forces in Cambodia, "Experience over more

than half a century on the Indochinese peninsula shows
that the aggressive plots of the Japanese fascists,
French colonialists, and U.S. imperialists as well as
the Chinese expansionists and hegemonists down to the
present have always treated Indochina as a target of
aggression and a unified battleground. . . . In their
plots to annex Indochina and expand into Southeast Asia,
the Beijing reactionaries cannot help but follow this
law."[13] Moreover, the record suggests to the Vietnamese
that just as aggressors must treat Indochina as a "unified battleground," so are the three countries able to
repel any aggression, including a nuclear superpower, if
they are united. Because Hanoi officials believe that
consciousness of a shared fate among the three peoples
is strengthened in dialectical reaction to each threat,
they firmly believe Indochinese unity is not only "irre-
versible" but is further consolidated by externally
mounted efforts to destroy it.

Implicit in the foregoing is a relatively compla-
cent attitude toward protracted tensions with neighbors,
as long as the costs can be controlled. It is clear,
too, that the men now in power in Hanoi cannot accept
the reconstitution of Laos and Cambodia as "neutral
buffers" if that means having governments in Vientiane
and Phnom Penh that are weak, divided, and vulnerable to
penetration by powers besides Vietnam. Because schemes
for coalition governments like that proposed by ASEAN
for Cambodia could have this result, such schemes are
unacceptable to the Vietnamese. So would be any lesser
forms of real power sharing.[14] Vietnamese diplomats
acknowledge Thai concerns but note that relative to
Thailand's U.S. and Chinese guarantees they can rely
totally only on their own national strength and paramount position in Laos and Cambodia. This has become so
basic in Vietnamese thinking that leaders in Hanoi hardly distinguish between consolidating friendly regimes in
Laos and Cambodia and defending their own country.
Hanoi's ties with Moscow are almost certainly subordinate to its aim in Indochina. Relations with the Soviet
Union are of course enormously important as a source of
economic and military assistance and as a counterweight
to the Chinese, but in the absence of unstinting Soviet
support for the Vietnamese army in Cambodia as well,
Hanoi would face more risk than benefit in facilitating
the Soviet Union's attempt to encircle China. It is
thus quite unrealistic to expect Moscow to force a Cambodian settlement on Vietnam that dilutes Hanoi's influence in Phnom Penh, except in the unlikely event that the
Soviet Union sacrificed important interests in Vietnam.

IDEOLOGICAL PERCEPTIONS

Notwithstanding that in international politics
realist views prevail over ideological ones, it would be
an error to overlook the influence of the latter in

Vietnamese perceptions and strategy.[15]   The Vietnamese
are in the early stages of consolidating their revolution, whose success they attribute to correct application of doctrine.   Though this doctrine may seem a mere
abstraction to some, this is abstraction the Vietnamese
take seriously.   Particularly in assessing long-term
trends and in attempting to predict internal shifts in
countries of concern to them, the Vietnamese rely heavily on ideological concepts.   Since the late 1960s, they
have joined the Soviets in maintaining that the "central
contradiction" in the present era places "three revolutionary currents" in opposition to capitalism and imperialism.   These currents are the socialist camp headed
by the Soviet Union, the national liberation movement in
the Third World, and the workers' movement in the capitalist countries.   As these currents gain strength, so
will the nations that coordinate their policies with
them, the theory predicts.

This theory combined with a doctrine of historical
inevitability reduces diplomacy and strategy to matters
of adjustment to the winning trends.   As a deputy foreign minister put it: "In assessing the situation for
purposes of making policy decisions, it is necessary
above all else to look at the trends.   Certain trends
are inevitable.   Those who see these trends and follow
them succeed, those who oppose them fail. . . . Vietnam
has been successful because it is on the side of the
growing number of countries that have won their independence.   Though these countries have economic problems, they are developing while peace is being consolidated."[16]   It follows that if statesmen have assessed
the trends correctly and devised policies that conform
to the winning trends, the nation will benefit from
change over the long run, regardless of trials in the
short term.   To the nostrum that patience assures success, ideology adds confidence that the trends have been
assessed correctly.

Marxism-Leninism also directs attention to internal
structures of class and power when assessing other societies' cohesion, capabilities, and external behavior.
Application of these ideas by the Vietnamese reflects
their own experience, however.   Convinced that they
achieved power by manipulating inequalities in their own
society, and confident that equality is the foundation
of their national solidarity and strength, Vietnamese
strategists are not much impressed by the aggregate
wealth of their neighbors.   What captures their attention is the unequal wealth distributions in these countries, which they regard as a cause of grave weakness.
Moreover, ideology predicts that these inequalities will
grow worse under capitalist-driven, export-oriented
development strategies.   Although they do not expect
revolutions identical to their own to occur, the Vietnamese are confident that rising social tensions will
preoccupy ASEAN elites in the future and make them eager
to remove sources of friction from the region.[17]

One of the main practical uses of Marxist-Leninist ideology is to sustain confidence despite setbacks. Indeed, ideology defines setbacks as abnormal events that require only tactical adjustment; these setbacks cannot be considered cumulative. The hope that Hanoi will see the direness of its straits as others see it founders on this confidence. Ideology also encourages the Vietnamese to anticipate the emergence of anti-imperialist, anticapitalist forces in the ASEAN countries that will divide these countries internally and provide incentive for ASEAN to settle its differences with the socialist bloc (and Vietnam). This expectation reduces concern about ASEAN's concerted support for Thailand over the long term. But this does not imply that Hanoi wishes to divide ASEAN itself to the point of collapse. For who but China would pick up the pieces? The Vietnamese moreover are ideologically predisposed to view the ASEAN nations as part of the Third World striving to perfect their independence and therefore potentially within the "current" on whose ascendancy the Vietnamese count for their own safety.

As for global strategy, the Vietnamese have been remarkably consistent in seeing their own struggles as alternatively central or peripheral to those of a socialist camp headed by the Soviet Union.[18] In this conception, it is the "internationalist duty" of communist states to support the camp member that at a given time finds itself at the focal point of conflict between socialism and imperialism. Soviet leadership is assumed by the Vietnamese not only for reasons of history and capability, but because China broke with the camp at the very moment Vietnam most needed the support of a united bloc in its war with the United States. Thus, an ideological interpretation of alliance obligations influenced Hanoi's decision to align with Moscow in the Sino-Soviet dispute. Obviously, the Vietnamese interpretation also has been self-serving, as all interpretations of alliance obligations tend to be, but the ideological context encourages the Vietnamese, as long as they are actively engaged in conflict with bloc enemies, to expect support as a moral right.

REALIST PERCEPTIONS

The influence of realpolitik is readily apparent, however. Forced to choose between competitive patrons in the last war, Hanoi leaned toward the one that had most to give, particularly for aerial defense of the North and the equipping of main force divisions, and away from the one that was turbulent and inward-looking. The Soviet Union was a reliable supplier of crucial military hardware; China during the same period refused to coordinate with the Soviets against the United States, was distracted by the Cultural Revolution, and mounted a challenge to Soviet leadership of the

Communist bloc.   China, to the Vietnamese, also seemed
more willing than the Soviets to improve relations with
the United States at Vietnam's expense as the war neared
its end.[19]   Since that war, the Soviet Union has been
viewed as the only possible counterweight to a hostile
China.   Ideology was certainly the last thing on the
mind of the Hanoi diplomat who told me "In all of history, we have been secure from China in only two conditions.   One is when China is weak and internally divided.   The other is when she has been threatened by
barbarians from the north.   In the present era, the
Russians are our barbarians."[20]
      Ideological concepts shape responses, perhaps sig-
nificantly through the analysis of trends, but experience has imparted to the Vietnamese a fine appreciation
for the realities of power, which is their principal
basis for assessing present threat and planning strategic security.   Thus, the Vietnamese regard the United
States as imperialist, an enemy by definition, but they
no longer consider the United States a significant direct threat: U.S. leaders have the "lesson" of Vietnam
before them and domestic opposition to interventionism.
The Indochina foreign ministers' meeting in January 1985
urged the United States to "assume a responsible role in
contributing to long-term peace and stability in Southeast Asia," which barely disguised the hope that U.S.
aversion to Pol Pot would develop into support for the
suppression of the Khmer Rouge and restraint in supporting the noncommunist Khmer resistance.[21]   The Vietnamese
moreover vastly prefer U.S. to Chinese influence in
Thailand because U.S. aims are limited and its power
declining in Southeast Asia by comparison with China.
      Japan is more problematic.   On the one hand, Japan
is a natural market for Vietnam's raw materials and
potentially its major source of hard currency earnings
and noncommunist investment and assistance.   The Vietnamese have realistic expectations of gaining significantly from economic ties with Japan in the future.
Despite the suspension of Japanese government credits
since 1979, two-way trade between the two countries has
continued at levels in excess of $100 million per year
(down from a postwar peak of $270 million in 1978), and
Japan is the source of roughly half of all private
credit disbursed to Vietnam from the convertible area.[22]
On the other hand, Japan is the most important forward
base of U.S. power in the Pacific, a direct threat to
the sea link with Vladivostok on which Vietnam increasingly depends.   Japan's location gives it and its allies
the potential to cut off Soviet assistance to Vietnam in
the event of hostilities.   Sea-lanes that ASEAN, U.S.,
Japanese, and Chinese strategists see bristling with
Soviet ships look like extremely vulnerable supply lines
to the Vietnamese.[23]   The inescapable conclusion for
Hanoi is that Japan's defense cooperation with the
United States or China, or its rearmament as long as

Japan is still capitalist and antipathetic to the Soviet Union, poses a threat to Vietnam.

Japan's support of ASEAN on the Cambodian question is said by Hanoi to disguise a cynical attempt to strengthen its economic position among the ASEAN states and, in cooperation with the United States, to play the role of "regional gendarme" in Southeast Asia.[24] Any tendency on the part of Japan to rearm, defend its sea-lanes, or to join with the United States, China, and South Korea in containing the Soviet Union is viewed with deep misgivings in Hanoi. The newspaper Quan doi nhan dan (People's Army), for example, described the spate of moves by Prime Minister Yasuhiro Nakasone in 1983 to bolster Japan's contribution in the Western Pacific as a "new phase in Japan's service to American global strategy."[25] Though principally concerned at present with what they perceive as Japan's subservience to the United States, in projecting future power shifts the Vietnamese regard Japan as the only country besides China capable of expanding in the region. Thus one foreign ministry official speculated that China's "four modernizations" and pursuit of a hegemonistic foreign policy might produce a defensive reaction in Japan in the form of a military buildup and resurgent militarism; such activities would present Vietnam with a dual threat from the north that Vietnam could offset only by cooperating still more closely with the Soviet Union. Increased Soviet access to naval and air facilities, he indicated, could not be ruled out in that event.[26]

Hanoi is similarly ambivalent with regard to ASEAN for a mixture of historical, ideological, and pragmatic reasons. The organization was founded by the region's anticommunist regimes partly in reaction to instability in Indochina, and two of its members, Thailand and the Philippines, assisted U.S. efforts to destroy the communist revolution in Vietnam. Following the war's end in 1975, Hanoi expressed hostility toward ASEAN as an instrument of U.S. imperialism, an emergent successor to the Southeast Asia Treaty Organization (SEATO), and a group of nations whose independence was still in thrall to Western capital. In Vietnamese eyes, ASEAN elites were a mixed bag of militarists, "feudalists," and stooges of a neocolonial world order. The ASEAN concept of a Zone of Peace, Freedom, and Neutrality (ZOPFAN) was found wanting for not including "independence," i.e., an end to military ties with the United States and dependency on Western capital.

But Hanoi softened these views in 1978 as it sought to preempt opposition to its planned move into Cambodia. It has continued to speak in tones of relative moderation. Though the Soviets may have nudged Hanoi to strike a less strident note, the Vietnamese recognized it was in their own interests to adopt a rhetorically conciliatory posture and to draw the ASEAN states into dialogue.[27] Without yielding anything to Cambodia,

Hanoi needed to placate fears that had united ASEAN
behind Thailand and that could facilitate China's penetration of the region. Hanoi also wished to capitalize
on the fact that ASEAN's natural leader, Indonesia,
shared the Vietnamese view of China as the principal
long-term threat.

Thus, Vietnam's strategic security concerns over-
rode its ideological distaste. The objectives were to
obtain acceptance of Vietnam's position in Cambodia and
to preempt tendencies in ASEAN to seek reassurance from
Great Powers hostile to Vietnam. These objectives required Vietnam to improve relations with ASEAN states,
preferably on a bilateral basis but on a multilateral
one as well. Hanoi therefore has subscribed to the
Malaysian proposal "to turn Southeast Asia into a
nuclear-free zone and to materialize the ZOPFAN concept
[without insisting on inclusion of 'independence'] pending a solution to the Cambodian problem." [28] The manifest hope of these moves, aside from offering bait for
ASEAN to move toward a Cambodian settlement on Vietnam's
terms, is to encourage those in ASEAN who wish to minimize Great Power involvement in the regon and to dis-
courage ASEAN's transformation into a military alliance. [29] A victory for the Philippine New People's Army
or for anti-Marcos politicians responsive to demands for
closing U.S. military facilities in the Philippines
would be highly favorable to Vietnam. Ideally, in
Hanoi's view, these developments could lay foundations
for a Southeast Asian united front against China in
tacit cooperation with the Soviet Union.

Nevertheless, for the present and foreseeable future, Vietnamese leaders perceive their country, in
their words, as "surrounded by enemies." This perception combined with trust only in their own determination
and ability to defend themselves has caused Hanoi to
maintain the world's fourth largest military establishment. Of total armed forces numbering 1,227,000 in
1984, the People's Army numbered 1 million. In almost
continuous combat since its founding in 1944, and with
some tactical as well as strategic victories over three
Great Powers to its credit, the People's Army is the
most experienced, battle-hardened armed force in Asia
today. A 15,000-man air force, a 12,000-man navy, a
60,000-man air defense force, and assorted border defense forces and auxiliaries round out the figure for
standing regulars. These are supported by a 500,000-man
quick reinforcement reserves, a 2.5 million-strong
"strategic rear" reserve, and militia that number somewhere between 1 and 3 million. [30]

The overwhelming emphasis given to ground combat
forces (56 infantry divisions averaging 10,500 men each)
and popular territorial defense is the legacy of two
long revolutionary wars against technologically superior
foes. It is also a response to the post-1975 threat
environment. Professional elements in the military
proposed at the end of the last war that this structure

be streamlined in exchange for technical modernization, but this argument was overriden by a need to use the military in economic construction (the People's Army has, in addition, 7 engineering and 15 economic con- struction divisions of about 3,000 men each) and then by the looming conflict with Cambodia and China. Since 1979, when the Chinese attack on the northern border was met primarily by local militia, regional forces, and a trainee division, the People's Army has deployed from 20 to 25 infantry divisions (roughly one-half of all assets including support units) north of Hanoi. Obviously, that is the direction from which the major short-term threat is seen to come. Another 3 divisions have been stationed continuously in Laos since 1965, and about 12 remain in Cambodia. The small navy's 6 frigates and assorted large patrol craft are adequate for coastal patrol and surveillance. The air force, with 290 combat aircraft consisting primarily of MIG-21s (and MIG-23s a virtual certainty if Thailand obtains the F-16A), is inexperienced in support of ground combat and weak in transport but overshadows its neighbors in aerial inter- ception; it also is acquiring large model helicopters useful in counterinsurgency. Although these forces give the Vietnamese confidence that they can cope with any threat on the horizon, including a "second lesson" from China, the cost is dear (military expenditure as a proportion of Gross National Product must rank among the highest in the world; the army takes a large proportion of technical school graduates, etc.). That cost com- bined with an inability to manufacture any but the simplest equipment and ammunition forces Vietnam to obtain an estimated $1 billion annually in foreign mili- tary assistance, overwhelmingly from the Soviet Union. Though Vietnamese military spokesmen flatly deny that any integration with Soviet strategic planning has taken place,[31] Soviet military support of Vietnam is a rela- tively cheap way for Moscow to see that more than 250,000 troops hostile to China are stationed on the latter's southern border and to secure Vietnam's parti- cipation in surveillance of the South China Sea. It also assures that Vietnam will have the means not only to defend its northern border but to pursue its goals in other parts of Indochina.

SECURITY RESPONSES:
CONSOLIDATING INDOCHINESE UNITY

Meanwhile, the Vietnamese believe their security requires them to strengthen solidarity among the three Indochinese countries at almost any price. How does Hanoi intend to do this? For the present it can shore up client regimes with its own army and advisory assis- tance, which is not difficult in Laos where the govern- ment originated in decades of revolutionary warfare under Vietnamese tutelage. But this is costly in Cambo- dia where the Vietnamese have had to construct a government from scratch in the teeth of domestic and international opposition. The idea of federation was abandoned long ago, and the Vietnamese seem genuinely aware that such a move now would only play into the hands of their adversaries. Periodic summits, semiannual foreign ministers' meetings, exchanges of technical teams, and a Vietnamese advisory presence are satisfactory to coordinate policy. If the Vietnamese have a model, it could be the Soviet role in Eastern Europe; though they do not themselves draw this parallel, they do not object when it is made.

But the Vietnamese do intend to promote "economic integration," in the words of a senior foreign ministry official. National committees for cultural and economic cooperation were formed in all three countries in early 1983 and held their first joint meeting in July. The appointment of fairly powerful Central Committee members to head each national committee indicates the importance attached to this goal. But the committees have only consultative powers, and their goal is a very distant one. It could hardly be otherwise, given the extremely low level of economic development in each country and the fact that although they have "cooperated" in military matters for years, as the Vietnam committee's deputy director put it, economic cooperation is "a new problem for us."[32] "Cooperation" in fact consists almost entirely of Vietnamese assistance to the other two countries, and priority is given to development of food self-sufficiency. No proposals for complementary development or for industrial coproduction were on the agenda as of spring 1984. Nor had linking intra-Indochina cooperation with Council for Mutual Economic Assistance (CMEA) activities been mentioned in any of the committees' joint meetings. Cooperation on truly major projects such as Mekong Basin development has been ruled out for lack of capital. The main physical links built up to the present are improvements to portions of the Ho Chi Minh Trail complex astride the Annamite Cordillera, a 286-km petroleum pipeline from Vinh in Vietnam's Nghe Tinh province to Route 13 in Laos, which each country separately manages on its respective territory,[33] and the extension of Route 9 to connect Savannakhet with Da Nang,[34] which the Vietnamese acknowledge will never provide Laos access to the sea that is as cost-efficient as the rail link across Thailand.[35] Transnational institutions, not to mention economic integration in the accepted sense of the term, hardly seem likely to emerge in the foreseeable future.

More interesting for what it reveals about the Vietnamese orientation to "cooperation" is the spirit in which Hanoi gives assistance. Vietnamese Communists in the past admired the relative egalitarianism of their neighbor's traditional societies, and "cooperation" is conducted among putative equals. The party moreover has attempted for decades to indoctrinate its cadres in respect for ethnic minorities and other people of Indochina, as the cooperation of these groups has been crucial to the attainment of party objectives. But the Vietnamese take naturally to the role of senior partner and patronize other groups. ("Matronize" might be a better word--see below.) The historian Alexander Woodside has suggested that this attitude resonates with Confucian "cultural evangelism" and "hierarchical vision of inter-state relations," reinforced by a "psychologically defensive imitation" of the way Vietnam was treated by Western colonial powers.[36]

Whatever the source, the tone is certainly present, particularly with regard to Cambodia, as in a triptych of poems, one of which is entitled "Orphaned Younger Sister," written by Le Duc Tho during a visit to Cambodia.[37] In spring 1984, Foreign Minister Nguyen Co Thach described the Phnom Penh regime as a "child" that Vietnam had to put on its feet and encourage to walk alone.[38] Though Thach's purpose was to emphasize Hanoi's determination not to let Phnom Penh become permanently dependent on Vietnam's defensive shield, the language was strikingly similar to that of Emperor Gia Long (1802-1819), who said: "Cambodia is a small country. . . . And we should maintain it as a child. We will be its mother, its father will be Siam. When a child has trouble with its father, it can get rid of suffering by embracing its mother. When the child is unhappy with its mother, it can run to its father for support."[39] Given that the Khmer Rouge could not survive without Thai connivance in China's support, the Vietnamese might well see the child as unhappy with its father, therefore running to its mother. Though they have done more than any other Vietnamese elite to expunge traditional negative stereotypes toward neighboring peoples, the Vietnamese Communists draw tremendous pride from protecting and developing other societies. In fulfillment of their "internationalist duty," not to mention their own security requirements, the Vietnamese find confirmation of Vietnam's full sovereignty and membership in the modern world community. These tremendously important psychic satisfactions are made all the more intense by the considerable sacrifice at which assistance is given.[40]

A last option for consolidating Vietnamese hegemony over Indochina could be Vietnamization in the form of settlement and eventual absorption of Laos and Cambodia. This spectre has been raised principally by Khmer resistance groups and their ASEAN supporters, who charge that Vietnamese in the hundreds of thousands already have settled in Cambodia with Hanoi's encouragement and assistance. But evidence of settlement of this magnitude is thin. Hanoi's principal concerns regarding settlement have been to curb the movement of smugglers, black marketeers, draft dodgers, and political dissidents seeking refuge or opportunity in Cambodia's post-1979 disarray, yet to permit some settlement that might help economic recovery. It is doubtful that the aim is

assimilation. Policy documents that have come to light
suggest an aim of regulating an ongoing movement so as
to guarantee that Vietnamese in Cambodia will contribute
to the economy, not to turbulence.[41] The Vietnam-
Cambodia border is closely patrolled to stop unauthor-
ized crossings,[42] and a plan to screen settlers already
in Cambodia was being discussed in spring 1984.[43] As
for numbers of settlers, they are undoubtedly higher
than the 56,000 Vietnamese (and over 60,000 Sino-Khmer)
cited by Phnom Penh in mid-1983, the last time estimates
were given.[44] But migration is said to have tapered off
due to tighter controls and, on the part of law-abiding
Vietnamese, to memory of earlier treatment at the hands
of the Khmer.[45] Hanoi foreign ministry analysts add
that an officially sponsored program of massive settlement of the kind alleged would provoke Cambodian, ASEAN,
and world opposition and be self-defeating.[46] However,
Hanoi sources refer to the 500,000 Vietnamese who lived
in Cambodia up to 1970 as precedent for a sizeable
community that might be tolerated again, which reveals
striking obtuseness given the reasons that this community subsequently was reduced nearly to zero.[47] It is
possible that opinion in Hanoi is divided on this issue,
with some officials willing to consider implantation of
Vietnamese communities in certain areas for security
reasons (à la Israel's West Bank) if other means are
seen to fail.

Hanoi does not seem to have perceived any significant failures in its strategy toward Cambodia thus far,
however. Building a new Cambodian party, state, and
army has proved more difficult than the Vietnamese initially anticipated but is explained by the fact that few
educated Khmer survived the Pol Pot years. Khmer resistance forces made minor gains rather than fading away
during 1983 and 1984, but this was attributed to external support and diplomatic constraints on use of force
along the Thai border. China persists in applying pressure on Vietnam's northern border, but no "second lesson" has materialized, and Beijing's search for balance
between Moscow and Washington, the Vietnamese believe,
constrains Chinese action against Hanoi.

The main fear of the Vietnamese has been that the
Phnom Penh government and the Khmer people might become
dependent on the People's Army for protection and grow
apathetic about the Khmer Rouge threat. Two "traps" are
evident: one is Khmer dependency leading to an intermin-
able Vietnamese military involvement; the other is pre-
mature Vietnamese withdrawal that would permit the Khmer
Rouge--and behind them the Chinese--to return.[48] The
unprecedented attacks by the Vietnamese on all major
border encampments of the resistance in the 1984-85 dry
season were part of an attempt to avoid both of these
traps through more vigorous military action. The immediate objective was to disprove claims that the resistance forces had grown stronger and, of course, to roll
back their progress, which the attacks did. But the

strategy can be justified only if it helps to shift the burden to Phnom Penh.

In the respite, therefore, the most urgent objective has been to consolidate the Phnom Penh apparatus at all levels in the densely populated basin around the Great Lake. It was calculated that if Phnom Penh could mobilize the resources of this, the "inland front," it would be able to handle the skirmishing at the "border front" with reduced Vietnamese assistance. The Vietnamese also have formed joint command structures for Vietnamese and Cambodian units in the field to stiffen the latter as nonessential Vietnamese troops are withdrawn.[49] Though attention, especially from the United States, ASEAN, and China, has focused on the presumed purpose of annual withdrawals to appease foreign opinion, the withdrawals also are consistent with Hanoi's desire to put the Khmer on notice that they must do more to defend themselves. From these adjustments of strategy, it can be concluded that if China and Thailand (or others including the United States) continue to supply a viable Khmer resistance, the Cambodian conflict is likely to evolve into a civil war between externally supported Khmer parties. Although Thai military leaders have suggested that the partition of Cambodian territory might be an acceptable outcome of such a conflict,[50] the Vietnamese categorically rule this out.

THE CHALLENGE AND THE RESPONSES

Vietnam has the means and determination to persist in its present course indefinitely, albeit at great cost to itself. Success in that course implies the consolidation of an Indochina bloc under Hanoi's predominant influence, easy access for the Vietnamese military to the Mekong Basin, protracted tension between Vietnam and China, and strengthening of security ties between Vietnam and the Soviet Union. These outcomes in turn would redistribute power on the mainland to Thailand's disadvantage and might lead to further entrenchment of the Soviet military presence in Vietnam. In response, Thailand already has sought reassurance from China and the United States at the same time it has diverted capital from economic to military development. These trends in Thai policy tend to divide ASEAN, as members not directly threatened by Vietnam grow impatient to end a confrontation that invites intrusion by the least trusted of the Great Powers. Though unlikely, an ASEAN split over these issues could drive Thailand to go it alone in alliance with China, the United States, or both. Alternatively, Thailand would have the option of accommodation and neutrality, leading toward the Burmanization of mainland Southeast Asia.

Over the near term, however, no radical change in the broad contours of conflict or alignment seems likely. Though Vietnam clearly has the upper hand in

Cambodia and can maintain it for as long as it is willing to station sizeable forces there, it is not evident
at this writing that it can unilaterally impose a stable
outcome based exclusively on its own security interests
without mortgaging its future welfare. Perhaps more
obviously, neither can Thailand, ASEAN, and their supporters impose their preferred outcome by pressuring
Vietnam as they have up to now. However, ASEAN has a
powerful incentive to continue backing Thailand: if
Thailand lost ASEAN's support, Bangkok might feel con-
strained to adopt an even less pleasant option than its
present one. The one aim shared by the regional con-
testants--a balanced relationship between Southeast
Asian countries and Great Powers to minimize opportunities for the latter to interfere in national and regional affairs--thus far has been held hostage by both
Vietnam and ASEAN in their demands for concessions over
Cambodia. Diplomatic deadlock, low intensity conflict,
and military buildups by all the major players therefore
seem likely to continue.

This prospect poses much the same problems for the
United States as it has since 1978. Washington must
seek a resolution of the Cambodian question in such a
manner as to reduce Soviet opportunities for expanded
influence and maintain ASEAN unity and sound U.S.-ASEAN
and U.S.-China relations. At first the United States
did this by acquiescing in China's strategy of "bleeding" Vietnam through diplomatic isolation and support
for the Khmer Rouge. Washington also helped to sustain
ASEAN resolve to extract concessions from Hanoi. Although these policies were useful in demonstrating U.S.
solidarity with China and Thailand, they did nothing to
evict Vietnamese troops from Cambodia, added incentive
for Hanoi to expand Soviet military access to Vietnamese
facilities, and associated U.S. policy, if only indirectly, with support for the Khmer Rouge. They also
abdicated influence to China. U.S. policy thus helped
to confirm the belief in Hanoi that Vietnam could rely
only on itself to extinguish the threat posed by a
China-backed Khmer Rouge and on close ties with the
Soviet Union to offset Chinese pressure. It was after
several years of what Hanoi considered diplomatic patience that in 1984 it ordered its army to attack in
major force on the border of Thailand. Vietnamese
forces in regimental strength crossed that border several times. With the Khmer resistance camps removed as a
buffer, the scene was set for a confrontation that could
force the United States to choose between a politically
unpalatable involvement or abandonment of a treaty ally.

It is in the U.S. interest to avoid having to make
that choice. This can be done by facilitating efforts
to liquidate the Khmer Rouge, which may require a larger
security commitment to Thailand to reassure Bangkok for
the loss of this "buffer" and to mitigate repercussions
in Thailand's relations with China. Sustaining the
noncommunist Khmer resistance with "humanitarian assist-

ance" is useful as a show of solidarity with ASEAN but should not be given with any expectations of obtaining a share of real power for noncommunists in the Phnom Penh government. Because there is little the United States realistically can do to modify Vietnam's relations with the Soviet Union, it is in the U.S. interest to support ASEAN efforts to find common ground with Hanoi on regional order over the long term. For the order desired by ASEAN, shared in large measure by Hanoi, is more compatible with U.S. interests than the regional polarization and encroachment of Chinese and Soviet influence that the policies of all the Great Powers, including those of the United States, thus far have exacerbated.

NOTES

1. For background and analysis, see David W. P. Elliott, ed., The Third Indochina Conflict (Boulder, Colo.: Westview, 1981); and William S. Turley and Jeffrey Race, "The Third Indochina War," Foreign Policy 38 (Spring 1980):92-116.
2. See Sukhumbhand Paribatra, "Strategic Implications of the Indochina Conflict: Thai Perspectives," Asian Affairs: An American Review 11, no. 3 (Fall 1984):30-35.
3. For futher comparison, see R. B. Smith, "Thailand and Viet-Nam: Some Thoughts Toward a Comparative Historical Analysis," The Journal of the Siam Society 60, part 2 (July 1972):1-21.
4. Henry Kissinger, White House Years (Boston: Little, Brown, 1979), p. 433.
5. "Tho cua Trung uong gui cho cac cap Dang bo," 3 December 1930, in Dang Cong San Viet Nam, Ban chanh hanh Trung uong, Van Kien Dang, 1930-1945 (Party Documents, 1930-1945) (Hanoi: Central Committee Commission for the Study of Party History, 1972), p. 190. This volume, marked "Luu hanh noi bo" (for internal distribution), is an unexpurgated documentary record.
6. "An nghi quyet cua Trung uong toan the hoi nghi noi ve tinh hinh hien tai o Dong duong va nhiem vu can kip cua Dang," (10-1930)," Van Kien Dang, p. 87.
7. "Truyen don giai thich viec doi ten Dang," (n.d.), Van Kien Dang, p. 188.
8. "Tho cua Trung uong gui cho cac cap Dang bo," p. 191.
9. For a detailed analysis of this split, see Huynh Kim Khanh, Vietnamese Communism 1925-1945 (Ithaca, N.Y.: Cornell University Press, 1982), pp. 99-119.
10. Vo Nguyen Giap, Nhiem vu quan su truoc mat chuyen sang Tong phan cong (The Military Mission in Transition to the General Offensive and Uprising) (Ha Dong Committee for Resistance and Administration, 1950), p. 14, in Library of Congress, Orientalia/ South Asia 4 microfilm collection, P. T. Chau, ed., Vietnamese Communist Publications, item 40.
11. Joseph J. Zasloff, The Pathet Lao: Leadership and Organization (Lexington, Mass.: Heath, 1973), p. 13.
12. Circular dated 27 November 1953, quoted in War Experiences Recapitulation Committee, Vietnam: The Anti-U.S. Resistance for National Salvation 1954-1975: Military Events (Hanoi: People's

Army Publishing House, 1980), trans. Joint Publications Research
Service no. 80968 (Washington, D.C., 3 June 1982), p. 62.

13. Gen. Le Duc Anh, "Quan doi nhan dan va nhiem vu quoc te
cao ca tren dat ban Cam-Pu-Chia" (The People's Army and its Lofty
Internationalist Mission in Friendly Kampuchea), Tap chi Quan doi
nhan dan (People's Army Journal) (December 1984), p. 32.

14. Phnom Penh spokesmen have ruled out any dilution of the
power monopoly held by the Communist party. See comment that
"internationally supervised elections" must be in accord with the
PRK constitution by PRK Foreign Minister Hun Sen on Phnom Penh
Radio, 11 December 1984, in Foreign Broadcast Information Service,
Daily Report: Asia & Pacific (hereinafter FBIS-APA), 14 December
1984; and Hun Sen's statement that "the leading role of the KPRP
cannot be questioned" in interview on Budapest Radio, 30 May 1985,
FBIS-APA, 31 May 1985.

15. For an analysis that emphasizes ideological influences in
Vietnamese views, see Gareth Porter, "Hanoi's Strategic Perspective
and the Sino-Vietnamese Conflict," Pacific Affairs 57, no. 1
(Spring 1984):7-25.

16. Interview with Vo Dong Giang, 31 March 1983. Giang
subsequently became minister of state for Foreign Affairs.

17. Such views were expressed to the author by several
sources in Hanoi's Ministry of Foreign Affairs.

18. See Gareth Porter, "Vietnam and the Socialist Camp," in
Willam S. Turley, ed., Vietnamese Communism in Comparative Perspective (Boulder, Colo., Westview, 1980), pp. 225-264.

19. The Vietnamese retrospective on this break is the Ministry of Foreign Affairs "white book," The Truth about Vietnam-China
Relations over the Last Thirty Years (Hanoi: Foreign Ministry of
the Socialist Republic of Vietnam, 1979).

20. Private communications with the author.

21. Communiqué of the 10th Indochina Foreign Ministers'
Conference, Radio Hanoi, 18 January 1985, FBIS-APA, 23 January
1985.

22. Japan Trade Organization, Bangkok, and International
Monetary Fund, "Socialist Republic of Viet-Nam--Staff Report for
1984," 18 May 1984, appendix I, p. 20.

23. A map in Quan doi nhan dan (People's Army), 1 October
1983, emphasizes the U.S. emplacement in the Western Pacific as
virtually encircling Vietnam and threatening sea communications to
the north.

24. Quan doi nhan dan, 1 July 1983.

25. Quan doi nhan dan, 26 January 1983; also Quan doi nhan
dan, 7 March, 4 and 24 April, and 25 and 28 September 1983.

26. Phạm Binh, director of the International Relations Institute, Ministry of Foreign Affairs, 21 April 1984. Also see Binh's
paper, "Prospects for Solutions to Problems Related to Peace and
Stability in Southeast Asia," presented at the CSIS-IRS meeting in
Hanoi, February 1984, The Indonesian Quarterly 12, no. 2
(1984):221-222.

27. One Foreign Ministry official told this writer in 1983
that Hanoi had dropped its insistence on inclusion of "independence" in the ZOPFAN concept on discovering it was "offensive" to
ASEAN countries, particularly Indonesia, though the ASEAN countries, he went on, "still depend on others and need to complete

their independence in the sense of reducing this degree of dependence."

28. Communiqué, Radio Hanoi, 18 January 1985.

29. Vietnam News Agency, Hanoi, 2 February 1985, FBIS-APA, 4 February 1985.

30. The International Institute for Strategic Studies, The Military Balance 1984-1985 (London: IISS, 1984), pp. 110-112.

31. Interview with Col. Nghiem Tuc, deputy editor of Quan doi nhan dan, 23 April 1984.

32. Interview with Pham Bao, 24 April 1984.

33. Vientiane Radio, 9 March 1985; FBIS-APA, 3 April 1985.

34. Vientiane KPL, 5 December 1984; FBIS-APA, 7 December 1984.

35. Pham Bao interview.

36. Alexander Woodside, "Vietnam and Laos: The Continuing Crisis," paper presented at the meeting of the American Historical Association, Washington, D.C., December 1969.

37. Nhan dan (The People), 18 January 1984.

38. Interview with Nguyen Co Thach, 25 April 1984.

39. Manuscript chronicle quoted in David P. Chandler, A History of Cambodia (Boulder, Colo.: Westview, 1983), p. 116.

40. Pham Bao, in the interview cited above, said: "Vietnam despite its own difficulties has given Cambodia an average of $30 million worth of assistance every year since 1978. This was mostly food at first, but now it includes consumer goods and capital goods. The Soviets give more--over $50 million worth annually--and additional aid is received from international organizations. Vietnam's $30 million is large in relation to its capacity."

41. Circular no. 38, PRK Council of Ministers, 9 October 1982; and Circular no. 240, People's Revolutionary Party of Kampuchea Central Committee, 13 September 1982. For discussion, see William S. Turley, "Is Hanoi Trying to Vietnamize Kampuchea?" Asian Wall Street Journal, 20-21 May 1983.

42. This was affirmed to the author by "land people" refugees, including recently arrived draft-age males, in Dongrak camp on the Thai-Cambodian border, 25 March 1984.

43. Interview with PRK Deputy Foreign Minister Kong Korm, 3 April 1984.

44. Press Department, Ministry of Foreign Affairs, "Policy of the People's Republic of Kampuchea with Regard to Vietnamese Residents" (Phnom Penh, September 1983), pp. 7, 8.

45. Thach interview. Following the overthrow of Prince Sihanouk in 1970, the military government instigated or tolerated attacks on Vietnamese civilian residents in Cambodia. Thousands died, and others sought refuge in Vietnam. Under Pol Pot, the remainder either fled or were killed.

46. These points were made in collective discussion with members of the International Relations Institute, 24 March 1983; also see Turley, "Is Hanoi Trying to Vietnamize Kampuchea?"

47. The figure is widely accepted as a reasonably accurate estimate. A senior official, interviewed 31 March 1983, made the unattributable comment that "it is normal for Vietnamese to live in Cambodia, but treatment of them has not always been good." Lengthy commentary in Quan doi nhan dan, 27 September 1983, portrayed the 500,000 Vietnamese who lived in Cambodia before 1970 as mostly

working folk who shared the Khmer's suffering under colonial rule.
In rare comments on the subject, Khmer antipathy to the Vietnamese
under Lon Nol and Pol Pot is either glossed over or ascribed to
instigation by U.S. and Chinese anti-Vietnam policies.

48. This was the point of Thach's reference above to Cambodia
as a "child" needing to stand alone to stimulate further growth.

49. Anh, "Quan doi nhan dan va nhiem vu quoc te."

50. The idea has circulated among Royal Thai Army officers
for some time. Gen. Pichit Kullawanich, commander of the First
Army Region, is a powerful proponent: "Maintaining that the nation-
alists would not be able to drive out the Vietnamese from Kampuchea, Lt. Gen. Pichit said the future of Kampuchea is that the
country will be divided in zones controlled by the Vietnamese and
the resistance." Bangkok Post, 24 April 1985; FBIS-APA, 26 April
1985.

9 ASEAN:
Patterns of National and Regional Resilience

Donald E. Weatherbee

In December 1978, a unified Vietnam, led by a skilled, cohesive communist elite that disposed of the largest and most battle-tested military force in the region sent its military machine into action across international boundaries, turning the Association of Southeast Asian Nations' (ASEAN) border regions into a zone of conflict and in effect making the Thai-Kampuchean border ASEAN's strategic border with Vietnam. The vague forebodings and looming menaces that had plagued the ASEAN security managers since the communist victories in Indochina in 1975 took on concrete form with this dramatic example of a potential adversary's willingness to use force in pursuit of external political objectives. No matter how complex the factors may have been in Hanoi's decision-making with respect to the invasion of Kampuchea, for a worried ASEAN, the first Southeast Asian "domino" had fallen to aggressive Vietnamese expansionism.

ASEAN's confrontation with Vietnam occurred in a wider regional strategic environment that had since 1975 been made more dangerous for ASEAN by the seeming withdrawal of the U.S. power presence and the apparent political detachment of the United States from local security interests. The relative diminution of U.S. Great Power in the region was accompanied by a higher profile for the USSR in its virtual alliance with Vietnam and the intrusion of Chinese power in direct support of Kampuchea. The changed regional distribution of power directly impinged on military force planning in the ASEAN states (Brunei, Indonesia, Malaysia, the Philippines, Singapore, and Thailand). Although the ASEAN states could not militarily influence the Great Power balance, they did feel the need to redress the local balance of regional military power in order to deter and if necessary repel any Vietnamese thrust across ASEAN strategic frontiers. These frontiers include not only the bleeding Thai-Kampuchean border but the potential conflict zone in the South China Sea where unresolved

201

boundaries pit five of ASEAN'S six members against
Vietnam and the People's Republic of China (PRC).

The intensity of the Vietnamese threat was shaped
by a Vietnamese order of battle that was quantitatively
and qualitatively superior to any the ASEAN states had
available.[1] As Goh Keng Swee, then Singapore Minister
of Defense, put it in mid-1979: "The dominant feature in
the relationship between the Indochinese and ASEAN
states is the superiority of the armed forces of the DRV
[Democratic Republic of Vietnam] over those of ASEAN
singly or collectively. . . . In any military contest
between the two sides--assuming there is no third power
intervention--the outcome would be quick and decisive."[2]
The realistic view in ASEAN security circles held that
as long as ASEAN major power asymmetries marked ASEAN-
Vietnamese relations, Vietnam's putative hegemonic ambitions might remain unchecked. The policy response was
an unparalleled period of ASEAN militarization. It is
this we consider here.

In a semi-ideological sense, ASEAN's efforts to
increase its indigenous security capabilities has been
encapsulated in the (originally Indonesian) concept of
"national resilience." In the abstract, "national resilience" means the total mobilization and utilization
of all of a nation's tangible and intangible resources
in defense of its interests. Construed more instrumen-
tally, "national resilience" has become a euphemism for
beefed up military establishments. As Indonesia's President Suharto warned in his 1981 Independence Day address: "In this turmoil filled world, whoever wishes to
preserve his independence must be ready to take up arms
to defend it."[3]

A closer examination of the ASEAN states' actual
defense planning--the way in which scarce resources are
deployed--is perhaps a better guide to real concerns
about security than the nuanced and diplomatic rhetoric
of the conference halls where the ASEAN elites are ever
alert to the impact of their words on extra-ASEAN powers
and to the self-conscious requirement of a generalized,
if simplified, lowest common denominator consensual
posture. The informing value of defense planning for
the relationship between security policy and threat
perception is particularly relevant when we realize that
planning for enhanced military capabilities in the face
of threat requires mental projection of the threat beyond an immediate crisis. The way in which investment
is made in military development may be a more objective,
longer term measure of threat perceptions than the ver-
balizations of the moment because "the needs to acquire
arms and increase military spending is closely related
to the country's perception of its security situation."[4]
Given the fact that there is a long lead time between
decisionmaking and manifestation when it comes to new
defense capabilities, it is obvious that ASEAN's acquisition of new capabilities is directed to security goals

beyond the demands for the immediate crisis over
Kampuchea.

Preparing for defense is expensive. Faced with a
changed security environment in the late 1970s, the
ASEAN states indicated what their new security priorities were in the reallocation of scarce state budgetary
resources. The period 1979-1982 saw a sharp upward jump
in defense expenditures. ASEAN's rising defense budgets
were meant to finance increases in military personnel,
infrastructure development, acquisition of modern weapons systems, and training. Historically in ASEAN
Southeast Asia, defense planning, force structure, and
tactics have been responses to threats originating from
internal insurgencies. ASEAN military establishments
were built around counterinsurgency (COIN) warfare. The
post-1978 militarization programs in the ASEAN states
have focused on the creation of a conventional warfare
capability, particularly in the strengthening of naval
and air arms, the poor relations in COIN.

If defense policy is to be rational so as to maximize investment, the priorities adopted have to reflect
an appreciation of the capabilities of potential enemies. Although the potential enemy may not be explicit-
ly named, the identity is implicit in planning. It is
obvious that the new conventional warfare capabilities
of the ASEAN states are not geared to Great Power intervention or nuclear threats but to a strategic and tactical assessment of threat in which self-defense capabilities do provide a measure of security in deterring
or repelling aggressive force from a regional enemy.
Realistically--if not diplomatically--the threats con-
trolling ASEAN's military policy seem to be based on the
perceived linkage between Vietnam's possible intentions
and its real capabilities.

THE MILITARY PROGRAMS OF THE ASEAN STATES

Malaysia

Nowhere in the region has the shift from COIN to
conventional preparedness been more dramatic than in
Malaysia. A closer look at the Malaysian military response to the new security environment is instructive
for ASEAN as a group. The Malaysian Armed Forces (MAF)
have been turned around at great financial cost to face
a potential external threat. Between 1979 and 1982, the
total defense and security budget increased by nearly
200 percent. Despite later efforts at savings in
straitened economic circumstances, in 1983 defense still
ate 5.8 percent of Malaysia's Gross National Product
(GNP), more than any other ASEAN country.[5] The Fourth
Malaysia Plan (1981-1985) had built into it a military
expansion program that had as its goal the acquisition
of the means to deter or repel any attack by a regional

aggressor. A sustained developmental emphasis was given to national defense: "A substantial programme for national defence will be carried out to increase the capability and effectiveness of the armed forces to meet any external contingency" (emphasis added).[6]

When in 1980, the then Prime Minister Hussein Onn announced the government's intention to embark on a massive militarization program, he stressed that Malaysia "was in a politically disturbed region and this requires us to strengthen our defences."[7] More directly to the point, the MAF chief of staff stated that expansion of the armed forces was necessary, "to meet external threats posed by developments in Indochina."[8] The military development program is placed in the context of "comprehensive defense," which means, "to put it bluntly," in Deputy Prime Minister Musa Hitam's words, "If you dare attack us, we will give you a bloody nose. Then we will bleed you to death."[9] Realistically, of course, this can only apply to regional conventional power.

The 100,000-man Malaysian Army has in its training and exercises moved substantially away from COIN to conventional warfare preparation.[10] The directive from the top to the brigade commanders is "to prepare the army in the event of a powerful external aggression."[11] When the full planned force of 120,000 is reached, the army will be double the size of the 1979 establishment. The army is still essentially a light infantry force relying on the M-16. It is deficient in artillery, antitank weapons, and air defense. In 1983, as part of the effort to build up its conventional warfare capabilities, the army created a cavalry corps and began to accept the delivery of twenty-five new British Stormer ATPCs along with twenty-six new Scorpion AC90 light tanks. The MAF's new mission is represented in tactical and strategic planning and exercises in which the "opposing" force seems to have the command structure, disposition, and tactics of the Vietnamese. This can be seen in the conventional warfare defense exercises of the Gonzales series held in 1980, 1981, and 1982.

The long-term combat development program for the Malaysian Air Force is designed to give it a new image and role in the country's defense strategy. Historically, the MAF has operated in support of internal security and counterinsurgent warfare. The new emphasis is to enhance the MAF's conventional warfare capabilities. At the end of 1982, an internal debate on Malaysian defense doctrine became public, and protagonists of the air force and navy called for greater resources to defend a country split into two halves by water as well as to protect the important maritime resources in Malaysia's exclusive economic zone (EEZ, i.e., a coastal area beyond the twelve-mile territorial limit over which a state claims an exclusive right to use for economic purposes). Some argued that the air force needed a minimum of 200 combat aircraft to do the job.[12] For the time being, however, it will remain a small air force with a planned three squadron (fifty-nine aircraft) fighter/ground attack force; one squadron of F-5E/F Tigers armed with AIM-9P Supersidewinders and two with the forty A-4 Skyhawks that are being reconditioned by the Grumman Corporation from the eighty-eight mothballed Skyhawks purchased by Malaysia in 1982. At the end of 1983, two RF-5E armed reconnaissance aircraft were delivered.

Malaysia's still expanding navy has on order two German-built corvettes that will be armed with Exocet missiles, four Italian minehunters, and additional off-shore patrol boats and fast attack craft. It already deploys eight Exocet-armed guided missile fast attack craft. Reflecting more extensive maritime surveillance responsibilities, a naval air wing is planned. The upgrading of the air base at Labuan in East Malaysia, which in 1984 became Federal Territory, and the planned new base at Miri in Sarawak will provide facilities for an air umbrella over Malaysia's South China Sea claims. Realistically, in terms of Malaysia's maritime interests and defense responsibilities, the navy's capabilities must be addressed in terms of joint operation or coalition warfare with other friendly navies in the region.

Budgetary constraints have forced a severe cutback and rephasing of some infrastructure projects and procurement programs. By mid-1982, revenue shortfalls caused the government to review its development budgets. The major casualty was the Gong Kedak air base at Pasir Puteh, Kelantan that accounted for more than half of the air force's expansion budget in the Fourth Malaysia Plan. Relative austerity--compared with the expansion budgets of 1979-1982--prevails today. Defense development in the 1985 budget is pegged at $183 million--23 percent less than in 1984, which itself represented a cut of 15 percent from 1983.[13]

The goals of military modernization and expansion remain intact despite the slowdown in the pace of achievement. The pause in the swift expansion is perhaps managerially desirable in that it now allows for attention to consolidation and absorption. The slowdown also allows time for a reassessment of strategic requirements. This seems implied in the emerging defense position of the Mahathir government, which recognizes that Malaysia can only ward off the first waves of any external aggression after which it will have to depend on friends to come to its military assistance.[14]

Malaysia's geostrategic problems were considerably complicated when it militarily occupied the Terembu Layang-Layang atoll in the South China Sea in the summer of 1983 (although the decision was apparently taken in 1981). This brought Malaysia into bilateral territorial conflict with Vietnam in the Spratly group of islands, islets, and reefs. General Tan Sri Zain Hashim warned that Malaysia would use whatever force was necessary to repel an attempt to expel Malaysian forces from the

island.[15] The occupation took place in the framework of
Exercise Pahlawan, the first full-scale combined forces
exercise in Malaysia's maritime zone. The two-month
exercise was seen as a demonstration that Malaysia was
serious about defending its claims. Malaysia also
claims Amboyna Key, sixty-four kilometers northwest of
Terumbu Layang-Layang, which has been occupied by Vietnam since 1978. Malaysia's injection of its power presence into the disputed South China Sea area has given
new strategic importance to the island of Labuan where
the Malaysian military presence is being strengthened.

Singapore

On his first official visit to Singapore in late
1981, Malaysia's Prime Minister Mohamad Mahathir remarked that he could not "see why Singapore has to
bolster its defenses except to complement the defense
capability and greater resilience of this region against
any external threat to the security of the area."[16]
This was rhetorically interpreted by Singapore's Prime
Minister Lee Kuan Yew to mean that the Singapore Armed
Forces (SAF) "should be there to augment Malaysia's
armed forces to meet any threat of external aggression."[17] This illustrates the political strategy behind
the development of the SAF: not only is the strategy for
the defense of Singapore, but it is also to prove to its
neighbors that Singapore would be a useful ally in
any collective effort to maintain regional peace and
security.

Singapore's defense policy is based on the premise
that "if you want peace you should prepare for war.
Countries which have, in the past, not taken the trouble
to prepare themselves for defense, have been overrun by
foreign countries."[18] But how does a small island nation of 2.5 million, sea- and air-locked in the embrace
of larger neighbors, defend itself? The Singapore strategy has been called that of the "poison shrimp" or
"porcupine"--both small but dangerous animals to preda-
tors. Brigadier General Lee Hsien Loong (son of the
prime minister and fastest rising star in the Singapore
political constellation) has noted that a small state
must fight to win. Conventional forces must be built up
that are "better equipped and better organised than
their opponents, which means exploiting technology and
human talent to the full."[19]

Starting from scratch after separation from Malaysia in 1965, Singapore has built a small (55,500)
conscript-based military force that is probably the best
equipped and trained in the region. The SAF is more
than just a "poison shrimp."[20] At the heart of the SAF
is its air force, probably the most advanced air force
in the region. The concentration of capital resources
on air defense maximizes Singapore's modern technologi-

cal base with the ability to operate and maintain sophisticated weaponry. It has an inventory of more than 160 combat aircraft with, at its core, one squadron of twenty-four F-5Es and two squadrons of reconditioned A-4s. An additional six F-5Es are scheduled for delivery. There are also two squadrons of older Hawker Hunters. Air defense is based on four SAM squadrons armed with old Bloodhounds, Rapier, Swedish RBS-70, and, its newest addition, the improved Hawk missile system. As Singapore continues its planned, constant modernization and upgrading, the air defense will be augmented by the purchase of four Grummons E2C Hawkeyes with sophisticated airborne radar surveillance systems at a cost of $450 million. The first is to be delivered in 1987. In justifying the deal, Minister of Defense Goh Chok Tong stated that "we must continually maintain our air defense capability to ensure Singapore's security in a world of constant turmoil."[21]

In 1984, Singapore chose the French company Aerospatiale's Super Puma transport helicopter over Sikorsky's UH-60 and British Westland's Sea King. The buy is for twenty-two with options for twelve additional. At least seventeen of these helicopters will be assembled by Samaero in Singapore, a joint venture company of Aerospatiale and Singapore Aerospace Maintenance Company. The Super Puma is a weapons platform as well as a transport. In the regional geostrategic context we note that the aircraft can be outfitted for antisubmarine warfare as well as equipped with antiship missiles.

The Singapore Navy's combat force consists of six Luersson missile gunboats armed with Gabriel II SSMs. These, together with a variety of patrol craft, are deemed sufficient for a mission that is geostrategically limited. The government decided not to make a major investment in high cost naval systems, preferring to build up the air force.

The army is a conscript force of 45,000 based on a twenty-four-month national service. This is the only nonvoluntary force in ASEAN. Its combat strength consists of three infantry brigades and an armored brigade. The SAF is equipped with 350 AMX-13 light tanks. It has been described as a "well organized, reasonably equipped, and cohesive force capable of home defence and some power projection abroad in a coalition context."[22] Since 1983, SAF has occupied a permanent camp complex for its jungle training in Brunei's Temburong district, north of Brunei Bay. There it has a training party of one hundred regulars. National servicemen rotate through on a six-month basis. In 1983, a Singapore infantry company participated in joint exercises with the Brunei-based British Ghurka regiment at Tutong in western Brunei. The army also jointly exercises at company strength with the Australian Army in Australia. Ties to the Five Power Defense Arrangement are symbolized by the continued presence of New Zealand forces in Singapore.

Brunei

When the U.S. Commander-in-Chief, Pacific (CINCPAC) Admiral William Crowe made the first official CINCPAC visit to ASEAN's newest member state in October 1984, he remarked that he was "extremely encouraged by the Royal Brunei Armed Forces' rapid development" and believed it was capable of protecting the country's sovereignty.[23] Given a population of just over 200,000 and the expenditures on defense, Brunei may be the "garrison state" of the region. In 1984, defense was allocated more than 12 percent of the Brunei budget. In the run up from 1978 to independence on 1 January 1984, substantially more than U.S.$1 billion was spent on weapons acquisitions for the 4,000-man force. These include three Exocet-armed fast attack craft, six Bolkow 105 helicopter gunships, sixteen Scorpion light tanks, and a Rapier air defense battery.[24]

The Royal Brunei Air Force (RBAF) essentially has two missions. The first is internal security in a rapidly changing political and social environment historically dominated by the rebellion of 1962. The second is protection of Brunei's sources of wealth, the on- and offshore oil fields. In this respect Bruneian military capabilities are linked to the indefinitely continuing presence of the British Ghurka battalion based at Seria. We have already noted the Singaporean military presence in Temburong. When the Brunei 3rd infantry battalion is formed, it is expected that it will be based in Temburong.

Brunei's external environment is strategically dominated by Malaysia. Malaysia's new legal regime for Labuan and the military buildup there make common security understandings between Malaysia and Brunei pressing with respect to their bilateral overlapping maritime jurisdictions and the wider problem of Vietnamese and PRC claims in the South China Sea ASEAN EEZs. Naval cooperation with Singapore began before independence and includes annual joint exercises called Pelican.

Indonesia

Indonesia's Second Strategic Development Plan (1979-1983) provided the framework for a major effort at rebuilding and reorienting the Indonesian Armed Forces (Angkatan Bersenjata Republik Indonesia, or ABRI). From a territorially based internal warfare force, ABRI was to be given the capabilities to meet conventional threats along its borders as well as assume the responsibilities of surveillance over Indonesia's extensive archipelagic maritime jurisdictions and EEZ.[25] Although not abandoning its territorial warfare doctrine, Indonesia's military program since 1979 reflects a geostrategic appreciation that the borders of the nation are in its maritime zones, and hence, ABRI must be prepared to

meet the enemy at that border. The magnitude of
Indonesia's maritime defense and surveillance tasks
cannot be overestimated. Within its jurisdictions are
some 2.5 million square miles.

ABRI's commander, General Mohamad Andi Jusuf, took
over in 1978 a military force that was ill-trained, ill-
equipped, and under-strength for the changing regional
security needs (all weaknesses that had been demonstrated by the East Timor campaign to suppress the
secessionist revolt by East Timor residents). To build
up national resilience in ASEAN's southern flank required a substantial investment of new resources. The
defense and security development budget (as opposed to
the routine or operational budget) jumped 500 percent
between 1978 and 1983. This was made possible by the
flow of wealth from Indonesia's petroleum exports. Although Indonesia's defense expenditures were in absolute
terms the largest in ASEAN, they still remained only
about 7 percent of the total development budget.[26] If
General Jusuf's 1978-1982 period was characterized by
military expansion fueled by oil revenues, his 1983
successor General Benny Moerdani's program for ABRI is
one of consolidation and rationalization in a budgetary
framework of austerity (a response to the sharp drop in
Indonesian oil revenues).

ABRI's current force level is about 280,000 men of
whom 210,000 are in the army. It is claimed that the
army was expanded to one hundred combat battalions under
Jusuf, many of which were not up to authorized strength.
General Moerdani has admitted that "from the very beginning we have counted that of the 100 battalions only
about 20 battalions are really the combat troops."[27]
The army's conventional warfare capabilities are centered on its Army Strategic Command (Komando Strategic
Angkatan Darat, or KOSTRAD) under the direct control of
the ABRI commander. KOSTRAD is made up of three infantry brigades (nine battalions), an armored brigade (ten
battalions), and an artillery regiment (three battalions). Two of the infantry brigades are airborne. With
existing lift capacity and the redeployment of elements
of KOSTRAD from Java to Ujung Panjang in Sulawesi, the
army can be quickly deployed anywhere in Indonesia. It
is from KOSTRAD that any forward strategic projection
would be possible. There is a separate special forces
elite command of 4,000 paracommandos also under the
direct control of the ABRI commander. The KOSTRAD units
are the first recipients of upgraded weapons. The
KOSTRAD armored battalions have adopted the AMX-13 light
tank as their battle armor; there are about one hundred
in the inventory with another one hundred on order. A
heavy vehicle repair center in Bandung keeps a mixed inventory on Saladins, Saracens, and Ferrets operational.

Outside of KOSTRAD, during 1984 and 1985, the territorial command structure of ABRI has been reorganized
to simplify and shorten the lines of command. The four
Theater Commands (KOWILHAN) into which Indonesia was

divided are being abolished. Under them the seventeen Area Commands (KODAM) are being reduced to eight and the Jakarta command. Parallel territorial command structures by the other services are being elminated. The eight Naval Area Commands (KODAL) are being changed to Eastern and Western Fleet bases at Surabaya and, when constructed, the new base at Teluk Ratai in West Sumatra. The base originally estimated to cost U.S.$5 billion is an element of Indonesia's new strategic orientations to the South China Sea and straits approaches to the archipelago.

Although modest in size, the Indonesian Navy (ALRI) is becoming a technologically advanced force and already possesses some interdiction capability. At the heart of the new navy are three Dutch built 1,500-ton corvettes armed with four Exocet MM-38 SSMs. Plans for two more have been delayed because of budgetary shortfalls. There are four Korean-built Exocet-armed fast attack craft. Two German-built type 209 submarines (with a third on order) also have a strategic defense role and give antisubmarine warfare (ASW) training. Four ex-U.S. Jones class frigates and two ex-Soviet Riga class frigates are still in service along with numerous other attack, patrol, and auxiliary vessels. Indonesia's latest major naval acquisition is the purchase of three ex-Royal Navy Tribal class frigates, three of seven built between 1962 and 1964 and designed originally for service in the Persian Gulf and Red Sea.

The post-1965 Indonesian Air Force (Angkatan Udora Republik Indonesia, or AURI) inherited not only the taint of complicity in leftist adventurism but an inventory of obsolescent and unserviceable Russian aircraft. The rebuilding of AURI has focused on creating a reaction force capable of supporting ground and naval operations. According to General Moerdani it is overmanned and is a major target for rationalization. The ABRI commander has unfavorably compared AURI's 27,000 men and 100 aircraft to Singapore's 7,000 men and 150-160 aircraft.[28] There is a combat force consisting of a squadron of F-5Es, two squadrons of ex-Israeli A-4 Skyhawks, and a COIN squadron of OV-10F Broncos. The acquisition of three Boeing 737s fitted with side-looking radar that give 100-mile coverage from each side of the aircraft will allow the full width of Indonesia's EEZ to be monitored on a mission range of 3,000 miles.

A very important component of AURI is its transport fleet. Given the geostrategic requirements, lift is vital to Indonesia's security. Twenty-one C-130 Hercules are at the core of the transport squadrons, which also fly an assortment of lighter transports including the Indonesian-assembled CN-212 and eventually the military version of Indonesia's CN-235. The planes are the products of the aerospace company PT Nurtanio, the centerpiece of Indonesia's nascent defense industrial complex. In addition to the fixed-wing aircraft, PT Nurtanio "produces" [assembles] a variety of rotary wing

aircraft including the German BO-105 gunship, the French
Super Puma, and the Bell 412. In 1986, it will begin to
assemble the BK-117. Nurtanio's director of technology
has indicated that a fixed-wing combat aircraft is
planned for the future.[29]
    General Moerdani has shown great concern for Indo-
nesia's air defense capabilities. AURI accepted delivery of the first two French Thomson radar units in
September 1983. These will be used to control F-5
intercepts. In addition to its combat aircraft Indonesia has deployed since 1982 the Swedish Bofors RBS-70
Giraffe SAMs. General Moerdani was very impressed by
Vietnam's air defense system when he visited there in
February 1984. It may have been coincidental, but within days after his return, he told the Indonesian Parliament that an advanced SAM system was necessary for
Indonesia.[30] After looking at a number of possibilities
including the U.S. Vulcan and Chapparal, Indonesia
placed in December a £100 million order with British
Aero Space for the Rapier system, one of the largest
recent defense orders placed by Indonesia.
    The testing of ABRI's newly acquired conventional
warfare capabilities has focused on the northern approaches to Indonesia. Indonesia's 21 March 1980 declaration of its EEZ was immediately followed by the largest combined forces exercise ever held by Indonesia,
which deployed thirty-five battalions over 15,000 square
miles of West Indonesia with the "front" established
north of the Natunas island group. Special attention
has been given to the establishment of a forward base on
Natuna Besar from which Indonesia can project power into
the South China Sea. In 1981, a new runway was opened
at Ranai Air Force Base that can take any aircraft in
AURI's inventory. It is known that other ASEAN air
forces have operated through Ranai. The special marine
unit formed in 1982 dedicated to the protection from
seizure of offshore platforms can operate from there.
Regular naval deployments are now made into the South
China Sea zone as well as combat air patrols.

The Philippines

    Of the military establishments of the ASEAN states,
the Armed Forces of the Philippines (AFP) has probably
been the least affected by perceptions of new external
threats. This does not mean that military expansion and
modernization to some degree have not occurred. Such
changes have been stimulated, however, by internal security developments; external security is largely conceived of as coming under the U.S. security umbrella.
The United States and the Philippines have a joint
defense plan for the Philippines in case of an external
attack worked out through the Philippine-U.S. Mutual
Defense Board (MDB). The Philippine alliance relationship with the United States is unique in ASEAN and with

the U.S. base facilities is seen as crucial to U.S. efforts to counterbalance growing Soviet military power in the region.

The AFP was the bulwark of the martial law adminis-tration and remains the effective guarantor of regime stability.[31]   Its size has ballooned from less than 60,000 in 1971 to 150,000 today.   The defense budget leapt from $82 million in 1972 to $1 billion in 1980 to more than $2 billion in 1984.   The AFP'S expansion in the first instance was largely caused by the military requirements of the Moro insurgency in the south.   The rapidly expanded intake, training, and deployment of officers and men to the bitter war in the south had a corrosive effect on traditional military values, and a breakdown in civil-military relations persists and in fact was exacerbated under the conditions of martial law.   Now it is the growing potential of the New People's Army (NPA) that tests the AFP's internal secu-rity role.   The NPA has taken the initiative across the length and breadth of the archipelago, not infrequently confronting the AFP in battalion strength.[32]   The AFP remains geared essentially to COIN operations.   The challenge, however, is as much political and economic as it is military.

The Philippines is an archipelagic state with a large maritime zone.   The navy is essentially a coast guard, and the air force has a basic ground support mission.   It is U.S. forces in the Philippines that face any possible strategic challenge--with one major and important exception.   The United States is not committed to the defense of claimed Philippine sovereignty in the Spratlys in the mid-South China Sea where the geopoli-tics of petroleum is at play.   There the Philippines militarily confronts Vietnam.   The Philippines has sought to upgrade its capabilities to defend its garri-sons in the Spratlys and has strengthened its support base on Palawan.

Continuing budgetary constraints have prevented the AFP, in the words of the justification for the U.S. security assistance program to the Philippines, "from sustaining and modernizing forces and equipment."[33] These budgetary problems have been exacerbated by the increasing reluctance of the U.S. Congress to assent to the requested military assistance appropriation for the Philippines.   Congress has preferred to change the mix of the aid package promised the Philippines in the con-text of U.S. base rights.

Thailand

Sustaining and modernizing forces and equipment have not been the problem for Thailand.   Thailand's front line status has justified large claims on its budgetary resources by the military.   The Royal Thai Armed Forces defense mission has been reoriented from

the internal war against the armed guerrillas of the
Communist party of Thailand to a more immediate threat
posed by the large, hostile Vietnamese armed presence in
the Thai-Kampuchean border area and the longer range
security concerns posed by uncertainty in estimating
Vietnam's further ambitions. Given that Thailand has
historically considered the trans-Mekong area of crucial
strategic importance, Thai security is seen as menaced
by the projection of Vietnamese power there especially
when that power is supported by an external actor that
is perceived as a potential threat--the USSR.[34]
    The Thai-U.S. connection has been a major factor in
enhancing Thai military readiness. In both the Carter
and Reagan administrations, the United States has publicly reiterated the U.S. commitment to Thailand under
the Manila Treaty with pledges of support in the event
of external aggression. As a demonstration of U.S.
support, the United States accelerated delivery of military hardware in the pipeline and substantially upped
its level of military assistance. President Ronald
Reagan has expressed his "full support" to Prime Minister Prem Tinsula-Nond for the modernization of Thailand's defense.[35]   Since 1982, the United States has
also engaged in extensive annual joint combined Cobra
Gold military exercises with Thailand.
    In the framework of the concept of total defense,
Former Thai Supreme Commander Saiyud Kerdphol has stated
that the present military preparations are sufficient to
meet the external threat by itself.[36] In the conventional war planning, the reequipping and restructuring
of the armed forces and the reserves are directed to
increasing Thai capability to block a Vietnamese land
thrust from Cambodia and through the Laotian tail.[37]
The threat would be aggravated in the event the internal
political situation deteriorated and the external enemy
was able to link up with internal forces. Much of the
growing Thai army political/military doctrine seems
designed to justify the army's preeminent position in
the political system. National defense still claims
nearly 20 percent of the budget, a figure that has been
fairly constant since 1979. Although in some parliamentary circles there may be criticisms of the drain on
scarce resources by military spending, the institutional
dominance of the military buttressed by the fact of the
bleeding border has allowed the government to resist the
kind of sharp defense cutbacks felt elsewhere in the
region.
    The force improvement program of the 160,000-strong
Royal Thai Army (RTA) has concentrated on creating a
more credible deterrent to conventional threats from
Soviet-supported Vietnam.[38] This has meant upgrading
its armor to include eventually 200 M-48 medium battle
tanks as well as its antitank rocket and missile inventory. The RTA receives the lion's share of the defense
funds--in 1984 more than half. Actually, in terms of
the wider security environment the continued concentra-

tion of resources on the army may reflect traditional patterns of intramilitary institutional relations more than strategic orientation.

The navy has acquired missile capability. It has in commission three fast attack craft each equipped with four Exocet SSM as well as three with Gabriel SSM. Four additional Exocet-armed attack craft are under construction in Italian yards. Larger ships include six older frigates. A new frigate and two corvettes are on order. Although Thailand has an Indian Ocean coast, the fleet operates basically in the Gulf of Thailand. One of the navy's major deficiencies has been the absence of sophisticated airborne radar systems for surveillance. Intelligence-sharing arrangements may have made the radar unnecessary. It is possible that at least two submarines may be added to the fleet although no order has been made.

The mission of the Thai Air Force has been essentially COIN. There are two air defense squadrons flying F-5Es and an attack squadron of F-5As. Thailand's new concerns about air defense has thrown into sharp relief the great importance of access to U.S. high-technology weapons systems and electronics. There is sometimes, however, a question of absorptive capabilities. The hasty delivery by the United States of the Redeye SAM to Thailand--the first to Asia--is an example. The weapon apparently has not been integrated into the RTA's air defense. In mid-1984, the U.S. Department of Defense informed Congress that it planned to sell $207 million of upgraded command, control, and communication equipment to Thailand to "strengthen Thai air defenses and thereby reduce the possibility of armed aggression against Thailand."[39] This should probably be placed in the context of the proposed F-16 purchase and the desire to create a modern tactical air defense force.

ASEAN and the F-16 Issue

The most critical current defense question for Thailand has been the issue of the purchase of two squadrons of F-16As. It has been Thailand's insistence since 1983 on acquiring the F-16A that has posed the issue of the export of F-16As to ASEAN and its implications for the regional balance of power. Currently, the most advanced combat aircraft in ASEAN air force inventories is the F-5E (Thailand, 34; Singapore, 24; Malaysia, 13; Indonesia, 11).[40] These 82 planes through four nations balance the 180 MIG-21s that are the combat backbone of Vietnam's air force. Thailand has argued the need to develop an offensive counterstrike air capability that can operate in the expected MIG-23 environment. The acquisition of a more advanced plane now will enable the Thai Air Force to keep abreast of modern weapons technology and maintenance and prevent any lag from developing.

Although willing to provide an export replacement for the F-5Es, the United States has been reluctant to provide an export license for the top-of-the-line F-16A, preferring to promote either the lesser-powered F-16/79 or the Northrop F-20, both especially designed for export. Thailand, however, has insisted on the F-16A, making the issue a political test of the strength of the claimed U.S. commitment. The question was high on Prime Minister Prem's agenda for his April 1984 meeting with President Reagan. In the wake of the 1984-1985 Vietnamese "dry season" offensive along the Thai-Kampuchean border, Congress was officially notified of the intention to grant the export license for the F-16A to Thailand and did not move to block the sale.

There are strong arguments to be made against the sale, not the least of which is the cost. For Thailand, the proposed sixteen-plane package would cost $500 million. One plane and its logistic tail cost about as much as raising and equipping an army division.[41] It is also argued that the scenarios in which the F-16A would really come into play are the least likely in Thai-Vietnamese relations. Finally, it can be suggested that the introduction of the F-16A into a Southeast Asian air force would be escalatory; it would guarantee Soviet transfers of MIG-23s to Vietnam, force budgetarily straining F-16A purchases on other ASEAN countries, and result in the internal reallocation of defense funds from instrumentally more utilitarian purposes.

In Indonesia, for example, although ambiguity about the role of the air force continues to abound in Indonesia's defense doctrine, General Moerdani is committed in principle to keeping the air force at the technological edge with the F-16A as the replacement for the F-5Es if a U.S. export license could be obtained.[42] Indonesia's military development budget has suffered severe entrenchments, and any buy will have to be delayed. On the other hand, the opportunity costs may be acceptable if only not to fall behind Singapore in terms of air combat capabilities. Singapore had taken an option on eight F-16/79s, but it is expected that this would be modified to the F-16A if a policy exception were made for ASEAN countries.[43] Confirmation that Singapore would be first in line after Thailand came with its specification of the Pratt and Whitney F100 engine that powers the F-16A.[44]

ASEAN DEFENSE COOPERATION

The concept of national resilience is complemented by the notion of regional resilience. In defense terms this means that as each ASEAN member increases its capabilities to defend itself the region as a whole becomes more capable of withstanding external aggression, especially from Vietnam. The question is how will the capabilities of the ASEAN members relate to one another militarily for regional resilience. We have sketched the national military responses to the post-

1978 regional security environment. How do these responses become associated in any meaningful fashion? The Thais use the phrase "collective political defense" to characterize their common efforts to eliminate from the region "adverse external interference."[45] But at what point, if any, will "collective political defense" give way to collective military defense?

Although ASEAN leaderships recognize that the members of the grouping have strengthened their armed forces and have forged consensual diplomatic and political ASEAN positions on crucial security issues, they continue to deny that the pattern of security cooperation that has evolved at an ever accelerating pace is leading to a military alliance. Foreswearing alliance, however, does not mean that intensified cooperative defense-related activities cannot take place. Perhaps the most visible element of increased defense cooperation has been the pattern of ASEAN joint military exercises on a bilateral basis. A partial listing of 1984's exercises suggests the structure of the evolving network of military relationships. (The Roman numeral following the code name indicates the number in the series of similar exercises in previous years.)

> Sing-Siam IV: March/April, Singapore-Thailand naval exercises.
> Air Thamal III: April, Thailand-Malaysia air exercise.
> Elang Indopura III: May, Indonesia-Singapore air exercise.
> Malindo Jaya XI: May, Indonesia-Malaysia naval exercise.
> Karipura Malindo III: Fall, Malaysia-Indonesia army exercise.
> Elang Malindo IX: September, Malaysia-Indonesia air exercise.
> Sea Garuda V: September, Indonesia-Thailand naval exercise.
> Englek VII: October, Indonesia-Singapore naval exercise.
> Malapura I: The first joint naval exercise between the Malaysian and Singapore navies was held in the South China Sea at the end of July 1984.
> ADEX: The ADEX exercises are joint air defense exercises testing the Integrated Air Defense System (IADS) for Malaysia and Singapore under the 1970 Five Power Defense Arrangement. The pattern has been for Australian air units based at Butterworth to exercise separately with Malaysia and Singapore. ADEX 84-3, held in June 1984, was a breakthrough. For the first time, Malaysian fighters operated out of a Singapore base.

Several points should be made about this list and the many prior exercises. With the exception of ADEX, they are all bilateral. Other ASEAN bilateral exercises are carried out with friendly non-ASEAN powers such as Australia, New Zealand, and the United States. The emphasis is on naval and air exercises. In part this is because they are are easier to organize and execute. The scenarios are for the defense of maritime and air-space and do not involve "games" of projecting ASEAN power to the Kampuchean-Cambodian border. The fulcrum for ASEANizing of military exercises seems to be Indone-sia. The Philippines' role in this kind of regional resilience seems to be that of hosting the U.S. bases.

With respect to ADEX, Australia will remain an active participant in the IADS even though it will have withdrawn from its base at Butterworth in Malaysia its remaining Mirage squadron by 1988. It has agreed to rotate through the new F-18As for a minimum of sixteen weeks a year beginning in mid-1988. Both Malaysia and Singapore endorse continuity in at least a symbolic Australian presence and seeming contribution to regional defense and stability. Existing air-warning capabili-ties for IADS will be augmented by Malaysia's acquisi-tion of a $180 million Hughes Aircraft HADR system. Moreover, although it is highly improbable that the new E2Cs will fly only in Singapore's very limited airspace, this acquisition too should be viewed in the context of the IADS.

Singapore's strategic military planning problem rests on a fundamental political problem: finding a regional role for the Singapore Armed Forces acceptable to its neighbors. Singapore officials have been the most insistently outspoken in favor of expanding the pattern of military cooperation beyond the bilateral. After his September 1982 summit with President Suharto, Lee Kuan Yew publicly called for raising the level of joint exercises from bilateral to trilateral and even-tually all-ASEAN exercises.[46] This would, he argued, enhance the deterrent capability of the member states' new military strength. His call fell largely on deaf ears. In a surprising, perhaps even gadflyish initia-tive, Indonesia's late ex-Vice-President and Foreign Minister Adam Malik in spring 1984 returned to the idea but in an even more direct fashion. Malik called for a joint all-ASEAN military exercise to be held in Thailand as a clear demonstration to Vietnam of ASEAN solidarity and determination.[47] Not surprisingly, Malik's bold proposal was warmly received only by Singapore. The then Colonel Lee Hsien Loong, SAF chief-of-staff, de-scribed the notion of an ASEAN joint military exercise in Thailand as "viable." His comment was made in Kuala Lumpur where he was on an official visit--his first--to further strengthen the good relations between the armed forces of the two countries.[48]

Singapore's contention that there should be in-creased military cooperation within ASEAN was taken up again in July 1984 when Singapore Second Minister for Defense Yeo Ning Hong, citing the Soviet military build-up, stated that "we must leave no stone unturned to

ensure continued peace and stability. The military
capabilities of the ASEAN countries should be enhanced
to the level necessary to meet external threats and
deter aggression."[49] This was quickly rejected by Philippine Foreign Minister Thinsulinonda Tolentino who
said, "I don't think the times require a change in the
policy and purpose of ASEAN," adding, "I don't think the
idea of military cooperation is even developing."[50] Indonesia also reacted coolly, turning down Singapore's
call for an ASEAN "military alliance" to face external
threats. It did not, however, rule out the possibility
of intensifying military cooperation in the existing
bilteral framework.

One area that has often been mentioned as ripe for
greater ASEAN cooperation is the standardizing of weapons systems and joint purchasing of components. Proposals for procurement cooperation and ASEAN defense-
industrial complementarity stumble, however, on the fact
that Singapore's existing technological and industrial
base would threaten the infant defense industries in
other ASEAN countries. Singapore's defense industries
are world class in terms of competitiveness.[51] Malaysia, for example, talks of standardization of weaponry
as it plans to manufacture its own assault rifle on a
joint venture basis with a European arms manufacturer.
Indonesia is replacing the M-16 as the standard infantry
weapon with the Belgian FNC 5.56 rifle manufactured
under license in Bandung. Meanwhile Singapore is trying
to sell its own assault rifle on the global market.
There is great resistance in Malaysia and Indonesia to
defense interdependence with Singapore. Indonesia's
General Moerdani has put it bluntly: under no circumstances, he has told the Parliament, will Indonesia buy
armaments from Singapore.[52]

At the core of regional resilience is the implicit
strategic alliance that has developed between Indonesia
and Malaysia.[53] For Indonesia, Malaysia is its strategic frontline as well as buffer. For Malaysia, Indonesia is a reliable strategic partner in the geographic
lock they hold on the vital sea- and air-lanes of communication in the Malaccan Strait region. There is an
appreciation of their common security interests in the
South China Sea zone. A 1982 treaty defines Malaysian
rights within the Indonesian archipelagic maritime zone
and preserves Malaysia's communications access between
Peninsula Malaysia and Sabah and Sarawak. The accord
also provides for Malaysian rights of naval maneuver and
exercise as well as joint security operations between
the two countries. The two countries jointly exercise
their navies and air forces in Indonesia's maritime and
airspace north of the Natuna Island. At the end of the
September 1984 Elang Malindo air exercise, Malaysian
Major General Mohammad Ngah stated that the two countries would present a united front against challenges or
threats from other countries.[54] For his part, General
Moerdani has said that Indonesia was prepared to help

Malaysia defend its territorial claim to the disputed Layang-Layang atoll.[55]

In 1984, the scope of the twelve-year-old Malaysian-Indonesian Border Agreement was revised and broadened. The new agreement extends the existing pattern of military cooperation to all borders--including maritime borders--between the two nations and covers the joint use of naval and air forces. According to reports, Indonesian sources said that the new agreement was the "most comprehensive security arrangement Indonesia had with a neighbour," but that similar arrangements could be considered with other ASEAN countries.[56] Even more interesting is the fact that at the signing of the new agreement, Malaysia's Deputy Prime Minister Musa Hitam seemed to place it within the context of the increasing Soviet naval presence in Southeast Asia by stating: "Maybe we have to arrange a new strategy on how to take more appropriate methods to protect our own interests in this strategic area."[57]

It must be noted, however, that Singapore occupies a strategic position in the same area as well. Its capabilities, together with Brunei's, if placed in a regional maritime and air defense context would add substantially to deterrence or interdiction. The number of SSM-capable vessels operated by the four navies, for example, is not insignificant. Nor is their airpower at the existing F-5 level to be dismissed as long as a potential adversary is operating at a MIG-21 level. The political problem is how to enhance what is in fact an Indonesian-Malaysian de facto alliance with the greater cooperation with Singapore in order to create an effectively integrated defense system. Recent events in Malaysian-Singapore defense relations point in the direction of greater cooperation through the first joint exercising between the two countries. It will not be alliance, however; it will be a broadening of the developing ASEAN security entente.

THE EXTRAREGIONAL CONTEXT

Malaysia has consistently rejected moves to change the "informal" and bilateral basis of security cooperation in ASEAN. In reiterating the Malaysian opposition to converting ASEAN into a "defense network," Deputy Foreign Minister Abdul Kadir Sheikh Fadzir expressed nonaligned Malaysia's concern about the wider political implications of such a move. He emphasized that "Malaysia's policy was to avoid such bloc formation moves" because ASEAN's members "are not prepared to be military outposts in the forward defence line of foreign powers."[58] The fear that tighter military association might lead to greater alignment is of particular concern at a time when Malaysia and Indonesia are consciously seeking a more equidistant posture between the United States and the Soviet Union. Moreover, there is concern that the

conversion of ASEAN into an overt defense instrument
would make it even less likely that political structures
could be devised to bridge the gap between ASEAN and
Indochina. The formal militarization of ASEAN runs
counter to the newly reinvigorated goal of a Southeast
Asian Zone of Peace, Freedom, and Neutrality (ZOPFAN).

Vietnam has singled out Singapore's "war machine"
for bitter attack as a major source of regional tension.
In commenting on Singapore's efforts to turn ASEAN into
a military alliance and its plans to build "a unified
weapons depot to prepare for war against the Indochinese
countries," Hanoi attributes this to Singapore's "one
sole objective which is to serve the aggressive and
expansionist policy of the American imperialists and the
Chinese hegemonists." [59] Deep suspicion of ASEAN military cooperation also colors Soviet judgment of the
grouping. ASEAN is depicted by the Soviets as under
constant pressure by the capitalist powers interested in
turning ASEAN into a military alliance directed against
the regional forces of "social renovation and progress," [60] i.e., the Indochinese countries and the USSR.
In the Soviet analysis of Indonesian policy one of the
positive elements offsetting the policy's "right-wing
tendencies" is that Indonesia actively resists the militarization of ASEAN. The Soviets see this resistance as
based on Indonesia's correct understanding that the
real threat to regional security does not arise from
Indochina. [61]

The Soviet comment quoted above points up the political fracture line in ASEAN that militates against a
common security strategy at the most minimum level of
self-defense against a direct aggression. As the fear
of a Vietnamese blitzkrieg has receded, singularly different long-term threat perceptions in the ASEAN region
have become manifest. [62] Indonesia and Malaysia feel
that the years of confrontation with Vietnam over Kampuchea have made the region vulnerable to Chinese political ambitions and strategic designs. There is concern
that the de facto Thai-Chinese alliance could have a
destabilizing impact in the long run. In this respect,
although the continued U.S. political-military presence
in the region is welcomed as a necessary ingredient in
the Great Power regional balance of power, especially
given the Soviet-Vietnamese link, it does not require
Jakarta or Kuala Lumpur to mortgage their future options
vis-à-vis the playing out of Sino-Soviet rivalries to
U.S. global security interests.

CONCLUSION: THE COSTS OF MILITARIZATION

Trends emerging from the prolonged crisis over
Kampuchea seem to be leading to a permanent hard division of Southeast Asia into two conflicting blocs facing
one another militarily across the Thai frontlines and in
the South China Sea. If this proves to be the case, the

costs of this division should be calculated. They are
both direct and indirect, political and economic. Let
the future accountants simply take note of the opportunity costs of a high level of conventional military
preparedness in ASEAN with the reallocation of scarce
resources to weapons systems such as the F-16A. We also
should be aware of the heightened stresses on the fragile domestic political institutions of the ASEAN states
as demands for more defense in an atmosphere of chronic
insecurity enhance other institutional claims of the
military. Moreover, as in the case of Singapore and its
neighbors, the creeping militarization of ASEAN has
reinforced old antagonisms and suspicions as newly developing military capabilities are measured against
possible future intentions. Will the balance sheet show
that the investment of half a decade in attempting to
redress the local balance of power contributed to national and regional resilience as broadly conceived?

NOTES

1. The standard source for order of battle comparisons is
The Military Balance published annually by the International Institute of Strategic Studies, London; see also, G. Jacobs, "Vietnam's
Threat Potential to ASEAN," Asian Defense Journal (May 1982):16-27;
Douglas Pike, "Vietnam, a Modern Sparta," Pacific Defense Reporter
(April 1983):33-39.
2. Goh Keng Swee, "Vietnam and Big-Power Rivalry," in Rich-
ard Soloman, ed., Asian Security in the 1980's: Problems and Poli-
cies for a Time of Transition (Santa Monica, Calif.: Rand Corpora-
tion R-2402-ISA, November 1980), p. 113.
3. Suharto, 17 August 1981, text as reported in Foreign
Broadcast Information Service, Daily Report: Asia & Pacific, 21
August 1981, p. N-7.
4. Khaw Guat Hoon, "Weapons Proliferation and Security in
Southeast Asia," in Robert O'Neill, ed., Insecurity: The Spread of
Weapons in the Indian and Pacific Oceans (Canberra: Australian
National University Press, 1978), p. 153.
5. This according to Deputy Defense Minister Abang Abu Bakar,
Straits Times, 3 March 1983.
6. Fourth Malaysia Plan, 1981-1985 (Kuala Lumpur: National
Printing Office, 1981), p. 185.
7. Speech to UMNO's 31st General Assembly, text as given by
The Star [Penang], 5 July 1980.
8. General Tan Sri Sany Jaffar, quoted by the Straits Times,
12 March 1979.
9. Deputy Prime Minister Musa Hitam, "Malaysia's Doctrine of
Comprehensive Security," Foreign Affairs Malaysia, 17, no. 1 (March
1984):97.
10. In addition to the Military Balance, in general for
Malaysian force structure, see Harold Crouch, "A Strict Division,"
Far Eastern Economic Review, 20 October 1983, pp. 46-51; Col. John
M. Fitzgerald, "Malaysia: Defense in Transition," Pacific Defence
Reporter (March 1984):23-28.

11. Brig. Gen. Mustafa Awang, quoted by the New Straits Times, 6 April 1981.

12. Straits Times,, 4 January 1983.

13. Asian Wall Street Journal Weekly, 29 October 1984, p. 22; Far Eastern Economic Review, 1 November 1984, p. 42.

14. Straits Times, 22 October 1984.

15. Straits Times, 20 September 1983.

16. Straits Times, 18 December 1981.

17. Straits Times, 19 December 1981.

18. Goh, "Vietnam and Big-Power Rivalry."

19. Brig. Gen. Lee Hsien Loong, "Security Options for Small States," speech to the Singapore Institute of International Affairs, 16 October 1984.

20. In addition to The Military Balance, in general for Singapore's force structure, see Kirpa Wong bin Rahim, "The Singapore Armed Forces," Pacific Defense Reporter (November 1980):56-58; Patrick Smith and Philip Bowering, "The Citizen Soldier," Far Eastern Economic Review, 13 January 1983, pp. 26-32.

21. Straits Times, 1 January 1984.

22. Special correspondent, "Singapore: The Reserves Provide the Teeth," Pacific Defense Reporter (October 1983):20.

23. Straits Times, 12 October 1984.

24. In addition to The Military Balance, in general for Brunei's force structure, see Hans Indorf, "Brunei--The Vulnerabilities of a Mini-state," Pacific Defense Reporter (September 1984):46-49.

25. In addition to The Military Balance, in general for Indonesia's force structure, see Donald E. Weatherbee, "Indonesia: A Waking Giant," in Rodney Jones, ed., Third World Regional Powers and the Future of Conflict (New York: Praeger, in press).

26. Indonesian budgetary data are contained in the annual Ministry of Finance report, Nota Keuangan dan Rancangan Anggaran Pendapatan dan Belanja Negara. It should be noted, however, that a substantial proportion of Indonesia's defense expenditures has been based on off-budget revenue sources. These too have contracted as Indonesia is forced to adjust to a post-oil era.

27. Interview in Tempo, 15 October 1983.

28. Tempo, 15 October 1983.

29. Harmono Pusponegara as quoted in the Indonesia Times, 14 March 1984. For a general discussion of Indonesia's defense industries, see Donald E. Weatherbee, "Indonesia's Defense-Industrial Complex," in James Katz, ed., Sowing the Serpent's Teeth: The Implications of Third World Militarization (Lexington, Mass.: Heath, 1986).

30. Straits Times, 21 February 1984.

31. In addition to The Military Balance, in general for the Philippine's force structure, see Khalid Abdullah, "The Armed Forces of the Philippines: Security Through Development in the 1980s," Asia Defense Journal (June 1982):20-35; Larry A. Niksch, "The Philippines: Uncertainties after the Aquino Assassination," Pacific Defense Reporter (February 1984):21-29.

32. U.S., Congress, Senate, Committee on Foreign Relations, The Situation in the Philippines, staff report (Washington, D.C.: GPO, 1984).

33. Congressional Presentation, Security Assistance Programs FY 1985, p. 89.

34. Sukhumbhand Paribatra, "Strategic Implications of the Indochina Conflict: Thai Perspectives," Asian Affairs 11, no. 3 (Fall 1984):32.

35. "Take-off for F-16s," Far Eastern Economic Review, 26 April 1984, p. 17.

36. General Saiyud Kerdphol, "The Meaning of National Security," ISIS Bulletin 1, no. 2 (October 1982):13.

37. For a general assessment of Thailand's security options, see Hans Indorf, "Thailand, the Front-line State," Pacific Defense Reporter (April 1982):36-44.

38. In addition to The Military Balance, in general for Thailand's force structure, see Hans Indorf, "Thailand: A Case of Multiple Uncertainties," Pacific Defense Reporter (September 1983):23-35.

39. Straits Times, 27 June 1984.

40. The figures are as given in The Military Balance, 1984.

41. "F-16 Counter-attacked," Far Eastern Economic Review, 25 October 1984, p. 50.

42. Jakarta Post, 19 December 1984.

43. Straits Times, 18 March 1985.

44. Aviation Week and Space Technology, 27 May 1985, p. 15.

45. Air Chief Marshal Siddhi Savetsila, minister of Foreign Affairs of Thailand, "ASEAN's Contribution to Asian Security," ISIS Bulletin 2, no. 4 (October 1983):30.

46. "A New Call for Unity," Asiaweek, 22 October 1982, p. 24.

47. Kompas, 8 May 1984.

48. Straits Times, 10 May 1984.

49. Straits Times, 23 July 1984.

50. Straits Times, 25 July 1984

51. For Singapore's defense-industrial complex, see Michael Richardson, "Singapore's Defense Industry," Pacific Defense Reporter (May 1983):69-75.

52. Straits Times, 21 February 1984.

53. In general for the Indonesian-Malaysian relationship, see James Clad, "Alike But Different," Far Eastern Economic Review, 18 April 1985, pp. 23-30, especially pp. 25-27.

54. Antara, 29 September 1984.

55. Straits Times, 4 December 1984.

56. Ibid.

57. Malaysian Digest, 31 July 1984.

58. Ibid.

59. Quan doi nhan dahn, 5 March 1984.

60. See, for example, A. Grebenschikov, "ASEAN in the Strategy of Washington and Tokyo," Far Eastern Affairs (January 1984):38-47; Y. Plekhanov, "ASEAN in Washington's Plans," International Affairs (Moscow) (June 1984):81-85.

61. V. Andreyev, "Indonesia: Growing Pains of Development," International Affairs (Moscow) (May 1984):59-66.

62. A good overview of ASEAN's differential threat perceptions is Robert O. Tilman, The Enemy Beyond: External Threat Perceptions in the ASEAN Region (Singapore: Institute of Southeast Asian Studies, 1984); for Indonesia, Malaysia, and Singapore, see Donald E. Weatherbee, "The View from ASEAN's Southern Flank," Strategic Review 11, no. 2 (Spring 1983):54-61.

10 ANZUS: The Alliance Transformed

Michael McKinley

ANZUS is a treaty that embodies anxiety. When the negotiations that led to its establishment commenced in early 1951, there was anxiety about the sort of arrangement that would guarantee Australian and New Zealand security in an age of British incapability. This worry was more keenly felt in Australia than in New Zealand, but both countries had perceived, during several years, a need for the United States to succeed Britain in guaranteeing their vital interests. The pressure, therefore, for this arrangement, ultimately called the ANZUS treaty, came from Australia and New Zealand—not from the United States. The United States had steadfastly taken the position that no formal treaty was necessary.

However, gradually the U.S. position changed. First, U.S. solidarity and appreciation grew as Australia and New Zealand sent ground forces to Korea. Second, all three nations were similarly concerned about the entry of the People's Republic of China into the Korean War and the threat China's action posed to Asian security. Third, the United States, partly in response to Chinese military activity, desired a "soft" peace with Japan and hence needed to obtain the support of U.S. allies who still feared a revival of Japan, a prime reason for the ANZUS treaty. Fourth, the United States, Australia, and New Zealand shared a concern for communist imperialism in general and regional communist expansionism based on the Asian mainland. Without doubt, also, there was at that time a sense of shared values, similar history, and common purposes that made a high level of close cooperation possible and natural.

Nevertheless, Australia and New Zealand differed as to the purpose and importance of the treaty. Australia wanted a formal arrangement more than New Zealand did, but the nature of the arrangement each sought also admitted differences between them. New Zealand, for its part, wanted a unilateral declaration by the United States that it would protect New Zealand, like that

given to Canada in 1938. This had an obvious attraction
to Wellington because, if effected, it would not require
that New Zealand give much, if anything, in return.
Australia's preferences for a formal trilateral treaty,
with provision for consultation, won out, however. Although New Zealand had to accept a formal treaty with
reciprocal obligations, the diplomatic liaison between
the three countries was seen as an intimate and effective one, both reassuring and comforting. Indeed, according to Frank Corner, former secretary of the New
Zealand Department of Foreign Affairs, the easy access
that Australian and New Zealand officials had to their
counterparts during various U.S. administrations was a
cause for envy among representatives in Washington of
other countries and to many of their governments.[1] In
short, the experience of the lesser powers in ANZUS
confirmed findings made by scholars that small powers
can have disproportionate influence over their larger
ally.[2]

Insofar as Australian and New Zealand defense was
concerned, the benefits attributed to ANZUS seemed to
expand with the passage of time. As the 1978 New Zealand Defence Review stated: "ANZUS has been accepted by
successive New Zealand Governments as the ultimate guarantee of security in the region."[3] Others, however,
held (and still do) a much more skeptical assessment of
ANZUS: that it is in reality a useless piece of paper
because each party is bound only to "consult" and only
to "act to meet the common danger according to its
constitutional processes." Indeed, as Desmond Ball
wrote in 1983:

> The ANZUS Treaty itself, however, is neither an abso-
> lute nor watertight guarantee, and nor is it the pri-
> mary determinant of United States military assistance
> to Australia and New Zealand. Whether or not the
> United States would come to the assistance, and the
> conditions on which it would be forthcoming, would
> depend essentially on the calculation of interests made
> by the United States Government at the time.[4]

Ball was alluding, in this passage, to the essentially equivocal nature of the U.S. guarantee under
ANZUS in certain circumstances. He was able to cite not
only two historical examples of U.S. equivocation but
also certain scenarios in which the United States, its
willingness notwithstanding, would be unable to provide
other than incidental help.[5] Implicit in ANZUS, therefore, is a continuing element of uncertainty caused by
the potential differences between what Australia and/or
New Zealand might hope for, and how much any particular
U.S. president and the Congress can or will deliver.

Nevertheless, as the aforementioned Defence Review
statement indicates, this did not prevent the New Zealand government from weaving for itself considerable
faith (supported by hope and inference) in what it

called the "ultimate guarantee" of ANZUS. For New Zealand, the price of this guarantee seems seldom to have
been in evidence. The benefits of alliance were
stressed while its costs were seen either as inevit-
able--in which case they were beyond argument--or hid-
den, in which case they were also beyond argument. New
Zealand defense came to be viewed, almost as reflex, in
an ANZUS framework. In Australia, where perceptions of
defenselessness were more acute, the treaty also was
invested with faith. Encouraged by Liberal-Country
party (coalition) governments who were in power for most
of the time, a strong populist sentiment emerged there,
as well, in favor of the alliance. In an interview in
March 1985, the Minister of Defense, Kim Beazley, outlined five areas of defense and foreign policy where the
cooperative relationship under the ANZUS rubric was
important: (1) intelligence exchange, (2) direct influence with the U.S. government, (3) special access to
U.S. equipment, (4) special opportunities for military
exercises, and (5) defense science cooperation.[6] New
Zealand documents also confirm these advantages.[7] In
short, Australian and New Zealand views mutually reinforce the proposition that ANZUS represents a vital defense asset against threats to the South Pacific and its
environs.[8]

SECURITY THREATS TO OCEANIA AND
THE NEW CHALLENGE TO ANZUS

    Although ANZUS originally was assumed to cover the
area north of Australia and New Zealand, it has over
time developed a certain elasticity of scope. Consequently, it now very definitely includes the South Pacific and, with somewhat less emphasis, the Indian Ocean.
The region north of Australia has always exercised the
minds of Australian security planners, and a number of
chapters in this volume attest to why this has been, and
should be, the case. Because the Indian Ocean is not
within the focus of this work, it is excluded from
further consideration; however, the expansion of ANZUS
coverage to that area reflects some of Australia's more
enduring defense preoccupations during recent years.
    Oceania, by comparison, does not command the same
attention. Indeed, the South Pacific must currently be
one of the very few areas of the world in which local
powers can produce threat assessments that are both
brief in content and mild in nature. "Fortunate" or
"benign" are terms that have been used by both Australian and New Zealand ministers to describe their local
security environments. Nevertheless, there are certain
disturbances in Oceania's tranquility.
    Those disturbances fall under three categories--the
establishment of a South Pacific Nuclear-Free Zone
(SPNFZ), tuna fishing, and French colonialism.[9] As
regards the first, a SPNFZ treaty was endorsed at the

16th South Pacific Forum in Rarotonga (the Cook Islands) in August 1985 by eight of the thirteen eligible states present. As an Australian initiative, it was, however, a compromise between the global interests of the United States and the regional aims of the Pacific island states. Thus, it banned the acquisition and testing of nuclear explosive devices, the storage and dumping of nuclear wastes, and the stationing of nuclear weapons in the South Pacific. Significantly, however, it did not prevent the testing of delivery systems, the transiting of the zone by nuclear-capable vessels, nor did it prevent access to such vessels (member governments were left to decide their respective policies).

Tuna fishing rights also have the potential of distancing the small regional states from the United States. What states such as Kiribati seek is a regional management or licensing system that goes some way toward national self-sufficiency. Yet in recent times, the only country willing to provide tangible recognition of this objective has been the Soviet Union. Furthermore, Moscow's offer of U.S.$1.05 million in access fees to Kiribati, and its subsequent acceptance, has been viewed with some trepidation by the states of the South Pacific. For the alliance, the significance of the proposed Soviet venture lies in the possibility that it might be corrupted into something more than fishing access rather than in any suggestion that Kiribati has undergone a transformation to communism. But for Kiribati, the Russian offer equals 10 percent of the republic's national budget.[10]

Where ideological conviction does play a damaging role is in the popular, regional demands for New Caledonian independence by the native Kanaks of the French island possession. Essentially, this brings French colonialism and Melanesian nationalism into conflict, and with it, the possibility of further external intervention beyond the already minor involvement of Libya (for provision of training to a small number of Kanaks). In this circumstance, all the nations of the South Pacific Forum insist that France expedite independence and prevent further expressions of extraregional interests.

The ANZUS alliance will also have to take into account the fact that there are some problems riveting the region--independence and nuclear-free zones--for which aid is an inappropriate and irrelevant "solution." In turn, this implies that Australia (and New Zealand, arguably) will need to demonstrate their Pacific character toward the popular aspirations of the South Pacific. Nevertheless, although some of these demands, such as a comprehensive SPNFZ, are probably not in the realm of achievement, others, such as a tuna fishing regime or New Caledonian independence, very definitely are. Both are manageable. Because of this, future assessments of the level of threat in the South Pacific and the levels of credibility and confidence in ANZUS will be deter-

mined by the alliance partners' responses to what are,
comparatively speaking, still mere disturbances.
    Nevertheless, the irony of the situation outlined
in the foregoing is that it clearly presents the lesser
challenge to ANZUS in Oceania. The real challenge now,
if not strictly a security threat, originates with a
member state. It takes the form, curiously, not of
aggression but of a mode of behavior and policy imple-
mentation that threaten the fundamental cohesion both of
ANZUS and of other treaties and arrangements underwrit-
ten by the United States. That state is, of course, New
Zealand, and the policy, that of banning vessels described as nuclear from its territory and waters.

NEW ZEALAND'S NON-NUCLEAR POLICY VIS-À-VIS ANZUS

    New Zealand's non-nuclear policy can be interpreted
in three ways: first, as a revulsion against nuclear
arms in general; second, as a desire to insulate New
Zealand's immediate region--the South Pacific--from both
nuclear weapons and superpower competition and confrontation; and third, as a move to effect New Zealand's
security by distancing New Zealand, as far as possible,
from any association with nuclear weapons that might
cause it to be a target should war break out.[11] As with
New Zealand's original impetus toward the ANZUS treaty,
the current policy strongly suggests an anxiety about
the state of the world; it is, moreover, a condition
that found official expression more than two decades
ago.
    As long ago as 1963, a New Zealand government took
the formal decision never to permit the storage, testing, or manufacture of nuclear weapons on New Zealand
soil. Because there is no evidence that any of these
were real prospects, this decision serves just to date
official New Zealand opposition to nuclear defense,
however that might be defined. Subsequently, the Labour
party after 1966 and the Labour government of 1972-1975
came to oppose visits by nuclear-powered craft, however
armed, as well as visits by any craft that might be
carrying nuclear weapons. A measure of the changed
conditions in which the alliance once operated is to be
had from the fact that the latter's request of its
allies to refrain from bringing nuclear-powered and
nuclear-armed craft to New Zealand was honored--as was
the succeeding (National party) government's wish to
host such vessels.
    The government elected in July 1984 has followed
the old Labour policy. Accordingly, its official policy
is that the craft of all allied forces that would otherwise be permitted to visit New Zealand must conform, in
positive terms, to two criteria: not only must they be
conventionally powered, but also "demonstrably conventionally armed" (emphasis added).[12] In implementa-
tion, however, this policy has not been applied compre-

230

hensively. For example, U.S. combat aircraft, F-16s, capable of carrying nuclear weapons visited New Zealand in October 1984 for Exercise Triad 84. Yet in February 1985, the New Zealand government rejected a U.S. request to allow the visit of the U.S.S. Buchanan, a twenty-three-year-old Adam class guided missile destroyer, configured with the ASROC system--an antisubmarine rocket capable of being armed with either conventional or nuclear warheads.

Under Prime Minister David Lange, the nominally binding position on all craft admits other ambiguities as well. Until the United States canceled the exercises scheduled for ANZUS (trilateral) participation, the New Zealand government adopted a curious stance on what was and was not permitted for its own forces. By extending its non-nuclear policy to such exercises, the New Zealand services were precluded from any involvement in military exercises designated as nuclear. As Prime Minister Lange has repeated on numerous occasions, his government is determined to state unequivocally that New Zealand wants no part of nuclear weapons.

In point of fact, however, the New Zealand government's policy was just the opposite--equivocal. On 21 February 1985, Minister of Defense Frank O'Flynn announced to Parliament that, despite the above prohibitions, the Royal New Zealand Navy (RNZN) would be allowed to exercise with nuclear-capable vessels outside New Zealand territorial waters. The minister justified this provision on the grounds that New Zealand recognized the right of passage of all vessels on the high seas--which was, and remains, true--but the difficulty arises in attempting to posit this as a basis for exempting the RNZN from government policy.[13] The RNZN, after all, is no more compelled to exercise with ships in international waters than it is with ships in New Zealand waters. But beyond these inadequacies in logic lies a more salient feature of the non-nuclear policy: to date the Labour government has chosen to implement it selectively and in the process has both undermined the credibility of New Zealand's avowed opposition to nuclear weapons and craft and sown the seeds for misunderstanding of its position.

Regarding ANZUS, according to official statements, the New Zealand government remains committed to the ANZUS alliance. But there are two facets of this commitment that deserve special consideration. The first is that ANZUS is only what the New Zealand government defines it to be; the second is that New Zealand's commitment is to ANZUS as a conventional alliance. Thus the prime minister denied that ANZUS obliges New Zealand to accept nuclear weapons and stated that his country has no wish to be defended by nuclear weapons.[14] He defined the value of ANZUS as follows:

New Zealand is a member of ANZUS because we see its

usefulness as a conventional alliance to us and to our region. It is a useful means of interaction among the conventional forces of three countries of broadly similar outlook and interests in the region.[15]

Elsewhere it is also clear that Lange's government continues to subscribe to the "ultimate guarantee" interpretation of ANZUS. In Canberra, in April 1985, he foresaw the "inevitability" of an ANZUS response, despite his government's current equivocation, if one of the three partners were attacked.[16] By so determining the parameters and contingent expectations of ANZUS, i.e., maintaining a non-nuclear policy while expecting a U.S. response in case of invasion or attack, the New Zealand policy on ANZUS might be summarized as a qualified commitment to general alignment.

The above assessment, of course, begs the question "aligned to what?" ANZUS, clearly, is not what it used to be; indeed, after February 1985, the impasse caused by New Zealand has brought into extensive currency the term "inoperative." But this term is taken to apply only to the level and nature of defense cooperation in conditions short of war within the treaty framework. As a result, the core obligations of ANZUS--to consult and act to meet the common danger, in accordance with constitutional processes--remained intact, at least until late September 1985, and were reaffirmed by both Australia and the United States as well as by New Zealand. But this situation, in which the lowest common denominator prevailed, was far from ideal because it emphasized the changed character of the tripartite relationship and underlined the potential for further deterioration of the alliance as it had been known. As the New Zealand government moved closer toward entrenching its non-nuclear policy in legislation, and as diplomatic attempts in September 1985 failed to resolve the essential differences between it and the United States, this potential was realized. In the wake of Deputy Prime Minister Geoffrey Palmer's visit to Washington in the fall of 1985, U.S. statements indicated the extent to which New Zealand had fallen from grace within the alliance.

In this matter, the prospects for rehabilitating New Zealand-U.S. relations, and the treaty as a tripartite alliance, are less than favorable. Public opinion in New Zealand, although solid in its support of ANZUS, has also consistently arrayed itself behind the Labour government's non-nuclear policies. If anything, the trend is toward increased support for Labour on both its weapons and craft proscriptions. The Labour party as a whole, moreover, is further to the left than its subsidiary Parliamentary party and has established constraints on what will and will not be tolerated in the government. Both, however, regard the nuclear ban as one of "principle" and certainly one that is "nonnegotiable."

As Deputy Prime Minister Palmer phrased it, no amount of persuasion, friendly or otherwise, will "cause us to deviate from our policy."[17]

Palmer's declaration does, however, contain elements of exaggeration; survey data have revealed the existence of a body of opinion that might desert the Labour government if its non-nuclear policies resulted in damage to New Zealand's export trade and/or New Zealand's exclusion from ANZUS. In effect, these costs, even imposed separately, would reduce the absolute majority support the New Zealand government now enjoys to a level below 40 percent (based on early 1985 data). If the Labour government is interested in survival beyond the next election, scheduled for 1987, such reservations will have to be borne in mind. Similarly, in a radically changed international threat environment, Labour could be deflected from its current policies. But deflection, or slight modification, is all that might be contemplated: given the strength of Labour's commitment, it must be regarded as highly unlikely that pressures from any of the sources outlined above could produce the abandonment of the non-nuclear policy.[18]

In this matter it should be appreciated that the New Zealand Labour party during the last few years has resolved to withdraw on a fairly regular basis. More recently, at the party's 1985 conference, it resolved to withdraw also from the Five Power Defense Arrangement with Australia, Britain, Malaysia, and Singapore. It also adopted resolutions in favor of nonalignment and neutrality and urged the government to grant permission for the Soviet airline Aeroflot to use Christchurch Airport for deploying Soviet fishing crews. At the same conference, motions were also put (and lost) to close down the U.S. military support operation for Antarctica and cut defense expenditures.

The possible election of the major opposition party, the New Zealand National party, to government is not, however, guaranteed to herald a substantial change. National has been obliged to reexamine its position on numerous issues, and the indications are that it is somewhat less committed to retaining all of its traditional open-door policies regarding visits by allied nuclear-capable vessels. Even if National should resume these policies, it is a moot point whether a resumption would make any difference to the alliance. The present imbroglio has obviously hurt the confidence that existed between New Zealand and its two ANZUS partners. Confidence will not be restored merely by a change of government in Wellington; it will take time. Even then, such restoration is not, perhaps, a realistic expectation. If a future National government should be in power and opposed by a Labour party whose policies were substantially the same as they were in 1985, then ANZUS in general would have only succeeded in becoming partly political (this presumes no change in the attitudes and practices of Australia and the United States). Little

confidence, therefore, could be expected to emerge from
a situation in which the operability of the treaty on a
day-by-day basis was being challenged in a fundamental
way every three years or less. In turn, this suggests
that a critical juncture was reached, and passed, in
ANZUS in early 1985. But unlike many critical junc-
tures, this one admits no rational or even foreseeable
return to the former status quo.

THE ANZUS RESPONSE

In terms of the security disturbances in the South
Pacific, as an alliance ANZUS is virtually silent, although the partners to it have been active in varying
degrees. It was on Australia's initiative that the
SPNFZ was proposed and on a U.S. initiative that a
belated attempt was made to revive the idea of a regional tuna fishing management regime. Both measures, however, are imperfect--the former because it is hardly
comprehensive and the latter because it comes so late
and was virtually forced on the U.S. government by the
Soviet Union's intervention. Expediency has, therefore,
been the determinant in each of these cases, and it has
prompted skepticism with the regional attention span of
Australia and the United States and the affinity they
claim with the countries of Oceania.

Dissatisfaction is also a factor in two other sets
of bilateral relations, notably between Australia and
the United States and between Australia and France. In
the former case, Canberra's discontent originated in
what it saw as Washington's unbecoming silence in the
face of French arrogance in the Pacific, particularly
with respect to continued nuclear testing at Nururoa
Atoll and the sinking of the Greenpeace protest vessel
Rainbow Warrior in Auckland harbor by French agents in
July 1985. Accordingly, in the course of an address in
late September 1985, the Australian ambassador to the
United States, Rawdon Dalrymple, delivered a firm diplomatic warning to the United States that its tardiness in
this regard did nothing for the confidence that the
South Pacific nations placed in the good offices of the
alliance partners. Nevertheless, this was dissatisfaction between close allies and expressed without rancor
or intensity.

As regards French decolonization, it was both Australia's and New Zealand's view that France should expedite the peaceful transition of New Caledonia to an
independent, multiracial society. At the same time,
both countries have condemned the soliciting of any
outside support that might entail the use, or threat of
use, of violence and terrorism to achieve legitimate
political objectives. Whether such expressions of support and caution for the Kanak people will have any
effect is questionable. France in this situation has
shown little willingness to accept outside counsel; on

the contrary, it has for the most part sharply resisted Australian and New Zealand overtures and proceeded at a pace dictated almost entirely by self-reliance.

The most visible consequence of the French attitude was a bitter response by Australian Foreign Minister Bill Hayden during the course of his address before the United Nation's General Assembly on 1 October 1985. In response to an extended period of official obfuscation by the French, then its grudging admission that French agents were responsible for the sabotage of Rainbow Warrior, Hayden attacked France not only for continuing to conduct its nuclear testing program within the new SPNFZ, but by implication berated it for ingratitude-- his charge was based on the fact that no countries sacrificed more lives in defense of France in World War I than Australia and New Zealand. His remarks were an attempt to rectify the "softness" or compromises that many observers saw in the SPNFZ treaty and a reassertion of Australia's identification with the Pacific community.

According to these responses, ANZUS was in effect following the practice in which Australia and New Zealand oversee the preservation of regional security in the South Pacific (even when it involved a certain amount of chiding of the United States). Thus, New Zealand's non-nuclear policy challenge to ANZUS was consistent with this practice, as was the U.S. response to it. Initially, the U.S. government engaged in a time-biding exercise in the hope that New Zealand would soften its position. For some seven months, no request was made of the new government in Wellington to host U.S. Navy vessels of any description. Australia also made no attempt to influence New Zealand, but this nonintervention grew from the more negative expectation that external attempts to influence matters would be unwelcome and counterproductive.

The event that moved the United States away from its initial stance was the rejection by New Zealand of the U.S.S. Buchanan. In its aftermath, the irreconcilable nature of U.S. conventions and New Zealand policy became apparent. With the former refusing to offer vessels that conformed to the Labour government's requirements, or to confirm or deny whether its vessels were carrying nuclear weapons, the latter's refusal to grant port access was assured. In turn, so was U.S. reaction and retribution, which involved drastic reductions in the levels of defense and intelligence cooperation. In effect, ANZUS was rendered "inoperative" as a trilateral security relationship, and New Zealand underwent a change in classification--from ally to friend.

Just as New Zealand signified its intention to provide a basis in legislation for its policy, pronouncements from the Reagan administration became progressively stronger and more punitive. In anticipation of the event, U.S. Under Secretary of State for Political Affairs Michael Armacost gave notice that the United

States could "renegotiate a new treaty arrangement, or perhaps there are other ways the legal eagles in our respective governments can define for transmuting a trilateral alliance into a bilateral alliance." [19]

Notwithstanding U.S. willingness to negotiate a new treaty, there is, and is likely to be for some considerable time, a marked disinclination in Australia to move away from ANZUS. For a start, a new treaty could include provisions that are more restrictive in terms of U.S. commitment to ANZUS. In an age when Congress has become increasingly jealous of its constitutional role in the U.S. foreign policy process, this restrictiveness must be seen as a distinct possibility and one that the White House could prove powerless to circumvent. To labor the obvious: ANZUS is the embodiment of views that prevailed in 1951; to say that its provisions would automatically be transferred, undiminished, to a new treaty would involve a gamble. On these grounds alone, no Australian government could welcome moves leading to the dissolution of ANZUS.

In Australia, too, there are cautions against such a decision. In this regard, there is probably no more eloquent testimony than Prime Minister Robert Hawke's decision not to provide Australian support for the MX missile-testing program. He has argued that such support would put not only ANZUS, but the joint facilities and the visits by U.S. Navy ships to Australian ports, at "potential risk" in the event of war. Lange's position was seen as originating from those opposed to the original MX decision, in association with the left wing of the Australian Labour party (ALP), who it was felt would be able to muster sufficient numbers for the calling of a special Labour party conference to debate the whole alliance structure. Hawke felt strongly about the issue: "I won't be a prime minister of this country where those issues of central and continuing importance to our security are at risk." [20]

In this light, it would appear that a treaty renegotiation could not be undertaken without considerable disruption to prevailing views in the governing (ALP) party in Australia. In all probability, the outcome in Australia would be as uncertain as in the United States, and hence the caution on Australia's part against ever entering renegotiation in the first place.

Canberra could also argue against a renegotiated treaty because of its potential effect on a future New Zealand government that wanted to resume the full range of alliance activities as they were understood prior to July 1984. Although this argument and its implications might be regarded as unlikely (in itself) to restore New Zealand to its prior status in ANZUS, such a restoration would nevertheless be that much more unlikely if, in the meantime, Australia and the United States had formalized their separatism.

Overarching these considerations, however, is the popular support for ANZUS within the Australian electorate as a defense asset. So firmly is this support rooted that moves to replace ANZUS would invariably be thought by the electorate to herald a dimunition in the U.S. commitment to Australia. Thus, in the face of New Zealand's initiative, Hawke's concern was to minimize the domestic risks to his government that could be caused by New Zealand's example and to maintain the vitality of Australia's relationship with the United States.

In order to diffuse any potential domestic risks, Canberra pursued the indirect approach. First, it waited, observing that any successful pressure on David Lange to change his government's position could result in the undermining of his leadership and New Zealand's assertion of an even harder line policy. Second, Canberra declared itself to be neutral in the dispute. Foreign Minister Hayden thus gave public assurances throughout late 1984 that Australia would neither act as "messenger boy" for the Reagan administration nor engage in "heavying" the Lange government over its stand. Somewhat fortuitously, Australia's stance in this period was facilitated by the lack of opportunity New Zealand had to exclude vessels banned under its policy.

In January 1985, however, the policy of limiting domestic risks conflicted with alliance maintenance, or at least was regarded as too passive a strategy to guarantee it. The Buchanan rejection demanded more, and more was forthcoming on three fronts--rebuke, isolation, and denial--from Australia (which reacted in obvious concert with the United States). The rebuke took the form of a strongly worded letter, reportedly sent without cabinet concurrence, from Hawke to Lange. In it, the former wrote that Australia "could not accept as a permanent arrangement that the ANZUS alliance had a different meaning, and entailed different obligations, for different members."[21] Within weeks, isolation and denial were achieved simultaneously using a number of measures--including the cancellation of scheduled trilateral military exercises, the cutting off of intelligence, and, perhaps most importantly, the postponement by Australia (as host nation) of the July 1985 ANZUS council meeting.

Yet, concurrently, Canberra also attempted to ameliorate New Zealand's situation. Thus, as a result of a joint defense ministers meeting in Wellington in April 1985, new words were found to express what consensus there was rather than what issues divided them: "demonstrable and important shared defence interests and a clear need to collaborate on regional security issues."[22] By this formula, basic differences on the alliance were subordinated to an agreement on more Australia-New Zealand (ANZAC) exercises and plans for closer defense industrial cooperation and coproduction. In addition, Australia agreed not only to help New Zealand overcome its external intelligence deficit by establishing and maintaining discrete ANZAC cells that

would handle information not U.S.-sourced, but also to
meet the associated cost these measures entailed. Australia thereby imposed additional burden on an already
stretched defense budget, and with it, elicited criticisms from the Australian right that the government was
either subsidizing or condoning a New Zealand policy
that was inimical to its own interests as already defined by Hawke.

Although criticisms were refuted, it is more difficult to challenge the illogic of Closer ANZAC Relations
(CAR) that the April agreements effectively entail.
Conversely, to embark on CAR now would seem to involve
New Zealand in an association that will be almost as
disagreeable for its policymakers as the nuclear dimensions of the alliance with the United States. The
point, though, is less that the New Zealand government
has failed the test of rational public policy, but that
the Australian government appears committed to a compounded illogicality.

WELLINGTON AND CANBERRA: DIFFERENT PERCEPTIONS AND CAPABILITIES

In terms of sheer defense muscle, it is easy to see
why a new military and political philosophy of closeness
to Australia seems imperative to New Zealand. Defense
spending figures are revealing in this regard.[23]   New
Zealand's defense budget is about one-half Australia's
in terms relative to Gross National Product and has been
steadily shrinking. In 1985-86, New Zealand will spend
about $504 million (in U.S. dollars) on defense (barely
5 percent of total government spending) compared with
Australia's more than $4.6 billion (9.5 percent of the
total). For this reason, any comparison of the force
levels and weapons systems of New Zealand with Australia, or any other regional power, can only be inappropriate. To be sure, in Australia's case, the discrepancy
reflects Australia's proximity to Asia, the vulnerablity
of its northern shores, and its immense natural wealth.
New Zealand, on the other hand, because of its remoteness, the vast ocean that surrounds it, and its relative
paucity of natural resources, perceives no external
threat.

New Zealand

In 1983-84, the cost of New Zealand's defense totaled $470 million. This represented 2.3 percent of
Gross Domestic Product (GDP) and 4.2 percent of government expenditure. Australia spent more than $4.95 bil-
lion, accounting for 9 percent of its total budget. By
1985-86, the disparity was even more striking. In June
1985, New Zealand allocated $504 million to defense--a
figure that represented an 18 percent boost over 1984-85

levels. Total expenditures forecast thus rose to $4.6 billion. To place these figures in perspective--the total New Zealand defense budget is just $2.1 million more than the increase allocated to defense in Australia for 1985-86. One other comparison is also revealing. Among the Western industrialized nations, only Austria, Finland, and Luxembourg spend a lesser proportion on defense.

Approximately one-half of the New Zealand total is accounted for by expenditure on personnel, 17 percent by capital equipment, and approximately 6 percent by forces overseas, mainly the New Zealand presence in Singapore (which includes one of the country's two infantry battalions). Although defense expenditures have increased in real terms since the late 1970s, New Zealand's military capabilities are, to say the least, modest even for a country of 3.3 million people.

In practical terms, New Zealand's 13,000 military personnel and associated equipment represent a working museum, a memorial to the bygone era of the Forward Defense Strategy when New Zealand and Australia envisaged holding at bay whatever threat was extant in Southeast Asia with the considerable help of their dominant alliance partners. The strike force elements without exception are artifacts belonging to modes of thinking that did not survive intact beyond the 1960s; moreover, their obsolescence is so consummate as to render them of questionable utility in a conflict involving any regional power.[24] The Royal New Zealand Air Force (RNZAF), for example, must be one of the few air forces in the world that possesses fighter-type aircraft (which don't even have air-to-air radar) slower than its transport aircraft. In this light, ANZUS's resources, in a strictly military sense, were not improved by New Zealand's active membership, nor, by the same criterion, should they be disadvantaged by its removal.

The prospects for a change in this situation are not bright because New Zealand has suffered from certain economic disadvantages, which are likely to persist.

> New Zealand has had to face the difficult task of creating and maintaining a viable defence force in a society whose wealth is still largely agricultural, with a small population and reliant entirely for its armed forces on a volunteer system in a relatively prosperous society. The task has been further complicated by the fact that the defence environment is principally maritime, and therefore requires a defence profile which includes a viable sea and air capability. These areas of defence however, are at the same time the most capital intensive and technologically sophisticated. However, the changes that have taken place in New Zealand's defence situation over the last decade have been accompanied by spiralling equipment and training costs, in an economic climate which has brought increasing financial constraints. [25]

The magnitude of such constraints can be gauged by reference to just a few economic indicators. Up until the last two years of the Muldoon (National party) government (1982-1984), inflation was of the double digit variety--15.8 percent in 1982, 12.6 percent in 1983, and currently 15 percent. Growth in the Gross National Product (GNP) has also been unspectacular--3.2 percent in 1982; 0 percent in 1983. At the same time, burdens on the economy have been aided and abetted by the fact that the exchange rate was fixed too high. But other factors also had their influence, including a budget deficit, in 1983-84, equal to 9 percent of the GDP--and a foreign debt, in 1982, of $10.2 billion (against a 1982 GDP of only $22.8 billion). Together, these fiscal practices had the effect of dumping New Zealand into a higher foreign debt per dollar of GNP than even Brazil has incurred. It also lost New Zealand the top credit rating it had previously enjoyed among the banks of New York.

Some hope is held for the long-term future of New Zealand's overall economy because the strategy of the Lange Labour government currently is in the control of what can only be described as "free marketeers." Not only have all exchange controls been terminated and the exchange rate floated (effectively devaluing the New Zealand dollar considerably), but the government has abolished all the price controls, wage controls, interest rate controls, most of the industrial subsidies, agricultural subsidies, export subsidies, and state corporation subsidies introduced or intensified by the previous conservative government. It intends to introduce a goods and service tax on everything, including food, and hopes to use the tax revenue so gained to obtain across-the-board reductions in income tax. Just as surprising, it is also dismantling much of its welfare state--something that, ironically, once placed New Zealand in the forefront of "progressive" nations.[26]

It is possible, however, that for all of the Labour government's endeavors, the country wil be unforgiving of its impoverishment in real terms in the immediate future and will remove Labour from office in 1987. This could very well return a National government whose economic policies would be basically reactions (and reactionary) to those of Labour. But in large part, the success or failure of the economic experiment will depend on how the rest of the trading world treats New Zealand. There are grounds for pessimism here because New Zealand's foreign exchange faces competition on all sides from grossly subsidized production such as that from the Common Market.

Economics aside, New Zealand has, however, made contributions to the ANZUS security relationship. But they are of an order much less significant than, for example, some of the U.S. installations in Australia.[27] In a war-fighting sense, the most important New Zealand installation is the Defense Communications Unit,

Tangimoana, north of Wellington, a signals intelligence
(SIGINT) operation under the national control of the
Government Communications Security Bureau. Its particular function is to provide high frequency direction
finding (HF-DF) data to a global network directed to
what was formerly known as the Naval Ocean Surveillance
Information Center (NOSIC) at Suitland, Maryland, but is
now known as the Naval Operational Intelligence Center
(NOIC). The end product of this intelligence is the
location of all naval vessels, especially Soviet naval
vessels (including submarines), on a worldwide basis.
On its own, Tangimoana is of extremely limited strategic
value. If Tangimoana were to be lost to the system, a
replacement could be located elsewhere in the South
Pacific without the alliance suffering any serious intelligence degradation.

In sum, New Zealand's alliance-relevant defense
installations are not really comparable to Australia's
or the United States'. Under certain conditions, installations in Australia would invite a priority nuclear
strike; such is probably not the case in New Zealand.[28]
But even if this crude litmus is disregarded, the nature
of New Zealand's military and strategic contribution to
ANZUS had more to do with the fact that it existed than
with any actual functional attribute.

Australia

For Australia, history, the international environment, and domestic considerations cause the country to
see the world in much less sanguine terms than New
Zealand does. In World War II, the Japanese bombed
Darwin and then penetrated the defenses of Sydney harbor
with midget submarines. These are reminders to Australia that there was peril out of the north, and the view
still has currency even if the origins of the peril have
changed.

For some time now, Australia's suspicious glance
has been in the direction of Indonesia and its operations in East Timor and particularly along the border
with Papua New Guinea. It is here, for example, that
the old Eurocentric notion of the Far East becomes a
distortion. For policymakers in Canberra, this is the
near north, and the closeness is worrying. Despite
frequent and reasonably cordial diplomatic exchanges
between Australia and Indonesia, there has also been an
attempt by Canberra to "signal" Jakarta that there are
limits to what will be tolerated. To this end, it was
announced, in August 1984, that the Royal Australian Air
Force (RAAF) would be locating its 75th squadron, with
the new FA/18 tactical fighter, at Tindal, near Kather-
ine, in the Northern Territory. This expensive (in
excess of $168 million over the first five years) proj-
ect is part of the development of northern defense from
Learmonth in the northwest through Derby, Darwin, and

Townsville in the northeast, and in conjunction with the
Jindalee over-the-horizon radar system. When these
deployments are coupled with the planned rotational
deployment of other FA/18s to the Butterworth Air Base
in Malaysia, there is a clear message to the Indonesians
(and others admittedly) that Australia is prepared to
defend its regional interests. On paper anyway. As
Exercise Kangaroo 83 proved, even allowing for its arti-
ficial nature, the Australian Defense Forces were
stretched to the limit by the insertion of only 200
"invaders" supported by limited airstrikes in the Pilba-
ra region of northwest Australia.

At the risk of appearing to overemphasize Australia's near north, two Indonesian strategic assets sharpen
Australia's concern. The first is the quite long-
standing agreement between Indonesia and the United
States governing the use of various strategic waterways
(e.g., Ombia-Wetar Straits) that U.S. Navy vessels use
to transit from the Pacific to the Indian Ocean. The
agreement implies that Indonesia enjoys U.S. confidence.
The second is the recent appointment of Assistant Secretary of State for East Asian and Pacific Affairs Paul
Wolfowitz as U.S. ambassador to Indonesia. As a "hawk"
who has easy and direct access to the White House, and
as the main orchestrator of U.S. policy on ANZUS, Wolfowitz's appointment indicates that Washington is paying
increased attention to Indonesia. In the light of Department of State and Pentagon anxiety over the future
of the Philippine bases, Wolfowitz's appointment has
been seen as significant in Australia. The fact that,
in 1984, he sparked a minor diplomatic row by making
extremely trenchant comments about Minister for Foreign
Affairs Bill Hayden and Australia's foreign policy under
him, must serve to indicate likely U.S. assistance in
the event of Australian difficulties with Indonesia.

Notwithstanding the worrisome potentialities of
Indonesia, Australia is determined on a closely supportive role in U.S. global strategy. In no area is this
more abundantly clear than in the area of nuclear strategy and the operation of the Australian-U.S. joint facilities at Pine Gap, Nurrungar, and North West Cape.[29]
From the limited public debate and governmental disclo-
sures that have occurred, it is apparent that Pine Gap
and Nurrungar play two intertwined roles. The first is
a stabilizing, verification role as regards arms control
agreements and an early warning role in respect of
missile launches. The second is a destabilizing nuclear
war-fighting role that facilitates counterforce target-
ing of Soviet missile silos. In addition, Pine Gap
provides the United States with a vital covert electronic surveillance capability that cannot be located in any
other part of the world.

According to Desmond Ball, the strategic intelligence function of Pine Gap has always overshadowed its
arms control functions to the point that the United
States is able, with the information it obtains, to

conceal certain nuclear strategic activities from Soviet scrutiny.[30] Under the rubric of strategic intelligence, facilities at Pine Gap also are able to monitor Chinese, Soviet, and Australian communications--official as well as private.

The third facility, as contentious as the other two, is the communications station at North West Cape that provides (among its functions) very low frequency signals to the U.S. fleet of nuclear-powered ballistic missile submarines. In the current state of submarine ballistic missile and associated technologies, this facility is extremely important. Such is the marked superiority of the United States over the Soviet Union that many U.S. commentators with a working knowledge of the various technologies credit the U.S. Navy with a move toward acquiring a first strike capability.[31] More conservative observers, however, deny that this situation is likely in the foreseeable future, yet they also point to policies that, taken together, are strategically destabilizing.[32] (This is, of course, denied by Australian and U.S. government officials who claim that, even if the capabilities are of a first strike nature, and some resist this suggestion, the United States does not adhere to a first strike strategy.)

Overall, then, these facilities fall in function somewhere between support for a doctrine of deterrence that is in a state of erosion and a nuclear war-fighting resource. By the second classification, they are all priority nuclear targets, and this has been confirmed by both U.S. and Australian government testimony. Nevertheless, the possible cost to Australia of hosting the latter is thought by successive governments to be worth the maintenance of the former. Neither under a coalition government nor an ALP government is this likely to change. Indeed, Prime Minister Hawke has put his future on the line insofar as their security of tenure is concerned. In March 1985, he went as far as to say he would not be prime minister if the hosting arrangements for the joint facilities were repudiated.[33] Thus, whether a benign or malign view is taken of these installations, they are regarded by the two largest ANZUS partners as vital.

The joint installations are also nonnegotiable instruments of U.S. policy. Prime Minister Hawke concurs in this, but it is Washington's attitude toward them that is more interesting. Whereas a number of Australian commentators have ascribed diplomatic leverage to the fact that the bases exist on Australian soil, this claim is rejected out of hand by senior U.S. officials. According to David Emery, deputy director of the U.S. Arms Control and Disarmament Agency, the bases are on Australian soil because the Australian government recognizes the very important role they play in promoting peace and in negotiation: they are, therefore, not bargaining chips in intra-alliance relations.[34]

Assertions of this nature have been common through-

out the history of the joint installations. Probably
the most frequent denies that they are, operationally
speaking, U.S. installations over which Australia has
even limited control. Yet the public record is quite
clear on the historical unilateralism of the United
States: in 1973, for example, during the Yom Kippur War,
the facilities at North West Cape, Pine Gap, and Nurrungar were placed on full alert, with North West Cape
being used to communicate the general U.S. alert to both
conventional and nuclear forces in the region to assume
Defense Readiness Condition 3 (DEFCON 3).[35]   At no stage
in the proceedings was the Australian government informed.[36]   In 1984, in the context of the Gulf War
between Iran and Iraq, a cabinet paper warned that the
current lack of Australian control was such that the
U.S. installations could be used without Australian
knowledge to initiate and support action to protect U.S.
interests in the Middle East.[37]   Hence, by any stand-
ards, Australia has been prepared to sacrifice considerable autonomy with regard to the three main U.S. bases
in the country. It hosts, and will continue to host,
U.S. facilities that by their very nature involve a
surrender of sovereignty in the area of war fighting and
possibly nuclear war fighting.

In other, related areas a similar pattern has been
followed--Australia is host to a number of high frequency direction-finding facilities and an OMEGA navigation station with unique military functions. The government has also agreed to allow research in Australian
establishments to be undertaken on a weapons system that
is directly relevant to the Strategic Defense Initiative
(Star Wars) of the Reagan administration.[38]   (The operation of a plethora of other U.S. installations with
varying degrees of strategic relevance is not examined
here.) Nevertheless, from the above brief considerations, there can be no doubt about Australia's extensive
involvement in the U.S. strategic posture. There is
also no doubt that New Zealand's objective of a closer
ANZAC relationship must be tempered by the fact that it
will involve a close alliance with the country that is,
effectively, a U.S. strategic satrap. For New Zealand
policymakers, there is unlikely to be any relief from
this fundamental orientation, under any Australian government, in the forseeable future.

New Zealand pleas for a nuclear-disarmed world, or
at least a nuclear-free Pacific Ocean are, given the
foregoing, unlikely to be accommodated. Certainly, New
Zealand might expect some support from Australia in the
disarmament/arms control sphere, and much is likely to
be made by Australia of its membership in various United
Nations organs, its membership in the Conference on
Disarmament, and its appointment of an ambassador for
disarmament. But none of these is likely to satisfy New
Zealand in the long run because what New Zealand wants
is what Australia cannot possibly provide--the abolition
of the current nuclear world, not its reform.

CAR, therefore, is a massive irony. It would actually subvert and make less credible New Zealand's policies. Whereas those policies now can be characterized as progressive, perhaps revolutionary, because they involve a fundamental rearrangement of long-established practices and understandings, Australian security policies point toward a closer identification and integration with U.S. nuclear strategy. In other words, the ANZAC connection will more closely involve New Zealand with a country that has acquired many of the same characteristics that caused New Zealand to distance itself from another country--the U.S.--in the first place. In turn, this would mean that New Zealand, in the guise of greater security and independence, had only "Japanized" itself--seeking neither to hear, speak, nor see the evil it purports to abhor.[39] In return, Australia might provide and encourage a sense of closeness, but it will do so on its own terms and with a qualified generosity, much like the shelter granted to a difficult child by a previous marriage.

A TREATY IN LIMBO

In such circumstances, it might be thought that New Zealand would, indeed should, withdraw from ANZUS. Instead, the situation admitted an irony in that, until September 1985, New Zealand steadfastly maintained a nonposition on withdrawal from ANZUS. On the contrary, it had, according to Prime Minister David Lange's statements, a continuing, strong commitment to the alliance. One extension of this position was that the onus of any attempt to disestablish ANZUS or to isolate New Zealand within it would be on Australia and the United States. Another extension of New Zealand's position was that any attempt by Australia and the United States to negotiate a separate treaty would signify the demise of ANZUS by unilateral withdrawal.

Expulsion of New Zealand from ANZUS was even less of a likelihood, again for a simple reason: the treaty contains no provisions for expulsion of a member state-- only withdrawal from the Council as specified by Article X, which requires that one year's notice be given to the government of Australia.

Nevertheless, it is significant that since withdrawal (albeit from the Council) was at least contemplated when the treaty was established, and given also that New Zealand was the least of the three powers to sign it, the possibility exists that ANZUS remains viable at the current level of operability between Australia and the United States. This is an intellectual and not a political judgment; the various political dimensions to the present situation could persuade these two countries to move toward a new formal alliance. The same political dimensions also could deter both from

such an initiative in view of the uncertainties that
must attend it.

Even more ironic than New Zealand's position on
withdrawal was its proposal of a Pacific Regional
Defense Arrangement; it was ironic because David Lange
(in Raratonga during the August 1985 South Pacific Forum), the prime minister of the militarily weakest state
in ANZUS, proposed the arrangement yet made no mention
of a role for Australia, upon whom New Zealand is increasingly dependent, both militarily and economically.
It is impossible, therefore, to conceive how New Zealand, which lacks the military and surveillance capabilities to coordinate a regional security arrangement, can
be taken seriously in strategic terms.

Within a month of Lange's proposal, however, the
central question of New Zealand's continued membership
in ANZUS was readdressed and this time in more realistic
terms. In the wake of the deputy prime minister's visit
to Washington and the evident failure of the U.S. and
New Zealand governments to reach a compromise, Lange
denied that there was "any possibility" of a return to
the traditional defense relationship between the two
countries. He therefore stated his preparedness to
scrap ANZUS "in the interests of harmonious relations
with Australia and the U.S." In doing so, he provided
one of the more telling indicators of the morbidity of
ANZUS as it has been known.

In geostrategic terms, to be in New Zealand is to
be lonely. So many negative indicators can be adduced
in support of this fact that it is perhaps more useful
to concentrate on the few positive indicators that make
the same point. Surrounded by vast oceans, New Zealand,
quite simply, is remote from anywhere except Polynesia,
Australia, and the southern polar ice--so much so that
one is tempted to borrow Henry Kissinger's famous depre-
ciation of Latin America and apply it: "a dagger pointing at the heart of Antarctica." Whereas some Australians fear that their country's endowment of natural
resources could provoke some form of attack or incur-
sion, New Zealand's main bounty is agriculture, and the
notion that someone might want to invade for this is
simply fantastic. Whereas Australia is preoccupied with
the near north of its strategic environment, the New
Zealand prime minister in 1969, Keith Holyoake, met with
considerable derision when he attempted to explain his
country's minimal commitment to the Vietnam War in terms
of the "logic" of geography. As was quickly pointed out
to him by David McIntyre, New Zealand's front line could
be placed in Southeast Asia only with the aid of a
spurious "logic": "It is helpful to remember that London
is closer to Hanoi than Christchurch is. Even Disraeli,
who said the 'key of India' was Constantinople, never
claimed that the outer defences of the Straits of Dover
stretched to the Gulf of Tonkin."[40]

Against this background, New Zealand is very much

cast into shadow--a small group of islands behind an
island continent that does not even possess the geostrategic importance that, say, Gibraltar enjoyed in
previous times, or that Australia, in relative terms,
has had thrust upon it now. In short, in geostrategic
terms, if New Zealand did not exist, it would not have
to be invented. The readiness with which the Reagan
administration has been prepared to cut off intelligence
to Wellington in the current impasse suggests that the
U.S. government is well appraised of the distinction
between convenience and necessity with regard not only
to the value of facilities in New Zealand but also the
country's strategic assets.

CONCLUSION

     Against the detachment of New Zealand from ANZUS,
the security challenges faced by Australia and the
United States remain manageable. Although Australia
would obviously welcome U.S. support for its concerns
about France's activities and tuna fishing rights, the
transformation of ANZUS from a trilateral to a bilateral
arrangement is the single most important security event
in the South Pacific and one that the remaining two
partners will need to accommodate.
     New Zealand's non-nuclear initiative undoubtedly
will have an extended effect, but to what end is impossible to say. In Western Europe, the Mediterranean, and
Northeast Asia, there are countries that will not only
give New Zealand's policies close consideration but will
take encouragement from them as well. Thus, for the
United States, the transformation of ANZUS is less important in itself than is its potential consequences in
areas of greater strategic significance.
     For all the potential disturbance this transforma-
tion implies, it is nevertheless possible to view New
Zealand's detachment in positive terms. Outside the
formal treaty arrangement, the ripple effect may be
obviated to a marked degree because the New Zealand
example presents other countries with stark decisions.
Moreover, because nearly every other country in the
world resides in a more threatening environment than the
South Pacific, the irony of the New Zealand stance could
be that states will stay within the bounds of traditional alliance behavior for fear of the costs and uncertainties that occur outside them. In New Zealand's
case, excommunication is not complete. There is a clear
desire, albeit illogical on the basis of the evidence
presented, that Closer ANZAC Relations will develop
between Australia and New Zealand and that the latter
wants to reestablish the close bilateral relationship in
nonsecurity areas with the United States that existed
prior to 1985. What might emerge, therefore, is a
relationship between New Zealand and ANZUS (or its successor) similar to the relationship between the neutral

Republic of Ireland and NATO. It probably satisfies no
one completely, but neither does it upset anyone
mightily.

In the prevailing circumstances, Australia and the
United States will be obliged to take into account a
fundamental disagreement between them and New Zealand.
To use an analogy, New Zealand is playing Luther to the
Alliance's Council of Trent. New Zealand sees itself as
the Reformation character and is energized by its cri-
tique of the existing world strategic order and its
departure from the gospel of international cooperation.
If Australia and the United States respond favorably to
Lange's démarche, they will only be conceding the fact
that, as with the Council of Trent, there was a need to
admit certain imperfections--an occasional greedy friar
or lecherous nun--the modern equivalent being the wide-
spread dispersal of nuclear weapons to innocent places
like the Southwest Pacific. But what the Council of
Trent understood and what Australia and the United
States will need to comprehend is that the real target
is not the abuses in orders but the orders themselves.
Luther did not want monks to be more chaste. He wanted
no more monks.

At issue are the conflicting views of the world
held by New Zealand, Australia, and the United States.
The former has decided that remoteness will continue to
ensure its invulnerability. It make no sense, then, to
criticize New Zealand policies merely because they do
not conform to another reality, for reality is just a
darkness that is sometimes penetrated by lightning that
can be put to good use. And the good use depends on
what is seen. Clearly, the Labour government is acting
on the basis of its own perceptions and shows every
indication of continuing to do so.

For Australia and the United States, the view of
the world is, to persist in the metaphor, illuminated by
the lightning of anxiety and threatening constellations
of forces. Again, it is of no matter whether the view
afforded is accurate--the belief derived from it exists
and that, at the bottom, is what counts. It is according to this belief that the current state of ANZUS has
developed and its future will be determined. Logic,
political accountability, and responsibility demand
nothing less.

NOTES

1. See an article entitled "ANZUS Expert Sets Record
Straight," in the Evening Post (Wellington), 14 February 1985.
Frank Corner, in addition to being the former secretary of the New
Zealand Department of Foreign Affairs, was also at various stages
in his career New Zealand's ambassador to Washington and his country's permanent representative to the United Nations. He took part
in the ANZUS negotiations and was present at the treaty's signing.
2. Ole R. Holsti, P. Terrence Hopmann, and John D. Sullivan,

248

Unity and _Disintegration_ in _International_ _Alliances_: _Comparative_
Studies (New York: Wiley, 1983).
3. New Zealand Department of Defense, _Defence_ _Review_ _1978_
(Wellington: Government Printer, 1978).
4. Desmond Ball, "The ANZUS Connection: The Security
Relationship Between Australia, New Zealand and the United States
of America," _Arms,_ _Disarmament_ and _New_ _Zealand_: _The_ _Papers_ and
Proceedings _of_ _the_ _Eighteenth_ _Foreign_ _Policy_ _School_ _1982_ (Dunedin:
Department of University Extension, University of Otago, 1983), p.
79.
5. Ibid., pp. 79-82.
6. _National_ _Times_ (Sydney), 8-14 March 1985.
7. For a detailed account of New Zealand's benefits, see
Briefing _Papers_ _Prepared_ _for_ _the_ _Minister_ _of_ _Defence_, a series of
papers supplied to the Minister of Defence, the Hon. F. D. O'Flynn,
on taking up his appointment and released by him on 19 October
1984. In particular, see Brief Two.
8. See Andrew Mack, "The Pros and Cons of ANZUS," Paper
presented to the Fabian ANZUS Conference, Lorne, Victoria, 4-5 May
1985.
9. On these matters I am particularly indebted to Dr.
Richard Herr of the Department of Politics, University of Tasmania,
for making available his paper on the 16th South Pacific Forum
entitled, "What's Happening to the Neighbourhood? Australia's South
Pacific Relations."
10. Ibid., p. 6.
11. For expositions and explanations of New Zealand's non-
nuclear policy, see _New_ _Zealand_ _Foreign_ _Affairs_ _Review_ 35 (January-
March 1985), for three addresses by Prime Minister David Lange (pp.
3-17), and one address by the High Commissioner to Australia, Mr.
Graham Ansell (pp. 47-51), hereafter cited as _NZFAR_ 35.
12. Ibid., p. 3.
13. Minister of Defense Frank O'Flynn has said that RNZN
vessels would be allowed to participate in joint exercises provided
they did not involve any use, or simulated use, of nuclear weapons
or maneuvers necessary for their use. Source: _Evening_ _Post_ (Wellington), 22 February 1985.
14. _NZFAR_ 35, p. 5.
15. Ibid., p. 13 (David Lange, Address to the United Nations
Conference on Disarmament, Geneva, 5 March 1985).
16. _Australian_ (Sydney), 18 April 1985.
17. _Dominion_ (Wellington), 26 January 1985.
18. For an extended discussion of issues raised in this
section, see Michael McKinley, _ANZUS,_ _New_ _Zealand_ _and_ _the_ _Meaning_
_of_ _Life_: _An_ _Assessment_ _of_ _the_ _Labour_ _Government's_ _Non-Nuclear_
Policy _and_ _its_ _Implications_ _for_ _the_ _Alliance_ (Canberra: Legislative
Research Service, Parliament of the Commonwealth of Australia,
forthcoming).
19. _Age_ (Melbourne), 31 July 1985.
20. _Australian_ (Sydney), 6 March 1985.
21. _National_ _Times_ (Sydney), 25-31 January 1985.
22. _Australian_ (Sydney), 4 April 1985.
23. Data used in this section is taken in part from _The_
Military _Balance_ _1984-1985_ (London: International Institute for
Strategic Studies, 1984), pp. 96-97, 106, hereafter cited as _The_
Military _Balance_.

24. Further discussion of this subject will be found in J. H. Beaglehole, "New Zealand: Highly Professional, But Upgrading a Slow Process," Pacific Defence Reporter (July 1984):15-19; Robert Miles, "Will God Defend New Zealand?" New Outlook (November-December 1984):36-38; and Dalton West, "The 1983 Defence Review: Prospects and Implications," New Zealand International Review 9 (May-June 1984):2-6.

25. J. H. Beaglehole, "New Zealand: Highly Professional, But Upgrading a Slow Process," p. 20.

26. See, for example, "New Zealand Labour Is Getting It Right," Weekend Australian (Sydney), 8-9 June 1985.

27. Desmond Ball, "The ANZUS Connection," pp. 71-75, 86; see also Peter Wills, "Spy vs. Spy," New Outlook (March-April 1985):27-30.

28. Ball, "The ANZUS Connection," pp. 88-93.

29. The complete list of U.S. installations in Australia is very much longer than these three. For a full analysis, see Desmond Ball, A Suitable Piece of Real Estate: American Installations in Australia (Sydney: Hale and Iremonger, 1980).

30. "U.S. Bases--What Hawke Didn't Say," Weekend Australian (Sydney), 9-10 June 1984.

31. See, for example, Journal of the Federation of American Scientists 33 (December 1980):3-8.

32. See World Armaments and Disarmament SIPRI Yearbook 1979 (London: Taylor and Francis, 1979), pp. 427-452; "Anti Submarine Warfare," Strategic Survey 1980-1981 (London: International Institute for Strategic Studies, 1981), pp. 31-36; and Joel S. Wit, "Advances in Anti-Submarine Warfare," Scientific American (February 1981):31-41.

33. Australian (Sydney), 6 March 1985.

34. Australian (Sydney), 10 December 1984.

35. Defense Readiness Conditions--DEFCONS for short--range from 5 to 1, with 5 being a normal peacetime condition and 1 being the ultimate state of emergency or "maximum force readiness."

36. Ball, A Suitable Piece of Real Estate, p. 16.

37. National Times (Sydney), 25-31 May 1984.

38. This refers to Australian research conducted at the Australian National University in Canberra and the Department of Defense Materials Research Laboratories in Victoria on the development of a "rail gun"--kinetic energy weapons system capable of launching projectiles at velocities approaching the speed of light. Its conventional applications are obvious--point defense for naval vessels against anti-ship missiles--but its strategic applications are even more significant--earth-based and space-based ballistic missile defense.

39. The allusion here is to the Japanese non-nuclear policy that is subverted by their practice of completely respecting U.S. nondisclosure policy and allowing clearly nuclear-capable vessels to be based in, or visit, Japanese ports, etc.

40. David McIntyre, "The Future of the New Zealand System of Alliances," Landfall 84 (December 1967):342. Also see W. David McIntyre, Britain, New Zealand and the Security of South East Asia in the 1970s (Wellington: New Zealand Institute of International Affairs, 1969), pp. 19-32.

Part 4

Future Prospects

11 Emerging Trends and Policy Implications for the Asian-Pacific Region and the United States

Lawrence E. Grinter
Young Whan Kihl

The Asian-Pacific region in the mid-1980s has become second only to Europe as a center of global strategic trends with important policy implications for the entire world. The political-military-economic environment of Asia and the Pacific has radically changed during the decade since the 1975 communist victories in Indochina. These changes have been produced primarily by three critical developments: (1) Soviet and Soviet client military expansion, which benefited from (2) the power vacuum created by U.S. military withdrawals, which in turn has been partially compensated for by (3) the impressive economic growth of the noncommunist Asian countries. The U.S. policy of disengagement and with-drawal from Asia has been reversed. This reversal began late in the Carter administration when President Carter was forced to respond to the Soviet invasion of Afghan-istan in December 1979. The policy has continued since 1981 with the Reagan administration's more activist policy in East Asia, i.e., beefing up the U.S. force presence and supporting regional forces and security initiatives.

In looking ahead, the Asian-Pacific region promises to be both dynamic and volatile in the late 1980s. The emergent trends and patterns in the region will continue to involve the major powers including the United States and the Soviet Union, as well as other regional powers. Diplomatic and power realignments since the 1970s among the major powers in the region have been far-reaching: particularly the U.S. exit from Indochina, Vietnam's invasion of Kampuchea, the 1978 Sino-Japanese friendship treaty, the 1979 U.S.-Chinese normalization, the abroga-tion of the Sino-Soviet alliance in 1980, and the emer-gence of the Association of Southeast Asian Nations (ASEAN) as a growing counterweight to Vietnam. Today China, Japan, ASEAN, and a host of smaller countries and entities in the region stand against the USSR, Vietnam,

253

and North Korea. In short, although the region's power
has diffused, its anticommunist stance has grown more
evident and stronger.

In this concluding chapter some of the future prospects in the region—both short term and long range—are
explored. The chapter concludes with policy implications for the region and recommendations for the United
States.

THREE REGIONAL TRENDS

1. The Soviet military buildup will continue.

The Russians have every right to a Great Power role
in Asia and the Pacific. Three-quarters of their territory and most of their energy and mineral resources are
located in the region. But they view East Asia as an
insecure, often threatening zone, and as a result, their
Asian policies have been at times heavy-handed, long on
threat and military power, but short on constructive
political and economic proposals. In responding to what
the USSR sees as threats to its security, it has emerged
as the greatest military threat to the region. Not
surprisingly, Moscow and the communist governments it
backs in Pyongyang and Hanoi have created exactly the
situation that is most harmful to them short of war: the
near unanimous distrust and opposition of most other
states in Asia and the Pacific including China and the
creation of a de facto security system opposing them led
by the United States, China, Japan, and ASEAN. For its
achievement of military predominance in East Asia, and
its encirclement of China, the USSR pays a heavy price
in diplomatic isolation and regional opposition. The
Russians, victims of their own paranoia, have created a
self-fulfilling prophecy. Given the steadiness and
harshness of Soviet policy in Asia and the Pacific in
the last few years—consistent through four Soviet heads
of state—it is safe to predict that the Russians will
continue both their policy of political-military expansion and their support of Hanoi's and Pyongyang's belligerent activities.

2. The United States will continue to slowly rebalance
   the military scales in East Asia.

Rejecting the earlier policies of withdrawal and
retrenchment by the Carter administration, the Reagan
administration has reversed the U.S. military decline in
Asia and the Pacific by gradually modernizing and expanding U.S. and allied combat power. But this reversal
is not, in and of itself, going to regain U.S. military
superiority in the region. The Russians have too much
momentum. To reverse the Soviet dominant situation
would require drastic measures such as a major Japanese
military expansion in Northeast Asia and possibly the

conversion of ASEAN into a formal military alliance in Southeast Asia. Neither development is likely to occur in the next few years. Thus, the United States and its Asian-Pacific allies must rely on incremental improvements of their combat power and continuing readjustments in their defense burden-sharing.

3. East Asia will continue to be the world's most dynamic trade and investment area.

This fact makes it possible for the Asian-Pacific countries to build up their defenses gradually without undue strain. Of course, Japan--East Asia's richest major country--could double or triple its defense spending without any appreciable effect on its economy. Increasing interdependence and cross-penetration by Asian-Pacific countries of each other's economies will occur as the "Gang of Five" countries (Japan, South Korea, Taiwan, Hong Kong, and Singapore) continue to act as the region's economic engine. The newly industrialized countries of the region--South Korea, Taiwan, Hong Kong, and Singapore--are following Japan's example. Relying on export-led strategies of economic growth, they have become exporters to North America, Western Europe, and Third World countries and are also assisting the less-developed countries. These industrializing countries will be followed by other ASEAN countries led by Brunei, Thailand, and Malaysia, perhaps less by Indonesia and the Philippines. With East Asian economies averaging 6 to 9 percent Gross National Product (GNP) growth rates in recent years, their ability to pay for arms is also becoming easier. Thus the needed reorientation in security burden-sharing in East Asia is made economically simpler, although for political reasons, many Asian states are fluctuating on the question of reliance on the United States. Finally, among the communist countries, China, a de facto U.S. ally, and North Korea, still an adversary, have made some economic progress. The Chinese "responsibility system" mixes capitalism and socialism in effective ways. North Korea, which first turned outward in the early 1970s only to fail, has now, given China's example, turned outward again and begun to attract very limited foreign investment. Vietnam, however, seems caught in the result of its militarism, political repression, and economic mismanagement as it strives to dominate Indochina.

REGIONAL IMPLICATIONS

The three regional trends depicted above will be accompanied by a further diffusion of power in the region and considerable flux in individual states' security policies. A host of cross-cutting dilemmas have emerged that affect both the capitalist and communist countries of the region.

Alliance Dilemmas

Among the allied countries, South Korea (the Republic of Korea, or ROK) will become increasingly self-sufficient militarily as an expanding economy allows South Korea to produce more of its own defense capabilities. Moreover the ROK is on the threshold of becoming an economic competitor of the United States in certain trade areas. Still dependent on the United States for its strategic protection, South Korea may move into the arms trade field, supplying ASEAN and other Third World countries with weapons, technology, and, possibly, advisers. Japan's external security policies also are changing but in subtler--although perhaps more comprehensive--ways than South Korea's. Japan, in fact, is on the threshold of being an important supplier of militarily usable high technology, and it already has these kinds of arrangements with the United States and China. Moreover, Japan may move into accelerated economic aid arrangements with some ASEAN countries that could have indirect military ramifications. Japan's view of its security responsibilities is broadening and maturing both regionally and globally, although Japanese public opinion still supports a benign and passive security role for Japan's armed forces. However, Japan's real defense problem lies close to home in the security situation of the sea named for Japan. It is here that a doubling or tripling of Japan's defense expenditures, in close coordination with the United States and possibly South Korea, could have a serious impact on the Soviet Pacific Fleet's mobility and war plans. How much longer Japan can afford to proceed in a passive defense direction, as the Soviet military expansion continues, is a matter of serious concern for Japan's allies.

In Southeast Asia, the most beneficial security-related development that each of the ASEAN countries could experience is orderly economic development and stable political transitions. If radical forces, for example, took over the governments of either the Philippines, Indonesia, or Thailand, the ripple effects throughout ASEAN would be extremely serious. One has only to recall the chaos that Indonesia's former President Soekarno reaped. Moreover, in the event of a radical takeover of any country, ASEAN's position against Vietnam also would be seriously jeopardized, and Hanoi and Moscow would surely move to exploit the situation.

In the South Pacific, New Zealand's current posture of "nuclear allergy" appears to be no longer resolvable within the Australia-New Zealand-United States (ANZUS) alliance. Although New Zealand has essentially dropped out of ANZUS as an operational factor, U.S.-Australian security cooperation, the heart of the alliance, remains firm.

For the allied countries of East Asia, then, the dilemma is how to balance threatening external environments against the demands of rising local economies and emerging political transitions and also make effective and increasing contributions to a revamped allied security system.

Communist Country Problems

Among the Asian communist countries serious schisms are well evident. China, hostile to the USSR, is arming itself against the Russians and the Vietnamese with the aid of Western technology. Vietnam, dependent on the USSR for extensive military and economic assistance, displays tension with its Russian advisers and undoubtedly desires a more independent foreign policy. In Indochina, historic ethnic frictions among the Khmers, Laos, and Vietnamese have complicated Hanoi's drive to dominate the area. North Korea seeks to balance its relations between Moscow and Beijing with renewed Soviet military support but is now also seeking--along the lines of the Chinese model--to attract Western investment. These realities, especially China's hostility toward the Soviets and the Vietnamese, that Beijing selectively employs as pressure points around its periphery, complicate Soviet expansion in the area.

Likely Conflict Zones, Problems, and Transitions

The Sea of Japan's Security
Control of this sea may be the single most critical political-military question in East Asia because it impacts on all the major powers as well as the two Koreas. In spite of Japan's benign, reticent perception of the Soviet and North Korean threat and Tokyo's continuing efforts to conciliate Moscow, will the enlarging Soviet presence and pattern of intimidation push Japan into new security measures? Will trilateral security cooperation inevitably follow between the United States, Japan, and South Korea? Isn't this a strategic necessity anyway, particularly in air and sea defense coordination, as the Soviet threat mounts in Northeast Asia?

The Sino-Soviet Border
The border continues to be heavily armed and there are no likely prospects for force reductions in the area. U.S., European, and Israeli technology and weapons are now going into China to help bolster China's defenses against the USSR. How far should Western military aid proceed in this regard? Does it intensify the ongoing arms race on the Sino-Soviet border? Does it further complicate relations between the People's Republic of China (PRC) and Taiwan?

The Korean Arms Race

The Korean Demilitarized Zone (DMZ) is the most heavily armed 155-mile strip in the world. How much farther will the Korean arms race proceed before either a saturation point is reached or an accidental war occurs? Should there be a deliberate policy of restraint on arms sales and technology by the external suppliers to the two Koreas? Perhaps such restraint already exists--the United States took seven years after agreeing "in principle" to sell F-16s to South Korea before the first deliveries were made, and Russian MIG-23s were not supplied to North Korea (the Democratic People's Republic of Korea, or DPRK) until June 1985. What about creating a nuclear-free zone on the Korean peninsula? What conventional arms restraints and political accommodations, resulting from inter-Korean dialogues and/or four-power conferences on Korea, would have to accompany such a development?

The South China Sea and the Spratly Islands

The combination of potential oil reserves and territorial ambitions by the littoral states will produce continuing friction in the South China Sea. For example, Vietnam, Malaysia, China, Taiwan, and the Philippines have already staked claims, and military skirmishes have resulted. Some of these countries are reorienting their defense capabilities from internal defense to external preparedness because of both the offshore problem and Vietnamese/Soviet activities. No evident supranational authority seems likely to be created that will help resolve these conflicts. Within ASEAN, cooperative devices and policies to moderate these problems, which exist in prototype form in terms of joint military exercises and cooperation, could be accelerated.

Indochina

Whether Hanoi is motivated by ideology, chauvinism, or legitimate security concerns as the Vietnamese politburo interprets them, the Socialist Republic of Vietnam, with full Soviet backing and a growing conventional military arsenal, shows no clear signs of relinquishing its military occupation and tutelage of Kampuchea and Laos. Complicated by Sino-Soviet rivalry in the area and increasing Soviet, Chinese, and some U.S. arms transfers, the implications of this Third Indochina War are very serious for Thailand, the rest of ASEAN, and the United States. Should the war widen, could Thailand defend against a concerted Vietnamese attack without outside support? Would that support in turn further divide Southeast Asia and increase Sino-Soviet tensions? Would the United States inevitably be dragged into these events?

The Philippine Situation

Next to the warfare in Vietnamese-occupied Kampuchea, the instability in the Philippines is the most critical

internal violence problem in East Asia. The New
People's Army (NPA) evidently has at least 12,000 ac-
tives in the field that are supplied in part from
abroad, including, reportedly, the Soviet Union. The
stakes are high because of U.S. military dependence on
Subic Bay Naval Base and Clark Air Base and ASEAN's
benefit from the U.S. presence. ASEAN is still fragile
enough that it could be traumatized if a critical member
government fell. Nothing, of course, would please Moscow and Hanoi more as they would be sure to accelerate
efforts to exploit the situation. Are there possible
ASEAN initiatives, political, economic, or military,
that could help defuse the situation in the Philippines?
Since U.S. military projection out of Subic and Clark
benefits ASEAN, perhaps the anti-U.S. sentiment in the
Philippines could be reduced by a multilateralization of
the bases with ASEAN forces. Or perhaps ASEAN diplomats
could offer to mediate between Manila and the NPA.
Could ASEAN markets be opened more to Philippine products? In short, can the Philippine situation be re-
gionalized to the allies' benefit?

Critical Political Transitions
Six Asian countries are likely to experience critical
political transitions in the next few years that bear on
the region's stability. These are: North Korea, where
Kim Il-Sung's son, Kim Jong-Il, will take over; South
Korea, where Chun Doo Hwan may turn over the government
to a civilian; China, where Deng Xiaoping, in his eight-
ies, wishes to ensure a stable transition; the Philippines, where a difficult political transition has
created considerable instability; and Indonesia and
Singapore, where both President Suharto and Prime Minister Lee Kwan Yew are expected to retire.

RESPONSES

These prominent problems and challenges will make
for both a dynamic and dangerous Asian-Pacific region in
the last half of the 1980s. For the allied countries of
East Asia both multilateral and individual policy responses are required. The three most critical security
problems, where multilateral responses seem most appropriate and necessary, are in the Sea of Japan, Southeast
Asia, and on China's northern border. Growing Soviet
intimidation of Japan and South Korea is very likely to
push the two countries into some kind of closer security
cooperation. The logic is on the side of such cooperation because the historical problems between Japan and
Korea are no deeper than those between Germany, France,
and England, for example, countries that fought each
other to total exhaustion twice in the twentieth century, but also have joined the world's most viable
alliance since 1947.
In Southeast Asia, ASEAN is on the verge of broad-

ening its multilateral diplomatic and economic position
against Vietnam's Soviet-supported aggression to include
a security dimension as well. If this cooperation could
also result in a decrease of territorial squabbles among
ASEAN countries--especially regarding offshore and ju-
risdictional questions--it would be doubly beneficial.
It is important that ASEAN not jeopardize its own regional resilience.

Regarding tension on the Sino-Soviet border, all of
East Asia has a stake in the outcome there. In the
absence of a Sino-Soviet normalization, China's turn to
the West for military assistance in defending against
the USSR is drawing a sympathetic, multilateral response. There are risks, however, to Western involvement here. Too extensive a Chinese military buildup,
for instance, could trigger Russian overreactions or
frighten China's noncommunist neighbors or both. There
is also the chance that China might use Western weapons
against countries other than the USSR.

POLICY IMPLICATIONS FOR THE UNITED STATES

The United States can encounter the twentieth century's final fifteen years in East Asia from a position
of some confidence and equanimity about the overall
direction of and trends within the region. As always,
the Soviet Union and its clients seek to upset the
region's stability and economic and political progress
through military intimidation (such as violation of
Japanese and Philippine air and seaspace), state-
sponsored terrorism (the Rangoon bombing), and subversive measures (such as Soviet Embassy activities in
Manila). These are not inconsiderable facts. They
produce an insecure external environment for many countries in the region.

But in contrast to Soviet policies and behavior is
the stunning economic growth of the noncommunist Asian
and Pacific countries and the benefits this growth provides. In short, U.S. allies and friends have more to
gain, and more to lose, than ever before. Thus, although the U.S. ability to undertake unilateral diplomatic and military actions in the area is reduced, the
Asian countries are more able to increase their own
share of the region's security burdens. Therefore it is
imperative that the United States develop a long-term
strategy and policy for Asia and the Pacific based on
two fundamental premises: (1) the continued deterrence
of the USSR and its friends through increasingly multilateral security actions among the United States and its
Asian partners; and (2) the continued advance of the
prosperity of East Asia and the United States through
reciprocal and more equitable trade and tariff
arrangements.

Recommendations for U.S. policy proceed from these
two strategic principles and are as follows:

1. Reaffirm the U.S. commitment and determination to help defend the region so as to provide the security environment for continuous economic growth and political stability.
2. Support increased efforts to multilateralize the defense of the Sea of Japan, and its three critical straits, thereby seeking to bring Japan, South Korea, and the United States together in accelerated military planning and operations in the area.
3. Support the emergence of ASEAN as a de facto military alliance and back ASEAN's policy of keeping the pressure on Hanoi until Vietnam withdraws its combat forces from Kampuchea.
4. Support the selective arming of communist China against the USSR, provided guarantees can be obtained that China will not use these arms against any other country than the USSR.
5. Expand the Rim of the Pacific (RIMPAC) naval exercises to include ASEAN members and South Korea, in addition to the current U.S., Canadian, and ANZUS forces and Japanese observers.
6. Support more liberalized trade in the area among Asian-Pacific countries, based on General Agreement on Trade and Tariff (GATT) principles of mutual benefit and nondiscrimination so as to open markets to all Asian-Pacific countries that promote orderly ecomonic and political development.

CONCLUSION

The management of Asian-Pacific security in the future must reach beyond previously mechanistic applications of geostrategic tactics and instead should actively plan the desired future political, economic, and military contours of the region. The key criteria for allied policy planning must be continued deterrence of the USSR and promotion of equitable economic progress among friends. Security responsibilities and military burden-sharing need to be made more reflective of the individual Asian-Pacific nation's actual and emerging capabilities. In the final analysis, the Asian-Pacific region probably has the most promising future of any area in the world. Creative diplomacy, market economics, liberalized political systems, and realism in security matters will be the essential ingredients in fulfilling this promise in the years ahead.

Appendices

APPENDIX A.   U.S. PACOM Area Military Personnel, December 31, 1984

Location	USA	USN	USAF	USMC	Total
Alaska	21	850	3	159	1,033
American Samoa	2				2
Australia	22	401	297	8	728
Bangladesh	2			6	8
Burma	3		2	6	11
China	5	3	3	11	22
Diego Garcia		1,321	13		1,334
Guam/TTPI	91	4,621	3,947	377	9,036
Hawaii (incl. afloat)	19,268	22,907	6,614	8,723	57,512
Hong Kong	12	14	6	11	43
India	5	3	5	20	33
Indonesia	13	14	13	11	51
Japan	2,633	7,850	14,597	20,566	45,646
Johnston Island	147		5		152
Korea	29,232	362	10,806	62	40,462
Malaysia	6	1	2	8	17
Midway Island		13			13
Nepal	2			6	8
New Zealand	2	50	10	6	68
Philippines	56	5,034	9,193	627	14,910
Singapore	3	14	3	9	29
Sri Lanka		3		6	9
Thailand	62	9	29	13	113
Afloat/Embarked					
7th Fleet		16,880		2,775	19,655
3rd Fleet		79,185			79,185
USPACOM Conus Forces					
Ashore Conus		38,035		41,935	79,970
Total	51,587	177,570	45,548	75,345	350,050

Source: DOD Report "Worldwide Manpower Distribution by Geographic
Area," USPACOM AREA DOD Personnel, assigned as of 31 December 1984,
Source: J13, Unclassified, p. 23.

263

APPENDIX B. Selected General Purpose Forces in Asia-Pacific, Part 1

	Japan	Taiwan	South Korea	United States	Subtotal
Ground forces	155,000	330,000	540,000	71,200[a] (approx.)	1,096,200
Aircraft	350-- 40 interceptors; 50 F-15 support fighters 12 C-130 transports and others	480-- F-15 fighters; 30 F-5F fighters with 60 more F-5E/ F-5Fs on order	440-- 220 F-5E through F-5F series	400-- 260 F-5A incl. 230 in 7th Fleet and Pacific Air Force components	1,670 (approx.)
Naval vessels	66 major units; 34 destroyers 18 frigates 14 attack submarines (diesel)	36 major units; 23 destroyers 9 frigates 3 corvettes 2 attack submarines (diesel)	22 major units; 11 destroyers 8 frigates 3 corvettes and numerous large patrol craft	3 carrier task forces; 2 battleships and assorted other major units	---
Main battle tanks	1,020 (approx.) Type 74 and Type 61	309 M-48s	1,200 M-47/48	850-900[b] (approx.)	3,400 (approx.)
Defense budget as % of GNP (1982)	0.93	7.8	6	7.2	---

Sources: Military Balance 1984-1985 (London: IISS, 1984); Research Institute for Peace and Security (Tokyo), Asian Security, 1984.

[a] In South Korea, 29,000; in Japan, 2,100 army, 25,100 marines, 15,100 air force--part of which could be used as backup infantry during wartime; and in the Philippines, 700 marines.
[b] U.S. MBT figures equivalent to one infantry division minus one brigade in Hawaii and one infantry division component in South Korea.

Selected General Purpose Forces in Asia-Pacific, Part 2

	USSR	North Korea	Vietnam	Subtotal	China
Ground forces	400,000[a] (approx.)	700,000	1,000,000	2,100,000 (approx.)	3,160,000 (approx.)
Aircraft	2,200	740 (MIG--17s/19s Su 7s/9s)	290	3,230	5,300 (approx.)
Naval vessels	149 major surface conbatants; 110 submarines; 1-2 VSTOL carriers	21 submarines; 4 frigates; 24 fast attack missile craft; 33 large patrol craft; 155 fast attack gunships	6 frigates; 10 fast attack missile craft; 39 fast attack gunships plus assorted patrol craft	---	2 nuclear attack submarines; 100 diesel submarines; 36 major surface combat ships
Main battle tanks	1,950-2,000 (approx.)	3,000 (approx.) Type 59; T-54/55/62 T-34	2,400 (approx.) Type 59; T-54/55/62 T-34, and M-48s	7,300 (approx.)	11,450 (Note: Western public estimates vary widely)
Defense budget as % of GNP (1982)	12-16	10.2	---	---	8

Sources: Military Balance 1984-1985 (London: IISS, 1984); Research Institute for Peace and Security (Tokyo), Asian Security, 1984.

[a] In Soviet Far East, 52 divisions = 460,000 (approx.); 9,500 Soviet personnel detached to Vietnam; 500 detached to Laos (number of Soviet personnel detached to North Korea unavailable).

Select Bibliography

The following bibliographical items are limited to ones published since 1982-1983, and they are listed under two separate headings: (1) general Asian-Pacific security, and (2) specific materials focusing on issues pertaining to the region, subregions, and specific Asian countries. As a rule, all the materials cited in individual chapters, plus others known to the editors, are included. Books, articles, reports, journals and periodicals, reference guides, and selected newspaper articles are also included.

ASIAN-PACIFIC SECURITY

Air University Review
Armacost, Michael H. The Asia-Pacific Region: A Forward Look. U.S. Department of State, Current Policy, no. 653, 29 January 1985.
Armed Forces Journal International
Asia Pacific Community: A Quarterly Journal. Tokyo.
Asia-Pacific Defense Forum
Asia Yearbook 1984. Hong Kong: Far Eastern Economic Review, 1984.
Asian Defence Journal: Monthly. Kuala Lumpur.
Asian Security, 1984. Tokyo: Research Institute of Peace and Security, 1984.
Asian Survey: A Monthly Review of Contemporary Asian Affairs. Berkeley.
Benjamin, Roger, and Robert T. Kudrle, eds. The Industrial Future of the Pacific Basin. Boulder, Colo.: Westview Press, 1984.
Buckingham, William, ed. Defense Planning in the 1990's. Washington, D.C.: National Defense University Press, 1984.
Clausen, A. W. "The Pacific Asian Countries: A Force for Growth in the Global Economy" (address). World Affairs Journal 3 (Spring 1984):55-56.
Defence Attache
Defence of Japan, 1984. Tokyo: Japan Defense Agency, 1984.
Defense and Foreign Affairs
Defense Monitor: Monthly. Wasnington, D.C.

268

Disam Journal

Garrity, Patrick, J. "Soviet Policy in the Far East." _Asia-Pacific Defense Forum_ (Summer 1983):14-20.

Hofheinz, Roy, Jr., and Kent E. Calder. _Eastasia Edge._ New York: Basic Books, 1982.

Hsiung, James, Ed. _U.S.-Asian Relations: The National Security Paradox._ New York: Praeger, 1983.

International Defense Review

International Security

International Security Yearbook 1984/85. Boulder, Colo.: Westview Press, 1985.

Journal of Northeast Asian Studies

Luttwak, Edward N. _The Grand Strategy of the Soviet Union._ New York: St. Martin's Press, 1983.

McMillen, Donald, ed. _Asian Perspectives on International Security._ London: MacMillan, 1984.

Military Balance, 84-85. London: International Institute of Strategic Studies, 1985.

Morrison, Charles E., ed. _Threats to Security in East Asia-Pacific: National and Regional Perspectives._ Lexington, Mass.: D. C. Heath & Co., 1983.

O'Neill, Robert, ed. _Security in East Asia._ New York: St. Martin's Press for the Adelphi Library, 1984.

Pacific Affairs

Parameters: Journal of the Army War College.

Polomka, Peter. "The Security of the Western Pacific: The Price of Burden Sharing." _Survival_ (January-February 1984).

Sakonjo, Naotoshi. "Security in Northeast Asia." _Journal of Northeast Asian Studies_ 2 (Spring 1983):87-97.

Segal, Gerald. _The Soviet Union in East Asia: Predicaments of Power._ Boulder, Colo.: Westview Press, 1983.

Shaw, Yu-Ming, ed. _Asian Pacific Security: A Multi-national Perspective._ Taipei: Asia and World Institute, 1984.

Shultz, George. _The U.S. and East Asia: A Partnership for the Future._ Address before the World Affairs Council, San Francisco, Calif., March 5, 1983. Department of State Bulletin, 31-6 (April 1983).

Solarz, Stephan J. "The Soviet Challenge in Asia." _Asia Pacific Community_ 24 (Summer 1984):1-27.

Strategic Review

Strategy

Stuart, Douglas T., and William Tow, eds. _China, the Soviet Union, and the West: Strategic and Political Dimensions in the 1980s._ Boulder, Colo.: Westview Press, 1982.

Survival: A Quarterly Journal. London: International Institute of Strategic Studies.

Thomas, Raju G. C., ed. _The Great-Power Triangle and Asian Security._ Boston: Lexington Books, 1983.

Tow, William, and William Feeney, eds. _U.S. Foreign Policy and Asia-Pacific Security: A Transregional Approach._ Boulder, Colo.: Westview Press, 1982.

U.S. Department of Defense, _Soviet Military Power._ Washington, D.C.: GPO, April 1984.

U.S. House of Representatives, Committee on Armed Services. _Report of the Delegation to East Asia._ 98th congress, 1st session, November 16, 1983.

U.S. House of Representatives, Committee on Foreign Affairs. The Soviet Role in Asia: Hearings. 98th congress, 1st session, 1983.

Whelan, Joseph G. The Soviets in Asia: An Expanding Presence. Washington, D.C.: Congressional Research Service, March 27, 1984.

Zagoria, Donald, ed. Soviet Policy in East Asia. New Haven, Conn.: Yale University Press, 1982.

SPECIFIC MATERIALS ON REGIONS/COUNTRIES/ISSUES

Abdullah, Khalid. "The Armed Forces of the Philippines: Security Through Development in the 1980s." Asia Defence Journal (June 1982):20-35.

Barnett, Robert W. Beyond War: Japan's Concept of Comprehensive National Security. Washington, D.C.: Pergamon-Brassey's, 1984.

Bello, Walden. "U.S. Military Bases in the Philippines." Southeast Asia Chronicle 89 (April 1983):3-19.

Byers, R. B., and Stanley C. M. Ing. "Sharing the Burden on the Far Side of the Alliance: Japanese Security in the 1980's." Journal of International Affairs 37, no. 1 (Summer 1983):163-175.

Chandler, David P. A History of Cambodia. Boulder, Colo.: Westview Press, 1983.

Chang Pao-min. Kampuchea Between China and Vietnam. Singapore: Singapore University Press, 1984.

------. "The Sino-Vietnamese Territorial Dispute." Asia Pacific Community 24 (Spring 1984):43-48.

Cumings, Bruce. "Korean-American Relations: A Century of Contact and Thirty-Five Years of Intimacy." In Warren L. Cohen, ed. New Frontiers in American-East Asian Relations. New York: Columbia University Press, 1983, pp. 237-282.

------. The Two Koreas. Headline Series no. 269. New York: Foreign Policy Association, 1984.

Curtis, Gerald L., and Sung-joo Han, eds. The U.S.-South Korean Alliance: Evolving Patterns of Security Relations. Boston: Lexington Books, 1983.

Dibb, Paul. "Soviet Capabilities, Interests and Strategies in East Asia in the 1980s." Survival 24, no. 4 (July-August 1982): 155-162.

Duiker, William J., Vietnam Since the Fall of Saigon. Athens, Ohio: Ohio University Center for International Studies, 1985.

Feeney, William. "The United States and the Philippines: The Bases Dilemma." Asian Affairs 10, no. 4 (Winter 1984):63-85.

Fitzgerald, John M. "Malaysia: Defense in Transition." Pacific Defence Reporter (March 1984):23-28.

Fung-wai, Frances Lai. "Japan's Defense Policy and Its Implications for the ASEAN Countries." Southeast Asian Affairs, 1984. Singapore: Institute of Southeast Asian Studies, 1984.

Gass, Henry B. Sino-American Security Relations. Essay 84-2. Washington, D.C.: National Defense University Press, 1984.

Gayner, Jeffrey, and Gregory Hung. "New Opportunities for U.S.-Thai Relations." Asian Studies Center Backgrounder. Washington, D.C.: Heritage Foundation, April 9, 1984.

270

Grebenschikov, A. "ASEAN in the Strategy of Washington and Tokyo."
Far Eastern Affairs (January 1984):38-47.
Grinter, Lawrence E. The Philippine Bases: Continuing Utility in a
Changing Strategic Contest. National Security Affairs Mono-
graph 80-2. Washington, D.C.: National Defense University
Press, 1980.
Hitam, Musa. "Malaysia's Doctrine of Comprehensive Security."
Foreign Affairs Malaysia 17, no. 1 (March 1984).
Horiguchi, Robert Y. "Vigorous Soviet Buildup." Pacific Defence
Reporter 11, nos. 6/7 (December 1984-January 1985):33-37.
"Indonesia-Vietnam Relations in Regional Perspective." The Indo-
nesian Quarterly 12, no. 2 (1984).
Indorf, Hans. "Thailand: A Case of Multiple Uncertainties." Paci-
fic Defence Reporter (September 1983):23-35.
------. "Thailand, The Front-Line State." Pacific Defence Re-
porter (April 1982):36-44.
------. "Brunei--The Vulnerabilities of a Mini-State."
Pacific Defence Reporter (September 1984):46-49.
Jackson, Karl, and M. Hadi Soeastro, eds. ASEAN Economic Develop-
ment and Regional Security. Berkeley: University of California
Institute of East Asian Studies, 1984.
Jacobs, G. "Vietnam's Threat Potential to ASEAN." Asian Defence
Journal (May 1982):16-27.
Kihl, Young Whan. "North Korea in 1983: Transforming 'The Hermit
Kingdom'?" Asian Survey 24, no. 1 (January 1984).
------. "North Korea in 1984: 'The Hermit Kingdom' Turns Outward!"
Asian Survey 25, no. 1 (January 1985):65-79.
------. Politics and Policies in Divided Korea: Regimes in Con-
test. Boulder, Colo.: Westview Press, 1984.
Kim, C. I. Eugene. "Civil-Military Relations in the Two Koreas."
Armed Forces & Society 11, no. 1 (Fall 1984):9-31.
Kim, C. I. Eugene and B. C. Koh, eds. Journal to North Korea:
Personal Perceptions. Institute of East Asian Studies Re-
search Papers and Policy Studies 8. Berkeley: University of
California Press, 1983.
Kim, Samuel C., ed. China and the World: Chinese Foreign Policy in
the Post-Mao Era. Boulder, Colo.: Westview Press, 1984.
Kim, Young C. "North Korean Foreign Policy." Problems of Commu-
nism (January-February 1985):1-17.
Koh, Byung Chul. The Foreign Policy Systems of North and South
Korea. Berkeley: University of California Press, 1984.
Lake, Anthony. "Dealing with Hanoi: What Washington Can Do." In-
dochina Issues 49 (August 1984).
Lee, Chae-Jin, and Hideo Sato. U.S. Policy Toward Japan and Korea:
A Changing Influence Relationship. New York: Praeger, 1982.
Leifer, Michael. Indonesia's Foreign Policy. London: George Allen
& Unwin, 1983.
Mediansky, F. A., and Dianne Court. Soviet Union in Southeast
Asia. Canberra: Australian National University, 1984.
Mendl, Wolf. Western Europe and Japan Between the Superpowers.
New York: St. Martin's Press, 1984.
Morrison, Charles E. Japan, the United States and a Changing
Southeast Asia. New York: University Press of America for the
Asia Society, 1985.
Nakagawa, Yatsuhiro. "The WEPTO Option: Japan's New Role in East

Asia/Pacific Collective Security." *Asian Survey* 24, no. 8 (August 1984).

Niksch, Larry A. "The Philippines: Uncertainties after the Aquino Assassination." *Pacific Defence Reporter* (February 19984):21-29.

------. "South Korea in Broader, Pacific Defense." *Journal of Northeast Asian Studies* 2, no. 1 (March 1983):85-99.

Olsen, Ed. "Security in Northeast Asia: A Trilateral Alternative." *Naval War College Review* (January-February 1985).

------. *U.S.-Japan Strategic Reciprocity.* Stanford, Calif.: Hoover Institution Press, 1985.

Paribatra, Sukhumbhand. "Strategic Implications of the Indochina Conflict: Thai Perspectives." *Asian Affairs: An American Review* 11, no. 3 (Fall 1984):30-35.

Pike, Douglas. "Vietnam: A Modern Sparta." *Pacific Defence Reporter* (April 1983):33-39.

Plekhanov, Y. "ASEAN in Washington's Plans." *International Affairs* (Moscow) (June 1984):81-85.

Pollack, Jonathan D. *China and the Global Strategic Balance.* Santa Monica, Calif.: Rand Corporation, 1984.

------. *The Lessons of Coalition Politics: Sino-American Security Relations.* Santa Monica, Calif.: Rand Corporation, 1984.

Porter, Gareth. "Hanoi's Strategic Perspective and the Sino-Vietnamese Conflict." *Pacific Affairs* 57, no. 1 (Spring 1984):7-25.

Reed, Robert F. *The U.S.-Japan Alliance: Sharing the Burden of Defense.* Washington, D.C.: National Defense University Press, 1983.

Rhee, Sang Woo. *Security and Unification of Korea.* Seoul: Sogang University Press, 1984.

Richardson, Michael. "Singapore's Defence Industry." *Pacific Defence Reporter* (May 1983):69-75.

Rosenberger, Leif. "The Soviet-Vietnamese Alliance and Kampuchea." *Survey* 27, nos. 118/119 (Autumn-Winter 1983):214-215.

Savetsila, Siddhi. "ASEAN's Contribution to Asian Security." *ISIS Bulletin* 2, no. 4 (October 1983).

Scalapino, Robert A. "Asia in a Global Context: Strategic Issues for the Soviet Union." In Richard H. Solomon, ed. *The Soviet-Far East Military Build-up.* Dover, Mass.: Auburn House Publishing Co., 1986.

Scalapino, Robert A., and Jun-Yop Kim, eds. *North Korea Today: Strategic and Domestic Issues.* Institute of East Asian Studies Korea Research Monograph 8. Berkeley: University of California Press, 1983.

Scalapino, Robert A., and Jusuf Wanandi, eds. *Economic, Political, and Security Issues in Southeast Asia in the 1980s.* Berkeley: University of California Institute of East Asian Studies, 1982.

Scully, William. *The Korean Peninsula Military Balance.* Backgrounder no. 2 of Asian Studies Center. Washington, D.C.: Heritage Foundation, 1983.

Segal, Gerald, and William Tow, eds. *Chinese Defense Policy.* Champaign: University of Illinois Press, 1984.

Shultz, George P. *Challenges Facing the U.S. and ASEAN.* U.S. Department of State, Current Policy, no. 597, 13 July 1984.

272

------. Economic Cooperation in the Pacific Basin. U.S. Department of State, Current Policy, no. 658, 21 February 1985.

Sigur, G., and Y. Kim, eds. Japanese and U.S. Policy in Asia. New York: Praeger, 1982.

Simon, Sheldon W. "China and Southeast Asia: Protector or Predator?" Australian Outlook 39, no. 2 (August 1985).

------. "Regional Threat Environments in Asia: Problems of Aggregation." In Edward Olsen and John Juricka, eds. Armed Forces in Contemporary Asian Societies. Boulder, Colo.: Westview Press, 1985.

Sutter, Robert G. "U.S.-Soviet-PRC Relations and Their Implications for Korea." Korea and World Affairs 7 (Spring 1983):5-20.

Tilman, Robert O. The Enemy Beyond: External Threat Perceptions in the ASEAN Region. Singapore: Institute of Southeast Asian Studies, 1984.

Tow, William T. "U.S.-Japan Military Technology Transfers: Collaboration or Conflict?" Journal of Northeast Asian Studies 2, no. 4 (December 1983).

Turley, William S., ed. Confrontation or Coexistence: The Future of Vietnam-Asian Relations. Bangkok: Chulalongkorn University Press, 1985.

U.S. House of Representatives, Subcommittees on Asian and Pacific Affairs. Hearings: United States-Philippine Relations and the New Base and Aid Agreement. 98th congress, 1st session, June 1983.

Warner, Denis. "Japan's Global and Regional Strategic Perceptions." Pacific Defence Reporter 11, no. 11 (May 1985).

Weatherbee, Donald E. "Indonesia: A Walking Giant." In Rodney Jones, ed. Third World Regional Powers and the Future of Conflict. New York: Praeger, in press.

------. "Indonesia's Defense-Industrial Complex." In James Katz, ed. Sowing the Serpents' Teeth: The Implications of Third World Militarization. Lexington, Mass.: D. C. Heath, 1986.

------. Southeast Asia Divided: The ASEAN-Indochina Crisis. Boulder, Colo.: Westview Press, 1985.

------. "The View from ASEAN's Southern Flank." Strategic Review 11, no. 2 (Spring 1983):54-61.

Weinstein, Martin E., ed. Northeast Asian Security after Vietnam. Champaign: University of Illinois Press, 1982.

Wolfowitz, Paul D. Recent Security Developments in Korea. U.S. Department of State, Current Policy, no. 731, 12 August 1985.

------. The U.S.-China Trade Relationship. U.S. Department of State, Current Policy, no. 594, 31 May 1984.

Yager, Joseph A. "The Security Environment of the Korean Peninsula in the 1980s." Asian Perspective (Seoul) 8, no. 1 (Spring-Summer 1984):85-105.

Yoshitsu, M. Caught in the Middle East: Japan's Diplomacy in Transition. Lexington, Mass.: Lexington Books, 1984.

Contributors

Lawrence E. Grinter is professor of national security affairs, Air Command and Staff College at Maxwell Air Force Base. He has published widely in his field and undertaken numerous studies for the National Security Council, the office of the Secretary of Defense, and the Joint Chiefs of Staff.

Young Whan Kihl is professor of political science at Iowa State University. He has written and co-authored several books including _World Trade Issues: Regime, Structure and Policy_.

Marian Leighton is an analyst with the Defense Intelligence Agency. She has worked as a freelance Soviet specialist for Radio Liberty and has published widely on Soviet foreign policy and international relations.

Michael McKinley is a lecturer in international relations and strategic studies in the Department of Politics at the University of Western Australia.

Leif R. Rosenberger is a Soviet foreign affairs specialist with the Defense Intelligence Agency. From 1979 to 1980 he was a special lecturer in international relations at Providence College.

Sheldon W. Simon is professor of political science and director of the Center for Asian Studies at Arizona State University in Tempe, Arizona.

Robert Sutter is a specialist in Asian affairs with the Congressional Research Service of the Library of Congress. He has held assignments with the Department of State, the Senate Foreign Relations Committee, and the Central Intelligence Agency.

William T. Tow is an assistant professor of international relations at the University of Southern California. He has written widely on East Asian security and U.S. foreign and strategic approaches to the Asian-Pacific.

William S. Turley is an associate professor of political science at Southern Illinois University, Carbondale. He was a Ford Foundation Research Associate in Vietnam from 1972 to 1973, and a Kennedy-Fulbright Professor at Chulalongkorn University, Bangkok, from 1982 to 1984.

Donald E. Weatherbee is the Donald S. Russell Professor of Contemporary Foreign Policy at the University of South Carolina. He was a Fulbright Fellow at the Institute of Southeast Asian Studies, Singapore, from 1981 to 1982, and has published widely on Southeast Asian affairs.

Index